A European Television

D0625409

`חל

WITHDRAWN

2 0 JUN 2022

York St John

3 8025 00545548 3

2 0 JUN 2022

A European Television History

Edited by
Jonathan Bignell and
Andreas Fickers

YORK ST. JOHN
COLLEGE LIBRARY

WILEY-BLACKWELL

A John Wiley & Sons, Ltd., Publication

© 2008 by Blackwell Publishing Ltd
except for editorial material and organization © 200* by Joe Bloggs [this line not
needed if Wiley-Blackwell holds copyright to editorial material]

BLACKWELL PUBLISHING
350 Main Street, Malden, MA 02148-5020, USA
9600 Garsington Road, Oxford OX4 2DQ, UK
550 Swanston Street, Carlton, Victoria 3053, Australia

The right of Jonathan Bignell and Andreas Fickers to be identified as the authors of
the editorial material in this work has been asserted in accordance with the UK
Copyright, Designs, and Patents Act 1988.

All rights reserved. No part of this publication may be reproduced, stored in a
retrieval system, or transmitted, in any form or by any means, electronic,
mechanical, photocopying, recording or otherwise, except as permitted by the UK
Copyright, Designs, and Patents Act 1988, without the prior permission of the
publisher.

Designations used by companies to distinguish their products are often claimed as
trademarks. All brand names and product names used in this book are trade names,
service marks, trademarks, or registered trademarks of their respective owners. The
publisher is not associated with any product or vendor mentioned in this book.

This publication is designed to provide accurate and authoritative information in
regard to the subject matter covered. It is sold on the understanding that the
publisher is not engaged in rendering professional services. If professional advice or
other expert assistance is required, the services of a competent professional should
be sought.

First published 2008 by Blackwell Publishing Ltd

1   2008

Library of Congress Cataloging-in-Publication Data

A European television history / edited by Jonathan Bignell and Andreas Fickers.
p. cm.
Includes bibliographical references and index.
ISBN 978-1-4051-6339-2 (hardcover : alk. paper) —
ISBN 978-1-4051-6340-8 (pbk. : alk. paper)   1. Television broadcasting—
Europe—History. I. Bignell, Jonathan. II. Fickers, Andreas.
PN1992.3.E78E87 2009
791.45094—dc22
2008031717

A catalogue record for this title is available from the British Library.

Set in 10.5/13pt Galliard by Graphicraft Ltd, Hong Kong
Printed and bound in Singapore by Markono Print Media Pte Ltd

The publisher's policy is to use permanent paper from mills that operate a
sustainable forestry policy, and which has been manufactured from pulp processed
using acid-free and elementary chlorine-free practices. Furthermore, the publisher
ensures that the text paper and cover board used have met acceptable
environmental accreditation standards.

For further information on
Blackwell Publishing, visit our website at
www.blackwellpublishing.com

Contents

List of Contributors   vii

Acknowledgements   ix

1   Introduction: Comparative European Perspectives on   1
    Television History
    Jonathan Bignell and Andreas Fickers

2   Early TV: Imagining and Realising Television   55
    Knut Hickethier

3   Institutionalising European Television: The Shaping of   79
    European Television Institutions and Infrastructures
    Christina Adamou, with Isabelle Gaillard and Dana Mustata

4   Searching for an Identity for Television: Programmes,   101
    Genres, Formats
    Jérôme Bourdon, with Juan Carlos Ibáñez, Catherine Johnson
    and Eggo Müller

5   TV Nations or Global Medium? European Television   127
    Between National Institution and Window on the World
    Sonja de Leeuw, with Alexander Dhoest, Juan Francisco
    Gutiérrez Lozano, François Heinderyckx, Anu Koivunen
    and Jamie Medhurst

6   American Television: Point of Reference or European   154
    Nightmare?
    Ib Bondebjerg, with Tomasz Goban-Klas, Michele Hilmes,
    Dana Mustata, Helle Strandgaard-Jensen, Isabelle Veyrat-Masson
    and Susanne Vollberg

7   European Television Events and Euro-visions: Tensions   184
    between the Ordinary and the Extraordinary
    Rob Turnock, with Alexander Hecht, Dana Mustata,
    Mari Pajala and Alison Preston

8   European Television Audiences: Localising the Viewers   215
    Mats Björkin, with Juan Francisco Gutiérrez Lozano

9   Conclusion: Reflections on Doing European Television   229
    History
    Andreas Fickers and Jonathan Bignell

10 European Television Archives and the Search for   257
    Audiovisual Sources
    Andy O'Dwyer

Index   264

List of Contributors

Christina Adamou is Lecturer in Film at the Aristotle University of Thessaloniki, Greece.

Jonathan Bignell is Professor of Television and Film and Director of the Centre for Television Drama Studies at the University of Reading, UK.

Mats Björkin is Senior Lecturer in Film Studies at the Department of Culture, Aesthetics and Media, at the University of Gothenburg, Sweden.

Ib Bondebjerg is Professor of Film and Media Studies and Head of the Department of Media, Cognition and Communication at the University of Copenhagen, Denmark.

Jérôme Bourdon is Senior Lecturer in Television Studies and Head of the Department of Communication, at the University of Tel Aviv, Israel.

Sonja de Leeuw is Professor of Dutch Television Culture in the Department of Media and Culture at the University of Utrecht, the Netherlands.

Alexander Dhoest is Lecturer in Communication and Media Studies in the Department of Communication Studies at the University of Antwerp, Belgium.

Andreas Fickers is Associate Professor of Comparative Media History in the Faculty of Arts and Social Sciences at the University of Maastricht, the Netherlands.

Isabelle Gaillard is Lecturer in Contemporary History in the Laboratoire de Recherche Historique Rhône-Alpes at the University of Grenoble, France.

Tomasz Goban-Klas is Professor of Media and Communication in the Department of Media and Communication at the University of Krakow, Poland.

Juan Francisco Gutiérrez Lozano is Associate Professor of Media Studies at the University of Málaga, Spain.

Alexander Hecht is curator/television archivist at Österreichischer Rundfunk (ORF) in Vienna, Austria.

François Heinderyckx is Professor of Communication Studies in the Department of Information and Communication Studies at the Free University of Brussels, Belgium.

Knut Hickethier is Professor of Media Studies in the Department of Media and Communication at the University of Hamburg, Germany.

Michele Hilmes is Professor of Media and Cultural Studies in the Department of Communication Arts at the University of Wisconsin–Madison, USA.

Juan Carlos Ibáñez is Professor of Media Studies in the Department of Audiovisual Communication at the University Carlos III, Madrid, Spain.

Catherine Johnson is Senior Lecturer in Television History and Theory in the Department of Media Arts at Royal Holloway, University of London, UK.

Anu Koivunen is Research Fellow in the Christina Institute for Women Studies at the University of Helsinki, Finland.

Jamie Medhurst is Lecturer in Film and Television History in the Faculty of Arts, University of Wales Aberystwyth, UK.

Eggo Müller is Associate Professor of Media Studies in the Faculty of Media and Culture at the University of Utrecht, the Netherlands.

Dana Mustata is an international PhD research fellow in the Institute of History and Culture at the University of Utrecht, the Netherlands.

Andy O'Dwyer is a technologist and project manager at BBC Future Media & Technology in London, UK.

Mari Pajala is Lecturer in Media Studies at the University of Turku, Finland.

Alison Preston currently heads the PSB and media literacy audience research programmes at Ofcom, UK.

Helle Strandgaard-Jensen is a PhD candidate in the Institute for Culture and Identity at the Roskilde University Centre, Denmark.

Rob Turnock is Senior Researcher in the Department of Media Arts at Royal Holloway, University of London, UK.

Isabelle Veyrat-Masson is Director of the 'Communication and Politics' Laboratory at the Centre National de Recherche Scientifique, Paris, France.

Susanne Vollberg is Senior Researcher at the University of Leipzig, Germany.

Acknowledgements

The editors would first like to thank the team of contributors whose work is presented in this book. While the long opening and closing chapters of the book were jointly written by us, the other chapters are the result of collaborative research coordinated for us by their lead authors, namely Christina Adamou, Mats Björkin, Ib Bondebjerg, Jérôme Bourdon, Knut Hickethier, Sonja de Leeuw and Rob Turnock. The lead authors drew on the expertise of other international scholars whose names are listed at the beginning of each chapter, and who comprised Alexander Dhoest, Isabelle Gaillard, Tomasz Goban-Klas, Juan Francisco Gutiérrez Lozano, Alexander Hecht, François Heinderyckx, Michele Hilmes, Juan Carlos Ibáñez, Anu Koivunen, Catherine Johnson, Jamie Medhurst, Eggo Müller, Dana Mustata, Mari Pajala, Alison Preston, Helle Strandgaard-Jensen, Isabelle Veyrat-Masson and Susanne Vollberg. The book's appendix on resources for television archival research was created by Andy O'Dwyer from the BBC, whose assistance in maintaining connections with the international community of television archivists was essential to the project.

The colleagues working with us on this book are fellow members of the European Television History Network, and it was at one of its meetings at the University of Utrecht that a discussion between Jonathan Bignell and Andreas Fickers first generated the idea for the book. Meetings with our contributing writers subsequently took place at ETHN workshops in Madrid and London, where the planning of the book's research was reviewed and finalised. We are grateful for the generous support of the people who organised these ETHN events, namely Gemma Camanez, John Ellis, Catherine Johnson and Sonja de Leeuw, and to the universities and research groups who hosted them. These stimulating intellectual and social gatherings enabled us to make very rapid progress in defining the content and working methods that have produced this book in a relatively short time. We also thank the staff of Wiley Blackwell Publishing, whose enthusiasm and commitment to this project have been constant throughout. Finally, we thank the community of colleagues, friends and family members who have not directly contributed to the book but whose ideas and support have sustained us and our contributors during the writing and editing process.

Jonathan Bignell and Andreas Fickers

1

Introduction:
Comparative European Perspectives on Television History

Jonathan Bignell and Andreas Fickers

There is currently no scholarly study of European television history. There are books on international television history (for example, Hilmes & Jacobs 2003, Smith & Paterson 1998), but these are compilations of separately authored chapters on national television histories without a common ground of shared questions or methodological reflections. In order to facilitate study of the complex and disparate development of television in Europe, this project defines chronological and thematic paths charting that development. The book is a systematic comparative historical analysis of television's role as an agent and instance of technological, economic, political, cultural and social change in European societies. An important aspect of this is that the development of television in Europe is uneven; for example Britain's national broadcaster began operating the 1930s while other nations had no developed television service until the late 1960s or even after. For this reason, the book is organised around critical debates rather than chronologically, and we introduce these debates in this introductory chapter. The book combines a structural historical approach (a comparison of the institutional development of television within different political, economic, cultural and ideological contexts) with a media-theoretical approach (theoretical work on the aesthetics of television as a medium and the intermedial relationships between television and other media). In this way *A European Television History* offers a unique historical and analytical perspective on the leading mass medium of the second half of the twentieth century.

Aims and Audience

The cultural identity of 'Europe' is a contested discursive and material space, which expands and contracts its boundaries, and changes over time. In this book we have followed Chris Barker's (1999: 172) understanding of identity in general in regarding European cultural identity as 'A temporary stabilization of meaning, a becoming rather than a fixed entity. The suturing or stitching together of the discursive "outside" with the "internal" processes of subjectivity. Points of temporary attachment to the subject positions which discursive practices construct for us.' Thus as the book proceeds we have removed the 'scare quotes' from around the term 'Europe' and its derivatives since the book as a whole consists of a debate both implicit and explicit about how television has taken part in the construction and deconstruction of Europe as a political entity, a rhetorical crux in different kinds of discourse, and a spatial territory acted upon by the implementation of different technologies, textual forms, and modes of distribution and reception. 'Since words do not refer to essences, identity is not a fixed universal "thing". Cultural identity is not an essence but a "cut" or snapshot of unfolding meanings' (Barker 1999: 172). Television has played a role in the construction of Europe as a discursive entity, for example in television coverage of European Union politics, but with uneven and partial results. Work by Klaus Schoenbach and Edmund Lauf (2002) investigated the 'trap' effect for television to disseminate political information to people uninterested in politics and to influence them more than other media. They found that in 12 European countries during the 1999 European elections the effect was unimpressive, even when proportionally more television news coverage of the elections and fewer competing channels with alternative programming were available to viewers. Similarly, a comparative cross-cultural content analysis by Peter and de Vreese (2004) studied British, Danish, Dutch, French and German television news and in the majority of countries EU politics and politicians were marginally represented. But where the EU was covered, EU politics were more prominent than other political news, especially in public broadcasting, in countries with higher levels of public satisfaction with democracy, and during EU summits. They concluded that the Europeanisation of television news was more an illusion than a reality.

We have written this book in English in order to address the greatest possible range of readers, and this question of language mirrors questions of linguistic dominance in European television as well. English-language television programmes, primarily those made in the USA and next, those made in Britain, are the most exported within Europe and to elsewhere in the world for screening either with subtitled dialogue or with a dubbed soundtrack. Television advertisements are also sometimes shown in several different countries, with the same visual images but with a soundtrack made in another language. Audiences in Britain (and the USA) are notoriously resistant to watching programmes in languages other than English, but this is relatively unusual. For example, in Poland imported foreign-language programmes have the dialogue of all the speakers dubbed into Polish by a single actor; in France and Italy British and American programmes are shown with multi-actor dubbing; while in the Netherlands British and American programmes are shown with Dutch subtitles. The significance of linguistic variation, translation and the meaning of television as part of nationalism are clearly impacted by this,

since around Europe the import of television in non-native languages is immediately a marker of difference. In nations such as Belgium or Switzerland where
there are several languages of broadcasting, or in the regions within nations
such as Wales and Catalonia, the issue of identity and television takes another
distinctive form as part of the variation across the European mediascape,
further complicated by recent transnational channels such as Hellenic TV (Greek
language), Polonia (Polish), Al-Jazeera (Arabic) and Phoenix TV (Chinese).
Writing a comparative history of European television provides a forum for
assessing these differences in both temporal and spatial terms, and raising
theoretical questions of identity in a specific and significant context.

Thus our theoretical premise develops from the post-foundational theoretical work developed at first in Europe itself in the post-1945 arena of critical
theory, bringing together in different ways the insights of post-Marxist, structural and psychodynamic theories. An exemplar of this tradition is the British
academic Stuart Hall (1996: 1), who noted:

> There has been a veritable discursive explosion in recent years around the con-
> cept of 'identity', at the same moment as it has been subjected to a searching
> critique . . . The deconstruction has been conducted within a variety of disciplinary
> areas, all of them, in one way or another critical of the notion of an integral,
> originary and unified identity.

Academic studies of television have attempted a range of definitions of the
medium, primarily based on how the medium communicates, which have mainly
involved distinctions between television and cinema or radio. The subject's
analytical methodologies have derived from disciplines including film studies,
its methods of discussing audiences and television institutions have come from
sociology, and overall these ways of describing the development of television
can amount to different ontologies and histories of the medium. Charlotte
Brunsdon (1998: 96) has summarised this in terms of the issue of television
specificity, negotiating between 'on the one hand, radio (broadcast, liveness,
civic address), and on the other, cinema (moving pictures, fantasy), with particular attention . . . to debate about the nature of the television text and the
television audience'. Because of television's internal difference as a broadcast
form (so many different programmes, channels and modes of address), even
at one point in time in a single geographical region, it has proved very difficult
for critics and commentators to produce useful general insights into the medium.
This is even more the case once the history of the medium and its regional
variations across countries and regions are considered. As a result, this book
thematises this problem rather than concealing it, and the constituent chapters return repeatedly and comparatively to the different ways that television
as a referent of discourse has been rhetorically deployed in debates about its
history, its place in European spatial territories and political-economic structures, and its significance for audiences and commentators.

In the earliest European nations to develop television broadcasting, predictions of what television would be emphasised liveness and its ability to relay real-world actuality, although this actuality might include live staged performance. Television was considered unable to compete with cinema as spectacular entertainment, and these assumptions conditioned the ways in which realism, contemporaneity and the protection of the home as a viewing space were promoted. The connection of television technology to immediacy predisposes it to linear scheduling with fixed points for key programme types, and an emphasis in critical discourses on the issue of temporality, thus producing an obvious relationship with radio's similar theorisation in terms of time. Film, on the other hand, has been theorised in terms of space (the screen space, the cinema as social space), and this has fed into theorisation of television in the form of models of spectatorship, identification and point of view. The emphasis on television's live temporality remained central to the medium's self-presentation throughout the twentieth century, as work by Jérôme Bourdon (2000) showed. Although live broadcasting declined as a technical phenomenon, it remained as a regime of belief among viewers. Bourdon proposed a typology of liveness, from major live media events to the semblance of liveness in game shows, from edited and recorded programmes influenced by live television such as documentary to the minimal relevance of liveness to most television fiction.

The influential concept of television as a 'flow' was developed by the British theorist Raymond Williams in a study first published in 1974 (1990: 86), which claimed that 'in all developed broadcasting systems the characteristic organisation, and therefore the characteristic experience, is one of sequence or flow. This phenomenon, of planned flow, is then perhaps the defining characteristic of broadcasting, simultaneously as a technology and as a cultural form.' Williams is less interested in analysing specific programmes or forms of programme than in the experience of television itself. The normal and heterogeneous flow of material constitutes the experience of television and also carries a flow of meanings and values deriving from culture which express the structure of feeling of that culture. However, Williams developed this insight after travelling to the USA, and he uses the American television experience as paradigmatic of all television. American television becomes a horizon towards which all television seems to progress. Rick Altman (1986: 39–54) argues that flow is not a characteristic of television itself but part of a specific cultural practice of television. This is American commercial television, where audiences are measured and sold to advertisers, and flow is required to ensure that the television is switched on even if audiences are not watching it. If so, the fact that programmes flow does not illuminate anything about the texts which are part of this flow, or the ways in which audiences actually respond to them. Williams's concept of flow confuses a property of the text (the continuing flow of images) and a form of audience response (a flow of feelings and experiences).

Historiographies of European Television

Doing history depends, on the one hand, on the questions and conceptual frames guiding the interpretative look of the historian; on the other hand it is very crucially dependent on the availability and accessibility of sources. On the archival level, both the amount of material available (conserved) and the modes of accessibility differ from country to country. While some countries have a central audiovisual authority taking care of the cultural heritage of television (like INA in France, or Beeld en Geluid in the Netherlands), archival research in other countries is a highly complicated affair, often depending on the goodwill of individual archivists or informal connections and contacts. In addition to the different situations of access to the historical material, doing television history reflects the disciplinary backgrounds (literature and film studies, social sciences, history) and institutional contexts in which scholars are trained in specific methodological approaches or socialised in alternative interpretative traditions. It is therefore not surprising that the national contexts of television scholarship vary considerably as well.

As historiographical overviews of television and media history have shown (Anderson & Curtin 2002, Bernold 2001, Bleicher 2003, Bourdon 2000, Corner 2003, de Leeuw 2003, Fickers 2007, Keilbach & Thiele 2003, Maase 2004, Roberts 2001, Scannell 2004), the literature on television history in both academic and popular kinds of writing has concentrated on the emergence, development and political or social importance of the medium in strictly national contexts. Within these different national narratives, it is possible to detect five different phases of television historiography, reflecting the institutional embeddings of television as a public service or commercial medium and the intellectual agenda of television research over the years. A first phase of both popular and scholarly television literature which is often neglected in television historiography is the phase that we propose to describe as 'ego-history'. This comprises documents written by early television pioneers and popular writings about the technical miracle of 'seeing by electricity'. To a certain degree it is not really surprising to see that the long prehistory of television (around 75 years, if one starts it with the first serious experiments on picture telegraphy in the late 1870s and counts the post-war years as the real takeoff of television as a mass medium) has generated an extremely rich and fascinating literature shaping the horizon of expectation for the complex implementation of television as a newcomer in the mass media ensemble of the 1930s and 1940s. This prehistory of television has gathered some attention by media archaeologists like Siegfried Zielinski (1989) or André Lange, but still offers enormous potential for a cultural history of television. Such a history would be interested in the discursive construction of television both as a new communication technology and a new mode of aesthetic expression.

A 'serious' academic interest in television starts only in the 1960s, focusing on the institutional development of television and mostly interested in the reconstruction of the political or governmental contexts that shaped the emergence of television as a public service medium. This second phase of historical writing on television is characterised by large and voluminous studies, often initiated by or closely linked to the public service institutions themselves (see Bausch 1980, Briggs 1985). A curious characteristic of these institutional histories of television is, perhaps surprisingly, that they were almost exclusively based on the study of written sources, reflecting the political and social conflicts in broadcasting organisations but neglecting television as a visual, programme-driven medium.

The emergence of the third phase of television historiography was inaugurated by the advent of what we would like to call 'audiovisual consciousnesses' in the 1970s and 1980s. The most important consequences of this political change in philosophies of cultural heritage were to be found in the changed roles and responsibilities of television archives. In several Western European countries the 1970s and 1980s witnessed the emergence of large national institutions for the conservation of television material, such as the Institut National de l'Audiovisuel (INA), Deutsches Rundfunkarchiv (DRA) and the Nederlands Audiovisueel Archief (NAA). This went along with an increased scholarly interest in the study of television and the establishment of academic journals that included the *Historical Journal of Film, Radio and Television* and national and international associations for the 'advancement' of broadcast history. The most active of these associations included the International Association for Media and History (IAMHIST), Vereniging Geschiedenis Beeld en Geluid in the Netherlands, the Comité d'Histoire de la Radio/Télévision in France and Vereinigung Rundfunk und Geschichte in Germany.

One of the results of this crucial phase of enhanced archival protection, occurring alongside slowly improving conditions of access to television programmes, was the diversification of the research agenda in the late 1980s and early 1990s. A bundle of new historical questions, methodological approaches and theoretical perspectives deeply challenged the classical political and institutional approach to television history. While institutional questions remained on the research agenda – especially because of the wave of commercial and private television stations all over Europe in the 1980s – television as a professional practice and a cultural industry became a new and important field of interest. The research generated from this conjuncture was not so much driven by a historical perspective, but instead by the new interest in television from British Cultural Studies. Television Studies as an independent academic discipline emerged and promoted the study of the medium from new perspectives, mainly turning academic attention from a perspective centred on the sender of television communication to its receivers. This new interest in television audiences and the sociocultural dimension of television as a daily lived reality opened the door to the most recent phase of television historiography and scholarship. This current paradigm is influenced by inter-disciplinary or transdiciplinary approaches, and sets the agenda as one of studying television in its role as a prominent actor in the construction of cultural identities and as an agent in the transnational or global circulation of aesthetic forms and cultural meanings.

In a book that addresses television history across a large and changing geographic space and across a period of about seven decades, an evident starting point for terminology to describe and evaluate regional, national and transnational interrelationships is the concept of globalisation. This is itself a contested term, but we adopt Chris Barker's summary of its referent, which is: 'Increasing multidirectional economic, social, cultural and political global connections and our awareness of them including the global production of the local and the localization of the global. Often associated with the institutions of modernity and time-space compression or the shrinking world' (Barker 1999: 172). This work on globalisation forms a starting point but also a set of problems in considering space, time, agency, power and cultural meaning, since it addresses each of these and attempts to unpack their application to historiographical narrative: 'globalization and global cultural flows should not necessarily be understood in terms of a set of neat linear determinations, but instead viewed as a series of overlapping, overdetermined, complex and "chaotic" conditions which, at best, can be seen to cluster around key "nodal points"' (Barker 1999: 37).

Any discussion of European television needs to take account of the social and political significance of how transnational and national cultures of broadcasting work in relation to each other. What is at issue is the degree to which the meanings of television are dependent on the kinds of institutions which make and broadcast it, and the conclusions which can be drawn from studying television in terms of its ownership, organisation and geographical spread. There are inequalities in production funding, and different roles of domestic and imported programming in national television cultures, and it has been argued that 'world patterns of communication flow, both in density and in direction, mirror the system of domination in the economic and political order' (Sinclair, Jacka & Cunningham 1999: 173). Globalisation theses proposed by Herbert Schiller (1969, 1976), for example, have argued that the globalisation of communication in the second half of the twentieth century was determined by the commercial interests of US corporations, working in parallel with political and military interests. This discourse connects cultural imperialism with the dynamics of colonialism, arguing that the colonial empires of Britain or France have been replaced by commercial empires. Traditional local cultures are said to be eroded by dependencies on media products and their attendant ideologies deriving from the USA, with the effect of globalising consumer culture across regions and populations which become constrained to adapt to its logics and desires, despite the lack in some of these regions (in the developing world) of resources to participate in them. This cultural imperialism thesis, developed in the 1950s and 1960s, pays scant regard to local and national specificities in media organisation or consumption, nor to regional flows of media products.

Regional flows and institutional arrangements have been developed in Europe to foster and protect its television culture. The European Broadcasting Union (EBU) was formed in 1950 by 23 broadcasters across Europe and the Mediterranean, with further national members and associate members (some of them outside Europe, such as broadcasters from Canada, Japan, Mexico, Brazil, India and the USA) subsequently joining from the public service and commercial sectors. Based in Geneva, it promotes members' co-operation and represents their legal, technical, and programming interests (Brack 1976, Eugster 1983, Zeller 1999). The EBU runs Eurovision to pool programmes and coordinate joint programme purchases, and organised the relay of Queen Elizabeth II's coronation in 1953 to France, Denmark, the Netherlands and Germany, and the live *Television Summer Season of 1954* from Montreux, Switzerland. The Eurovision network is carried on satellite and terrestrial transmission stations, exchanging news footage since 1958 and since 1993 via Euronews in English, French, German, Italian and Spanish. Eurovision also coordinates joint purchasing of coverage of European sports programming. A further organisation, the European Audiovisual Observatory, was set up in 1992 by media practitioners and governmental authorities including the European Commission to improve the mechanisms for the flows of television across Europe, access to market and economic, legal and practical information, and to provide authoritative information about the television, cinema and video industries.

Because of the specific relations, actualised differently in different times and spaces, between European television and the television cultures, technologies and economies of US television, the important focus of much globalisation theory on US hegemony in electronic media is also relevant to this study. According to a feature article in the British *Radio Times* listings magazine (Eden 2006), the most popular programme in the world in 2007 was the American police drama series *CSI: Miami*. In the list of most viewed programmes around the world, compiled by comparing charts from most of the world's countries, American programmes dominate and include *Lost*, *Desperate Housewives*, *The Simpsons*, *CSI* and *Without a Trace*. Again, we emphasise not the teleological progress of US media hegemony in Europe, but the unevenness of the impact of different aspects of US television, and their contestation in specific contexts: 'the impact of Anglo-American television in a global context may be understood as the creation of a layout of western capitalist modernity which overlays, but does not necessarily obliterate, pre-existing cultural forms' (Barker, 1999: 42). Research by De Bens and de Smaele (2001) tracing the origin of films and series on 36 public and commercial channels from six European countries in 1997 confirmed the dominance of American drama and the limited distribution of European drama, despite the efforts of the

European Union to combat these tendencies by quotas and subsidies. Public channels broadcast a wider range of national, non-national European and American drama, with domestic drama series predominating over American series in prime-time on both public and commercial channels. De Bens and de Smaele found that European drama was constrained by considerations of language and cultural proximity in ways that American drama was not.

However, in relation to histories of European television, but also those of other temporal and spatial formations, globalisation is understood as generating or at least defining its own other, namely localisation. But Morley and Robins (1995: 116–17) caution against idealising the local, as a redemptive force that might rescue economies, identities and cultures from globalisation understood as its antagonist. Localisation in television is relational, and relative to globalising processes, and this can be seen in the presence of localisation initially as an other to national broadcasting (the setting up of regional television channels and forms in the UK and Spain, for example) and then to transnational and global television developments. Indeed, for global television institutions, whether commercial corporations or regulatory bodies, negotiations between rather than the overcoming of, global, national, regional and local television have been evident in recent decades.

Methodologies for Comparative and Interdisciplinary Histories of Television

Comparison as a methodological and/or theoretical concept is nearly as old as modern scientific thinking itself. As Jürgen Schriewer (2003: 9–54) has shown, the comparative method became a central tool in the scholarly development and disciplinary differentiation of modern science during the so-called scientific revolution. In the philosophy of language, anatomy, geography, law and religious studies, comparison and comparative studies both promoted and reflected the spectacular widening of the spatial and thereby historical horizons of European scholars in the era of enlightenment. In the late nineteenth century, scholars like Karl Marx, Max Weber and Emile Durkheim introduced the comparative approach into their works on social history and historical sociology.

The work of canonical historians like Marc Bloch, Charles Tilly or Hartmut Kaelble (1999) has demonstrated the scholarly benefit and intellectual potential of the comparative approach for understanding the complex nature of modern societies. But despite their common interest in using the comparative approach as a heuristic or epistemological tool for the interpretation of past realities, the definition of what a historical comparison is or should be varies considerably from author to author. Charles Tilly, in his 1984 essay *Big Structures, Large Processes, Huge Comparisons*, has considerably promoted the conceptualisation of comparative historical methodology by introducing four different forms of historical comparison. The first of these is the individual-ising comparison, interested in the study of alternative developments of a few comparative cases. His second category is the encompassing comparison, looking at the relatedness of different cases to a common institution (for ex-ample, economic development in Britain, Canada and India in relationship to the British Empire). Thirdly, Tilly distinguishes the variation-finding comparison, interested in a comparative study of a general or global process such as the national and regional paths of the process of industrialisation. Finally, he identifies the universalising comparison, which searches for common rules of historical developments or processes of historical change. Building on Tilly's and other conceptualisations, Hartmut Kaelble (1999) has developed a categorisation of comparisons, differentiating them by focusing on their heuristic motivation or intention. He thereby distinguishes the structural, the analytical, the clarify-ing and judging, and the comprehensive comparison, each of which are charac-terised by the interest or motivation for knowledge (*Erkenntnisinteresse*) of the researcher.

These classical approaches to the comparison of societies or civilisations in their political representation in the forms of nations are extremely rich and eloquent studies, but their status has been challenged by three subsequent conceptions. Each of the three has been more theoretically discussed than empirically tested, but is helpful to the project of this book. These models or concepts have been identified under the labels of 'transferts culturels' (cultural transfers), 'entangled history' and 'histoire croisée' (crossing histories). While the concept of transfer emphasises the mutual processes of reappropriation and resemantisation of cultural goods in the era of globalisation (Espagne 1999), 'entangled' histories apply this perspective with a special focus on the rela-tionships between colonising and colonised societies, aiming at breaking the Eurocentric angle of most studies (Conrad & Randeria 2002). Last but not least, the concept of 'histoire croisée' is inspired by a general scepticism towards the idea of more or less stable national milieus, languages, institutions or values and promotes the vision of deeply transnationalised modern societies (Werner & Zimmermann 2003). As we discuss below, these recently devel-oped methodologies and theories of history are highly suited to the histor-ical study of television.

Our account of Tilly's and Kaelble's work noted that each of them has been eager to systematise both the different functions and forms of historical com-parisons. In contrast to this rather mechanistic approach to the question of comparison, Michael Werner and Bénédicte Zimmermann, as two of the main protagonists of 'histoire croisée', have criticised the classical comparative approaches for being too rigid and formalised in the use of their categories, and most significantly, for neglecting the relational and fluid character of the categories and objects of comparison their work has identified. Inspired by the heuristic concept of 'double reflexivity' proposed by the British sociolo-gist Anthony Giddens, Werner and Zimmermann (2006: 32) propose to explore processes of cultural transfer by questioning 'scales, categories of analysis, the relationship between diachrony and synchrony, and regimes of historicity and reflexivity'. In their article 'Beyond Comparison: Histoire Croisée and the Challenge of Reflexivity', summarising their basic theoretical assumptions, Werner and Zimmermann (2006) present five central questions or problems, reflecting the methodological implications of the 'histoire croisée' concept. The first of these is the question of the observer and the impact that the researcher's perspective has on the problem at hand. The second problem that Werner and Zimmermann identify is the scale of comparison and how this scale or scope determines the issues and results of a study. Third is the problem of the definition of the object of comparison, which clearly sets boundaries on the topic and thus also limits the comparison's conclusions. Fourth, the conflicts between synchronic and diachronic logics are highlighted since comparative studies of single time periods versus historical analysis across time periods will raise different problems. Finally, Werner and Zimmermann identify the difficulties arising from the various kinds of interaction between the objects of comparison.

Some of the claimed gains of reflexivity made by Werner and Zimmermann lose a certain revolutionary touch when the rich literature on the philosophy of history is considered, though some of that literature (for example Johann Gustav Droysens' *Historik*, published in 1868) is now little known. Nevertheless, their accentuation of the intersection of both heuristic categories and the constructed objects of study have interesting insights to offer for television historians as much as historians of other aspects of culture. In highlighting that entities and objects of research are not merely considered in relation to one another but *through* one another, they invite historians to look at the complex processes of interaction, circulation and appropriation between objects of study, and in doing this, to conceptualise these entities and objects as dynamic and active, rather than stable or immobile, as is often assumed in comparative approaches. This process-oriented dimension of the 'histoire croisée' concept is especially fruitful for a cultural history of the media, since in our view that history should be interested in phenomena of adaptation, resistance, inertia and modification in the complex trajectories of cultural transfers of forms and contents.

At the present time, comparative research in media history remains the exception. As Michele Hilmes (2003b: 1) has stated: 'Most histories of broadcasting have stayed within national boundaries. Comparative studies have been few, and largely confined to discussion of structures, laws and economies. The tricky business of comparative cultural studies of the media remains largely unexplored.' This is also true for television history in particular, within the larger disciplinary field of media history. While national disparities have been widely researched, they have hardly been analysed at all from a comparative perspective. There are a few exceptions, such as Jane Chapman's (2005) study which explicitly addresses the problem of comparative media history, but even that suggestive work presents a rather eclectic compilation of historical findings and is clearly focused on the history of written media, especially newspapers. A sophisticated theoretical and methodological reflection about comparative historical analysis has been absent. This book offers both structural comparisons, such as the analysis of different television institutions, and analytical comparisons of the societal impact and cultural meaning of television in different times and places, together with comparisons ranging across a variety of both synchronic and diachronic historical perspectives.

Key Theoretical Concepts

This book is divided into chapters that are arranged thematically, each focusing on a specific set of historiographical problems and brief case studies that explore these problems in specific contexts. Across the book as a whole, there are recurrent research questions that our contributors have used to guide their studies. In the remainder of this chapter we illustrate what these guiding questions are, to outline for readers how the tensions in writing a comparative history of European television address the medium as a hybrid mediating interface that offers a terrain not only to narrate a history but also to question the process of historiography in relation to the medium. To make this process clear, we offer in this section a chain-narrative of pairs of concepts, chosen to highlight the methodological stakes and challenges of this book.

Television spheres: private versus public

One of the most prominent metaphors and iconographic strategies to promote and advertise television in the early years was to present it as a 'window to the world'. The seductive promise was that television would offer completely new kinds of mediated participation in world affairs or public entertainment. Without the need to leave the domestic sphere, the viewer would be able to travel to all corners of the world, and become a witness to the most distant happenings while sitting comfortably on a sofa. As 'armchair theatre', television combined the experience of simultaneity (liveness) with a new form of spatial transgression that deeply challenged the public–private relationship. Of course television was not the first medium to offer these possibilities for mediated experiences of immediacy and simultaneity. Radio historians like Paddy Scannell (1996), Susan Douglas (1987, 2004) or Michele Hilmes (1997) remind us that the fascination and ontological quality of early radio listening left probably much deeper impressions of wonder and amazement on the individual and in the collective memories of its public than did television a few decades later. The religious vocabulary often used when trying to describe the listening experience is a powerful sign of the imaginative force of the medium (Peters 1999). As 'picture radio', television added the visual to this mediated experience of the distant, but probably borrowed most of its imaginative power from associations with the cinematographic dispositif and not from radio broadcasting.

Despite these differences between early radio and television discourses, both deeply challenged the notion of the public sphere and the classical situations of mass communication. As Paddy Scannell (1996: 69) has argued, radio had reversed the public–private relationship 'because in all its output it speaks to the domestic and private, it has the pervasive effect of bringing the values that attach to the private realm into the public domain'. Television reinforced this by making the invisible visible. By introducing a television camera into the sacred space of a church or into the private apartments of the Pope, for example, television enabled a thitherto unknown intimacy and complicity with persons, places and situations, creating a strong feeling of eye-witness and authenticity by means of televised images and narratives. This new form of medial participation was most prominently experienced in early television events like the Coronation of Queen Elizabeth II in 1953 or major sporting events like the World Cup Football Championship and the Olympics. The inherent quality of television as a broadcast medium to create imagined communities or to shape collective viewing experiences still is one of the most powerful ingredients of the attraction of television as a mass entertaining and mass information medium.

But the apparently total access to the private sphere that is witnessed in contemporary 'reality TV' formats is of course by no means representative of the history of European television. It must be seen as the result of a gradual process of the public conquest of private space, and a lowering of taboos and rights to privacy step by step. But this inversion of the private–public relationship was at all times a contested and publicly debated process. This can be demonstrated by the case of the French presidential elections in 1953. Inspired by the successful transmission of the British Coronation festivities in June 1953, for the first time in the history of the French Republic the French public broadcaster Radiodiffusion-Télévision Française (RTF) decided to cover the presidential elections taking place at the convention hall in Versailles on live television. The election procedure started on 17 December 1953, but no one had foreseen that it would take 13 ballots to finally designate René Coty as the new French president. After six days of interminable discussions and failed initiatives, the programme director in charge finally decided to stop the live coverage with the justification that this 'spectacle' would produce a negative image of the French political class and democratic culture abroad. The journalist of *Le Monde*, Michel Droit, commented on this unfiltered insight into the strange parliamentary culture of the Fourth Republic with a biting question, asking whether the transmission of parliamentary debates should be seen as a new form of entertainment programme or as a serious means of political information (Cohen 1999: 38). Despite the fact that political broadcasting today, especially at election time, has been increasingly staged by means of formats that offer visual and dramatic forms of entertainment (such as graphical representations or combative interviews), this episode of French television history shows that there were various forms of political, moral or cultural resistance to the televisual takeover of the public sphere. This process has been catalysed with the advent of commercial television stations all over Europe beginning in the late 1970s.

Within a few years of its first broadcast on Dutch television in 1999, *Big Brother* had been adopted with some nationally specific variations in diverse television territories. The antics of its contestants varied, as did the reaction of the programme's broadcasters to content that could be considered offensive or potentially challenging to the norms expected of television in different nations. For example, the first British series of *Big Brother* included contestants stripping off their clothes, covering themselves with paint and creating imprints of themselves on the walls of the house. By contrast, the American *Big Brother* contestants talked a lot about sex and relationships, but remained modestly clothed and no sexual liaisons took place. In the Netherlands the contestants were more uninhibited than in Britain, and there was some sexual activity, but the programme was not permitted to be screened at all in some Muslim nations beyond the borders of the EU. These differences cannot be explained by simply drawing on national stereotypes, and are instead the result of two main forces. One of them is the regulatory environment for television in different countries, where some words or images could not be broadcast (though live streaming over the internet had lower thresholds in this respect), and the other is the internalisation of norms of privacy in social life in particular cultures, inflected by the fact that the contestants knew they were on television and therefore must have modified their behaviour in relation to what they expected that television could and should show. What look like national differences between individuals in reality TV must in fact be national differences between how people who know they are on television adapt themselves to what they think television is and can do. Notions of privacy and the use of television by non-professionals to air personal concerns are also relevant to participation in talk shows, since they allow 'ordinary' people to express themselves. But work by Kathleen Dixon and Sonja Spee (2003), for instance, showed in the case of the Flemish talk show *Jan Publiek* that participants negotiated shifting and even contradictory identities with other participants, the host, the producers and the conventions of the programme as well as discourses of gender and class, but were unable to voice their feelings and opinions because of their inexpert media literacy.

Television spaces: national versus transnational; regional versus global

Although the private–public relationship has a distinctive spatial connotation, we propose to differentiate between television spheres and television spaces.

While the notion of 'spheres' refers to the philosophical concept of a communication-based public sphere laid out in the work of Jürgen Habermas, the term television spaces stresses the topographical and geographical dimension of political communication communities. For media historians, talking about communication spaces has the advantage of emphasising the importance of linking the transmission and reception of information to the physical contexts of both the distribution and the appropriation of mediated communication. While philosophers or theoreticians of communications sometimes tend to idealise or deterritorialise diverse phenomena of mediated interaction from their concrete and situational performance, the early history of television teaches us how important it is to confront the public discourse about television with the 'real' spread of television, both in terms of transmission coverage and the average percentage of households equipped with a television set. For both parameters we see substantial differences when comparing European nations in the 1950s, 1960s and even in the 1970s. The realisation of so-called 'television nations' (Bernold 2001: 8–29) was a process which reflected the different economic dynamics of European states in the phase of 'modernization in restoration' (Schildt & Sywottek 1993), and even within countries the development of television infrastructures varied considerably. The expansion of television coverage from urban to rural areas was a lengthy process and mainly funded by state capital spending. It produced many inequalities and at least in the early days of television, it reinforced embedded separations between centre and periphery that were expressed as distinctions between the city and the countryside. While nationwide coverage of television signals was realised in Britain by the mid-1950s, the same national reach only happened in France or the Netherlands some ten years later.

This gradual construction of the television nation was paralleled from a transnational point of view by a techno-political instrumentalisation of television, most prominently illustrated in the different choice of black-and-white line standards by the leading European television nations. The effort to establish dominance among the nascent national television industries was concretely expressed by the introduction of different television systems, when Britain introduced a 405-line standard, France an 819-line standard and the Germanic and Scandinavian countries a 625-line standard. This resulted in a serious complication of European programme exchanges and hampered the emergence of a European imag(e)ined community (Fickers 2007). Both the black-and-white line-standard debate and the similar national conflicts over colour television in the 1960s are powerful demonstrations of the nationalistic instrumentalisation of television and serve as historical correctives to unreflective but widespread discourses about the globalising or transnational scope and impact of television.

Global television infrastructures have been inflected in different national and regional contexts. But it has been widely argued that global consumerism, in terms of the tendency of commercial television institutions and advertising-financed television services to impact increasingly on European television culture, has had growing effects on the meaning of European television as a descriptive term and on the perception of television in Europe by audiences. The argument here, as stated by Stuart Hall (1995: 176–7), is that global consumerism

> spreads the same thin cultural film over everything . . . inviting everyone to take on western consumer identities and obscuring profound differences of history and tradition between cultures . . . Sometimes, cultures are caught between, on the one hand, the desire for mobility and material rewards of modernity and, on the other, the nostalgia for a lost purity, stability and traditional coherence which the present no longer provides.

In this respect, television organisation and television programming has experienced a perceived challenge to national identities. It is important to consider national identities not only as the structural residue of laws, political cultures and spatial geographies but also as discursive formations. Chris Barker, for example, defines national identity as: 'A form of imaginative identification with [the] nation-state as expressed through symbols and discourses. Thus, nations are not only political formations but also systems of cultural representation so that national identity is continually reproduced through discursive action' (Barker 1999: 174). This discursive action consists not only in discourses about television, but also the discourses of television. For instance, Angeliki Koukoutsaki's (2003) work on Greek television drama production since the 1970s demonstrated the importance of local context, where continual increases in programming hours for drama and the increasing subdivision of drama into specific genre types led to the evolution of nationally specific programme forms. The testimony of Greek television practitioners confirmed that the national characteristics of Greek television production, in a small and politically unstable context with a short history of television broadcasting, led to genre differentiation in part because of the constraints of local settings and financing. The discursive action of television making in Greece fed into the reproduction of national identity in the aesthetic forms of programmes.

To take another example, in the post-imperialist context of Britain Jeffrey Richards (1997: ix) recalls that

> It became unfashionable in the 1960s and 1970s to talk about national character and national identity because of their nineteenth-century overtones of race, empire and hierarchy . . . [but] ever since [the Falklands war in 1982] there has been a massive and continuing academic interest in questions of national identity, national character and patriotism. This has taken the form of an unending stream of conferences, articles, books and collections on Britishness, Englishness, national identity and so forth. It has resulted in some extremely good and some dismayingly shallow work.

It is useful in the context of this book to note that Richards goes on to argue that the discourses of national identity are then placed in the context of the regional and transnational fracturing of that identity, demonstrating how the conception of the nation itself can be understood as a mediating concept that points both outward and inward:

> The academic interest has been sharpened, widened and enhanced by Britain's uneasy relationship with Europe, the continuing struggle over the status of Northern Ireland, the rise of nationalist and Home Rule movements in Scotland and Wales, criticism of traditional British institutions such as the monarchy, the law and the Church of England and the ideological dominance . . . of Thatcherism with its nationalist rhetoric. The combination of circumstances has undoubtedly resulted in an intellectual and emotional crisis of national identity. (Richards 1997: xi)

The force of discourses of national identity in relation to European television is that they function to unite nations in response to perceived internal and external challenges.

But there are conceptions within national and regional ideologies that have operated as mediating links between nations or regions, demonstrating the actual hybridity and permeability of the European ideological space. One of these is children's television, comprising the programming made for it, the personnel creating it, and the sometimes extra-televisual textual properties on which it is based. Continental European animated programmes for children were reconfigured for British television in the 1970s and early 1980s, for example, and instantiate a series of methodological and theoretical issues about programme import, production and adaptation in the context of programmes aimed at young audiences. While animation has been dominated by US imports in Western Europe and there is a strong tradition of British animation, animation from continental Europe has been important to British television. The role of animation as a predominantly short-form programme type useful for gap-filling in British schedules, and for compliance with regulatory demands for children's programming, coexists with an industrial context of international programme, format and personnel exchange. The separation of image and sound tracks allowing re-voicing also conduces to its exportability. To name a few indicative examples, the stop-motion animation series *Barnaby* (1973) was based on French books by Olga Pouchine and made by the French producer Albert Braille and Polish animator Tadeuzs Wilkoz. British animation company Q3 translated them and sold them to the BBC for the slot formerly occupied by the originally French puppet series *Hector's House*. The drawn animation *Ludwig* (1977) was created by the Polish documentary film-maker Mirek Lang, who migrated to Britain in 1968 for political reasons, and worked on the series with his son Peter. Produced in Britain, the series illuminates the integration of European personnel into the British industry. The stop-motion series *The*

Moomins (1983), based on the Finnish Tove Jansson's books, was screened by ITV but reshaped from the Polish Semafor studio's original one-hour episodes into 100 five-minute stories. These brief examples indicate how complex the attribution of nationality can be, and how through the 1970s British children's television integrated European programming because of the transportability of children's animation as a form that could be re-voiced in different languages, the transnational links between children's literature publication and character ideas based on shared ideologies of childhood, and the conception of children's television production as a transnational market for programme makers and programmes.

The imagining of the nation, as Benedict Anderson (1983: 16) powerfully argued, has been actualised in concrete action, most obviously by means of war:

> It is imagined as a *community* because, regardless of the actual inequality and exploitation that may prevail in each, the nation is always conceived as a deep, horizontal, comradeship. Ultimately, it is this fraternity that makes it possible, over the past two centuries, for so many millions of people, not so much to kill, as willingly to die for such limited imaginings.

In television, the different television roles of the combatants in the Second World War are instructive here. In Britain television broadcasting ceased, while in Germany and in German-occupied France it continued at least for several years. In these nations where television continued during war, its function was to reproduce the hegemony of national identity, imagined in different ways depending on whether television was broadcast in an invading or in an occupied nation, despite challenges from internal and external agencies. As a general point, we concur with Smith (1991: 143) in his overview that: 'Of all the collective identities in which human beings share today, national identity is perhaps the most fundamental and inclusive . . . Other types of collective identity – class, gender, race, religion – may overlap or combine with national identity but they rarely succeed in undermining its hold, though they may influence its direction.' Theorists of television have emphasised that at the levels of production, distribution and consumption it is possible for the significance of global television to change, and argue that globalisation is not a natural and unstoppable process. In production, global television corporations can be restrained by national or local laws and regulations which make them operate differently in different places. Global distribution networks may transmit the same television programme over a very wide area, but the ways in which the programme is received (by whom, how, and the significance of receiving global television in a particular society) will be different in different contexts. John Sinclair and his fellow authors (Sinclair et al. 1999: 176) explain that 'although US programmes might lead the world in their transportability across cultural boundaries, and even manage to dominate schedules on some channels in particular countries, they are rarely the most popular programmes where viewers have a reasonable menu of locally produced programmes to choose from'. The theory of globalisation is a way of addressing both processes which homogenise television and those which reduce differences, but also a way of addressing processes of differentiation. Furthermore, globalisation theory brings together approaches to television which concern economic, institutional, textual and reception practices.

Television institutions: public service versus commercial television

Broadcasting evolved from prior technologies that included the telegraph, the telephone and wireless (radio) ship-to-shore communication, and services based on these technologies provided both point-to-point and point-to-multipoint communication. The verb 'to broadcast' was adopted to express the idea of scattered, undefined, anonymous dissemination of information on radio waves, and derives from the farmer's method of hand-sowing grain by casting it broadly, letting seeds fall where they may. The physical properties of radio waves mean that they are not affected by political or geographical boundaries, and from the first this made them an issue for cross-border negotiation and legislation. Radio clubs, national amateur associations and popular magazines testify to the first stage of a 'radio boom' even before the emergence of broadcasting in the modern understanding of the term. It was the First World War that brought an abrupt end to this first phase of the boom, though inaugurating another. The exclusive use of radio frequencies for military purposes in all countries involved in the war not only demonstrated the military and political importance of radio technology in times of crisis, but even more significantly instituted a process of state-controlled use of radio frequencies as means of private or public communication. The concept of broadcasting was the result of 'a concerted effort on the part of big business and government, feeding on the elite public's fear of the masses, to change that vision to the highly centralised, one-way, restricted-access system that is broadcasting' (Hilmes 2003b: 29).

From a transnational historical perspective the process of institutionalisation of radio broadcasting after the First World War must be interpreted as a process of national appropriation and social shaping of radio as a broadcast medium. While nearly all nation-states extended their existing authority over the legal regulation of wire communication technologies to radio transmissions (especially the allocation of frequencies), governmental intervention in the institutionalisation of broadcasting stations strongly varied from country to country. Three institutional models emerged, reflecting the political, economic and sociocultural structures of the hosting states: the commercial or private broadcasting model, the national or centralised model, and finally the public service model.

The influence of British television organisation in Western Europe has been very great, because of the early establishment of the BBC as a public service broadcaster in radio from 1922 and in television from 1936, and because of the broad acceptance of social-democratic ideologies in Western European societies. The organisation of the BBC as a semi-autonomous public corporation was inherited from the late Victorian corporations which had monopolies to provide services such as gas, electricity and water, distributed widely to domestic consumers and subject to regulatory standards despite central control by a single corporation. Their control of supply and freedom from competition was granted in exchange for a remit to operate for the public good. The BBC took seriously its aims to raise the standards of the entire national audience in terms of sophistication of taste, intellectual appetite and levels of knowledge, while supplying a range of material targeted at the diverse interests of a diverse audience, and this set up the expectations for television to be understood as a form of public service broadcasting. In addition to the paternalistic public service model as represented by the BBC, a whole range of alternative public service models existed in Europe. In West Germany, a federal public service model with independent broadcast authorities in each Land came into being, collaborating under the umbrella of a federal (but not state-controlled) agency. After having experienced a very liberal radio broadcasting system in the inter-war period, France experienced a strong centralisation and governmental control of both radio and television broadcasting after the Second World War, and this centralised public service model is probably the clearest example of the governmental instrumentalisation of broadcasting in a democratic political system. One of the most curious forms of public service model is to be found in the Netherlands, where the main political or sociocultural classes of Dutch society (*zuilen* in Dutch, perhaps best translated as 'pillars of society') each formed their own broadcasting association. Established during the institutionalisation of radio broadcasting in the 1920s, this 'pillarised' public service model is still existent. But interestingly, television was one of the most prominent actors in the process of 'de-pillarisation' of Dutch society in the 1950s and 1960s. The existence of only one channel fed by the limited amount of programmes provided by the different pillars in the early decades of television had the effect that audiences consumed all of the scarce output regardless of the originating pillar of the productions.

The main alternative to this model in Western Europe was that offered by the organisation of television in the USA, where corporations such as RCA and General Electric developed television production and reception equipment during the 1920s. It was not the government, the Hollywood film studios or individual entrepreneurs who worked on television but the firms producing radio equipment. Television was modelled on radio broadcasting, rather than cinema or the public services, and the radio broadcasters NBC and CBS promoted television as a market for their programmes. Television in the USA, like radio, used national networks supplying programmes to local stations, gaining income from commercials and sponsorship. This commercial model has rivalled that of public service television increasingly through the history of European television, in parallel with the gradual erosion of political ideologies of paternalism, social democracy and statism, in favour of compromises between public and private ownership, and consumerisation. In France in the era of de Gaulle, the ORTF channel was overwhelmingly sympathetic to the interests of the government and its management was appointed through government patronage, and the same was true of RTVE in Spain during the control of the state by the fascist regime.

In Eastern Europe, however, the institutions of television were closely controlled by the Soviet-influenced governments of the post-Second World War period until the revolutions of 1989. During that period, the prospect of citizens watching programmes and channels made in the West or beamed to them by satellites operated by Western corporations led to signal jamming, prohibitions on the use of satellite dishes and the development of regional systems of programme exchange closely related to the economic bloc of COMECON. The suspicion of commercial and foreign television in Eastern Europe derived from a quite different understanding of the functions of television in society, which were that it would publicise the decisions made by the ruling party, educate the population, and establish a channel of communication between the party and the people. The transition to western models of television distribution, marketisation and modes of address to the audience in Eastern Europe demonstrate a gradual movement from state control, with an emphasis on information, political programming and entertainment programmes based on state-approved national values, to increasing commercialisation and diversity. The Eastern European nations, however, exhibited some distinct differences in the degree of political control over their television services. In Romania, programming and production were closely controlled by the state, and the country's weak economy could contribute little to what from the outside seemed a very impoverished television culture. In Czechoslovakia, the Russian invasion of 1968 imposed rigid state control but western imports were commonly used because of the inability of domestic production or imports from fellow communist states to produce sufficient programming hours to fill the schedule. Similarly, in Hungary, by the mid-1980s significant numbers of hours of programmes were imported from Britain, West Germany and the USA.

The incursion of commercial television institutions into nations and regions formerly characterised by public service television or state television has been imagined as both an opportunity for democratisation, and as a threat to both cultural independence and the public good of the citizenry. In each of these different contexts, the nation has been seen as a residual entity, threatened either by a dominant form of television organisation that is perceived to be new and thus a harbinger of modernity, or as an alternative cultural form that offers a space of resistance. For the commercial television institutions, who are responsible to owners and shareholders which are likely to be transnational corporations such as banks, investment funds or media firms, the nation is an outmoded obstacle. As Morley and Robins (1995: 11) suggest: 'The imperative is to break down the old boundaries and frontiers of national communities, which now present themselves as arbitrary and irrational obstacles to this reorganisation of business strategies. Audiovisual geographies are thus becoming detached from the symbolic spaces of national culture, and realigned on the basis of the more universal principles of international consumer culture.' Since commercial television is associated with the USA as the dominant commercial broadcasting arrangement in the world, suspicion of commercial television has run alongside suspicion of US programming products and especially those targeted at youth audiences such as pop music programmes and channels, television screening of Hollywood cinema and American drama, and imported US children's programming. Each of these genres had commercial success, and throughout the second half of the twentieth century the critique of Americanisation, the defence of nationalism and the valuation of tradition have occurred around the totemic figures of the child and the teenager. There have been significant and ongoing debates in Europe about public service and state television, seen either as an old-fashioned and monolithic system which prevents change, or as a space in which television that challenges commercial values and aspires to artistic quality might find an audience. In this context, the comparative analysis of both institutional structures and of European television programmes illuminates the variant grounds for valuing structures and programmes, as more or less conducive of social change, or more or less worthy of consideration as creative and interesting.

The processes of globalisation are open to regulation by individual nations, rather than being an autonomous and unstoppable process, and global markets are regulated by contracts and by international and national laws. But the transnational European organisations which oversee international television agreements generally support the lowering of national restrictions and quotas, because they seek to create a free-market economy in communications. The European Free Trade Association, for example, has provided support for cross-border television exchanges which are based on the principles of unrestricted commercial exchange. The apparently free and uncontrollable television market is not a natural fact and depends on political decisions about deregulation and competition in television by nation-states and groupings of states. The European Parliament issued the Television without Frontiers Directive in 1989, for example, which insists that the majority of programming in member states must originate from within that state. The Directive has been periodically updated and modified since its creation, taking account of new developments in technology, and has gradually weakened its requirements to allow a more commercial market approach to television in Europe. Countries and regional groupings of countries tend both to deregulate and to encourage globalisation, but also to introduce further regulation to protect their societies against it. However, in the global television landscape the concepts of society and nation are diminishing in usefulness. As the sociologist Anthony Giddens (1990) has argued, the concept of society as a unit bounded in time and space loses its force when, for example, live television news or sporting events confuse the sense of time and space by broadcasting across time zones.

Television audiences: active versus passive audiences

As much as nations are, audiences are also imagined communities, which are summoned into existence by specific discourses. For broadcasters, audiences may be conceived as commodities which can be sold to advertisers, or as relatively homogenous national communities defined by their occupation of a national broadcasting footprint and who are addressed as citizens of that territory. In northern and western European nations where television developed earliest in the years following the end of the Second World War, a relatively prosperous and urban or suburban middle class were those who could most easily afford the time and expense of watching television. The expansion of private space (larger rooms, more bedrooms and big gardens, for example) made space for television, but also created social dislocation and intense consciousness of social status. Television was regarded as a remedy for these problems because of its creation of social cohesion through collective viewing by both families and extended friendship networks. Television thus stimulated social talk that was given new interest by television programmes and supported public service ideals, which were to encourage viewers to expose themselves to a range of programme genres, some of them requiring concentration and promoting self-improvement. Notions of discrimination, taste and active viewing that were already evident in discourses about radio listening were available as rhetorical structures for articulating the uses and gratifications of television in the 1930–50 period.

In the early days of television, the medium was not only in search of its identity as a new player in the existing mass-media ensemble, but it was also in search of its potential audience. In distinction to the USA, where television was promoted as a private and commercial activity for the entertainment of a domestic public right from the beginning of a regular service that started during the New York World's Fair in 1939, many European countries envisaged and often organised television as a public and communal viewing experience. Before the Second World War, home and 'theatre television' developed side by side, and it was by no means clear at that time that the domestic setting would become the dominant model of television viewing (West 1948: 127–68, Winker 1994). The two leading television countries of the pre-war years, Britain and Germany, realised large screen projection for television broadcasting in cinemas or specially created *Fernsehstuben* (television viewing rooms). Philip Corrigan (1990) reports that in 1937 there were more than a hundred public venues for watching television in Britain, which included railway stations, restaurants and department stores. Audiences sometimes as large as a hundred people watched television collectively. The Nazi government in Germany in the 1930s was interested in the propaganda value of television broadcasting, and partly in competing with the large American corporations that were investing in television production and television sets. Staging the Olympic Games of 1936 in Berlin was a stimulus to German television, and broadcasts were received not in individual homes but in viewing rooms established in cities, and some of the buildings used for television screening could hold audiences as large as four hundred. But industrial corporations in Germany had considerable political influence during the Nazi era, and their plans to develop a domestic television receiver market meant that public screenings gave way to domestic viewing in the late 1930s (Uricchio 1989).

Among the small but privileged group of people who could experience television before the Second World War, a large majority did so in public viewing settings. While the concept of public viewing in combination with large-screen projection slowly died out in the post-war years, even domestic reception was often a collective experience. Numerous early television viewers recounted memories of the attendance of friends, neighbours or relatives (Bourdon 2003: 13) in what John Ellis (2002) has called television's 'age of scarcity'. And as the Italian example of the popular television programme *Non è mai troppo tardi* (*It's never too late*) shows, some television formats were even designed to reach a classroom audience. The programme was financed by the Italian Ministry of Education to promote literacy in rural regions, and was broadcast by the national public service broadcaster RAI between 1959 and 1968, for a mainly older audience who watched the programmes on a weekly basis in classrooms or municipal buildings. In France, also, teachers and municipal authorities inaugurated and promoted the formation of 'Télé Clubs', especially in rural regions, where people could attend television transmission once or twice a week. These gatherings mainly took place in primary schools and were followed by a public debate about the programmes, thereby attempting both to take television seriously as a 'high-culture' form and also to embed the new medium in a democratic discourse (Lévy 1999: 107–32).

But in the more prosperous households of the post-1980 period in Western Europe, the proliferation of television sets has made it common for different age groups and genders within the home to view different programmes in different rooms in different ways. Other domestic technologies such as video games, computers and mobile phones have rivalled the television as the centre of home leisure and also rivalled the collective experience of viewing. Across Europe, unevenly developing in a broadly west to east and north to south direction, audience fragmentation has been matched by new approaches in both academic studies and industry research to the issue of television viewership. The availability of multi-channel television in developed countries has the effect of diminishing audiences for terrestrial channels as hundreds of new channels split up the audience. For commercial channels, the splitting up of the audience threatens their income from advertisements, since smaller audiences mean less revenue from advertisers unless especially valuable sections of the audience can be targeted by their programmes. Falling audiences for non-commercial network terrestrial television channels – such as Britain's BBC – pose a threat to their right to funding, since they cannot expect viewers to pay television licence fees if they are rarely watching BBC programmes. But to try to grab audiences back by imitating the programme formats and audience address of commercial television programmes causes another problem for such channels, since duplicating the programme forms of their rivals means they have no claim to being an essential alternative to commercial television.

However, in both academic work and in the discourses of broadcasters' audience measurement, it has been increasingly recognised that audiences are fragmented, differentiated and often unpredictable. Stuart Hall (1996: 4) points out that this leads to a need for the historicisation of the concept of audience, because of the different ways in which audience has been discursively conceptualised over time:

> Identities are never unified and, in late modern times, increasingly fragmented and fractured; never singular but multiply constructed across different, often intersecting and antagonistic, discourses, practices and positions . . . Precisely because identities are constructed within, not outside discourse, we need to understand them as produced in specific historical and institutional sites within specific discursive formations and practices, by specific enunciative strategies.

In relation to television's mode of address by means of programme texts, interstitial programming such as commercial and idents, and the peripheral texts that enfold television programming in discourses such as listings magazines and press commentary, European television is part of a much larger process of identity formation for viewers. It can be argued in general, along with Chris Barker (1999: 5–6), that identity is

> the meeting point, the point of suture, between on the one hand the discourse and practices which attempt to 'interpellate', speak to us or hail us into place as the social subject of particular discourses, and, on the other hand, the processes which produce subjectivities, which construct us as subjects which can be 'spoken'. Identities are thus points of temporary attachment to the subject positions which discursive practices construct for us.

These processes of audience interpellation have taken a distinctive form in the twenty-first century because of the gradual adoption across Europe of interactive television.

Discussing interactivity in television is complex, because the term is used both to refer to the software of television, a text whose understanding and decoding involves the active input of a viewer, but also to television hardware, where digital technology enables viewers to make decisions about the programmes they are watching and how they are watched, such as their scheduling according to a menu of preferences accessed via a remote control button.

Theories of the active audience in television studies have established that audiences respond actively to texts, and engage with their meanings. But this is not the same as interactivity as it is more recently defined, since this refers to the intervention of the viewer in the text, in the form of a communication between the viewer and the source of the programme. The study of this issue is becoming increasingly important, not only because of the pervasive penetration of interactive television into the majority of European homes, but also because the heavy cost of producing this technology has given more influence to the big corporations that already seek to dominate the television landscape (Jenkins 2004). The concentration of media ownership has happened at exactly the same time as the kinds of media consumption have become more diverse and apparently more democratic. The power of the audience seems to exist at the same time as, and potentially in opposition to, the increasing power of media conglomerates.

Television technologies: transmission versus reception

The history of television in Europe (and elsewhere) has too often been assimilated into a narrative about the progressive improvement of technology. From the earliest mechanical devices for audiovisual broadcasting, through the introduction of magnetic tape in programme production and as home recording technology, to cable television and satellite transmission, it has too easily seemed that the history of television is driven by technological innovation. By contrast, however, technical innovations require the resources of large organisations, and the will to implement technologies in applications which can be represented and sold to a public. They require the stimulation of demand, and a framework of regulation and law to govern their implementation. Technologies cannot be seen as in themselves the drivers of the development of television in Europe, since recognition of a potential market, and both modes of viewing and offers of programme content that can be presented to this market, are preconditions for the adoption of a new television technology.

Television became a centralised business early in its development, in which large corporations and institutions controlled the facilities for programme production, and the networks for distribution from central transmission sources to the television audience. Whereas production and distribution involved a small number of centralised organisations, reception was differentiated and audiences were relatively passive and understood either as markets or as relatively unified citizenries. By contrast, in the late nineteenth century television technologies were imagined to be more like telephone systems (Gripsrud 1998: 20–1), in which people equipped with small television recording devices would make and send pictures and sound to domestic receivers in a much more personal, unregulated and cheaper form than actually became the case. Politically, therefore, television might have been a popular medium, in the sense that it could have been made and received by individuals and informal networks. The two decisive factors in the actual development of European television were capitalist firms interested in developing new product lines for mass markets to purchase for domestic use, and national governments which co-operated to establish technical standards for television equipment and transmission systems. This also led to the creation of professional elites of highly trained technicians and production staff to undertake the making of programmes and a cadre of professionals to carry out the management of television.

Radio and television engineers without doubt played a crucial role in the infrastructural integration of the European broadcasting space. The transnational character of radio waves made them an issue of cross-border negotiation and legislation from the very beginning, resulting in the foundation of international, non-governmental broadcasting institutions. The International Broadcasting Union (IBU) was founded in 1925, the European Broadcasting Union (EBU) in 1950, and the Organisation Internationale de Radiodiffusion et Télévision (OIRT) in 1946. The EBU quickly became the most important platform for the development of a Western European television infrastructure (Zeller 1999). The first initiatives to realise transnational television transmissions in Europe were the bilateral experiments of the French and the British broadcasting corporations, leading to the 'Calais experiment' in 1950 and the 'Paris week' of 1952. The mutual praise lavished by RTF and BBC officials after the realisation of 'Paris week' in 1952 show that both the British and the French saw themselves as the pioneers of a coming European television era. This era started with the live coverage of the Coronation of Queen Elizabeth II in 1953, which was the first truly European television event. For the first time in television history, an event was broadcast live into five countries: Britain, France, Germany, Denmark and the Netherlands. From a cultural history perspective, the effect of this transmission on the public cannot be overestimated. The feeling of televisual participation created by the live transmission of motion pictures undoubtedly gave impetus to television development all over the world. Although the coronation transmission had been carried out by the national broadcasting institutions of the five countries involved and therefore was not an official EBU activity, its impact on the EBU was great. As Wolfgang Degenhardt (Degenhardt & Strautz 1999: 38) and others have shown, the technical expenditure was enormous, especially the costly equipment for the line-conversion of the pictures transmitted, but the propagandistic effect of this pioneer performance was worth more than money. Without doubt, the Coronation event shaped a new horizon of televisual expectations in many European countries and promoted the idea of television as a 'window to the world'.

Both on a material, institutional and symbolic level, television infrastructures are probably the most prominent witness of the hidden integration of Europe as a communication space. On the material level, the technical infrastructure of broadcasting, comprising transmitters, networks of relay stations, cables and satellite dishes is evidence of Europe as a technically connected communication space. Institutionally, European broadcast institutions (like the IBU, the EBU or the OIRT) have functioned as crucial gateways for realising transnational interaction, both technically and juridically as well as on the level of intercultural communication. Beyond their function as gateways they can be analysed as mediators of changing discourses about Europe. As networks for the flow of intercultural communication, broadcast infrastructures have shaped European communication spaces and thereby territories for the negotiation of European identities. The sonic and visual icons of Europe (for example, the symbolic force of the Eurovision hymn) represent Europe as a cultural space and demonstrate the discursive infrastructures (Fickers & Lommers 2009) that contribute to its formation.

The separate layers of European broadcast infrastructures are theoretical constructions, and in fact interact with each other in various ways. While political conceptions of Europe as a community of sovereign but legally committed nations have influenced the (fragmented) construction of a European broadcasting space, broadcast technologies (such as short-wave radio or satellites) have challenged the politicisation of the ether and offered unexpected possibilities for civilian, amateur appropriations of Europe as a transnational communication space. In this sense, the 'reversion of the public/private relationship' (Scannell 1996: 69) through broadcasting can be interpreted as a structural transformation of the European political public sphere. The early live Eurovision transmission opened up a window on just handful of Western European nations, but Telstar satellite transmission experiments in 1962 inaugurated the age of global television coverage. Only five years later, in the same year as the introduction of colour television in Germany, Britain, France and the Soviet Union, the first global television programme was broadcast around the world. *Our World*, a two-and-a-half-hour programme conceived by the BBC producer Aubrey Singer but realised in collaboration with the EBU, was transmitted to 31 countries and reached an estimated audience of 400 million viewers. Today, it is most famous for the segment starring the Beatles. Performing at the height of the Vietnam War, the group wanted to spread a message of peace and love to the world. They broadcast a live set, singing John Lennon's song 'All You Need is Love' which had been written specially for the occasion.

European commercial broadcasting by satellite began with ASTRA in 1989, and could be received by 56 million households (35 per cent of total households) in 22 European countries in 1995 (Collins 1990). ASTRA and its sister satellites are operated by a private Luxembourg company, SES, which leases satellite transponders to broadcasters. Their footprints extend from Iceland to northern Morocco and the Canary Islands to Budapest, and can be received by home receiving dishes or through cable networks. The media entrepreneur Rupert Murdoch was ASTRA's first client in 1988, for Sky Television in Britain and Western Europe, followed by German broadcasters for commercial entertainment channels, and the gradual financial success of the system led to the 1995 launch by the European Satellite Agency of its first satellite to compete with ASTRA. Transnational television institutions in Europe have provided exchange networks for news broadcasting that have created closed circuits among broadcasters in the region, producing a European news market. Raw television news footage is offered to broadcasters by news agencies such as Eurovision, and is accessed through the European Broadcasting Union (EBU). This network is connected other transnational exchange services, and six times a day satellite links exchange news footage between Eurovision and Asiavision, for example. Satellite technology enables the international news agencies such as Visnews and Worldwide Television Network to operate 24 hours a day, sending both raw footage and complete news packages to national and regional broadcasters. Because of the different languages of television broadcasting in different nations, the news agencies mainly distribute images without commentary. This makes it more likely that their news footage will be perceived as objective by news editors, and this impression is reinforced by the neutrally phrased written material which the agencies provide with the footage to explain what their pictures denote. The agency footage can have a range of meanings attached to it by the voice-over commentaries which individual news broadcasters add to it in programme packages.

Television discourses: between hopes and fears

Television is known for its engagement with the current time and space of its audience, the 'here and now', but in its representations of that spatial and temporal world tailored to the competences of its audiences, it has also functioned as a mechanism for utopian imaginings of the different. The hopes for television are part of a larger function of utopian thought in general, which both represents and actualises the possibility of change. As Levitas (1993: 257) has argued, utopian thinking may be

> understood more broadly as the desire for a better way of living expressed in the description of a different kind of society that makes possible that alternative way of life. There may be many reasons for finding utopian thought interesting, but the political importance of utopia rests on the argument that a vision of a good society located in the future may act as an agent of change.

The specific role of television in expressing utopias in its programming content, and also representing in its own form as a mass broadcasting technology the hopes for what media will offer to societies in the future is therefore connected to larger political and cultural utopianisms. Television has stood in Europe as a totem or currency representing greater transformations: 'Politically, utopia is important because of its potential role in social transformation. The absence of utopian thinking may then be construed as a problem because it paralyses political action or prevents it from cohering into a force capable of effecting fundamental change' (Levitas 1993: 257). The very presence of television as a technology, an aspect of social life, and a mediator of representations, has enabled utopian discourses to adopt television in various ways as an example or symbol of what a better future might be like.

As William Boddy, William Uricchio and Carolyn Marvon have demonstrated, the discourse surrounding the emergence of television as a new medium is part of a larger narrative pattern, reflecting the ambivalent role of technology in the process of modernisation. They argue that every time a new medium enters the existing mass media ensemble, 'the consequences of technical innovation, real and imagined, provoked both euphoria and unease within and without the communication industries' (Boddy 2004: 3). But these dialectical positions in relation to the benefits and the downsides of new communication technologies not only mirror the cultural or societal disputes about the role of media in modern societies. They also actively interfere in the process of technological development by shaping the horizons of expectation that influence both the developers and the users of new technologies.

Both the processes of invention and innovation of new media technologies, as well as their histories, seem to follow certain patterns of narration. The international saga of the invention and innovation of radio, television or the internet (among the other 'new' media that entered the mass media ensemble in the twentieth century) can be read as a serial technological drama. Following Bryan Pfaffenberger (1992: 286), we argue that these narrative patterns not only characterise historical storytelling about acts of invention and processes of innovation, but that the technological artefacts themselves implicitly have the momentum to shape specific paths of development:

> To emphasize the metaphor of drama, too, is to employ a richer metaphor than text. It is to emphasize the performative nature of technological 'statements' and 'counterstatements', which involve the creation of scenes (contexts), in which actors (designers, artefacts, and users) play out their fabricated roles with regard to a set of envisioned purposes (and before an audience), and it is also to emphasize that the discourse involved is not the argumentative and academic discourse of a text but the symbolic media of myth (in which scepticism is suspended) and ritual (in which human actions are mythically patterned in controlled social spaces).

There are three recurring narrative patterns discovered in analysing the history of television. The first is the metaphorical description of the act of invention, second the (melo)dramatic accounts of glory and failure in the process of innovation, and third the mythical charge that technology carries in techno-political regimes, and together they perfectly demonstrate the 'symbolic media of myth and ritual' and show the performative nature of the technological development of television (Fickers & Kessler 2008).

But the dramatic narratives of television are not limited to the prehistory of the medium, where the technical qualities of the invention gathered the most popular attention. Since the time when regular television services started, the message of the medium was as much the object of public debate as the medium itself. As Vincent Crone (2007) has recently demonstrated in relation to the Dutch case, both scientific and popular discussions about the harmful effects of television watching on the physical and mental state of its viewers have gone along with the development of television since the mid-1950s. These dramatic narratives occur in cyclical waves, and they should not be analysed as a rhetorical symptom accompanying television as a cultural form and as a technology, but as inherent parts of television as a discursive construction. It is of course the task of the media historian to contextualise these recurring narrative patterns and to interpret their cultural meanings or political and ideological implications, and the (few) existing publications with a media comparative focus encourage us to explore this methodological path (Damann 2005).

However, television is an emblem of the future as well as the present because it exemplifies postmodern fragmentation, the absorption of history into a continual present, and the reduction of spatial and cultural specificity, as Morley and Robbins (1995: 112) suggest: 'What is being created is a new electronic cultural space, a "placeless" geography of image and simulation.' Television might also be understood as preventing the progressive improvement of European societies, as Morley and Robins (1995: 112) continue:

> The formation of this global hyperspace is reflected in that strand of post-modernist thinking associated particularly with writers like Baudrillard and Virilio. Baudrillard, for example, invokes the vertigo, the disorientation, the delirium created by the world of flows and images and screens. The new global arena of culture is a world of instantaneous and depthless communication, a world in which space and time horizons have become compressed and collapsed. The creators of this universal cultural space are the new global cultural corporations.

For some, television embodies the end of history and thus the end of 'grand narratives' of utopian thinking. As Levitas (1993: 258) argues:

> postmodernity creates difficulties about thinking about the future. The spatial replaces the temporal, while the fragmentation of experience underlines the contingency of all interpretations of the world and renders problematic any commitment to an alternative, let alone an alternative future. The condition of postmodernity is one in which the future presents itself as foreclosed – or indeed fails to present itself at all.

However, this pessimistic narrative about postmodernity, very relevant to television since the medium has been seen as one of its chief embodiments, is challenged by the historical work on television that we present in this book. Levitas (1993: 258) continues:

> The claim that postmodernism and/or postmodernity have extinguished the utopian imagination is not altogether true, and this for two reasons. First utopian speculation continues although there have been changes, and quite important changes, in the space that utopia is able to occupy in contemporary culture. Second, the causes of these changes are not to be located solely or even primarily in the ideological sphere. They are not caused by a failure of the utopian imagination, but result from a more concrete problem, that of the difficulty of identifying points of intervention in an increasingly complex social and economic structure, and of identifying the agents and bearers of social transformation. It is difficult, therefore to imagine and believe in the transition to an imagined better future.

Work on the hopes and fears about television that have persisted in its history in Europe demonstrate these problems. Changes in television technology have always made it difficult to identify how television might offer better or worse futures for societies, though they have encouraged speculation about the issue. Some of the nodal points for this speculation and the airing of hopes and fears have included the invention of television itself, through to the changed understandings of television associated with video recording and consequent time-shifting. Currently, hopes and fears crystallise around the proliferation of channels made possible by new satellite and cable networks, and the new modes of delivery through digital streaming and the possibility to watch television on different kinds of receiver (computers, mobile phones, etc.). It is no more difficult or easier in the 2000s to assess the accuracy of hopes and fears for television than it was in the 1930s or 1950s. The complexity of television as a technology, institution, aesthetic form and mode of cultural experience have both permitted utopian thinking about it but also repeatedly disconfirmed both hopes and fears.

Television norms: high versus low quality

The dramatic narratives of television often include implicit moral or ethical appraisals, expressed in simple qualitative juxtapositions such as 'good' or 'bad' programmes, 'high' or 'low' cultural standard, and so on. Intellectuals, moral authorities (like churches) or political parties have all expressed their concerns about the basic standards of quality in programmes from the early days of television onwards. A recurrent pattern in these discussions about the quality of television is the tension between the 'serious' and the 'popular' mandate of television as a mass medium, and this is often exemplified by the differences between the European tradition of public service broadcasting and the American model of commercial stations. The academic field has paid extensive attention to the processes of so-called 'Americanisation' or 'Westernisation' of European cultural traditions in the nineteenth and especially the twentieth centuries. In the processes of transnational circulation and national appropriation of goods and meanings, the media have without doubt played a crucial role as mediators and actors of cultural transfer. But as both Valeria Camporesi and Michele Hilmes argue, it is important not to analyse these processes as one-way phenomena and examples of cultural imperialism from the USA to Europe, but to more carefully interpret them as complex forms of interaction, mutual construction and interdependent development between the two continents. The continents themselves are of course abstract constructions, simplifying and reducing the enormous diversity and complexity of cultural traditions and their national or regional specificities. As Valeria Camporesi has stated: 'This whole work of translation, resistance, adaptation, rejection, selective learning puts the very notion of "Americanization" to serious test' (Camporesi 2000: 199). While Camporesi's work concentrated on the relationships between the BBC and the USA in the inter-war period, Michele Hilmes (2003a: 26–7) has recently extended this warning about 'historical dualisms' to the whole history of broadcasting in the twentieth century:

> Now, as the national systems of control established in the early decades of the last century are breaking down under the forces of deregulation and globalisation; now that technologies such as satellites and the Internet provide us with new models of communication that defy centralised national control; now that corporate influence over the institutions of the State has rendered moot many of the old distinctions between private and public; now that our understanding of democracy as cultural as well as political means that the old 'one size fits it all' standards of the past can no longer be justified: we might re-examine the public vs. commercial, British vs. American dichotomy and turn our attention instead to the similar social functions of both systems.

Academic studies of television have had little interest in valuing programmes or television forms comparatively, while by contrast journalistic coverage, informal talk and professional discourse in the television industry place evaluative issues high on the agenda. The industry criteria of quality, as well as reflecting considerations of economic success and profile within institutional hierarchies, have also reflected a concern for aesthetics and professional skill, but the divisions between these types of valuation have tended to blur into each other. For example, the Golden Rose (Rose d'Or) festival for entertainment television in Montreux, Switzerland, began in 1961 as a means for national broadcasters to find low-cost programmes that could be presented as 'quality' television during the summer period when schedules were occupied largely with repeats and low-budget entertainment. This resulted in an international variety programme with a competition format that could be exchanged for productions produced in other countries. The first winner was the BBC's *Black and White Minstrel Show* and subsequent winners have included circus specials, sitcoms, game shows and cartoons including *The Muppet Show*, *The Benny Hill Show*, *Monty Python's Flying Circus*, *Cirque du Soleil*, *The Simpsons* and *Mr Bean*. Juries for prizes are designed to avoid domination by the most powerful producing nations, or by public service or commercial broadcasters. The expansion of the festival led to the demise of direct programme exchanges and instead the evolution of the event into a programme market, Videokiosk, in which representatives from up to forty nations bought and sold formats as well as programmes, and series as well as one-off specials. So the festival began from the start as a mechanism for fulfilling broadcasters' scheduling and supply needs, as well as a competitive contest for quality in light entertainment. Its subsequent evolution into a programme market simply makes explicit confusion between industrial imperatives and aesthetic criteria that were evident from the beginning.

The example of the Golden Rose shows that criteria of evaluation have common features across Europe, but there are also significant differences, and this book distinguishes and debates the ways that a programme (or a channel, or an evening's viewing) has been considered 'good' in different parts of Europe at different times. Quality television is an informal category that often separates prestigious dramas, documentaries, art films and adaptations of literary sources from 'popular' television. Although in recent decades academic television studies have taken popular television seriously, because it is the television most people watch the most, criticism in the press, and sometimes in the television industry itself, has evaluated popular television is unimportant, merely commercial, and lacking in artistic value.

John Fiske and John Hartley (1978: 125) argued that the discourse of television comprised a mixture of 'literate' and 'oral' codes. 'Literate' components are those shared with literary texts and other high-status forms of written communication which are 'narrative, sequential, abstract, univocal, "consistent" ', whereas features which are more similar to informal communication, spoken language or popular songs are 'dramatic, episodic, concrete, social, dialectical'. The literate codes of television underlie programmes' novelistic narrative structures and linear explanatory forms, and can be regarded as reproducing the unifying and official languages of social power, which impose an ordered worldview. On the other hand, the 'oral' features of television derive from organic communities and everyday discourses, and are thus a representation of popular culture. In the context of critiques of social control, and the valuation of ordinary people and their worldviews, the oral mode of television is a vital and progressive element possessing radical potential. Discourses of evaluation of quality have tended to value 'literate' modes while devaluing 'oral' ones, but the identification of 'oral' and popular aspects of television in Europe gestures towards academic studies' increasing desire to validate the ordinary viewer, popular culture and the contribution of television audiences to meaning.

The question of quality in television is closely connected with two contrasting cultural values, namely experimentation and heritage. Lowenthal (1997: ix–xi) argues that on one hand, heritage has a protective function in overcoming dissatisfaction with the present or recent past, or veiling the anxious prospect of an expected future. In these respects, the role of heritage is to be a consolation, and thus works to prevent change and progress. As a cultural phenomenon closely associated with nationalism, it may also have xenophobic resonances. However, on the other hand, heritage makes links between viewers and their ancestors and offspring, and has potentially positive benefits in creating bonds between individuals, national television communities, and regional groupings of television cultures across Europe. The heritage of television, and heritage in television programming content, can be understood as a mechanism and conduit for the production of a sense of shared history and the continuity of European identities of different kinds.

In contrast to some television cultures such as Britain, where heritage on television has developed a relatively specific meaning (as the adaptation of literary classics, programming about symbolic national landscapes, elite or popular institutions, and examples of well-known television from the past), some European television cultures have a much more contested and problematic notion of heritage. This goes to prove Michel Foucault's (1986: 82) point that

> we should not be deceived into thinking that this heritage is an acquisition, a possession that grows and solidifies; rather, it is an unstable assemblage of faults, fissures and heterogeneous layers that threaten the fragile interior from within or underneath . . . The search for descent is not the erecting of foundations: on the contrary it disturbs what was previously considered immobile; it fragments what was thought unified; it shows the heterogeneity of what was imagined consistent with itself.

Television rituals: ordinary versus event

The discursive construction of Europe, European identities and European spaces are most visible in so called European 'events'. Until recently, events have been the favoured objects of study of sociologists interested in the 'extra-ordinary', in social agency or collective activity transgressing quotidian or routine social behaviour (Knoblauch 2000: 33–50). Generally speaking, events as social happenings are planned and organised occasions of collective participation, whether in the form of either mediated or proximate participation. While events originally consisted in a bodily and physical experience of an organised happening by a larger group of people (such as Roman circus games lasting several days, a medieval conclave or a modern political event such as the Vienna Congress), modern communication technologies have deeply changed both the nature and the experience of social events. The live coverage of events by various media technologies has transformed the social situation of the happening: those who directly participate have themselves become the points of access for the unknown mass of mediated participants. Together they perform what Daniel Dayan and Elihu Katz have described as 'media events'. Focusing their investigation on television, Dayan and Katz (1992: 1) define media events as extraordinary experiences of medial participation: 'Audiences recognize them as an invitation – even a command – to stop their daily routines and join in a holiday experience. If festive viewing is to ordinary viewing what holidays are to the everyday, these events are the high holidays of mass communication.' While the definition of media events by Dayan and Katz has been criticised for being too rigid in its characterisation of media events as pre-planned and highly stereotyped forms of mediated social interaction (Wanning 2001), media sociologist Nick Couldry (2003) wondered whether they can be 'read' as expressions of social order at all or should be interpreted as medial constructions of collective identities.

Ordinary television is a repository of the accretion of different and often contrasting forms of representation and relations with audiences that play an important role in the constitution of cultural identities in Europe, especially national ones. Thus ordinary television can be understood overall as a narrative 'by which stories, images, symbols and rituals represent "shared" meanings of nationhood. National identity is a constitutive representation of shared experiences and history told in stories, literature, popular culture and . . . television' (Barker 1999: 68). In this respect, the functions of ordinary television are not as dissimilar as they might seem from the identity-forming functions of television events and television as itself an event, since these too work to focus conceptions of regional, national, transnational and global identities around a specific television moment. This moment may be one created for television, one already existing whose circulation is made possible by television and thus assumes a different character, or one that is relayed by television but remains tied in its form and significance to factors that are independent of its transmission. A significant example of a television event is the Eurovision Song Contest, beginning in 1956 and along with *Jeux Sans Frontières* one of the prime activities of the EBU. In 1954 there were fewer than five million television receivers in the continent, 90 per cent of which were in Britain, but the audience for the programme grew because of satellite transmission to reach North Africa, the Middle East and Eastern Europe. While Eurovision initially focused on sport, news and public affairs, in the 1950s the EBU wished to reduce the influence of American entertainment and expanded the San Remo Song Festival in Italy into a European television event. The first Contest was held in Lugano, Switzerland, and by the end of the twentieth century was watched by 600 million people in 35 countries. Early contests were dominated by ballads, contrasting with the American domination of national popular music by rock and roll, but by the late 1960s entries aimed at teen audiences began to predominate and songs either used

English lyrics or very simple, non-specific phrases such as 'La la la' (as in the winning Spanish entry of 1998). Rule changes in the later 1970s encouraged entries based on national folk traditions, but by the 1980s further influences from British and US pop choreography and eroticisation were combined with professionalisation and promotion by the music industry.

Television events in Europe contribute to new ways of thinking about time, space and relationships with the world. Since information circulates across different time zones, local time and the sense of familiar space can be understood as partial and local variations within a European or even global time and space. Local activity can be seen in the contexts of transnational and global problems and opportunities, where traditional and historic ways of understanding subjectivity, community or nation are overlaid or even replaced by transnationally dominant ways of thinking. Television events enable their audiences to witness different places and times of different nations and cultures, such as news broadcasting of the 1990s conflicts in the former Yugoslavia. In the years leading up to the revolutions in Eastern Europe in 1989, in some nations images of the apparently comfortable lives and abundant consumer goods of Western Europe aided the populations' desire for political change, and images representing western culture such as satellite broadcasting of MTV stimulated change in the Soviet Union in the late 1980s.

But in contrast to 'event television', ordinary television such as prime-time entertainment shows offers some evidence for the industrial and ideological homogenisation of television in Europe in the recent past. In the recently deregulated television cultures of Eastern Europe, factual entertainment programmes such as 'people shows' or 'makeover shows' have been developed in national versions deriving from formats successful in Western European cultures. Examples of these programmes include *Big Brother* (the most successful example), but also programmes featuring lifestyle and self-improvement documentary series and contests. Although there was widespread condemnation of these programmes for 'dumbing down' the audience (Biltereyst 2004), they have also been defended as 'just entertainment' and as a benefit of increasing viewer choice, as part of a generalised movement towards populism and the democratisation of television. The parallel between choice and democratic empowerment is of course a false one, though in principle there is no reason to regard choice as antagonistic to democracy. If viewers in newly commercialised television cultures, where consumer capitalism takes over from state control or paternalistic regulation, choose to watch makeover formats and other kinds of reality TV programming, this can be seen both as an embrace of the new culture of selfhood as a project of secular perfectibility, and also as a testing or ventilation of social anxieties about the processes of the commodification of the self and the body as things to be worked on, improved, modified and shown off. The pain involved in the exposure, testing, risking and failure of the self thus shown under construction is as much at stake as the pleasures of watching and identifying with contestants engaged in projects of self-improvement and self-analysis. The episodic serial process of pressuring, testing, exposing and judging selves and bodies in *Big Brother*, for example, can be seen as an opportunity for questioning the shift to body/self projects of perfectibility as well as a celebration of it.

The use of television as a medium in which makeover formats are translated and exchanged across different local and regional spaces in Europe draws attention to the temptation to take television as a causal agent of local and regional social change based on the specific form it takes in the USA. This is partly for the pragmatic reason that theories of television are readily available from US academics and theorists. It is also the result of the assumption that the model of television institutional organisation in the USA is the historic destiny of television in all contemporary societies. For example, the de-differentiation of space and time in transnational makeover forms and formats relates interestingly to theoretical work on the medium (based on its US forms) in the work of Margaret Morse. She argues that television is parallel to the freeway and the shopping mall, noting first the flow and movement in which billboards are driven past on an American freeway, and secondly the segmentation and multiplicity of products in the self-contained and privatised space of the shopping mall. For Morse (1990: 197), television, the freeway and the mall are 'derealized or *nonspace*'. Television can take the viewer anywhere in time and simulate the past (like the artificial village square of the shopping mall) and can also shift the viewer in space by offering visions of distant places that are rendered the same as each other as they rush past in an evening's viewing (like the infinite horizon and endless journey of the freeway). This produces a mobile subjectivity and an experience of distraction which is dislocated from traditional spaces and times at the same time as it simulates and commodifies them, turning them into products offered for the audience to choose. As in many theoretical accounts of the specific aesthetics and politics of the television medium, the metaphors used to analyse it connect television to America, postmodernism and feminisation in their connection with consumption, the erosion of boundaries and the liquidity of flow. So the argument is that makeover television abstracts the people who are transformed from their specific spaces and times of existence, making each made-over self and body equivalent to all the others that are subjected to reality TV's weekly transformations. Some reality TV formats are adapted to particular localised cultures, and the expectations about identity, private space and the role of television in different societies. However, the fact of transnational export of formats in itself represents an erosion of local particularity, and the adoption of television modes of address to viewers about identities and bodies that derive from western models.

Gamedocs have been traded in Europe as international formats that are locally produced, and this had previously been a distribution model adopted by the owners of more conventional game-show formats such as *The Price is Right* or *Who Wants to Be a Millionaire*. The pre-designed and tested formats of reality TV cost less to produce than wholly new programme ideas devised for specific national channels, and reduce the risk that new programmes face of finding the right audience and becoming popular. Annette Hill's work (2002: 325–6) on the different national audiences for *Big Brother* demonstrated the format's role as means to define the brand identity of individual national channels and to raise the profile of a channel. The first version of *Big Brother* was produced in Holland by John de Mol Productions for the Veronica channel. De Mol's company Dutch Endemol is owned by Spanish media company Telefónica, and formats that Endemol has devised include a range of reality TV variants such as *Fame Academy*, *Changing Rooms*, *Fear Factor* and *The Salon*. In the Netherlands, the first *Big Brother* series peaked at 6 million viewers when two contestants enjoyed a moment of physical intimacy, and healthy ratings for the programme assisted in making the format an attractive prospect for broadcasters in other countries, but perhaps equally important was the profile of the programme as evidenced by press and television coverage, which supported a rapidly growing public culture of talk, consisting largely of speculation about the contestants and the outcome of the competition. This word-of-mouth circulation of information has been a key aspect of *Big Brother*'s success internationally, and has the spin-off benefit of drawing viewers to the channel broadcasting the series and potentially keeping them watching it for other programmes in its schedule.

In Germany, *Big Brother* was produced by Endemol Entertainment for the RTL2 and RTL channels. Its success meant that a second series was commissioned during the summer run of the first series, so that a second series could begin in autumn 2000 as soon as the first one finished. RTL2 was a small broadcaster with an average 3.9 per cent share of the audience in *Big Brother*'s time slot, and the channel increased this to 15 per cent for the second *Big Brother* series. Then a third series was commissioned for the post-Christmas season (finishing in May 2001) but the ratings did not equal those of its predecessor. The opportunity to raise a minority channel's audience share was more dramatically demonstrated in Portugal, where TVI screened *Big Brother* (produced by Endemol Entertainment) from September to December 2000, gaining an average share over this period of 61 per cent in contrast to its normal average share of 9 per cent, and a peak share of 74 per cent in the series' final week. Similar success followed when a second *Big Brother* series was screened by the same channel. *Big Brother* in Spain was broadcast by Tele 5 (produced by Zeppelin Television) in April–July 2000. Tele 5 had a normal average share of 21 per cent, and although at the start of the *Big Brother* series the channel's initial share was 13.7 per cent, this rose to 30 per cent with a peak for the final episode of 70 per cent, when the ratings for this climactic end to the competition overtook those of the Champions League soccer semi-final. *Big Brother* in Belgium was on Kanal 2 (produced by Endemol Entertainment) from September to December 2000, and the channel's average share rose from 9 per cent to a peak of almost 50 per cent.

Similarly, *Big Brother* in Switzerland was on TV3 (produced by B&B Endemol) in autumn 2000 and increased the channel's share from an average of only 2.5 per cent to 30 per cent. *Big Brother* in Sweden did not get high ratings or audience share, but achieved high levels of publicity and profile for its broadcaster. The series was on Kanal 5 (produced by Metronome Television) in autumn 2000, and the channel's 10 per cent share remained steady during the run. However, the media profile of *Big Brother* in Sweden was a significant factor in Kanal 5's decision to commission a second series with a modified format. The ways in which personnel, format ideas, programmes and ways of interacting with television occur in different locations suggest at least the westernisation of ideas about the self, the body and community.

Television politics: democratic versus totalitarian

When television began in Europe in the periods immediately before and after the Second World War, all of its programmes were live because recording technology had not been perfected. On one hand, television gave and still gives viewers an experience of immediacy and credibility, because of its mythology of transcription or denotation. The dissemination of information and actuality beyond the local and personal experience of its viewers can be argued to broaden the experience and awareness of the audience. The political effects of this have been for television to assist national and European institutions in involving citizens in social and political debate and to contribute to the public sphere. On the other hand, television's necessary selectivity, conventions of representation and governance by television institutions and legal regulation empower television to relate the viewer to the world and separates the viewer from his or her experience of reality. If television substitutes mediated and partial versions of information and understanding for authentic experience, then its effect is to deter discussion and debate. For example, Wulf Kansteiner's (2004) work on the West German public television station ZDF between 1963 and 1993 showed that programming on the history of the Third Reich was interesting to viewers except during a brief period in the mid-1970s. However, the characteristics of this programming in the 1960s reinforced an apologetic tone that ignored the Holocaust, whereas in the 1980s a more self-critical representation developed though it still did not directly confront active Nazi perpetrators in the Holocaust or the people who passively witnessed it at the time.

Problems of the contribution of television in Europe to democracy, versus its relationship with social control or totalitarianism, are linked directly with understandings of the audience as a citizenry, and questions of passivity and consumerisation. For Chris Barker (1999: 230), 'television on a global scale has the capacity to contribute to democracy (via the principles of diversity and solidarity) through its range of representations, genres, arguments and information. However, the vision of television as a diverse and plural public sphere is seriously compromised by its almost complete penetration by the interest-based messages and images of consumerism.' A concrete example of this in recent history is provided in the work of Deborah Philips (2005) on television home makeover formats such as *Home Front* and *Changing Rooms* that mediate between the private, domestic space of the home and the public world of television. Expert designers become television personalities who act as 'tastemakers', contributing to pan-European processes of privatisation of property and the symbolic effects of rising housing costs so that an avowed democratisation of taste in these widely exported formats in fact confirms the superior knowledge and cultural capital of television experts to erase differences in personal taste in favour of its commodification.

The hope that television would be a strong agent of democratisation was part of the dramatic narrative of early television. There have been numerous statements to this effect by politicians and state officials, bearing witness to the extraordinary expectations of television as a means of democratic political communication. The first director-general of post-war public service television broadcasting in West Germany, Adolf Grimme, presented television in 1953 as the medial reincarnation of the classical ideal of democracy. For Grimme, what made politics in ancient times a publicly shared activity for all returns in the age of mass media, for television takes the place of the agora, or meeting-place of the whole nation in which direct democracy can be realised. Kurt Wagenführ, one of the most prominent German radio and television journalists, saluted Grimme by stating that the television camera in parliament would be an omnipresent eye of democracy, enabling a direct link between the inner sphere of the parliament and the whole German nation. A few years later, Gabriel Delaunay, Grimme's French equivalent and director-general of the Radio Télévision Française (RTF), made exactly the same historical comparison: 'The columns of the Forum Romanum, too fragile to resist time and wars, have collapsed. Politics had to take refuge in strange temples called "parliaments". But radio and television have given birth to a new conception of the Forum in installing it around every table of a household' (Delaunay 1958). The French television historian Évelyne Cohen (1999: 26) interpreted the political function of television during the de Gaulle years as a genuine 'national language', a privileged vehicle of national sentiment and community. Television's role as a stabilising force of the nation has been widely researched, but the transnational impact of programmes and people crossing the borders of 'television nations' needs to be researched in a much more detailed way.

Transnational news channels are one of the key examples for the debate about the impact of television on national political structures of news value and the public sphere. Complete news programmes are broadcast by satellite by the American institution CNN, which broadcasts to about 130 countries with content in major regional languages, and Britain's Sky News and BBC World. BBC World was launched in 1991 as BBC World Service Television, drawing on the global recognition of the BBC's radio World Service and using the radio service's 250 correspondents and 57 regional bureaux, as well as the BBC's television studios, technicians and reporters already stationed around the world. This scale of operation makes the BBC the world's largest newsgathering organisation. Half of BBC World's 24 hours of television consists of news programmes, each half an hour in length, and the other half is BBC current affairs, factual and entertainment programmes. BBC World is the biggest rival to the CNN network, and has a contrasting style. Rather than emphasising breaking news and live broadcast, BBC World is based around the journalistic comment on news which its correspondents and reporters can offer, and the very diverse international coverage which it can provide using World Service radio's expert staff. In 1992 the service reached three continents, constituting 80 per cent of the world's population. Soon deals had been negotiated for BBC World to be broadcast by satellite to continental Europe (including Russia), and the channel was the first to offer simultaneous translation of its English-language news programmes into other regional languages, then followed by CNN.

The selection of news stories on national television networks around the world, and the structure and form of news broadcasting there are influenced by CNN and BBC World because their global coverage and broadcasting have the effect of bringing its selection of stories to the attention of national broadcasters. These channels can also affect the events which are being reported, since coverage of events almost live can have the effect of altering the progress of a news event, for example by alerting officials to the perception of their actions abroad. However, it would be mistaken to claim that transnational news broadcasters have direct effects on shaping events or attitudes to them. Apart from the theoretical insight that television's effects need to be considered within national institutional, legal and cultural constraints which delimit and redirect them, there are specific restrictions on the gathering of news and the accessibility of transnational television news. Attempts to manage news broadcast journalists by national politicians is common, in order to influence the representation of events outside a particular country where a transnational television news broadcaster is operating. The influence of the broadcasters is limited also by the fact that their programmes are in English and/or the languages spoken by affluent elites who are attractive to advertisers, so that only a relatively privileged sector of many societies has access to the transnational channels.

The proliferation of television channels in recent years has given rise to new channels that address audiences who have been dissatisfied with competitors and who are most likely to produce negotiated readings of dominant television news agendas offered by national and transnational channels such as BBC World or CNN. The international channel al-Jazeera was launched in 1996 and initially broadcast only in the Arabic language from Qatar, funded by the country's ruling emir. Its aim was to offer a new kind of journalism to audiences in the Middle East, following western norms by reporting opposing views instead of the official news agendas and opinions of government sources in the region. But despite this aim for objectivity and neutrality, the channel repeatedly annoyed western governments, especially the USA, by broadcasting videotape messages sent to it by the anti-western Islamic organisation al-Quaeda. These videotapes featured Osama Bin Laden, widely regarded as the terrorist leader behind al-Quaeda and the instigator of numerous attacks on western targets, including the destruction of the World Trade Center in 2001. Al-Jazeera started a new English-language channel in 2006, al-Jazeera International, attracting prominent British and other non-Arab journalists to present its programmes. The opportunity to follow stories that have not received much coverage in existing national and international news, or have been covered from a predominantly western point of view, is the main thing that al-Jazeera offers to its audiences and journalists. But the perception that the channel is unlike CNN or BBC World in this respect also meant that some of its presenters and reporters were cautious about its links with political and religious movements attacking the Western powers. Al-Jazeera employs over 200 staff from 30 national backgrounds in its news team, which it claims will permit reporters with local knowledge to offer new perspectives on news stories. The agenda is to avoid the categorisation of news according to the stereotypes of western-based channels, so that items from Africa, for example, will not be driven by the narratives about famine, AIDS and war which have often dominated coverage of the region. The programme schedule of the channel is timed to match the time zones of its viewers, so that over one 24-hour period, moving East to West, it broadcasts for four hours from Kuala Lumpur, 11 hours from Doha, 5 hours from London and 4 hours from Washington. As well as offering English-speaking audiences new kinds of coverage, and a new balance of coverage that favours the developing world and non-western nations, the channel expects to attract audiences from Muslim backgrounds who cannot speak Arabic but are interested in the non-western perspectives of its journalists and may be resistant to coverage of news on western channels such as CNN or BBC. There are 1.2 billion Muslims in the potential global audience, but only about 240 million speak Arabic. The channel is initially available free of charge to viewers via cable and satellite, though broadband streaming on the internet is likely to follow. In Britain, the channel is carried by Sky and when it launched at the end of 2006, al-Jazeera hoped to find viewers in about eight million British households.

Work by Jean Chalaby (2005) showed that cross-border television channels operate in different ways and proposed a typology comprising ethnic, multi-territory, pan-European channels and transnational networks. His interviews with media executives revealed that each of the four types of cross-border television had different relationships with nation-states, geographical space and culture. The pan-European channels such as Eurosport and MTV (Chalaby 2002), broadcasting across Europe, localised their pan-European output in the 1990s by means of local advertising, dubbing or subtitling, local programming and the opportunity for local opt-out within a particular territory. As a business strategy, localisation has facilitated globalisation processes by allowing transnational media players to cope with cultural diversity and operate more efficiently as multinational institutions.

Television changes: old versus new

The narrative of European television history has often been assimilated into the narrative of globalisation. In some respects the creation of European political institutions, especially the EU and its progressive erosion of physical borders between nations, and laws permitting citizens to work in nations other than that of their home, have made the globalisation narrative more pertinent in Europe than in other regions of the globe. Morley and Robins (1995: 87), for example, connect this to the narrative of modernisation: 'It is through the logic of globalisation that [the] dynamic of modernisation is most powerfully articulated. Through proliferating information and communications flows and through mass human migration, it has progressively eroded territorial frontiers and boundaries and provoked ever more immediate confrontations of culture and identity.' Television has not only borne witness to these changes in news and documentary programming, for example, but can also been seen as an agent of the new because of the export and exchange of formats and programmes across national boundaries. Morley and Robins (1995: 87) continue, quoting the French historian Pierre Nora (1989: 7): 'Where once it was the case that cultures were demarcated and differentiated in time and space, now "the concept of a fixed, unitary, and bounded culture must give way to a sense of the fluidity and permeability of cultural sets". Through this intermixture and hybridisation of cultures, older certainties and foundations of identity are continuously and necessarily undermined.' Television's hybridisation of cultures by means of programme and format exchange, and the possibility to dub or subtitle images with locally specific languages mean that television can exemplify modernity both in its content and in the transnational harmonisation of transmission standards and broadcasting technologies through the twentieth century.

Karen Siune and Olof Hulten (1998) set up a series of oppositions between older media and new media. In relation to the institutional control of the broadcast networks, the distinction between 'old' and 'new' media landscapes is between monopoly and competition. The organisations dominating the two epochs also have different primary goals, since television institutions were originally part of a larger enterprise towards democracy, whereas they are now driven by survival and the struggle for success and profit. While both 'old' and 'new' institutional forms have as primary activities the management of selection processes governing what material is screened, and the programme mix that enfolds it, the 'new' institutions have much less control over programme production, because of the outsourcing and privatisation of production processes and facilities. For Siune and Hulten, the logic governing the activities of television institutions was formerly based on responsibility, whereas more recently that logic is drawn from the market and economics. The selection criteria have shifted from political relevance to sale, and the reference group for the institutions has changed from citizens to consumers. Their focus has changed from the decisions taken and the power structure to the process of policy making and new conflict dimension. The perspective of institutions is no longer that of the nation or media system, but of individuals and global reach. This changed television culture has led to debates (in Norway, for example, as Syvertsen (2003) explains) about the national regulation of television to protect national public service television from the perceived threat of media convergence, transnational television institutions and commercialisation.

If television is an emblem of the new, it is so in part because of its containment and processing of memories of the old. Its adoption of some of the modes of radio (centre to periphery broadcasting, national organisation and regulation, adoption of inherited formats, forms and modes of address – including some that were hitherto borrowed by radio from theatre and other kinds of performance or journalism) connect television both to the past and to other media. This ability of a 'new medium' to adopt, integrate and appropriate functions and forms, aesthetic conventions and narrative patterns of 'old' media, have recently been discussed under the label of 'intermediality'. As Frida Chapple and Chiel Kattenbelt (2006: 12) state, intermediality is associated historically with the exchangeability of expressive means and aesthetic conventions between different art and media forms. But intermediality is by no means a phenomenon of the television or internet era, but (as recently has been argued by theatre historians) a classical characteristic of live theatre performances. In film and literary studies, the concept of 'intertextuality' has been stressed to analyse the various ways and forms of relationships between different 'texts' and their mediated and appropriated meanings (Kristeva 1980). In addition to that, the term 'transmediality' has been introduced in media and communication theory to describe processes of translation both of content and aesthetic forms from one medium to another (often referred to as 'adaptations'). In recent times, two other notions dealing with these phenomena of translation, transgression or interaction between contents and forms have been circulating in the field of media studies that are the notion of 'remediation' and 'convergence'. While the term 'remediation' – most prominently advertised in the book of that title by Jay Bolter and Richard Grusin (1999) – mainly stresses aesthetic and narrative implications of digital media in the context of visual culture, 'convergence' as defined by Henry Jenkins (2006: 2) describes 'the flow of content across multiple media platforms, the cooperation between multiple media industries, and the migratory behaviour of media audiences'. With the exception of Jenkins's definition of 'convergence', which rejects the classical digital revolution paradigm that presumed that new media would displace or fully absorb old media, and stresses the importance of technological, industrial, social and cultural (user) contexts in both the circulation and appropriation of mediated texts and meanings, most media scholars have studied and analysed these processes while focusing on the textual or aesthetic dimension.

Reasoning about processes of remediation or convergence from a historical and comparative perspective obliges theorists to reflect more systematically on the interconnectedness and the directions of flows between the chosen objects of study, for example early television and radio or early television and film. Intermedial relationships have too often been analysed as one-way processes or flows, either by looking at the impact of old media on new by means of discourse analysis, or by analysing the impact of new media on old as an example of remediation. The real challenge of comparative media history from a 'histoire croisée' perspective would involve thinking of the processes of media in transition as processes of mutual co-construction, or simultaneous phenomena of invention of new and reinvention of old media, thus problematising the phenomenon of convergence and understanding it as a two-way flow.

The blurring of boundaries between spaces and times, newnesses and oldnesses in television produces not only an uncertainty about where television's specificity begins and ends, but also how this technology embedded in the home has impacted on the sense of what home means. Like the discourse on heritage discussed above, the history of television in Europe involves the continual negotiation of the meaning of the familiar (the old, the habitual, the domestic, the homely) and the unfamiliar (the new, the novel, the other, the uncanny).

Television ontologies: 'us' versus 'the others'

Television reproduces the familiar, in the sense not only of presenting it again, but also effectively creating and renewing it. This process delimits what is familiar and knowable but also what is other and alien. The task 'of catering to the various forms of "nostalgia" – for a sense of community, tradition and belonging – falls increasingly on the electronic media'. (Morley & Robins 1995, 4–5) For the history of television in Europe, this means investigating the different kinds of home that television has produced and supported, as well as those that it has repudiated. Here, home not only refers to the domestic context of reception and the images of domestic life that are offered and contested, but also the larger homes represented by regions, nations and transnational groupings. In this context, Europe itself as a common home is a key point of debate in this book. Morley and Robbins (1995: 89) suggest about this wider meaning of home and homeland (in German, *Heimat*):

It is around the meaning of European culture and identity in the new global context that this image – this nostalgia, this aspiration – has become politically activated . . . Yet Heimat is an ominous utopia. Whether 'home' is imagined as the community of Europe or of the nation state or of the region, it is steeped in the longing for wholeness, unity integrity. It is about community centred around shared traditions and memories.

The most famous example of a representation dealing explicitly with this issue is the German television serial *Heimat,* but versions of this television meditation on home and homeland in the context of a European belonging that is either welcomed or feared can be found in all television cultures across the continent. This in itself demonstrates the significance of this problem for European societies. 'Heimat is a mythical bond rooted in a lost past, a past that has already disintegrated: "we yearn to grasp it, but it is baseless and elusive; we look back for something solid to lean on, only to find ourselves embracing ghosts" ' (Berman 1983: 333). It is about conserving the 'fundamentals' of culture and identity. And, as such, it is about sustaining cultural boundaries and boundedness. To belong in this way is to protect exclusive, and therefore excluding, identities against those who are seen as aliens and foreigners. The 'Other' is always and continuously a threat to the security and integrity of those who share a common home (Morley & Robins 1995: 89). Programming strategies for multicultural programming have therefore been developed by commissioning editors and programme-makers in public broadcasting institutions to address both minority and mainstream audiences. As Leurdijk's (2006) study of this process in five west European countries showed, ideologies of universality, focusing on experiences like death, birth, love and friendship in factual entertainment or infotainment formats were developed to address urban and young audiences, producing moves away from west European heritages of social realism and away from older target audiences or recent immigrants.

Television has brought new ways of understanding the European symbolic spaces of locality, region or nation, and transnational symbolic spaces like the notion of the Cold War, a global 'war on terrorism' or a New World Order, for example, which change understandings of subjective place in the world. Because television broadcasts such a range of images of culture, such as versions of what youth and age, domesticity, work and gender might mean, for example, the tensions between national and transnational television in Europe have provided the possibility of reflecting on local cultures. Transnational television provides resources for viewers to think about themselves and their social environment, in the same ways that local or national television does. Sinclair and his fellow authors (Sinclair et al. 1999: 187) give this example from a British context: 'An Egyptian immigrant in Britain, for example, might think of herself as a Glaswegian when she watches her local Scottish channel, a British resident when she switches over to the BBC, an Islamic Arab expatriate in

Europe when she tunes in to the satellite service from the Middle East, and a world citizen when she channel surfs on to CNN.' Europe's television citizens negotiate their sense of place, time and community in relation to local, regional and global television cultures, and do so by borrowing from or resisting television structures, modes of address and representations. The diasporic communities in Europe have been given new ways of constructing identities by the transnational channels and cross-border distribution of television that began in the 1980s with satellite television. Aksoy and Robins (2000), for example, have shown how transnational television from Turkey included programmes from the state broadcaster TRT, a range of new commercial broadcasters, and channels specifically aimed at Muslim viewers. This diversity made it possible for Turkish viewers inside and outside Turkey to actively construct and reconstruct their identities and sense of place and belonging without a necessary anchorage to a singular symbolic and geographical reference point.

The Aims, Methods and Problems of this Book

Finally, we can draw these research problems together as specific manifestations of the greater conceptual tension between identity and difference. The three key questions addressed in this book are, first, what a comparative history might look like, as a discourse that acknowledges difference while functioning as a unified discussion. Second, this is a television history, so that how television operates to find an identity as a medium by establishing difference and similarity with other media is an important feature of the book. Third, we aim to write a history of European television, so that the identity of Europe as an entity (more accurately, as several overlapping kinds of entity) impacts on each of the preceding two issues. This chapter has outlined the central questions of the project and the methodological approach. Each chapter that follows begins with an introduction outlining central questions and introducing case studies and sources. The main body of each chapter comprises comparative analysis of the political, economic, aesthetic, ideological and social-cultural contexts of the development of the aspect of European television addressed, and specific case studies instantiating it. A conclusion and annotated bibliography complete each chapter. The questions addressed here are taken up in the concluding chapter, where we offer synthesising theses about the issues addressed across the book as a whole.

This book is the result of a real European co-operation, between 28 television scholars of 15 different nationalities (27 of them being affiliated to a European university), developing historical case studies of 15 European countries and 3 European regions. It is easy to demonstrate the adventurous character of this project, which may best be understood as a scholarly experiment by the rather small community of European television historians, driven by the intellectual belief that the field of media history has to break out of the national frames in which it has developed and grown since the 1950s and 1960s. Without diminishing the value and necessity of national media and television histories, we think that the transnational and comparative approach is a more adequate one for the study of television as an object and practice characterised by its placing on and across cultural borderlines.

In order to guarantee a real comparative perspective for each of the chapters we invited the members of the European Television History Network to form teams for collaborative writing. Under the editorial responsibility of a lead author, the teams discussed the scope and the case studies to be presented in each of the thematic chapters, inspired by the general design of the book as developed by the editors. With the exception of the first chapter on the prehistory and early visions of television, for which it proved to be problematic to create a writing team, the case studies that form the historical evidence of the chapters reflect both the national and scholarly profiles of their contributors. While each chapter reflects on the European dimension of its topic in a more general sense, the concrete comparative dimension is based on a necessarily limited number of case studies. The originality of this book lies not so much in the presentation of new case studies but in the comparative interpretation and analysis of these cases from a European perspective.

Neither the book nor the chapters therefore claim to offer a holistic view of Europe in all its geographical and cultural diversity, but instead pay attention to interesting, relevant and – at least in certain cases – representative moments in the history of television in Europe. This is a Europe which is in itself rather a discursive construction of fragmented, diverse and often diachronic narratives than a homogeneous and essentialist phenomenon. The eclectic structure of the book is both the result of the initial decision to build on the competences and expertise of our collaborators and is also a reflection of the existing landscape of academic television history in Europe. Despite the broad geographical scope of the case studies presented, ranging from Sweden to Greece in the north–south direction and from Wales to Romania on the west–east axis, we are painfully aware of a certain Western European emphasis in the book. Although we attempted to find and invite colleagues from Central and Eastern European universities to participate in the workshops organised by the European Television History Network that initiated this project, our success in finding partners in these countries remained rather limited. It is our greatest hope that this publication might help to further stimulate and initiate dialogue and scholarly collaboration of this kind. Nevertheless, thanks to the diversity of the personal and intellectual biographies of all the participants in this collective experiment, we hope to offer a book that reflects the spirit of European 'diversity in unity', witnessing an intellectual curiosity to explore the complexity of television as a cultural phenomenon and a unique academic and social engagement. This project is a truly collective, transnational and interdisciplinary experiment which we hope will prompt the further enrichment of comparative European television historiography.

References

Aksoy, A. and Robins, K. (2000) 'Thinking across spaces: transnational television from Turkey'. *European Journal of Cultural Studies* 3, 343–65.

Altman, R. (1986) 'Television sound'. In: Modleski, T. (ed.) *Studies in Entertainment: Critical Approaches to Mass Culture.* Bloomington: Indiana University Press, pp. 39–54.

Anderson, B. (1983) *Imagined Communities: Reflections on the Origins and Spread of Nationalisms.* London, Verso.

Anderson, C. and Curtin, M. (eds.) (2002) 'Writing cultural history: the challenge of radio and television'. In: Brügger, N. and Kolstrup, S. (eds.) *Media History: Theories, Methods, Analysis.* Aarhus, University of Aarhus Press, pp. 15–32.

Barker, C. (1999) *Television, Globalization and Cultural Identities.* Buckingham, Open University Press.

Bausch, H. (ed.) (1980) *Rundfunk in Deutschland* (5 vols.). Munich, DTV.

Berman, M. (1983) *All that is Solid Melts into Air: The Experience of Modernity.* London, Verso.

Bernold, M. (2001) 'Fernsehen ist gestern: Medienhistorische Transformationen und televisuelles Dabeisein nach 1945'. *Österreichische Zeitschrift für Geschichtswissenschaft* 12:4, 8–29.

Biltereyst, D. (2004) 'Reality TV, troublesome pictures and panics: reappraising the public controversy around reality TV in Europe'. In: Holmes, S. and Jermyn, D. (eds.) *Understanding Reality Television.* London, Routledge, pp. 91–110.

Bleicher, J. K. (2003) 'Fernsehgeschichte und ihre Beziehung zu Modellen der Mediengeschichte: Ein Forschungsbericht'. In: Bleicher, J. K. (ed.) *Fernsehgeschichte. Modelle – Theorien – Projekte,* Hamburger Hefte zur Medienkultur 2, pp. 3–22.

Boddy, W. (2004) *New Media and Popular Imagination: Launching Radio, Television, and Digital Media in the United States.* Oxford, Oxford University Press.

Bolter, J. and Grusin, R. (1999) *Remediation: Understanding New Media.* Cambridge, MA, MIT Press.

Bourdon, J. (2000) 'Live television is still alive: on television as an unfulfilled promise'. *Media, Culture & Society* 22, 531–56.

Bourdon, J. (2003) 'Some sense of time: remembering television'. *History & Memory* 15:2, 5–35.

Brack, H. (1976) *The Evolution of the EBU Through Its Statutes From 1950 to 1976.* Geneva, European Broadcasting Union.

Briggs, A. (1985) *BBC: The First Fifty Years.* Oxford, Oxford University Press.

Brunsdon, C. (1998) 'What is the television of television studies?' In: Geraghty, C. and Lusted, D. (eds.) *The Television Studies Book.* London, Arnold, pp. 95–113.

Camporesi, V. (2000) *Mass Culture and National Traditions: The BBC and American Broadcasting, 1922–1954.* Fucecchio, European Press Academic Publishing.

Chalaby, J. (2002) 'Transnational television in Europe: the role of pan-European channels'. *European Journal of Communication* 17, 183–203.

Chalaby, J. (2005) 'Deconstructing the transnational: a typology of cross-border television channels in Europe'. *New Media & Society* 7, 155–75.

Chapman, J. (2005) *Comparative Media History. An Introduction: 1789 to the Present.* Cambridge, Polity Press.

Chapple, F. and Kattenbelt, C. (eds.) (2006) *Intermediality in Theatre and Performance.* Amsterdam, Rodopi.

Cohen, E. (1999) 'Télévision, pouvoir et citoyenneté'. In: Lévy, M.-F. (ed.) *La télévision dans la République: Les années 50.* Paris, Éditions Complexe, pp. 23–42.

Collins, R. (1990) *Satellite Television in Western Europe.* London, John Libbey.

Conrad, S. and Randeria, S. (eds.) (2002) *Jenseits des Eurozentrismus: Postkoloniale Perspektiven in den Geschichts- und Kulturwissenschaften.* Frankfurt A. M., Suhrkamp.

Corner, J. (2003) 'Finding data, reading patterns, telling stories: issues in the historiography of television'. *Media, Culture & Society* 25, 273–80.

Corrigan, P. (1990) 'On the difficulty of being sociological (historical materialist) in the study of television: the 'moment' of English television, 1936–1939'. In: Syvertsen, T. (ed.) *1992 and After: Nordic Television in Transition.* Bergen, University of Bergen, pp. 130–60.

Couldry, N. (2003) *Media Rituals. A Critical Approach.* London, Routledge.

Crone, V. (2007) *De kwetsbare kijker: Een culturele geschiedenis van televisie in Nederland.* Amsterdam, Amsterdam University Press.

Damann, C. (2005) *Stimme aus dem Äther – Fenster zur Welt: Die Anfänge von Radio und Fernsehen in Deutschland.* Cologne, Böhlau.

Dayan, D. and Katz, E. (1992) *Media Events: The Live Broadcasting of History.* Cambridge, MA, Harvard University Press.

De Bens, E. and de Smaele, H. (2001) 'The inflow of American television fiction on European broadcasting channels revisited'. *European Journal of Communication* 16:1, 51–76.

Degenhardt, W. and Strautz, E. (1999) *Auf der Suche nach dem europäischen Programm: Die Eurovision 1954–1970.* Baden-Baden, Nomos.

Delaunay, G. (1958) 'La radio-télévision, puissance politique'. *Cahiers d'études de radio et de télévision* 18, 124.

de Leeuw, S. (2003) *Hoe komen wij in beeld? Cultuurhistorische aspecten van de Nederlandse televisie.* Utrecht: Utrecht University Press.

Dixon, K. and Spee, S. (2003) 'Deploying identity for democratic ends on *Jan Publiek*: a Flemish television talk show'. *European Journal of Women's Studies* 10, 409–22.

Douglas, S. (1987) *Inventing American Broadcasting, 1899–1922.* Baltimore, MD, Johns Hopkins University Press.

Douglas, S. (2004) *Listening In: Radio and the American Imagination.* Minneapolis, University of Minnesota Press.

Eden, J. (2006) 'Caruso control'. *Radio Times,* 5–11 August, 11–12.

Ellis, J. (2002) *Seeing Things: Television in the Age of Uncertainty.* London, I. B. Tauris.

Espagne, M. (1999) *Les transferts culturels franco-allemands.* Paris, Presses Universitaires de France.

Eugster, E. (1983) *Television Programming Across National Boundaries: The EBU and OIRT Experiences.* Dedham, MA, Artech.

Fickers, A. (2007) *'Politique de la grandeur' versus 'Made in Germany': Die Analyse der PAL/SECAM-Farbfernsehkontroverse als Beispiel einer politischen Kulturgeschichte der Technik.* Munich, Oldenbourg.

Fickers, A. and Kessler, F. (2008) 'Narrative topoi in Erfindermythen und technonationalistischer Legendenbildung: Zur Historiographie der Erfindung von Film und

Fernsehen'. In: Bodenmann, S. and Splinter, S. (eds.) *Mythos – Helden – Symbole: Legitimation, Selbst- und Fremdwahrnehmung in der Geschichte der Naturwissenschaft, Medizin und Technik.* Munich, Martin Meidenbauer, pp. 71–82.

Fickers, A. and Lommers, S. (2009, forthcoming) 'Eventing Europe: broadcasting and the mediated performances of Europe'. In: Badenoch, A. and Fickers, A. (eds.) *Untangling Infrastructures and Europe: Scales, Mediations, Events.* London, Palgrave Macmillan.

Fiske, J. and Hartley, J. (1978) *Reading Television.* London, Methuen.

Foucault, M. (1986) 'Nietzsche, genealogy, history'. In: Rabinow, P. (ed.) *The Foucault Reader.* Harmondsworth: Penguin, pp. 76–100.

Giddens, A. (1990) *The Consequences of Modernity.* Cambridge, Polity Press.

Gripsrud, J. (1998) 'Television, broadcasting, flow: key metaphors in TV theory'. In: Geraghty, C. and Lusted, D. (eds.) *The Television Studies Book.* London, Arnold, pp. 17–32.

Hall, S. (1995) 'New cultures for old'. In: Massey, D. and Jess, P. (eds.) *A Place in the World? Places, Cultures and Globalization.* Oxford, Oxford University Press, pp. 175–213.

Hall, S. (1996) 'Who needs identity?' In: Hall, S. and du Gray, P. (eds.) *Questions of Cultural Identity.* London, Sage.

Hill, A. (2002) '*Big Brother*: the real audience'. *Television and New Media* 3:3, 323–41.

Hilmes, M. (1997) *Radio Voices: American Broadcasting, 1922–1952.* Minneapolis, University of Minnesota Press.

Hilmes, M. (2003a) 'British quality, American chaos: historical dualisms and what they leave out'. *Radio Journal* 1:1, 13–27.

Hilmes, M. (2003b) 'Introduction'. In: Hilmes, M. and Jacobs, J. (eds.) *The Television History Book.* London: BFI.

Hilmes, M. and Jacobs, J. (eds.) (2003) *The Television History Book.* London: BFI.

Jenkins, H. (2004) 'The cultural logic of media convergence'. *International Journal of Cultural Studies* 7:1, 33–43.

Jenkins, H. (2006) *Convergence Culture: Where Old and New Media Collide.* New York, New York University Press.

Kaelble, H. (1999) *Der historische Vergleich: Eine Einführung zum 19. und 20. Jahrhundert.* Frankfurt a. M., Campus.

Kansteiner, W. (2004) 'Nazis, viewers and statistics: television history, television audience research and collective memory in West Germany'. *Journal of Contemporary History* 39, 575–98.

Keilbach, J. and Thiele, M. (2003) 'Für eine experimentelle Fernsehgeschichte'. *Hamburger Hefte zur Medienkultur* 2, 59–76.

Knoblauch, H. (2000) 'Das strategische Ritual der kollektiven Einsamkeit: Zur Begrifflichkeit und Theorie des Events'. In: Gebhardt, W., Hitzler, R. and Pfadenhauer, M. (eds.) *Events: Soziologie des Außergewöhnlichen.* Opladen, Leske & Budrich, pp. 33–50.

Koukoutsaki, A. (2003) 'Greek television drama: production policies and genre diversification'. *Media, Culture & Society* 25, 715–35.

Kristeva, J. (1980) *Desire in Language: A Semiotic Approach to Literature and Art.* New York, Columbia University Press.

Leurdijk, A. (2006) 'In search of common ground: strategies of multicultural television producers in Europe'. *European Journal of Cultural Studies* 9, 25–46.

Levitas, R. (1993) 'The future of thinking about the future'. In: Bird, J., et al. (eds.) *Mapping the Futures: Local Cultures, Global Change*. London, Routledge, pp. 257–66.

Lévy, M.-F. (1999) 'La création des télé-clubs'. In: Lévy, M.-F. (ed.) *La télévision dans la République: Les années 50*. Paris, Éditions Complexe, pp. 107–32.

Lowenthal, D. (1987) *The Past is a Foreign Country*. Cambridge, Cambridge University Press.

Maase, K. (2004) 'Schwerpunkt Mediengeschichte: Geschichtsmedien'. *Geschichte in Wissenschaft und Unterricht* 55, 564–642.

Morley, D. and Robins, K. (1995) *Spaces of Identity: Global Media, Electronic Landscapes and Cultural Boundaries*. London, Routledge.

Morse, M. (1990) 'An ontology of everyday distraction: the freeway, the mall, and television'. In: Mellencamp, P. (ed.) *Logics of Television*. London, BFI, pp. 193–221.

Nora, P. (1989) 'Between memory and history: les lieux de mémoire'. *Representations* 26, 7–24.

Peter, J. and de Vreese, C. (2004) 'In search of Europe: a cross-national comparative study of the European Union in national television news'. *Harvard International Journal of Press/Politics* 9, 3–24.

Peters, J. D. (1999) *Speaking into the Air: A History of the Idea of Communication*. Chicago, Chicago University Press.

Pfaffenberger, B. (1992) 'Technological dramas'. *Science, Technology & Human Values* 17:3, 282–312.

Philips, D. (2005) 'Transformation scenes: the television interior makeover'. *International Journal of Cultural Studies* 8, 213–29.

Richards, J. (1997) *Films and British National Identity: From Dickens to Dad's Army*. Manchester, Manchester University Press.

Roberts, G. (2001) 'The historian and television: a methodological survey'. In: Roberts, G. and Taylor, P. M. (eds.) *The Historian, Television and Television History*. Luton, Luton University Press, pp. 1–8.

Scannell, P. (1996) *Radio, Television & Modern Life: A Phenomenological Approach*. Oxford, Blackwell.

Scannell, P. (2004) 'Broadcasting historiography and historicality'. *Screen* 45:2, 130–41.

Schildt, A. and Sywottek, A. (eds.) (1993) *Modernisierung im Wiederaufbau: Die westdeutsche Gesellschaft der 50er Jahre*. Bonn, Dietz.

Schiller, H. (1969) *Mass Communications and American Empire*. New York, Augustus M. Kelly.

Schiller, H. (1976) *Communication and Cultural Domination*. New York, M. E. Sharpe.

Schoenbach, K. and Lauf, E. (2002) 'The 'trap' effect of television and its competitors'. *Communication Research* 29, 564–83.

Schriewer, J. (2003) 'Problemdimensionen sozialwissenschaftlicher Komparatistik'. In: Kaelble, H. and Schriewer, J. (eds.) *Vergleich und Transfer: Komparatistik in den Sozial-, Geschichts- und Kulturwissenschaften*. Frankfurt a. M., Campus, pp. 9–54.

Sinclair, J., Jacka, E. and Cunningham, S. (1999) 'New patterns in global television'. In: Marris, P. and Thornham, S. (eds.) *The Media Reader*. Edinburgh, Edinburgh University Press, pp. 170–90.

Siune, K. and Hulten, O. (1998) 'Does public broadcasting have a future?' In: McQuail, D. and Siune, K. (eds.) *Media Policy: Convergence, Concentration, Commerce.* London, Sage, pp. 23–37.

Smith, A., with Paterson, R. (1998) *Television: An International History* (2nd edn). Oxford, Oxford University Press.

Smith, A. D. (1991) *National Identity.* London, Penguin.

Syvertsen, T. (2003) 'Challenges to public television in the era of convergence and commercialization'. *Television & New Media* 4, 155–75.

Tilly, C. (1984) *Big Structures, Large Processes, Huge Comparisons.* New York, Russell Sage Foundation.

Uricchio, W. (1989) 'Rituals of reception, patterns of neglect: Nazi television and its postwar representation'. *Wide Angle* 11:1, 48–66.

Uricchio, W. (2004) 'Historicizing media in transition'. In: Thorburn, D. and Jenkins, H. (eds.) *Rethinking Media Change: The Aesthetics of Transition.* Cambridge, MA, MIT Press, pp. 23–38.

Wanning, S. (2001) 'Media events or media stories?' *International Journal of Cultural Studies* 4:1, 25–44.

Werner, M. and Zimmermann, B. (2003) 'Penser l'histoire croisée: entre empirie et réfléxivité'. *Annales* 58, 7–36.

Werner, M. and Zimmermann, B. (2006) 'Beyond comparison: histoire croisée and the challenge of reflexivity'. *History and Theory* 45, 30–50.

West, A. G. D. (1948) 'Development of theatre television in England'. *Journal of the SMPE* 51, 127–68.

Winker, K. (1994) *Fernsehen unterm Hakenkreuz: Organisation, Programm, Personal, Medien.* Cologne, Böhlau.

Williams, R. (1990) *Television, Technology and Cultural Form.* London, Routledge.

Zeller, R. (1999) *Die EBU. Union Européenne de Radio-Télévision (UER) European Broadcast Union (EBU): Internationale Rundfunkkooperation im Wandel.* Baden-Baden, Nomos.

Zielinski, S. (1989) *Audiovisionen: Kino und Fernsehen als Zwischenspiele der Geschichte.* Reinbek bei Hamburg, Rowohlt.

2

Early TV:
Imagining and Realising Television

Knut Hickethier

Like all new media, television was not the invention of a single person but the result of a common effort and a combination of a number of technical innovations. Similarly, although nations made various claims afterwards, television was not the invention of one single nation but the result of international activity. These inventions did not come from a single place or one country, but they did emerge in the nineteenth century in the European and North American context of industrialisation. Over a long period of time, scientists and radio amateurs worked on the accomplishment of television as it later became realised in the form of a broadcast programme medium. Indeed, it took more time to develop television than was necessary for the accomplishment of any other newer technological media device such as film, radio or even the internet.

The prehistory and early history of television can be divided into different periods in which – as always in historical periodisation – different trends overlap. The first period runs from the middle of the seventeenth century until about 1880 and can be considered as television's prehistory, in which basic scientific discoveries were made but in which television as a medium had not been thought of. A second period from 1880 until 1910 can be identified, in which inventors began to think about the transmission of pictures over a long distance and in which there was talk of 'television'. This period may be characterised as a period of technical imagination about and amateur experimentation with television. The third period begins in 1910, before the First World War, and ends in about 1933. It was marked by the fact that two major companies in the electrical industry attended to the development of television and tried to promote it. This third phase is characterised by technological developments at an industrial level and can – as Albert Abramson (1987) has done – be written as a history of patents. At the beginning of the 1930s, television was not only imagined as a programme medium, but the institutionalisation of television began with regular broadcasts of experimental programmes. Television entered the period of institutionalisation and scheduling. The

Second World War marked a break in the development of television. Between 1939 and 1945, its further development ceased or was maintained only on a restricted scale. The year 1945 begins the period of the definite establishment and implementation of television, leading to its introduction over nearly all of Europe within a period of 20 years. The post-war era marked the start of television as a mass medium.

The Contexts of Television Development

The scientific discoveries and technical inventions marking the beginning of television derive from the exploration of electricity. The broadcasting media of radio and television were the first mass media to be made possible only by electricity. As Albert Abramson (1987) has shown, radio and television emerged in the context of electrical telegraphy, which is based on the long-distance transmission of electrical impulses by means of a conducting cable. The exploration of electricity became more dynamic when, in the second half of the nineteenth century, industrialisation made electricity a viable source of energy on a significant scale and therefore introduced a new period of industrial expansion. From the 1870s and 1880s, experiments aiming to achieve the electric transmission of pictures gained importance. This did not just involve electrical experiments, but reflections about how to use these technologies for the further development of individual and social communication.

Telegraphy made the importance of electrical communication obvious, because it overcame the limitations of signal transport linked to the speed of living beings (messengers or stagecoaches, for example), the intricacy of mechanical and optical telegraphs, and the cruising speed of steam-powered means of transport (such as steamboats or railways). Telegraphy was essential for the imperial politics of the European powers, since it enabled decision makers to be quickly informed about any threatening activity in the colonies (Headrick 2000). Television became not only interesting as a geostrategic means of communication in that context, but also on a wider cultural scale. The development of television resulted from a growing interest in the acceleration of information exchange in general and the wish to obtain pictures of distant events that were unreachable by oneself. 'Tele-vision' in the sense of an accelerated vision of the whole world was a subliminal wish described by many fairy tales, myths and literary utopias (Lange 2001). The invention of television is therefore embedded in the cultural context of the leading European industrialised countries of the nineteenth and twentieth centuries. That cultural context must also be seen as embedded in the process of modernisation occurring in western societies. Television is both the result of, and the means to express, an industrial and cultural effort towards modernisation, and has strongly promoted this mission throughout the second half of the twentieth century.

Prehistories of Television: Technical and Cultural Developments before 1880

A number of developments created the framework for the development of television as a new technology and medium. One was the technical discoveries and inventions that took place within the exploration of electricity and alongside scientific discoveries in the broader context. Another was the cultural developments in the nineteenth century that occurred against the background of industrialisation. The final development discussed here will be the emergence and implementation of mass media like radio and cinema.

Technical and scientific conditions

At the same time as the discovery and exploration of electricity, a techno-scientific way of thinking emerged that was underpinned by a basic conviction: that all human wishes and ideas could be realised by technological means – if not instantly, then at least in the long-term (Hard & Jamison 2005). This strong belief in technological progress undoubtedly motivated many inventors and technical amateurs. Their work was driven not only by a curiosity to explore phenomena in their structure and nature, but also to control them and to make them usable. The development of storage technologies, from photography to the gramophone, film and the digital memory chip is based on the repudiation of the human brain as a site for storage, on the creation of collective memory and the wish for immortality (Zielinski 1999). Such deep motivations perhaps have an anthropological origin, but the wish to quickly get information about an event, if possible in the moment when it is happening, has cultural foundations. This ambition is deeply ingrained in Western thinking, and thus in the European mind. The idea of being informed about everything and of the ubiquity of the senses is not limited to one single European country. On the contrary, it can be found in many countries on the Continent and it motivated inventors and discoverers, especially in the leading industrial nations of Europe (Mattelart & Mattelart 1995).

This can be shown by taking a look at some of the stages in the exploration of electricity. In 1770, the Italian Luigi Galvani discovered the 'animal electricity' in living bodies; around 1820, the Frenchman André Marie Ampère invented the 'ammeter', a type of telegraph. The German Georg Simon formulated the basic laws of the relationship between amperage and voltage; the Englishman Michael Faraday defined the laws of electromagnetism and made the invention of telegraphy possible; the Scotsman James Clerk Maxwell conceived the theory of electricity that is still valid today; in 1820, the Dane Hans Christian Ørsted identified the relationship between electricity and magnetism. In 1833, the Germans Carl Friedrich Gauss and Wilhelm Eduard Weber sent the first telegram by means of an 8,000-foot-long telegraph line in Göttingen; in 1844, the first telegraph line in the USA was put into operation by Samuel F. B. Morse. In 1860, the Belgian Zénobe Théophile Gramme invented an electrical generator; in 1866, the German Werner von Siemens developed the dynamo; in 1877, Thomas Alva Edison improved the light bulb in the USA and, with the European Gramme and Siemens, he made street lighting and the creation of electricity networks possible.

These technical inventions and developments were based on scientifically inspired thinking, and in particular, theories of light were prototypical and crucial for the development of television. The theory of light could be understood as the principle of the new thinking, because it worked with two decisive models: the understanding of light as a stream of particles (Newton) and in the form of waves (Huygens). This dualism resulted, on the one hand, in the idea of the diffraction of light and, on the other hand, in the concept of the transmission of information by electromagnetic waves. At the beginning of the nineteenth century, the wave theory became predominant after the observation of interference phenomena of light by Young and Fresnel. Waves are, however, unthinkable without a medium in which they can diffuse. Following the analogy of the propagation of sound waves in solid objects and gases, the so-called 'ether' was therefore conceived as a medium for the diffusion of light (Cantor 1981). The theory of electromagnetic waves developed by Heinrich Hertz was closely related to this theory. In 1884, Hertz produced electromagnetic waves for the first time. The relationship between electric and magnetic phenomena was already known, but he was the first to produce electromagnetic waves and hence created the first radio waves that are the basis for radio broadcasting (Wiesbeck 1988).

The cultural and technical backgrounds

The cultural developments of the nineteenth century were also crucial for the emergence of television. The new techno-scientific thinking was deeply rooted in cultural traditions influencing the perception, experience and conception of the modern world. The most important phenomenon in changing cultural experiences was acceleration – at first the acceleration of vision (Borscheid 2004, Kern 1983). Thanks to the invention of the railway, people could travel faster through the landscape than by horse or carriage, they saw 'faster' and the landscape passed by smoothly. Because people could travel faster it seemed that distances decreased, places moved closer together and the world became smaller. Based on this new nineteenth-century experience of time and space, Marshall McLuhan (1989) later developed his thesis of the 'global village' – a world shrunk to local dimensions as a result of globalised mass media.

The long-distance transmission of information is also a product of the acceleration of perception. The invention of the telegraph took place in the first half of the nineteenth century, and the first optical telegraphs developed mostly for military reasons. From 1832, a telegraph line linked the Prussian capital Berlin with the Rhine city of Koblenz (over 340 miles). Similar systems developed in France and in England, where Barnard L. Watson invented an optical telegraph. In 1837 the American Samuel F. B. Morse invented an electric telegraph, and from 1847 the first electrical telegraph line in Europe was in operation between Bremen and Bremerhaven in Germany. From 1850 onwards, submarine cables were laid, first between Calais and Dover and in 1858 between Europe and North America, though the first permanent line was not established until 1866. In relationship to this development, news agencies arose to quickly spread information; in 1851, the Reuters agency was founded in London. Scientists like Hertz were working on wireless telegraphy by means of radio waves from 1898, and in 1899 the Italian Guglielmo Marconi started the first wireless telegraph service.

This acceleration of perception was most prominently experienced in western industrial countries like Britain, Germany and France. As 'laboratories of modernity', big cities like London and Paris were the most prominent loci of accelerated rhythms of life. It is no coincidence that this cultural sensitisation to acceleration increased at the end of the *fin de siècle*. This period is therefore often called the 'era of nervousness' (Radkau 1998), characterised by a new industrial way of life with its dissolution of the holistic thinking that still dominated agrarian societies. The emergence of leisure time as a result of standardised work flows in factories heavily catalysed the spreading use of mass media as a pastime activity.

Along with the acceleration in perception of time, the linearisation and standardisation of time itself emerged. Until well into the twentieth century, different local time zones existed even in smaller countries. The standardisation of time began in about 1840, when it became necessary for the synchronisation of railway schedules and telegraph communication between different places (Schivelbusch 1986). After many discussions, a standardisation of universal time and the division of the world in time zones was agreed upon at the International Meridian Conference in Washington in 1884. For the development of electromechanical television, this aspect of time standardisation became crucial because of the need for perfect synchronisation between the two rotating Nipkow discs inside early television equipment.

Accelerated communication over long distances did not only concern language and written texts, but increasingly the transmission of pictures also, because of a growing demand for visual representations linked to the expansion of mass media consumption. Literacy spread during the nineteenth century, but communication by pictures and illustrations nevertheless remained extremely popular. Large-scale panoramas and dioramas were created in the first half of the nineteenth century, and not much later photography was invented, by which the world could apparently be captured and pictured without human participation. In the middle of the century, the demand for visual entertainment was answered further as the illustrated press developed and picture

roduced, comic strips were invented and early experiments with
film took place.

₋ne First Television Ideas and Devices in Europe

The different developments and inventions that – in retrospect – contributed
to the emergence of television only slowly moved towards a conceptualisation
of television as a programme medium. The reasons for this 'slow development of a fast medium' (Elsner, Müller & Spangenberg, 1990) lay first of all
in the vague idea of what was being aimed for, secondly in the diverse and
undirected paths of technological developments, and thirdly in the fact that
the need for fast visual communication in society was not as evident as in the
second half of the twentieth century. However, it was very clear that television
was being worked on as a distribution and communication medium. It was
not conceived as storage medium, as the phonograph record was for the audio-
phonic field and film for the visual field. This is why when there was talk about
television in technical writings in the twentieth century, reference was always
made to phototelegraphy (Fuchs 1928) and radio. At the beginning of the
1930s, a clear distinction was also made between television and film.

The starting point, according to the early technical literature of the 1930s,
was the discovery of the photoconductivity of the chemical element selenium
by the engineers Willoughby Smith and Joseph May in 1873 during the lay-
ing of a transatlantic cable (Korn 1930). In 1878–9, the Portuguese Adriano
de Paiva, the Italian Carlo Perosino and the Frenchman Constantin Senlecq
came up with ideas for converting a picture into electrical impulses by means
of a selenium cell. De Paiva published a short paper called 'La Téléscopie
Electrique. Basée sur L'Emploi du Selenium' in 1880, and Senlecq published
the brochure 'Le Télectroscope' in 1881. In addition, the American George
R. Carey also claimed to be the inventor of television, because of an article
on selenium and television he had published in 1879, as had his compatriot
William E. Sawyer. But, as the German engineer Arthur Korn (1930: 1) declared
in his overview of the historical development of electrical television, those were
just ideas that 'were in the air'. From a technical point of view, they never
were put into practice. In addition to these very first thoughts about electrical production and transmission of pictures, the German Werner von Siemens
and the Englishman Shelford Bidwell had the idea of producing pictures not
only with one but with several selenium cells, while others promoted the idea
of producing pictures by means of electric rays (Hertz in 1887, Hallwachs in
1888, and Elster, Geitel and Rosenthal in 1908 with alkali cells). All in all it
was a tentative search for technical possibilities in an unknown field, and the
numerous publications of the 1880s and the 1890s about television witness
a great interest in it and great inventiveness in experimenting with the new
technology (Winston 1998).

Paul Nipkow's idea of electromechanical image dissection and composition is considered one of the key events of late nineteenth-century television development, because it is an example of sporadic devotion to a vague idea of what television might be, and because of the later implementation of some of his particular technical inventions. In 1883 Nipkow was a Berlin student of signalling technology and developed the idea of dissecting pictures into spots of light by means of a rotating disk with holes in it. These spots could then be captured by a selenium cell and transformed into electrical impulses. In 1884, he applied for a patent on this idea, but did not present anything more than a drawing and a few notes. His ideas were to be realised by others. Only a year later the patent had lapsed, because Nipkow failed to pay the annual fee. He abandoned television and became a signalling technician. It was only as part of the Nazi claim for television as a German invention that Nipkow, now in his seventies, was acclaimed 'the father of television' by Third Reich officials (Winker 1994). In 1883, Nipkow's idea was just one among many others. The Frenchman Lazare Weiller developed a mirrored drum for the dissection of pictures, the Englishman Henry Sutton worked with electrostatically charged liquids, the Austrian Jan Szczepanik used small mirrors and the German Ernst Ruhmer acoustic vibrations. Edmund Liesegang published a brochure about 'electric television (Phototel)', but meant rather a sort of phototelegraphy. Around the turn of the century more and more patents for television were applied for, in Russia by Wolfke in 1898 and Polumordvinow in 1899, and in Denmark by Valdemar Poulsen in 1898, for example (Abramson 1987).

Already in the 1920s, an argument in scientific magazines arose about which idea could count as being the origin of television. This question of authorship regularly surfaces in periods of techno-nationalistic instrumentalisation of technologies – especially under authoritarian regimes. But the argument about authorship is pointless, because there no single inventor of television. Television is a multi-authored invention and collective innovation, and owes its development to the persistent aspiration of technical, scientific, economic and cultural interests in the leading industrial nations of the nineteenth and twentieth centuries (Fickers & Kessler 2008).

From about 1900, technicians and scientists increasingly tried not only to produce ideas, but to develop functioning technical devices and to experimentally explore the problems of image dissection, transmission and synthesis. For the production of pictures, the Braun tube was developed by the German physicist Ferdinand Braun in Strasbourg. This glass vacuum tube could produce pictures on the fluorescent surface at the bottom of the tube thanks to an electromagnetically directed cathode ray. The number of inventions and technical devices phenomenally increased in European countries in the period leading up to the First World War, but two approaches clashed. On the image construction side, the dissection of pictures and their transformation into electric signals was carried out in an electromechanical way by means of a Nipkow disk or a variation on it. On the image reproduction side, the synthesis of the impulses back into pictures, on the contrary, could be carried out electronically by means of the Braun tube. This discrepancy between mechanical and electronic technologies persisted until the 1930s and hindered the development of television for a long time (Burns 1998).

Up to this point, it had been a characteristic in the development of media and communication technologies – from telegraph to telephone, sound recording to film and radio – that the technical principles of the recording and transmission side were similar. Only television remained for a long time a hybrid between a mechanical and an electronic device. This fundamental problem was first addressed in 1908 by the Russian scientist Boris L. Rosing. In his laboratory at St Petersburg University, he started scanning the pictures that arrived on the screen of a reception tube with an electron beam, which led the way to the development of an electronic camera. By 1911, he had already managed to build a camera that could produce very elementary pictures. Rosing's ideas were seized by Vladimir K. Zworykin, one of Rosing's students, who emigrated to the USA and worked at the laboratories of the Radio Corporation of America (RCA). In the early 1930s, he developed an electronic camera (the Iconoscope) that fundamentally contributed to the decisive breakthrough into all-electronic television (Abramson 1995).

However, the exchange between technicians and scientists mainly took place in the cities of Western and Central Europe, and in a 1965 retrospective the German television publicist Gerhard Eckert (1965: 11) was amazed at how much the idea of television occupied the brains of engineers, technicians and physicists all over the continent. These were not only private hobbyists or tinkering amateurs, but primarily scientists at technical universities who worked experimentally as well as systematically on the possibilities of television. In this field, the technical universities of Berlin, London, Paris and St Petersburg played a predominant role.

Television, Industry and the Development of Radio

Whereas in the first decade of the twentieth century, research around the idea of television was essentially carried out by universities, engineers' unions or scientific societies (such as the Institute of Radio Engineers in the USA or the Royal Television Society in Britain), the electronics companies, which were closely linked to the universities, began in the 1900s to take an interest in the technology of moving image transmission. This interest was on the one hand motivated by the hope of making money from the new telecommunication technology and the emerging market for media products; on the other hand, it was driven by national and often military interest in the new communications technologies.

The Influences of Radio and War

Radio technology came to the fore because its transformation into and appropriation as a communication technology proved to be easier and faster in comparison to television. Marconi had already demonstrated that the wireless broadcast of acoustic signals functioned even at very large distances (across the Atlantic), and the electronics companies, often on the orders of the army and with the financial aid of the state, concentrated on the establishment of wireless technologies for military communication. After all, it could be militarily decisive to be able to transmit information quickly over long distances. Most states had a wireless transmission monopoly within their territories and therefore authority over telecommunications. Within the different states, the often competitive companies merged or founded corporate affiliates (for example, in Germany Telefunken was created out of AEG and Siemens & Halske, and in the USA RCA was founded by American Marconi and General Electric). International patent pools and licensing agreements between these multinationals were established in order to share markets and avoid costly patent battles (Griset 1995: 37–64). Whereas in the field of radio technology, economic and national interests were closely linked, the state of television technology at that time was too rudimentary to satisfy similar state or military interests (Reiss & Zielinski 1976). The work on television therefore decreased during the First World War (Abramson 1987: 41). It was only in the interwar years that the electronics industry became the driving force in the development of television. At the beginning of the 1920s it became clearer and clearer that television as a broadcasting technology could become similar to radio, as an attractive medium of public entertainment. The already existing co-operations between technical universities, the electronics industry and state authorities were therefore promoted. However, the technical problems of television turned out to be complex and difficult.

Changes in the concept of television

Until the early 1920s, it was still unclear what the television medium should do. The early ideas had been defined by telegraphy, in which communication between two points was reciprocally established by means of a carrier and discrete signals were transmitted. This idea underlay the conception of phototelegraphy by cable and the dissection of a picture into discrete pixels that could be transformed into electric information using selenium or, later, alkali cells. But with the invention of film in 1895, the idea of television changed from the transmission of motionless pictures to animated pictures. The German scientists August Karolus and Arthur Korn, both professors at the Technical University of Berlin, therefore introduced the term 'telecinema' (Korn 1930: 12).

With the emergence of radio as a new mass medium in the late 1920s, radio became the dominant point of reference for the development of television.

The success of radio as a mass medium for information and entertainment now shaped the conception of television as a medium for programmes. This new conception had an impact on the research agenda of television engineers as well. Two ideas of television took a back seat: as a medium that could be used reciprocally (like the telephone or telegraphy), and – just as in the case of early film and radio – as a symmetric device for both recording and transmission. These two stagnated or were quashed in favour of one-way broadcast and reception technologies during the further development of both radio and television. For the state, it was increasingly undesirable that the radio listener or television viewer could become an independent (and therefore uncontrollable) sender. There was no interest in a dialogic medium, and here the close relationship between media technologies and political or social power is obvious. As Michele Hilmes (2002: 29) has stated, the concept of broadcasting was the result of 'a concerted effort on the part of big business and government, feeding on the elite public's fear of the masses, to change that vision to the highly centralized, one-way, restricted-access system that is broadcasting'.

From test assemblies to mechanical television

Four centres for the development of television evolved in the 1920s: London, Berlin, Paris and several places in the USA. Alongside people already active in the television business such as Bidwell in Britain, Weiller in France and Karolus and Korn in Berlin, two new faces came on the scene and pushed both the development and public promotion of television: the Hungarian Dénes von Mihály and the Scotsman John Logie Baird. The German firm Telefunken AG took both von Mihály and (occasionally) Baird to Berlin work on television at their laboratories. Baird was thus lured away from the BBC, which also aimed to further develop television in the mid-1920s.

But it was unclear where the technical journey of television should lead. Many engineers made detailed improvements, but a real breakthrough was not in sight. It was impossible to decide whether a mechanical, an electronic, a mixed system or a completely different technology would finally make television a reality outside the laboratories of inventors and major companies. In the USA, Zworykin began working on an electronic camera in 1923 and applied for first patents for his inventions, but the advantages of electronic television systems were still not visible. Baird, who as an independent inventor-entrepreneur was interested in quick success, constantly improved the electromechanical devices and could produce and transmit television pictures over a certain distance from the second half of the 1920s. Besides Baird in London, other scientists who were working on television systems used the mechanical principle, such as Philo Farnsworth in San Francisco (later in Philadelphia), Frank Gray in New York, Edouard Bélin in Paris and August Karolus and Fritz Schröter in Berlin. But Baird was perhaps the most driven among them and constantly presented new devices, not least to keep the interest of the public alive (Burns 2000).

By 1928, the possibility to produce and broadcast television pictures with 48 lines, even if they were still imprecise and unclear, existed in the USA as well as in Europe. In April 1928, the RCA in New York built the first television station (W2XBS) that broadcasted moving picture films. In May 1928, Denis von Mihály presented television broadcasts in Berlin, using a mechanical system. In July 1928 Baird demonstrated a colour television transmission, and in August a stereoscopic television broadcast. The number of announcements of television presentations increased, but often there is little left of the event but the newspaper announcement. Whether the technical demonstration really took place and, importantly, whether it was successful cannot be determined and is often very doubtful. In August 1928 von Mihály and Karolus presented their television devices for the first time at the International Radio Exhibition in Berlin. But Karolus could only broadcast slides whereas Baird could show moving pictures.

Popular interest in television was aroused in the mid-1920s thanks to many articles in popular magazines and newspapers. More and more, scientists were urged to present television experiments in public. Independent television inventors like von Mihály and Baird also tried to stimulate public interest in order to gain new investors for their costly ventures. From 1928 onwards, television was a permanent attraction at the popular radio fairs in London, Berlin or Paris (Riedel 1994). After a long phase of utopian and fantastic speculation in both popular writings and scientific literature, the discourse about television entered a phase characterised by the popular staging of television as a miraculous technology at industrial fairs and museums. The Deutsches Museum in Berlin, one of the earliest popular museums of science and technology, inaugurated a section featuring 'picture telegraphy and television' as part of their permanent exhibition in 1930 and dedicated a special show entirely to television in 1937. In the same year, television was prominently staged at the World's Fair in Paris, both in the French 'Palais de la Radio' and in the German pavilion. The World's Fairs in Paris and New York (1939), where the regular broadcast of television programmes in the USA was inaugurated, mark the phase of staging television as a politically and culturally important medium and industrial reality rather than a technical or scientific attraction.

In the USA, General Electric had established a television station (WGY) in Schenectady in August 1928. This station is said to have sent the 'first television broadcast' of a single play on 11 September 1928 (Abramson 1987: 125). Although the picture must have been very small and fuzzy, a whole programme was at least presented. A whole clutch of other experimental stations broadcasted television images in different ways (often only still pictures) with a number of lines between 24 and 60 and an image frequency between 7.5 and 21 pictures per second. These experiments were mostly received quite enthusiastically by the press. With the introduction of television, the Modern Age seemed to have arrived in a new way.

In the USA, RCA, General Electric and the Westinghouse Company largely financed Zworykin's work on the electronic camera. Zworykin had travelled around Europe (besides Germany, Britain and France, he also visited Hungary and Belgium) in 1928 to become informed about the newest developments, and he returned to the USA with many new ideas (Abramson 1987: 122–3). Zworykin especially found an energetic supporter in RCA's manager David Sarnoff, who promoted further experiments by Zworykin until around 1933. Zworykin mainly concentrated his work on the construction of an electronic camera (Iconoscope), but at the same time, he also considered the development of a reception tube (Kinoscope) in order to create an integrated all-electronic television system.

In Europe, Baird tried to get a frequency from the BBC for the broadcast of his television. After having only little success – the BBC was not impressed by the picture quality – he went to Berlin at the invitation of Hans Bredow, the German high commissioner on broadcasting matters, to try his system in programme service. Because of several difficulties, he returned to England in June 1928. Von Mihály's experimental programmes on the Berlin channel Witzleben were not successful either. In the USA, despite many experimental broadcasts and a big financing effort, television also remained unsatisfying.

Moreover, public criticism of television arose because the promises made about the new medium could not be kept. On the one hand, the mechanical systems in use produced unsatisfying picture resolution because of their small number of lines, and on the other hand, the development of an electronic camera did not progress either. Further developments were necessary in electronic cameras as well as in electronic image transmission. Alongside Zworykin and Farnsworth in the USA, these developments were carried out by the German researcher Manfred von Ardenne, who, financed by the radio producer Loewe, intensively worked on the production of electronic recording tubes (Schröter 1937).

Despite the need for further technical invention, broadcasting companies were established in the USA. Various companies aimed to get into the market early with their own television system, because they hoped to gain a commercial advantage. On 21 July 1931, Columbia Broadcasting System (CBS) inaugurated a television station and thus for the first time one of the big radio networks regularly broadcasted picture and sound programmes, amounting to about seven hours per day until 1933 (Abramson 2002: 169). In 1933, CBS ceased the programme service 'until better devices are available'.

The big attraction promoted by public television presentations was the fact that moving pictures could be broadcast over long distances without using a cable. It was therefore mainly the technical problems of doing this that fascinated the population. But the real attraction of the medium – its potential to witness events happening in distant places – could not be realised because the cameras were not powerful enough. The broadcast of films was no real alternative, since cinema presentations of a film on a large screen, now combined with the possibilities of sound since 1928–9, were much more attractive. The television picture on the small screen of the time – usually 6 inches

(15 cm) square and only 9 inches (25 cm) square at the beginning of the 1930s – hardly seemed to be suitable for a mass medium. The real break-through was still not in sight.

On the technical side, scientists in the USA and Britain experimented with the presentation of television on large screen projection systems in cinemas. In Germany, on the contrary, film was explored as a means for the production of live records. The 'Fernseh AG' (founded by the Bosch, Loewe Radio, Zeiss Ikon and Baird Television companies) developed an intermediate film-processing system. An event was recorded by a film camera, and then the film ran through a developing and fixing bath, and was then fed in front of an electronic kinescope and electrically scanned. This technology was principally used to broadcast the Olympic Games in Berlin in 1936, but it proved to be too expensive and was never used afterwards. Because of the development of the intermediate film process, the 'Fernseh AG' neglected research on an electronic camera, although the inventions of Ardenne would have led the way (Ardenne 1996).

In the USA, it was the union of General Electric, Westinghouse and RCA with its television laboratory under Zworykin's supervision that mainly promoted the development of electronic television. Although some companies, also in the American–European context, had cross-licensing agreements and patent pools, not all the new findings were communicated. The RCA, for example, did not disclose all of its inventions. In 1931 it had already used an image dissection tube for two years for outdoor shooting without the others knowing (Abramson 1987: 201). In Britain, Electric and Musical Industries Ltd (EMI), formed in 1931 from a merger of British Columbia Records and the Gramophone Company, became involved in television development and continued to operate the television system that had been invented by Baird Television.

Programme concepts

Although technical problems emerged again and again, the question of what television could be used for also kept people's minds busy. The special feature of this medium seemed to be the broadcast of moving pictures (in the early 1930s still separated from sound transmission), and this broadcast could take place almost simultaneously with the events that were broadcast. Even the intermediate film process with a time delay of about two minutes seemed to correspond to the idea of liveness – the technology was accepted as television-like. The up-to-date nature of television presented a real advantage compared to cinema, especially in the case of news broadcasts. Cinema newsreels still demanded one to two days of production time and therefore offered a lesser sense of actuality. The medial character of television therefore corresponded rather to radio than to the cinema. Television simply added the moving picture to the wireless transmission of sound. In the same way that film turned into an audiovisual medium in 1928 when sound was added to pictures, the sonic medium of radio seemed to turn into television thanks to the addition of moving images (Hickethier 2004).

Because of this medial similarity between radio and television, it seemed quite obvious that the programming structure of radio broadcasting should be transferred to the new medium. In Germany the discussion about the programme structure of television took place in the technical magazine *Fernsehen*. This magazine for the first time systematically stimulated a public debate about the future programme identity of television in Germany. The engineer Rudolph Thun pointed to the 'close relationship' between radio and television and described potential programme forms. Domestic reception of television – just like radio – was promoted as best use of the medium. This suggestion was not at all self-evident, however, after the extended experiments with the picture telephone and the cinema projection of television pictures that were made by the German Post Office. But the identification of film and television as distinct media was therefore very clear in the German case. Television was conceived in the same way as radio: news and short press releases, education and entertainment were seen as the pillars of future television broadcasting (Hickethier 1998). Both in programming and in its institutional development, radio formed the 'structuring framework' (Olivesi 1998) for television development in most European countries.

The First Television Programmes

The first half of the 1930s was marked by a period of economic depression in the USA and Europe. Given the fact that the technical inventions advanced only slowly, if at all, and a stable television broadcast of a contrastive and sophisticated picture still was not achieved, it seems only too logical that those companies that had invested in television development halted their commitment. The union of General Electric, RCA and Westinghouse in the USA had the impression that television could not be put into practice very soon. David Sarnoff, who always had promoted Zworykin's television activities, decided to concentrate research activities more on radio technology. EMI turned to the development of telecommunication in 1933, merged with the Marconi Wireless Telegraph Company in 1934, but then nevertheless pursued television activities. The Philco Corporation separated from Farnsworth, because it had lost the hope of developing its own television system and becoming an independent player in the field. In the early 1930s, the international situation was somewhat ambivalent and paralysed: on the one hand, the trust of the industry in technology was inconsistent, if not lost altogether, because of the lack of visible technical improvements; on the other hand, the companies hesitated to give up the large investments already made in the years before the depression. It was Zworykin's continuous work on an electronic camera and an adequate electronic reception system that finally broke the deadlock.

His improved iconoscope camera offering a high-definition television ⊦
especially, clearly demonstrated the limits of all electromechanical televisi∪.
systems in experimental operation at that time (Abramson 1995).

The path to the beginning of television

Despite the rather pessimistic appreciation of television by the industry, there
was still a public interest in television. From 1930–1 experimental broadcasts,
and often experimental programmes, were made in Germany, Britain and the
USA to test different programme formats and to check and improve image
quality and transmission stability. Whereas in Britain the BBC started the experimental service, the Reichspost undertook these experiments in Germany.
Later the Reichs-Rundfunk-Gesellschaft (RRG), responsible for programme
production, also participated in the technical experiments. From May 1934,
the RRG transmitted a small experimental schedule on three evenings per
week. In the USA, Sarnoff stopped RCA's experimental service in 1933, but
the British postal authority and also the BBC announced they would begin
an experimental service. These tests were carried out with two competing
systems: the 30-line system developed by Baird Television and the 180-line
system operated by EMI. Baird reproached EMI for not promoting British
interests but in fact being an American company because of the participation
of RCA. Their relationship was therefore dissolved: RCA sold its EMI shares
to render Baird's allegations groundless and to keep up in the competition
for the future television system to be used by the BBC.

To get to a decision on the system that should be used in Britain, a commission under Lord Selsdon was appointed on 16 May 1934 to investigate
the state of television development and to draft a report. Members of the commission travelled to the USA and to Germany to examine the respective devices.
On 14 January 1935, the report of the Selsdon commission was published,
recommending the introduction of high-definition television (with at least 240
lines). Baird Television and EMI-Marconi were to be given a chance to compete, but the television pictures of both systems had to be receivable on the
same device. It was recommended that the BBC should control the television
service (Abramson 1987: 214). Although EMI-Marconi with its 243-line system was – from a technological point of view – already ahead of Baird's system,
the company tried to develop an improved 405-line system before the experimental BBC broadcasts started. Already in the middle of April 1935 EMI managed to present a picture of 405 lines to the BBC television service (Briggs 1985).

The announcement that British television would soon go into operation
did not remain unrecognised by other countries. As a clear political reaction
to the British initiative, the German Reichspost in Berlin opened a regular
television service on 22 March 1935 with a schedule of two hours each weekday. They operated with an electromechanically produced picture of 180 lines
that is supposed not to have been very stable. On 19 August 1935, a fire in
the transmission complex put an end to the regular television broadcasts that

could only be resumed in 1936. In France, the ministry of Postes, Télégraphes et Téléphones who had also experimented with television announced the start of an experimental service with 60 lines for 26 April 1935. The low-definition mechanical television devices were built by René Barthélémy since the early pioneers of television in France (Weiller, Belin and others) had turned their back on television (Amoudry 1997). In the USA, the British announcement of both a 240-line system (Baird) and a 405-line service (EMI-Marconi) was met with scepticism. David Sarnoff saw no future for the electro-mechanical system but decided to consider the London experiences. Other companies, like Farnsworth Ltd and Bell Laboratories, felt challenged by British and German activities and planned television stations operating with the 240-line system that now became, in effect, a new standard. These developments reflected a new optimism in American companies who felt encouraged by the politics of the New Deal. But Europe and the USA were not the only places to experiment with television. In Japan, experiments had taken place at the Technological Institute in Tokyo since the 1920s. Those experiments were carried out by Kenjiro Takayanagis, who also travelled around Europe and the USA in 1934 to observe television developments. Back in Japan, he won support from the Japan Broadcast Corporation (NHK) and the Nippon Electric Company to promote his experiments. However, this work did not have an influence on European developments (Japan Broadcasting Corporation, 1967).

At the end of 1935, the international situation was as follows: EMI-Marconi possessed the leading system with 405 lines and even Baird Television could not catch up. The Farnsworth and Telefunken systems, which were linked to Baird, also lagged behind EMI's technology. Even in the USA, developments by RCA had not progressed to the same extent. However, regular television services now went into operation in different countries, but based on different technical standards. The open competition between Baird Television and EMI-Marconi in Britain demonstrated that television had entered the phase of marketing and industrial production. But at the same time, television became a symbol for national prestige and economic prowess. If Baird could threaten his competitors with the reproach of 'not being British', how much could television become a symbol for a nation's cultural-technical progress in a Europe of national tensions? In the second half of the 1930s, the technical problems clearly became of secondary importance compared to political ambitions.

Television as national symbol: Paul Nipkow's German television station (1935–44)

With the National Socialists' accession to power in Germany the whole radio system, which had been nationalised since 1932, was reorganised and put under the control of the Reich's Propaganda Ministry. All Jewish employees and those considered politically undesirable were eliminated from the institution. The small experimental television station operated by the Reichspost near the *Haus des Rundfunks* (Broadcasting House) in Berlin-Witzleben was now run by the *Reichsfunkgesellschaft* (the Reichs radio society) – as far as programming was concerned, and by the Ministry of Aviation as far as high-frequency technology was concerned. After the announcement of the Selsdon commission to begin a regular television service in Britain, the Nazis were eager to officially start their programme before the British. Rather in a rush, the first regular television broadcast went out on 22 March 1935. The *Reichssendeleiter* (National Programming Director) Eugen Hadamovsky wanted television viewers to be organised in *Fernseharbeitsgemeinschaften* (federal television committees), an idea that was soon dropped. Television would serve the propaganda of the Reich and was pompously advertised as a 'German invention'. In Hadamovsky's words: 'Fight for Germany to become the first nation in the world in which all our "national comrades" can watch television' (Hickethier 1998: 39). The director of National Socialist mass events Carl Boese became the first director-general of the station, which from 1936 was named after the inventor of the 'electrical telescope' Paul Nipkow. Television was staged in, so-called *Fernsehstuben* (public television rooms), mostly located in post offices. The programme, at first lasting one hour, could be watched by 20 to 30 viewers at a time and was subsequently repeated.

After a fire in the transmission complex in 1935, broadcasts stopped until 15 January 1936. As well as the broadcast of films, the live transmissions mainly consisted of artistic and cabaret performances, and – to a smaller degree – of outdoor events like football matches. In the case of outdoor transmissions, the intermediate film process was used. The coverage of the Olympic Games in Berlin in 1936 involved a mobile van, equipped with a large Farnsworth image-dissection camera (from the USA). In the public television rooms, 150,000 viewers are said to have witnessed the seven or eight hours of live broadcasts a day (Winker 1994). Although many practical experiments could be made during the Olympics, outside broadcasts proved to be extremely complicated and costly and were therefore abandoned subsequently. The attempts to broadcast the Nazis' Nuremberg rallies by means of a broadband cable from Nuremberg to Berlin were finally cancelled after two attempts in 1936 and 1937. Leni Riefenstahl's films of the Nuremberg rallies produced a strong propaganda effect that the television broadcasts on a small screen never matched. This lack of propagandistic effect made television uninteresting as a political tool for the leaders of the National Socialist Party. Television programming, mainly based on the idea of transferring well-known radio formats to television, was based on studio productions. Hans-Jürgen Nierentz, programme director from 1937, opted for fictional entertainment programmes, abbreviated versions of cinema films and advice shows that, from 1938–9 onwards, were broadcast live from the studio. Political or ideological subjects were mainly dealt with by newsreels and Nazi film productions.

Television in Germany under National Socialism did not get beyond this collective reception that was, in any case, limited to the cities of Berlin and Hamburg. The number of television rooms remained stable throughout the late 1930s, and there were never more than 20 to 27. The Minister of Propaganda, Joseph Goebbels, did not want to bring television into competition with cinema, whose propagandistic potential was fully developed. In 1939, the television industry prepared for the production of a cheap *Einheitsempfänger* ('standard' or 'uniform set') for private use. But due to the beginning of the Second World War, only about fifty sets left the factories (König 2004). However, a propagandistic interest in showing that television could operate even during the war prevailed. Television was used to entertain soldiers and to strengthen the morale of the troops. Each Saturday evening, a big entertainment show, *Wir senden Frohsinn, wir spenden Freude* (*We Send Joy, We Spend Pleasure*) was staged in the large domed hall of the *Reichssportgelände* (Reich sports arena) and broadcast live to the television rooms and military hospitals. Almost all the popular entertainment stars of the Third Reich performed there. On 21 June 1944, these television events were finally suspended. The programme forms that had been developed in this period were taken up again when television restarted in the Federal Republic of Germany in 1948. Many directors, authors and employees of the television service before 1945 participated in the reconstruction of a federal television structure in both West and East Germany.

The pre-war BBC television service in Britain (1936–9)

After years of experimental transmissions, on 2 November 1936 the BBC opened a regular television service in London. Already during the 'Radio-Olympia-Weeks' of August 1936, the BBC had presented a series of television programmes to the public. Their positive reactions convinced the BBC to start a regular programme service, but with alternating technologies: one week, the programme was transmitted with Baird's 240-line technology, the other week the programme came in 405-line quality over the EMI-Marconi system. After a fire involving Baird's television equipment in the studios at Crystal Palace, the dual pattern ceased on 5 February 1937 and the Post Office defined the 405-line system as the single national television standard. All programmes were produced at Alexandra Palace ('Ally Pally'), and the programming was – just as in Germany – mainly based on the radio model. Similarly to Germany, the BBC transferred successful variety and entertainment formats from radio to television. The programme at first lasted one hour, then two hours. Because of the availability of two studios (one equipped with Baird technology, the other with EMI-Marconi technology), the production facilities were rather generously equipped. Whereas German television produced rather droll stories, the BBC staged comedies, musical shows and even cartoons (Lazell 1991). Already during the experimental period, a first single play (*The Man with a*

Flower in his Mouth by Luigi Pirandello) was broadcast (14 July 1930), and Baird had realised a broadcast of the Derby horse race on 3 June 1931 (Eckert 1965: 11–12). Alongside these entertainment programmes, more serious formats like education programmes were presented in a lecture style. Radio again inspired the testing of possibilities in television, for, as in Germany, the BBC's post-war programme philosophy was mainly based on its experience in the three years before the Second World War (Corner 1991).

Even in political reporting, television began to demonstrate its possibilities. On 30 September 1938, the BBC television service reported live on the return of the British Prime Minister from Munich using outside broadcast. The pictures were transmitted by means of a wireless link to London and then broadcast from Alexandra Palace. Abramson (1987: 248) described this report as 'the first actual broadcast by television of a major news event as it was actually happening'. A year before, on 12 May 1937, the Coronation procession of King George VI had been transmitted using several outside broadcast vans equipped with different cameras, but the pictures were transmitted by cable and not wirelessly. In 1938 and 1939, several wireless outside broadcasts from sporting events (the Oxford and Cambridge Boat Race, the Derby races and Wimbledon tennis) were realised. In Britain, both public viewing (in cinemas) and reception in private homes were promoted. There are said to have been about 3,000 television receivers in the London area before the war (Abramson 2002: 265). Whereas the BBC broadcasted by means of the EMI-Marconi-system, Baird Television now tried to develop large-screen television projection apparatus to be used in cinemas. The first large-screen projections were demonstrated in the Palais Cinema in Kent in 1937, and Baird even staged colour television projections in the Dominion cinema in central London. He thus tried to promote television as a hybrid medium linking different media characteristics – a visionary thought but one that was ahead of its time.

Television experiments in France, 1938–9 and 1943–4

As the French electronics companies dealing with television were not or only partly involved in the patent agreements between RCA and Telefunken on the one hand and Baird Television and the Fernseh AG on the other hand, they have been less noticed in the history of technology (Fickers & Kessler 2008: 71–82). However, a first television presentation took place in Paris in 1931 and only one year later the first experimental service was started. In November 1935, the 180-line standard was introduced, which was increased to a 455-line standard in 1937. This created the basis for the first regular programmes broadcast from the Eiffel Tower in 1938 (Eckert 1965: 93). In France, programming was also based on radio principles, so that a mixed programme of entertainment and education developed. The programme service was suspended when the war began (Amoudry 1997: 123–214). When the German military occupied Paris in 1940 and wanted to abolish the aerial installation ᴜn the Eiffel Tower, Telefunken suggested continuing to operate it. The television station ran under German military control. Under the direction of Alfred Bofinger and Kurt Hinzmann, both experts in the field of the radio, a studio service was established in a dance hall called 'Magic City'. This curious episode of German–French collaboration ran from 7 May 1943 until 16 August 1944, and three to four hours of television programmes were broadcast by the *Fernsehsender Paris* station (Television Station Paris). There are said to have been about 1,200 receivers in Paris and its periphery (Kubler & Lemieux 1990, Truckendanner 1998). In a nostalgic look back at this period, two central figures in the Paris television service during the war, the French Jacques Poinsignon and the German Kurt Hinzmann, claimed that their central motivation had been to 'lay the foundation for European television in a peaceful and friendly manner'! (Hickethier 1998: 57–8).

Television after the Second World War

The beginning of the Second World War led to a worldwide stagnation of television development. If the programme service was not suspended as in Britain, it nevertheless remained at the same technical level. After the war, the situation changed dramatically. In 1945, the USA had nine television stations: three in New York, two each in Los Angeles and Chicago and one each in Schenectady and Philadelphia. There are said to have been 7,000 television receivers at that time (Abramson 1987). From 1946 on, a phenomenal increase in television viewers took place. In 1947, 178,000 television sets were constructed and in 1949 the number had increased to 2,421,000 (Hickethier 1998: 62). National penetration rates for television rose from 0.2 per cent in 1946 to 9 per cent in 1950. In 1955, 65 per cent of American homes were already equipped with a television set. In addition to the prosperity of post-war American industry, social and political factors shaped the rapid growth of television as the new leading mass medium in the USA. The so-called 'TV freeze' by the Federal Communications Commission (FCC) was a political setback, in which the FCC refused to allocate new television broadcast frequencies for black and white television stations between 28 September 1948 and 14 April 1952. They were pressuring the American television industry to develop a compatible colour television system, and the move ensured the monopoly and stable growth of the old radio networks (Boddy 1990: 42–64). But the housing act of 1949 laid the foundation for a revitalisation of domesticity and family life by promoting the government-sanctioned ideal of prefabricated suburban homes (Wright 2001: 240–62). The extremely high marriage rate and – as a direct result – birth rate in the post-war period (96.4 per cent of the female and 94.1 per cent of the male US population married in the late 1940s) inaugurated a baby boom, which reversed the declining birth rates of previous decades and revitalised the nuclear family as basic social construct

(Spigel 1992: 36–72) . In this very special economic, social and political environment, television began its career as a favourite family pastime activity.

In Europe, by contrast, the development of television resumed only slowly. To many people, television suddenly appeared as an 'American' medium that had to be adapted to the respective cultures of the European countries. The introduction of television now became a symbol for a new, modern lifestyle in a western world. At the same time the Cold War affected the development of television as a political medium. Especially in boundary regions where the opposed political camps' territories met and therefore were in reach of the enemy's television, television was directly involved in the ideological confrontation and became a 'window' on the world of 'the other'. In most Western European countries, television developed into a medium for the propagation of consumption, leisure and individualism; in the Eastern countries, it became a medium for the political socialisation of the individual and the subtle implementation of ideology and political values.

Post-war stages of the implementation of television in Europe

The post-war introduction or implementation of television as a mass medium in European countries can be divided into four stages. In the first stage, from 1945 to 1948, Britain and France continued the experiments carried out before the war. France resumed its television service very early, on 29 March 1945, and used the facilities of the *Fernsehsender Paris* left by the Germans. Britain resumed its regular television service on 7 June 1946. In a second stage from 1949 to 1954, which was a time of political tension between East and West, Italy's public service channel RAI began an official programme service on 26 February 1952, the Federal Republic of Germany's official service began on 25 December 1952, Denmark's on 1 October 1953 and Belgium's on 31 October 1953. The third stage occurred in the second half of the 1950s when the following countries inaugurated a regular television service: Sweden on 1 July 1957, Finland on 1 January 1958, Norway on 20 August 1960, Switzerland on 1 January 1958, Spain on 28 October 1956 and Portugal on 7 March 1957. Commercial television, which started in 1954 with Independent Television (ITV) in Britain, served as a model for some European micro-states such as Luxembourg and Monaco. Because they could not finance a television station by viewing licence fees, they opted for advertising revenues and deliberately broadcasted their programmes to reception areas in neighbouring states. In a last stage from 1961 onwards, some western countries at the edge of Europe introduced television, after it had become clear that television was the dominant new mass medium in the world. In Ireland television started officially on 31 December 1961, Gibraltar TV and Malta TV followed in 1962, and Greece began in 1966.

Comparison of the speed of television expansion in European countries shows that the expansion always followed the same pattern. After a first stage, in which the medium spread only slowly and was promoted by additional campaigns and through the broadcasting of major media events (like coronations or sports broadcasts), it reached a threshold of about 3–5 per cent of households equipped with a television set. In most cases, this was the 'critical mass' that catalysed a rapid expansion of television, reaching saturation within 10 to 15 years. After this first market saturation, the number of television sets increased much more slowly (Bonus 1968). Moreover, the expansion took place faster in countries that introduced television at a later point in time, clearly owing to the dramatically falling prices of sets that changed from luxury goods into consumer goods. After a long incubation period, television finally became the leading mass medium of social self-reflection in Europe at the end of the 1960s and beginning of the 1970s.

Is there a European television style?

Before the Second World War, a European style in television could not be detected. Television programmes in London, Berlin and Paris retained a local appearance. Political circumstances did not promote, and sometimes even hindered, exchange. Even between the technicians, transnational communication decreased, and the war finally broke all the ties. However, according to surviving records, there were structural similarities: the programming and formats showed clear resemblances, which reached from the newscast through the documentary to sport, the single play, the theatre broadcast, the cinema film and the evening entertainment show. Scheduling was concentrated on the evening, sometimes on the afternoon. Moreover, the broadcasts were limited in time and presented as a middle-class family event. The presentation style was nevertheless different. The Germans were rather formal, polite and official. In Britain, television was also polite, but also entertaining and, in accordance with BBC principles, not political. In France, television was entertaining in an improvised manner. However, in each case television was clearly addressed to the middle class. According to the television critic Gerhard Eckert (1965), a certain European style of television developed in the 1950s, despite the different institutional settings and political contexts. This European television style was shaped by the idea of a nationalised, largely independent media entity and persisted – despite the introduction of commercial television – as a dominant characteristic. Following Eckert, public service ideology with its strong educational and pedagogical emphasis is perhaps the strongest common denominator of the diverse and colourful European television landscape.

Note

Translated by Stefanie Dries from the original German; additional references by Andreas Fickers.

References

Abramson, A. (1987) *The History of Television 1880–1941*. London, McFarland & Co.

Abramson, A. (1995) *Zworykin: Pioneer of Television*. Urbana, University of Illinois Press.

Abramson, A. (2002) *Die Geschichte des Fernsehens*. Munich, Fink.

Amoudry, M. (1997) *René Barthélémy ou la grande aventure de la télévision française*. Grenoble, Presses Universitaires de Grenoble.

Ardenne, M. von (1996) *Entstehen des Fernsehens: persönliche Erinnerungen an das Entstehen des heutigen Fernsehens mit Elektronenstrahlröhren*. Herten, Verlag historischer Technikliteratur Freundlieb.

Bonus, H. (1968) *Die Ausbreitung des Fernsehens*. Meisenhain am Glan, Hain.

Cantor, G. N. (ed.) (1981) *Conceptions of Ether: Studies in the History of Ether Theories, 1740–1900*. Cambridge, Cambridge University Press.

Boddy, W. (1990) *Fifties Television: The Industry and its Critics*. Urbana, University of Illinois Press.

Borscheid, P. (2004) *Das Tempo-Virus: Eine Kulturgeschichte der Beschleunigung*. Darmstadt, Wissenschaftliche Buchgesellschaft.

Briggs, A. (1985) *BBC: The First Fifty Years*. Oxford, Oxford University Press.

Burns, R. W. (1998) *Television: An International History of the Formative Years*. London, Peregrinus.

Burns, R. W. (2000) *John Logie Baird: Television Pioneer*. London, IEEE.

Corner, J. (1991) *Popular Television in Britain: Studies in Cultural History*. London, BFI.

Eckert, G. (1965) *Das Fernsehen in den Ländern Westeuropas*. Gütersloh, Bertelsmann.

Elsner, M., Müller, T. and Spangenberg, P. (1990) 'The early history of German television: the slow development of a fast medium'. *Historical Journal of Film, Radio and Television* 10, 193–219.

Fickers, A. and Kessler, F. (2008) 'Narrative topoi in Erfindermythen und technonationalistischer Legendenbildung: Zur Historiographie der Erfindung von Film und Fernsehen'. In: Bodenmann, S. and Splinter, S. (eds.) *Mythos – Helden – Symbole: Legitimation, Selbst- und Fremdwahrnehmung in der Geschichte der Naturwissenschaft, Medizin und Technik*. Munich, Martin Meidenbauer, pp. 71–82.

Fuchs, G. (1928) *Die Bildtelegraphie*. Berlin, Georg Siemens.

Hard, M. and Jamison, A. (2005) *Hubris and Hybris: A Cultural History of Technology and Science*. London, Routledge.

Griset, P. (1995) 'Innovation and radio industry in Europe during the interwar period'. In: Caron, F., Erker, P. and Fischer, W. (eds.) *Innovations the European Economy between the Wars*. New York, Walter de Gruyter, pp. 37–64.

Headrick, D. (2000) *When Information Came of Age: Technologies of Knowledge in the Age of Reason and Revolution, 1750–1850*. Oxford, Oxford University Press.

Hickethier, K. (1998) *Geschichte des deutschen Fernsehens*. Stuttgart and Weimar, Metzler.

Hickethier, K. (2004) ' "Das Wunder der Technik": Die Genese eines Mediums durch die Erprobung anderer Medienparadigmen: das Fernsehen zwischen Telegrafie, Tonfilm und Radio'. In: Segeberg, H. (ed.) *Die Medien und ihre Technik. Theorien – Modelle – Geschichte*. Marburg, Schüren, pp. 183–206.

Hilmes, M. (ed.) (2002) *Connections: A Broadcasting History Reader.* Belmont, CA: Wadsworth Publishing.

Japan Broadcasting Corporation (ed.) (1967) *The History of Broadcasting in Japan.* Tokyo, JBC.

Kern, S. (1983) *The Culture of Time and Space: 1880–1918.* Cambridge, MA, Harvard University Press.

König, W. (2004) *Volkswagen, Volksempfänger, Volksgemeinschaft. 'Volksprodukte' im Dritten Reich: Vom Scheitern einer nationalsozialistischen Konsumgesellschaft.* Paderborn, Schöningh.

Korn, A. (1930) *Electrisches Fernsehen.* Berlin, Otto Salle.

Kubler, T. and Lemieux, E. (1990) *Cognacq-Jay: La télévision française sous l'occupation.*, Paris, Éditions Plume.

Lange, A. (2001) 'Le miroir magique: La vision à distance par le biais de l'électricité à la fin du XIXème siècle et l'historiographie des origines de la télévision'. *Recherches en communication* 14.

Lazell, D. (1991) *What's on the Box?* Cheltenham, Evergreen.

Mattelart, A. and Mattelart, M. (1995) *Histoire des théories de la communication.* Paris, Éditions la Découverte.

McLuhan, M. (1989) *The Global Village: Transformations in World Life and Media in the 21st Century.* New York, Oxford University Press.

Olivesi, S. (1998) *Histoire politique de la télévision.* Paris, L'Harmattan.

Radkau, J. (1998) *Das Zeitalter der Nervosität: Deutschland zwischen Bismarck und Hitler.* Darmstadt, Wissenschaftliche Buchgesellschaft.

Reiss, E. and Zielinski, S. (1976) 'Internationaler Medienzusammenhang: Am Beispiel der Entwicklung des Rundfunks in England, Frankreich und Deutschland'. In: Berns, H.-J. (ed.) *Massen/Medien/Politik.* Berlin, Argument, pp. 150–201.

Riedel, H. (1994) *70 Jahre Funkausstellung: Politik, Wirtschaft, Programm.* Berlin, Vistas.

Schivelbusch, W. (1986) *The Railway Journey: The Industrialization of Time and Space in the 19th Century.* New York, Berg.

Schröter, F. (ed.) (1937) *Fernsehen: Die neuere Entwicklung insbesondere der deutschen Fernsehtechnik.* Berlin, Springer.

Spigel, L. (1992) *Make Room for TV: Television and the Family Ideal in Postwar America.* Chicago, University of Chicago Press.

Truckendanner, P. (1998) *Der Fernsehsender Paris: Deutsch-französisches Okkupationsfernsehen (1942–1944).* Dissertation, University of Salzburg.

Wiesbeck, W. (1988) *Hundred Years of Electromagnetic Waves.* Berlin, VDE.

Winker, K. (1994) *Fernsehen unterm Hakenkreuz: Organisation, Programm, Personal.* Cologne, Böhlau.

Winston, B. (1998) *Media Technology, and Society: A History from the Telegraph to the Internet.* London, Routledge.

Wright, G. (2001) *Building the American Dream: A Social History of Housing in America.* Cambridge, MA, MIT Press.

Zielinski, A. (1999) *Audiovisions: Cinema and Television as Entr'actes in History.* Amsterdam, Amsterdam University Press.

3

Institutionalising European Television:
The Shaping of European Television Institutions and Infrastructures

Christina Adamou, with Isabelle Gaillard and Dana Mustata

This chapter focuses on key aspects of the creation and development of television institutions in Europe, with regard to comparing institutions in France, Greece and Romania, while also making extensive references to the European Broadcasting Union (EBU). The chapter does not aim to be an exhaustive study of television institutions in Europe, but the institutions chosen provide stimulating points of comparison, as they spread across Eastern and Western Europe. It should be noted that strong political control has been exercised on television institutions in all three countries, even though they have developed under different political situations. Of course, this is not meant to imply that the exercise of political control over television has been common throughout Europe. The chapter analyses the ways in which television was envisioned and realised, briefly highlighting an implied hierarchy in comparison with other media and placing emphasis on the strong links between television and radio. It focuses on the development and the problematics of public service broadcasting, a common imperative, differently interpreted. The chapter will also highlight the EBU's envisioned and actual role, in relation to public service broadcasting and the effort to convey the notion of a European identity, drawing parallels with public service broadcasting and problems with popularity within the boundaries of nation-states. The chapter addresses the complexity of political control in different political circumstances and it closes with an extensive reference to the advent of private television, emphasising the ways in which it was linked to issues of political control and public service broadcasting. The birth of television and the advent of private television – two key moments in television's development, the practices of censorship and the varying policy of public service – are inextricably linked to the ways in which television has been conceived.

The Birth of Television Institutions in Romania, France and Greece

The development of television in Europe has often followed the development of radio, not just chronologically but also with regard to the models of how broadcasting could be delivered, organised and used by its audiences. The comparative relationships in different European contexts between television and radio will be outlined, while also making brief references to television's relationship with other media, as television was variously thought to be their inheritor, a rival, or a supplement.

Radio and television were initially associated in France, Greece and Romania, but were gradually differentiated, as their techniques and modes of address were gradually differentiated. It is noteworthy that television's independence from radio, the growth of the television set market and the importance of the new medium were gradually developed in France, whereas communist governments in Romania actively created a market for the new medium, and the army dictatorship in Greece both censored television and took a very active interest in the development of the new medium by investing in the armed forces' channel. The communist government in Romania and the right-wing army dictatorship in Greece both treated television as a strong weapon in exercising political control. While censorship will be analytically discussed later, it is important to keep in mind that television's potential as a propaganda medium is present in its first steps.

The initial lack of adequate funding of television institutions in France led to programmes largely being derived from radio, cinema or theatre, whereas in Greece, the late arrival of television and lack of funding led to early television schedules relying heavily upon films, imported American series and theatrical forms of entertainment. Television gradually became more independent in the 1960s and first half of the 1970s in France and during the end of the 1970s in Greece, as the television set market took off.

There was an implicit yet evident hierarchy between media, whereby cinema was regarded as more important than television in France and Greece, and television regarded as more important than cinema in Romania. In all three countries, however, radio and television were initially joined in the same public service broadcasting institution and separated later, with television taking the lead, as it quickly became extremely popular.

The birth of television in Greece has a turbulent and telling prehistory, as companies were repeatedly invited to make offers for the creation of a television network, yet its creation was repeatedly postponed with ambiguous explanations. International contests for establishing a television network in Greece in 1952 and 1955 were effectively cancelled. A third contest, in 1958, was won by the Nippon Electric Co (based in Japan), but the network was not realised. In 1959, the Greek government signed an agreement with the

Italian national public service broadcaster RAI, only to cancel it later. In the same year, the Greek armed forces started broadcasting at a very small range (3 km). A small network was built in Thessaloniki in 1960 during the 25th International Exhibition, by the Public Electricity Corporation. Two years later, the Public Electricity Corporation began broadcasting in Athens, but that effort came to an end, as the government was quick to assign television broadcasting to EIR, the Hellenic Radio Foundation, the public service broadcaster. In 1964, the wedding of Constantine, former King of Greece, was broadcast by EIR and Eurovision in and around Athens. Lord Thompson suggested installing a network in Greece in 1965, but the government did not accept his proposal. Both the Greek armed forces and EIR started broadcasting experimentally in 1965 and more regularly in 1966. The armed forces, in fact, began experimental and regular broadcasting and news reports slightly earlier.

Television scholars are still quite hesitant to interpret the prehistory of Greek television. However, there was clearly an underlying conflict between the urgency to install a television network and the need for it to be national and public service, which was further complicated by the active involvement of the armed forces. In 1967, the year after television broadcasting eventually started, a dictatorship was imposed by the Greek armed forces, in a period of political turbulence that began in 1965 with the former king's involvement in the appointment of ministers. Television in Greece and its relationship to the state were formed under a dictatorship. The second Greek channel was directly controlled by the army, before and during the army dictatorship, but also for eight years after the dictatorship had fallen. Even though (according to a law of 1975) it was to be joined to EIRT by 1977, this did not happen until 1982. So the army was actively involved in television's development in Greece for 17 years; its role in propaganda will be discussed later on.

Although Greek governments seemed to take an active interest in the development of television, it has always been an expensive medium, so in both France and Greece it has had to struggle with inadequate funding. The funding for EIR was initially 750,000 drachmas, just enough for a camera, a monitor and a spotlight (Psalidas 1996). Thus, when experimental broadcasting began, they could only broadcast documentaries lent to EIR by foreign embassies and USIS (US Investigations Services), but original (cheap) programmes were quickly developed (Karter 2004: 23).

Television's importance as a mass medium seems to have been immediately acknowledged, although the television market was initially limited. Its late arrival to Greece, however, meant that the audience was prepared to accept it as part of their everyday lives. The television set market soared before the 9th European track events organised in Athens in 1969.

Although television in Greece gained its financial independence from radio and the two media were separated with a 1975 law, it nevertheless retained its ties with theatre and radio for many years. In 1974, the first democratic government after the dictatorship selected Dimitris Horn, a well-known and respected actor, as director-general and he in turn used radio presenters for the news, as they were more experienced (Karter 2004: 36–7).

The role of 'national interests' in joining radio and television in a public service broadcasting organisation is particularly noteworthy, not only in countries when television developed under a dictatorship, but also where it developed under democratic governments. In France, since 1793, with the Chappe system, the transport of ideas and news had been under state monopoly. However, during the 1920s and 1930s, unlike Britain or Germany, radio broadcasting was both public and private. At this time, experimental television depended on the General Post Office, like radio broadcasting, and was under state control (Amoudry 1981). During the Second World War, private radio broadcasting was compromised by the German enemy. Therefore, in 1944–5, public authorities decided that radio broadcasting ought to be public service and a state monopoly. Radio and television institutions were joined together as their techniques were similar and they were both to be mass markets and mass media. As a newcomer, television relied on radio, especially for its funding.

Most of the radio set makers became television set makers. Jean-Pierre Bouyssonnie, who was in charge of manufacturing radio and television sets at Thomson's group at the end of the 1950s, gave some explanations: Thomson started producing television sets because they 'were already in there. Think that we [Thomson] started manufacturing radio transmitters before World War II' (Bouyssonnie 2004).

Television did gradually become a mass medium. In 1949, a television set seemed to be an alien contraption: 90 per cent of the nation's homes had never watched it, according to a SOFRES poll, while about 80 per cent of households had a radio set (Rioux & Sirinelli 1998: 234). The television set was said to be 'a radio set with images' so that the audience would understand what it was (Flichy 1992: 31). In the mid-1980s, however, 92 per cent of French households owned a television set, which was known as the *télé* (telly), and 80 per cent were watching it every day, while about 70 per cent listened to the radio on a daily basis (BIPE 1984: 55). Television was taking over as far as popularity was concerned.

The funding for television was essentially based on licences derived from radio and television sets. Since 80 per cent of households owned a radio set in 1949, while 1 per cent owned a television set, radio fees, at the beginning, were to be used to finance the growth of television. But the new medium was much more expensive. There were only few television programmes which were often derived from radio programmes, cinema or theatre (Benoist 1953: 53).

A television programme that appeared in 1952, *36 chandelles*, was a French variety show presented by Jean Nohain, who had come from radio, and it was a copy of a radio show. It was inspired by the radio games that Jean Nohain presented, and in particular by *Reine d'un jour*, which rewarded a listener. The programme aimed to heighten the tension, and Jean Nohain covered parts of it as if it were a football match (Mousseau & Brochand 1982: 41). Most of the contemporary critics expressed reservations, as it was thought to be too close to radio, since the anchorman was talking too much. It was a long programme, recorded in a static way, and therefore it looked much more like a theatre play than a television programme. This was not the only programme derived from radio. At the end of the 1950s, *La caméra explore le temps*, a kind of historic show, was both inspired by a radio show *La tribune de l'histoire*, created by André Castelot, and by theatre. A historic plot, chosen from well-known plots and mysteries of French history, would be presented like a direct theatre play, prefaced by a presentation of the story (Veyrat-Masson 1997). Quite tellingly, *36 chandelles* disappeared during the 1960s. During this period, television took the lead. Radio started to develop new uses, while television was developing new programmes.

During the 1960s, the television set market became a mass market, while that of radio sets was less profitable. Most of the resources of the radio and television public service broadcasting were now derived from television licence fees: in 1964, the television share within the functional budget was 41.5 per cent, whereas radio's share was 25.4 per cent (Bourdon 1990: 13). Television was becoming the predominant medium, but at the same time, thanks to the transistor technique, radio was developing personal uses, especially among teenagers. Radio broadcasters, particularly in outlying areas, had understood they could obtain this new audience by programmes made for them, and television was not able to compete. *Salut les copains* (Europe 1, 1959) had big ratings, while the television programme *Âges tendres et têtes de bois* (1961) was not as successful (Sohn 2001: 68).

Radio and television were still public service organisations which faced a lack of funding. Furthermore, by the end of the 1960s they were complex corporations, with more than 10,000 engineers, technicians, presenters, directors, administrators and so on within the same institution. During the 1970s, public television channels had to compete with each other, within the realm of public service broadcasting. Public radio and television became independent. They were now complementing one another. But while illegal radio started breaking state monopoly, the arrival of satellite television partly forced public authorities to officially break this monopoly. It was not without consequences for public service broadcasting, as we will later show.

By 1955, state actors in Romania had already become receptive to the ways in which communications media, with their technological abilities of distributing information and linking private households to discourses taking place in the public arena, could be used for nationalistic and propagandistic purposes. After the First World War, due to Romania's great economic deficit and the dangers of Germany's expansionistic policies, discourses on nationalism became embedded into the post-war Romanian economy and national efforts were made towards the industrialisation of the country by means of technological developments and scientific research. State funding supported those scientific activities promoting a sense of the nation and capable of shaping the Romanian identity. A great deal of importance was given to applied sciences and technical schools, while attempts were made to integrate Romania into the ongoing European discourses favouring sciences over the humanities. Discourses heated up, claiming that national wealth consisted not solely of economic prosperity, but also of the nation's ability to keep up with Europe's scientific and technological trends. Already at that time, Silviu Brucan pointed out in the leading press organ *Scânteia* (Selejan 1992: 104) that the development of scientific activities was to support and promote a true national culture, a national culture that was seen to be at the centre of the party's interests. In the period of intense industrialisation and nationalisation dictated by the country's political and economic contexts, radio underwent a boom period, whereas scientific research began to be dedicated to television in the laboratory of the Sciences Faculty of Bucharest University and the first Romanian image transmitter was presented in Bucharest.

Upon such national discourses claiming that scientific research and technological developments can assert a nation's independence, integrate it within the European trends and help the process of industrialisation, proper social, economic and legal frameworks were created to support the further development of radio (Puia 1982: 62–3). State funding was created for the improvement of the national radio broadcasting network. The commercialisation of radio receivers to middle-class consumers was facilitated by the dropping of high customs taxes and the establishment of the *Radio Popular Factory* boosted the consumer market for radio sets, which then in turn generated a significant increase in radio broadcasting hours. The Romanian Radio Telephony Society was also turned into the Romanian Radio Broadcasting Society, a relevant new terminology which seemed to acknowledge the switch in radio from a technological and functional offspring of telephony to an institutionalised means of broadcasting, already pointing to the social function of communications technologies.

The expansion of state control over radio became even more visible during the Second World War, when radio was assigned a strict propagandistic mission that was to be asserted not only through Romanian folkloric music, but also through programmes with a strong political content, such as *Ora Ostaseasca Germano-Romana* (*The German–Romanian Military Hour*), *Ora Ostaseasca Italo-Romana* (*The Italian–Romanian Military Hour*), *Orase Romanesti* (*Romanian Cities*), *Transilvanenii si Cultura Romana* (*Transylvanians and the Romanian Culture*) (Denize 1999). Furthermore, local radio studios were set up in different regions of the country such as Transylvania and Moldova, so as to withstand the potential expansionist interests of international powers. Key moments in the course of the Second World War were broadcast live on radio, such as the proclamation of the end of Romania's alliance with Germany and the formation of the new government. At times of national threat generated by the war period, radio proved to be a solid tool in national preservation as well as in propagating state power and political interests to the nation.

The very path that the Romanian radio took – from a radio telephony society to a radio broadcasting society, from a technological medium to a communications means, an instrument of propaganda and a mechanism of representing political interests – is a strong argument that by 1955 Romanian influential circles had reached maturity in using technology in the interest of state power. That explains why unlike other technological innovations, television in Romania did not need any marketing contextualisation, nor did it involve power struggles between different actors within society. At that point in time, when the Communist Party had already seized power, television was just another efficient medium of propagating state ideology. In Romania, the introduction of television was thus a social achievement of political powers, rather than a more disputed product resulting from the dynamics between technology, economy and society. Television in Romania was a technology that was in the first instance appropriated, rather than circulated. Due to the fact that the invention and the technological development of television took place at the urging of political powers, the new medium did not involve a prior introduction, development and proliferation of the technology, but it was made to generate immediately a consumption of the new product and a domestication of the apparatus. In its incipient phase, television functioned as an extension of radio, not only technologically, but also socially, culturally and politically. The first technological developments of the medium were carried out in places such as the Sciences Faculty of Bucharest University and were presented at the Romanian Athenaeum in Bucharest – sites of national pride and political approval. From its first broadcast on 31 December 1956, television was placed under the supervision of the State Sub-secretary of Press and Propaganda, who supervised also the radio institution. The Romanian Radio Broadcasting Society became Romanian Radiotelevision Broadcasting. Staff were transferred from radio to television against their will: 'In 1958, I was transferred from radio – where I had been since I was a child – to television, the transfer being considered a punishment. I refused for a long time and tried to avoid the unwanted transfer . . . I was taken from the centre of radio with its current affairs, and brought to the periphery', confessed Alexandru Stark, a key figure in public Romanian television, years later (Munteanu 1972a: 50).

> In 1960, just like the rest of my colleagues, I was brought from radio – where I was a presenter – to the news department of television. Those were the crazy years of pioneering, when television was subject to radio from all points of view. Everything was live, 16 mm film was still a dream and the only illustrative materials used were photographs . . . Back then, television news was searching for its ideal form, being still tributary to radio. Cross-cuts were also used in television, alternating from one news presenter to another. (Florin Bratescu, in Munteanu 1972b: 40)

The transfer of people from one propagandistic medium to a new medium, such as television, insured not only the transfer of knowledge, but also the transfer of state control. The very first television programmes tried to promote the type of content developed by radio, but also just like radio, presented programmes with a strong social content. Programmes such as *Reflector* served as a watchdog for the wrongdoings in society and as an authority the public could appeal to in trying to solve cases of social injustice. This kind of programming had a double function: on one hand it promoted the ideology of the party; on the other hand, it contributed to the consumption of television. Indeed producers, presenters and the entire team involved were working 'in the spirit of the party documents' (Munteanu 1972b: 40).

The amount of political control over television institutions in Greece and Romania is by no means representative of all European countries. The BBC was created as a semi-autonomous corporation, yet political control has been extremely limited (Bignell 2004: 41). Sweden, as well as countries in southern Europe, considered it to be a model of independence, and professional documents and parliamentary reports referred to it (Bourdon 2007b). The federal public service model in West Germany also enjoyed independence from the state, while the plurality of Dutch broadcasting associations guaranteed that different views were broadcast. The direct political control of television in Greece and Romania, as well as the less direct yet still present political control in France, have inevitably created issues of censorship and propaganda, problematised the notion of public service broadcasting and seem inextricably linked to the monopoly of television.

Censorship and Propaganda

The birth of television and the formation of its relationship with the state, particularly in Greece and Romania, seem to be inextricably linked to practices of censorship and the use of television as a medium of propaganda. French governments have also been known to exercise censorship, although it may be more evident under non-democratic governments. Although television has been envisioned by some governments as a tool for moulding consciousness, censorship and propaganda have not always been successful. The BBC further established its objectivity during the 1956 Suez crisis, by presenting both the government's and the opposition's views, despite political pressure (Crisell 1997: 169–70). Also, in the countries in question, both television professionals and – perhaps more importantly – audiences have proved to be resistant and television a means of communication too complex to be controlled. The social and ideological context of the birth of television in Romania and its use as a propaganda tool are inextricably linked. They will be briefly discussed here, in order to allow for a comparison among the three countries.

Censorship in France and Greece will be discussed further, highlighting the complexity of political control in different political situations and in relation to the news, but also drama. Instances of censorship during, before and after de Gaulle's government will be used as examples, as well as instances of censorship during the dictatorship and the change of the director-general of the public service channels every time the government changes in Greece. A further aim of this discussion will be to problematise censorship and political control, usually conceived as immediate and direct.

As mentioned above, television in Romania was introduced as a highly nationalistic tool, imagined and intended as a mechanism for state propaganda and indoctrination. Its implementation did not ignite fierce power struggles as might have been the case in other countries, nor did it necessitate the existence of a prior consumer market. In fact, the advent of the new medium within society was a smooth and predefined process, which relied heavily on the prior experiences set forth by radio. It is the close adaptation of early television to the already existing radio as well as the prominent state control of radio that explains the *unprepared* and yet *predetermined* introduction of the medium of television in Romania.

Throughout the communist regime, the main themes of television broadcasting remained social investigation, national history, folk culture, international sports events, national scientific and technological achievements and socialist education. All such content was aimed at portraying the notion of a national, socialist identity. 'Starting with schools – the decisive factor in education – and ending with the modern mass media – radio, television and the press – everything must be subordinated to . . . increasing the socialist consciousness of the working people', declared Nicolae Ceauşescu at the Plenary Meeting of the Central Committee in November 1971 (Ceauşescu 1972: 95). Entertainment on Romanian communist television was scarce and controlled and was regarded as yet another form of manipulating the citizen, 'as a way of maintaining peace and potentially, keeping the citizen pleased' (Securitate Archives 1982: 105). Towards the end of communism in Romania, popular dissatisfaction with the regime, but also with public television, escalated. The public turned its back on national broadcasting, while tuning their aerials in to neighbouring countries and sending letters of dissatisfaction to the public institution (Securitate Archives, 1982: 261). Developing in the shadow of political interests, public television in Romania extended its loyalty to state power far into the institution's history.

The close relation between television and the state in Romania was manifested primarily by means of a tele-mediation of state power and ideology, which has characterised the institutional development of television in Romania. Both the introduction of television, as well as its post-communist liberalisation – manifested through integration with the EBU and simultaneously through the competition with the newly established private networks – constituted crucial moments in the history of the public broadcasting institution and were marked by a strongly defined relation to state power.

Television broadcasting in Greece started shortly before the dictatorship and, as a result, television's relation to the state was mainly formed during it. One might expect a break with that tradition under democratic governments and a complete reform of television's relation to the state, but despite the fact that changes have been made, they have not been sufficient enough to guarantee television's autonomy. The dictatorship in Greece was also well aware of television's power as a medium, even though it was a relatively new one in Greece. One of the dictators' first actions was to change EIRT's ident to a double-headed bird – the Greek dictatorship's symbol – and a soldier involved in a military march. YENED, the armed forces' channel, was actively involved in political propaganda as well as popular entertainment programmes and producing popular series (Valoukos 1998: 15). EIRT initially had to prepare for broadcasting the 9th European Track Events and thus television conformed to the dictatorship's strategy of 'bread and spectacle' that would supposedly keep people happy. All television programmes were censored, with more emphasis on the news. Although they appointed people who shared the same ideology in key posts, many of the personnel already working at EIRT at the time remained when dictatorship was imposed, and they were later condemned for not resigning from their jobs in public television during the dictatorship (Karter 2004: 36).

YENED, which can be translated as: the Armed Forces' Department of Information, had always been a propaganda tool. It had established its first radio station in 1948, during the civil war in Greece, so its involvement with television was the next step. As Karter states, its title does not clarify whether it was meant to offer information to the armed forces or information by the armed forces to Greek citizens (Karter 2004: 54). YENED's idents were cartoons that usually presented a soldier, a sailor or an airman, but also citizens abandoning their everyday activities (a man leaving a date or children who stop fighting) to run to take their place in front of their television sets. The idents are quite telling of YENED's twofold identity as a channel devoted to propagating the armed forces and seeking popularity. YENED's relation to the army ceased to exist when it was joined to ERT and named ERT-2, in 1982 (*Chronology of the Evolution of Greek Television*).

Television's relation to the state was a close one, particularly during the dictatorship, yet censorship was not always successful. Although the dictators were keen to exercise total control over television, some programmes seem to have escaped censorship. *Ekeinos ki Ekeinos* (*He and He*, EIRT, 1972–4) was a modernist drama series featuring two tramps talking (Valoukos 1998: 92). It was a minimalist, studio-based drama and much of the dialogue used metaphors and was open to different readings. Being an open text, it managed to escape censorship. In one episode, the two protagonists are once again in the park and decide to choose human company, warmth and friendship and to remain outside the system, referred to as 'the egg', that can offer them material goods, such as food and nice warm clothes. Although the dialogue was not particularly revolutionary, it was largely interpreted as cultural resistance to the dictatorship. The audience could read through the lines a much desired message.

Censorship and resistance by television professionals and audiences are often linked to non-democratic regimes. Censorship in Greece, however, did not cease when the dictatorship ended. Even the 1975 Greek Constitution, established after the end of the dictatorship, protected the press from censorship, but clearly stated that radio and television were exempt from such protection, being 'under the direct control of the state' (Dentoglou 1986: 13). Even to this day, it is customary for every new government to appoint a new director-general of ET (formerly EIRT), and even journalists and news presenters change accordingly.

Although the socialist party had criticised the right-wing government that followed the dictatorship for its policies of censorship and political control, they followed similar policies in often changing the board of ERT, promoting programmes that shared the government's ideology and projected its work (Papathanasopoulos 1994: 242). Although the news now also covered the statements and some conferences of other parties, the prime minister was said to appear more often on television than in parliament. A great deal of freedom was given to ERT by a socialist government in 1985, propagated as the 'spring' of television. Unfortunately, that was a short-lived experiment, since the prime minister claimed that too much emphasis was put on criticism of the government. It is noteworthy that during the last few months under a socialist government in 1989, political control of television augmented, on the basis of a claim similar to de Gaulle's. De Gaulle claimed to have the right to control television programmes, on the basis that the press was against him. PASOK, the Greek socialist party, claimed that their political opponents controlled the radio and the press, and therefore they would control television (Papathanasopoulos 1994: 243–4).

From the 1950s, French governments intervened and censored television programmes. Under the president of France Charles de Gaulle, this political control was quite direct, especially by the Ministry of Information. This political control had an impact on every type of programme, newsreels as well as entertainment, but was not always successful. The strikes against political control, like that of May 1968 (Bourdon 1990), may be the most obvious example of resistance to censorship, but it is certainly not unique.

When Max-Paul Fouchet talked freely about the Algerian war in January 1958 – before de Gaulle came to power – he was asked, in future, to submit his scripts to the government. He chose to resign instead (Bourdon 1998: 31). Censorship under de Gaulle was mainly focused on the news, but also censored films that deviated from the government's official version of recent history, such as *The Battle of Algiers* (dir. Pontecorvo, 1966), which was not broadcast.

However, commercial radio as well as the press was free to criticise the government, and thus a pluralism of opinions was allowed to exist. Although state monopolies made television as a medium more susceptible to political control, censorship during democracy could not be applied to all media. On the other hand, both the radio and the press were censored during the dictatorship in Greece and the communist regime in Romania. Some television professionals resisted political control by resigning. Perhaps more importantly, either by turning their aerials to neighbouring countries or reading (more?) into daring television programmes, audiences found ways to resist censorship and propaganda. Perhaps the largest flaw of policies designed to use television as a propaganda tool was that even if television professionals conformed, audiences would not react as the passive mass that some governments imagined them to be.

Public Service Broadcasting

A key co-ordinate in this discussion is the relative importance of notions of Public Service in different European contexts, and the different ways in which this notion was interpreted and problematised within broadcasting institutions, in relation to the regulation and political control of television as well as the creation of television schedules and programme formats. Public service broadcasting has been envisioned slightly differently in different European states. The role of 'public service broadcasting' was interpreted and practised very differently during the first years of television during the communist era in Romania and the army dictatorship in Greece, where it served state propaganda, as we have argued. However, there were also significant differences in the ways in which it was envisioned and practised in other European states. While the imperative to inform and form public opinion was particularly emphasised in Germany, in article 5 of the 1949 Basic Law, there were no official mandates in Spain or Italy. An official policy statement about public service broadcasting in France was only made fairly recently, in a 1964 law (Bourdon 2004: 285).

Public service television, in its various forms, has largely been successful in informing and educating, while entertaining has proved to be a more ambivalent part of its mission. There have also been many challenges to public service television, some of which will be considered here: the effort to create an audience identity – where the EBU will serve as an example, the processes of creating public service's own identity – which has undergone some transformations in Greece, and facing competition – with regard to France. Although this cannot be an exhaustive study, it will hopefully indicate the complexity of some of the challenges faced.

Television, as we have argued, was immediately acknowledged as a powerful medium of mass communication and it has been envisioned as a medium able to create identities by dictatorial and democratic governments, as well as the EBU. This vision of the medium led non-democratic governments to radical measures, while in the context of democratic societies both within nation-states and the EBU it led to the creative and open-ended imperative for the new medium to 'inform, educate and entertain'. Although the practices of non-democratic and democratic governments regarding the control of television institutions are far from similar, in both cases television was envisioned as a medium able to mould or influence audiences' opinions and identities.

The ideologies and visions surrounding television's birth in Greece, Romania and France have major differences, yet in all three cases television institutions were created to serve national interests. The first efforts to regulate international technological standards that would allow for exchanges of technology and programmes failed. The EBU and OIRT aimed at an international co-operation of television institutions, but actually divided Europe, until 1993. The EBU is a particularly interesting case of public service television that aimed to create a European identity, as programmes were met with different audience reactions than expected.

Before the Second World War, countries that had television networks had standardised the number of lines and images per second and each operated with a different system, e.g. Germany used 441 lines, the UK 405 and France 455 (Fickers 2006). The use of different operating systems was continued after the Second World War, partially, in countries like France, in an effort to protect the national industry of television set makers.

The IBU, founded in 1925 to regulate international broadcasting, was broken up after the war, partially due to the abuse of its technical centre by the German army during the war and partially due to the competition with OIRT. OIRT (Organisation Internationale de Radiodiffusion) was founded in 1946, based on a proposition by the Soviet Union. The EBU was born in 1950, in an effort led by the BBC to create a union for Western Europe (Fickers 2006). Even though the EBU was created in the aftermath of the Second World War, an era when there was a strong will for a united Europe, its creation as a reaction to the creation of OIRT confirmed that Europe was already split by the Eastern and the Western bloc. There was an initial agreement between 23 public service broadcasters, but it quickly expanded to include broadcasters from Mediterranean and Middle Eastern states and, since 1993, when OIRT and EBU merged, it also extended to the former Soviet and Eastern European countries. Apart from its technical and legal aims, the EBU aimed to create a common consciousness, a European identity (Bourdon 2007a).

Some of the efforts to reinforce a European identity were based on highbrow culture, such as *The Biggest Theatre in the World* (1962–71). This presented the work of playwrights such as Harold Pinter, Günter Grass and Shakespeare. However, it was not extremely popular, the plays were not met with the same level of appreciation in different national cultures and, perhaps more importantly, they were not perceived as part of a pan-European culture. On the other hand, light entertainment programmes, such as the *Eurovision Song Contest* (1956–) and *Jeux Sans Frontières (It's a Knockout)*, have been very – if unequally – successful. The notion of 'entertaining' has always been a slightly problematic part of public service in terms of quality. The success of such programmes, perceived as 'low-quality', and the resistance to the 'European' identity of more highbrow programmes, have problematised the notion of PSB within the EBU. Furthermore, both programmes favour antagonism: the audience's 'political voting' in the Eurovision song contest, according to political alliances or a widely accepted cultural affiliation between some nations, is indicative of differences and antagonism between clusters of nations/states, rather than the unity of Europe. The efforts to create a European identity seem to have failed for the same reason that censorship and propaganda partially failed. As Bourdon argues, 'European leaders long supposed that "mass communicating", top down, with the same contents, was a key move in forging a new collective consciousness and that television could achieve this all by itself' (Bourdon 2007a).

ERT, on the other hand, faced problems in establishing its own identity. EIR has always been committed to public service broadcasting and the early variety of programmes indicates the aim 'to inform, educate and entertain'. During the first two years of broadcasting, schedules included the news, a sports programme, a programme about cinema, *On Logos and Art* – a programme mainly about art and literature, *For You, Lady* – a 'women's' programme, theatre monologues with some of the best actors/actresses, children's programmes, history programmes and popular series, such as *The Saint* and *Bonanza* (Karter 2004: 30–2). However, as has been mentioned above, the notion of public service has repeatedly changed, according to different government policies.

The first socialist government in Greece, elected in 1981, also perceived television as a medium able to form a common identity and gave much emphasis to public service broadcasting, while new aims were set. The new principles of public service could be summarised as 'socialism, province, woman' and were supported by broadcasting television programmes about northern Greece, appointing a representative of the Greek Women's Union to the board of ERT and introducing political series. *Yes, Minister* was first broadcast in Greece in 1982 and the Greek series *Lavreotika*, based on the events of the workers' massive strike at Lavrio in 1896, was also produced and broadcast in the same year. Highbrow cultural programmes also appeared in 1982, which presented novels or 'quality' films (Valoukos 1998: 30–1). Although the socialist government's polices admittedly supported the 'high quality' of public service television, they were nevertheless geared towards promoting their own ideology. The line between public service and political control can be very fine and the evolution of public service in Greece seems to have been defined by television's relation to the state, rather than the audience.

Public service broadcasting in France initially also had political aims, as it was closely connected to the ideology that was prevailing after the Second World War in that country. Concerning the future of radio broadcasting, the immediate goal was to put on the agenda a programme about Resistance fighters (Eck 1999: 41). Choosing public service broadcasting for television was a way to provide the audience with cultural and educational benefits. Public service broadcasting has to be a quality service in the national interest (Bousser-Eck 1997: 4). The supply of programmes did not have to fit the demand. It had to give the audience what was, according to the broadcasters, good for it. At the same time, private television was created in the outlying areas, along the borders. These were the only areas where it competed with public service broadcasting with its commercial views.

But television was able to develop new popular programmes. There was a boom in series, especially imported from the USA (Bourdon 1989: 180). US-imported series accounted for about 80 per cent of serials and series in 1966. Series for children like *Rin Tin Tin* were the first to be broadcast. They were popular, as well as quite cheap. Like films, they were useful to provide television, especially the new second channel created in 1964, with more hours of programmes. Despite these popular programmes, and even if ratings were more influential, programmes were still running on the model of 1950s television. Documentaries, school programmes, dramas and news made up about 45 per cent of the total amount of hours broadcast on the first channel in 1967. Series, films and variety shows made up about 25 per cent. It was quite the opposite for the second channel. The channels were not competitors. They were said to be complementary.

In 1974, radio and television broadcasting was divided into seven different independent companies and the three television channels were now officially competitors and had to respond to audience demand. But they had not yet had to cope with total liberalism (the free play of the law of supply and demand), both in economics and politics. Gaining the audience was a much better way to achieve prestige and legitimacy than advertisers and money (Souchon 1978). As advertising was limited, the main financial resources were still licence fees. Radio and television public service broadcasting was still in the red (Commission d'enquête 1979: 36). Television and radio channels were now complementing one another, as television was initially an evening medium, the 'punctuation of the end of the day' (Derèze 1994: 52), while radio was a morning one. Radio was also becoming a social medium and people were listening to the radio while doing other things. Concerts, theatre plays, serials and sports were now disappearing in favour of musical programmes (BIPE 1984: 55).

Public service broadcasting also had to compete with broadcasters operating outside France. Public radio encountered much more serious difficulties: broadcasters were able to transmit to the whole country, while along the borders, television had to face competition. With the arrival of television advertising in 1968, the concept of public service broadcasting was endangered. Broadcasters were gradually becoming dependent on advertisers and in 1974 they were to compete with each other.

Public service broadcasting in France was able to supply three television channels and to expand its schedule, but it faced financial problems. At the beginning, public service broadcasting had to be financed both by public loans and licence fees. Public authorities were slow to vote for a public loan to build a network for television public service broadcasting, which also had the effect of slowing down the television sets market. Fortunately, there was a boom in the market during the 1960s which helped to increase the supply of programmes, especially through broadcasting a new channel. But radio and television public service broadcasting was still in the red until the arrival of private television, even with the introduction of advertising. Moreover, it was a big and complex institution and therefore difficult to manage. The status of this institution continued to change.

The Advent of Private Television

Competition, as we have argued, started before the birth of private television, with the introduction of advertising and the birth of other public service television channels. However, with the advent of private television, competition became one of the major challenges faced by public service television, not only in terms of popularity, but also appreciation. The advent of private television in France (1982) and Greece (1989) created new challenges for public service broadcasting that will be briefly discussed at the end of the chapter. In 1974, French public broadcasting split into seven entities. Radio broadcasting and television broadcasting were divided into different companies. There were three television channels which were now competitors. With the arrival of satellite television, it seemed to public authorities that they would, in a way, have to face the same problems that they had with radio before: television broadcasters operating from outside France were able to transmit to the whole country. At the same time, at the end of the 1970s, illegal radio started to appear in France. This prepared the movement towards commercial broadcasting. Private radio and television broadcasting was allowed in 1982 by a socialist government in France. Radio and television were entering a new era that challenged public service broadcasting.

When the first television channel became private in 1986, public channels were minority ones. The 1986 law was a turning-point: public service broadcasting now became 'public sector' broadcasting (Bourdon 1994: 274). Since it was more and more dependent on advertising, it had to compete with the private sector, losing more and more of its identity. In 1988, the socialist government tried to react by creating a cultural channel, which did not happen until 1992, whereas in 1995, an educational channel, France 5, the channel of knowledge arose. Even if the cultural channel ARTE, which formed a partnership with France 5, seemed to adopt the former concept of public service broadcasting, the audience share was quite poor.

Private television emerged in Greece in 1989 and immediately became very popular. The most popular drama series and sitcoms have consistently been produced for and broadcast by private television, since its birth. Public service television underwent a long and deep crisis and only during the last couple of years has it broadcast popular programmes, mainly focusing on big sporting events and imported American series, such as *Lost* or *Desperate Housewives*. While some of the original drama it produced received critical acclaim, it was not very popular. Although during the 1990s there was a widespread feeling that public service television ought to compete with private channels, it is nowadays accused of overspending and of following a 'populist' policy.

However, public service television's reaction to the popularity of private television in Greece has been more complex than that. While retaining some of the cultural and educational programmes on network television, ET also created new digital channels in 2006. Prisma+ is a channel aimed at people with special needs, making all programmes accessible to them, e.g. through the constant use of sign language. Cine+ is devoted to film, and European as well as American independent cinema makes up a large part of the schedule, while it also hosts Studio+, a music channel. Last but not least, Sport+ has broadcast some of the most important sporting events, as well as less popular ones, offering space to women's sport or handball. The new digital channels address niche audiences and even Sky, a private television channel, seems to follow the same policy, as it specialises in news, documentaries and reality TV.

As far as objectivity is concerned (always a major issue in Greece), although private networks' right- or left-wing ideology is often apparent, they are nevertheless believed to be more independent and private television is seen to guarantee at least a pluralism of opinions. The birth of private television was the outcome both of internal pressures and pressure from the EU, that promoted a 'television without borders'. After the local elections of 1986, the mayors of the three largest cities – who belonged to the opposition – stated that they would create radio stations and television channels, which was realised the following year (Papathanasopoulos 1994: 243–4). The law that deregulated radio and television followed shortly afterwards. Although private broadcasting is legal in Greece, it is noteworthy that broadcast licences have still not been given to private channels in Greece, despite the fact that they are well established, echoing perhaps governments' need to control television and the turbulent prehistory of the Greek public service television.

The advent of private television in Romania posed a challenge to public service broadcasting both in terms of popularity and in terms of appreciation, as private television was envisioned and proved to be more independent. The merger between OIRT and EBU in 1993 (re)defined the notion of public service television in Romania. The moment of this merger coincided in Romania with the rise of private networks, a phenomenon which provided comparative and competitive grounds for state television. At the time that Romanian national television joined the EBU and aligned itself to the EBU's missions of public broadcasting, the rise of private networks in Romania generated an Americanisation of television content. The competition that inevitably arose between state television and private networks ended up with a validation of American inspired values within the Romanian mass-media landscape.

Private television in Romania was hailed as independent television and the effort for independence was evident during the local elections of 1996. From its start on the audiovisual market in 1994, ProTV became the strongest private network, reaching an audience share of about 60 per cent. Shortly afterwards, ProTV became a promoter of democratic values in Romania, displaying heavily Americanised television content. The coverage of the 1996 elections put TVR and ProTV in direct competition. During the elections, TVR adopted a strongly partisan position towards PSDR – the ruling party. At the local elections in June 1996, although PSDR lost the elections, TVR celebrated the party as a winner, allocating hardly any air time for the actual party winner in the elections. The public broadcaster's partisan position towards PSDR – a party who had been in power since the 1989 Revolution and was a direct offspring of the former communist structures – continued during the presidential election campaign in September–November 1996, while the rest of the Romanian mass media held a favourable position towards the opposition. Three weeks before the presidential elections, ProTV began displaying a balanced coverage of the elections campaign. ProTV hired a private company for public opinion research, which revealed the electorate's intentions to vote for the opposition. On the night of 3 November 1996, when the results of the first private poll in Romania were issued, ProTV reached ratings of 98 per cent of its possible audience (Teodorescu 1998: 303–4). ProTV continued with pro-opposition broadcasts, which brought an increase in its audience up to 9 million. While the opposition was seizing power, ProTV was seizing the lead in audience shares.

While after the fall of the communist regime, public television was proclaimed free and independent from the state, it nevertheless continued its close relations to the state power. This became visible in the rise of private networks in Romania that engaged not only competition between public and private broadcasting networks, but also fierce competition between different political actors. The 1996 elections in Romania generated direct competition between TVR – the public broadcaster – and ProTV – a private network running since the end of 1995 and partly owned by the American consortium Central Media Enterprises. During the local elections in June 1996, PSDR, the ruling party, suffered major losses. While the rest of the mass media promoted the image of PSDR's defeat, public television fêted the party as an actual winner. Later that year, during the presidential elections, state television maintained its favourable position towards PSDR. It is interesting that the political competition for power paralleled the competition between public service and private television networks, which became tokens of bias-free, independent broadcasting. The great audience shares of ProTV showed the way the public was turning its back not only on Iliescu – PSDR's leader and a former Communist Party official – but also on state television, as a main supporting agent of Iliescu.

The struggle between TVR and ProTV, between PSDR and the Opposition, between the public and the private mirrored also a struggle between the *Europeanisation* and the *Americanisation* of the televisual landscape in Romania. A *Europeanisation* of broadcasting was marked primarily by public television's alignment with the EBU. However, a possible Europeanisation process, with all its implications, was doomed to fail within the Romanian context. One of the legal missions of the EBU was to establish programme exchanges, with the aims of promoting understanding of other cultures and ensuring programme variety, control, access to and reception of foreign content (Eugster 1983: 3). While during communism, television programming was limited and repetitive, programme variety was more than welcome in the new democratic era. However, due to both limited financial and personnel resources, the content variety that the public television could provide found itself inferior to what private networks, as well as cable television, could offer. Furthermore, controlled and institutionalised access to and reception of foreign content was a fierce reminder of the communist attempts to control television content and access to foreign programmes. Such *European* dimensions failed, thus, to change the highly politicised image of public service broadcasting. The lack of credibility that was cast on public television upon competition with private networks generated low audience rates for the public broadcaster, and thus any programming through EBU exchanges failed to gain successful audience ratings.

Technologically speaking, television in Romania made the switch from the Secam to the Pal system. This aligned Romanian television broadcasting with European broadcasting standards, yet at the same time generated, at consumer level, the need for improved, western television sets. Without proper state facilitation for a new television set market, the event caused further gaps between different social strata. Last, but not least, the sense of community, whether European or national, failed to be promoted by Romanian public service television. Newly produced national programmes decreased at the expense of foreign imports, while the scarce national content that was still present did not captivate public attention, either for lack of credibility or for its strong resemblance to communist television broadcasting. Instead, private networks and cable television with their abundance of American programming, diverse genres and satires against the state enjoyed greater popularity.

The rise of private networks in Romania in 1994 provided a defining tool for public service broadcasting, which had been until then the only television broadcasting medium on the market. The competition between the different broadcasters revealed the public institution as a politically manipulated medium and thus, the public missions of TVR became perceived as ghastly remnants of the communist regime. Once again the times of political crossroads in

Romania served to underline the institutional relations of public television to the state power. This rendered the public dimension of television indistinguishable from the public arena of power.

Both in Greece and Romania private television had a very large audience share, and it is perhaps noteworthy that only recently have the Greek public service channels started to increase their share, but the most popular programmes on public service television in Greece and on private television in Romania are imported American series. In all three countries competition with private television has been fierce. While TVR became a remnant of the communist regime in Romania, public service television in France reacted with the creation of public service channels that address niche audiences and particular interests, and Greek public service television had a mixed reaction of creating programmes and channels for niche audiences while also acquiring popular American series.

The chapter has discussed the creation of television institutions and markets with an emphasis on the visions and conceptions of television as a medium, and it has focused on countries where political control over the development, identity or mission of television institutions was exercised for long periods of time. Television's birth and the formation of its relation to the state are inextricably linked to each country's sociopolitical situation and therefore there are major differences among the case studies examined. A common denominator, however, was a conception of television as a medium able to form identities. This 'top-down' philosophy of communication has often led to policies of censorship and propaganda being imposed on public television institutions, which nevertheless have not always been successful, as both television professionals and audiences resisted them. The ideal of public service was often based on similar, yet certainly not identical, conceptions of television as a medium and has thus occasionally failed. The different notions of public service broadcasting and the practices of censorship highlight the complexity of political control over television but also draw attention to the similarities and differences in envisioning and broadcasting public service television, both within nation-states and parts of Europe. Perhaps the largest challenge faced by public service television has been the advent of private television, although responses to it as 'bad'/commercial or 'good'/objective television have greatly differed. Still, public service television seems to reinvent itself by addressing audience demand, rather than trying to create it.

References

Amoudry, M. (1981) *René Barthélémy ou la grande aventure de la télévision française.* Paris, Presses Universitaires Françaises.

Benoist, P. (1953) *Télévision, un monde qui s'ouvre.* Paris, Fasquelle.

Bignell, J. (2004) *An Introduction to Television Studies.* London and New York, Routledge.

BIPE (Office of economic informations and forecasts) (1984) *Le comportement des ménages en matière de radio, de télévision et de téléphone, 1972–1982*. Paris, BIPE.

Bourdon, J. (1989) 'Les professionnels de la télévision et les Etats-Unis'. In: Bertrand, C.-J. and Bordat, F., *Les médias américains en France*. Paris, Belin.

Bourdon, J. (1990) *Histoire de la télévision sous de Gaulle*. Paris, Anthropos/INA.

Bourdon, J. (1994) *Haute fidélité, pouvoir et télévision, 1935–1994*. Paris, Seuil.

Bourdon, J. (1998) 'Censorship and television in France'. *Historical Journal of Film, Radio and Television* 18:2, 231–5.

Bourdon, J. (2004) 'Old and new ghosts: public service television and the popular – a history'. *European Journal of Cultural Studies* 7:3, 283–304.

Bourdon, J. (2007a) 'Unhappy engineers of the European soul: the EBU and the woes of pan-European television'. *International Gazette of Communication* 69:3, 263–80.

Bourdon, J. (2007b) 'Self-inflicted imperialism: on the early Americanization of European television'. In: Urrichio, W. (ed.) *We Europeans? Media, Representations, Identities*. Bristol, Intellect.

Bousser-Eck, E.-H. (1997) *La radiodiffusion française sous la IVe République, monopole et service public (août 1944–décembre 1953)*. Doctoral thesis, Université Paris X–Nanterre.

Bouyssonnie, J.-P. (2004) Interview at the Chambre de Commerce Internationale, Paris, 28 November.

Brochand, C. (1991) 'La Radio–Télévision Française à la recherche d'un statut, ses programmes, son avenir'. In: de Bussière, M. et al., *Les années cinquante à la radio et à la télévision: journées d'études du 9 février 1990*. Paris, GEHRA.

Ceauşescu, N. (1972) *Report*. Bucharest, Romanian News Agency.

Chronology of the Evolution of Greek Television (Xroniko tis Ellinikis Tileorasis). Athens, ERT (Hellenic radio television) Museum-Archive.

Commission d'enquête du Sénat (1997) *L'argent de la télévision*. Paris, Flammarion.

Crisell, A. (1997) *An Introductory History of British Broadcasting*. London and New York, Routledge.

Denize, E. (1999) *Istoria Societatii Romane de Radiodifuziune*. Bucharest, Editura Societatea Romana de Radiodifuziune.

Dentoglou, P. D. (1986) *Radio, Television and Constitution* (3rd edn). Athens, Sakkoula.

Derèze, G. (1994) 'Médias et temporalités domestiques, une perspective ethno-logique'. In: Bertrand, G. et al. (eds.) *Temporalités de la télévision, temporalités domestiques*. Paris, INA/CNRS.

Eck, H. (1999) 'La Radiodiffusion–Télévision Française'. In: Jeanneney, J.-N. (ed.) *L'Echo du siècle: Dictionnaire historique de la radio et de la télévision en France*. Paris, Hachette.

Fickers, A. (2006) 'National barriers for an *imag(e)ined* European community: the technological frames of postwar television development in Europe'. In: Hojbjerg, L. & Sondergaard, H. (eds.) *European Film and Media Culture*. Copenhagen, Museum Tusculum Press, University of Copenhagen, pp. 15–36.

Flichy, P. (1992) 'La télévision, genèse socio-technique d'un objet'. *Culture technique* 24, 26–34.

Karter, G. N. (2004) *Hellenic Radio Television: History and Stories (Elliniki Radiofonia Tileorasi: Istoria kai Istories)*. Athens, Kastanioti.

Mousseau, J. and Brochand, C. (1982) *L'aventure de la télévision, des pionniers à aujour-d'hui*. Paris, Nathan.

Munteanu, N. C. (1972a) 'Stark de la Radio la T.V.' *Cinema*, May.

Munteanu, N. C. (1972b) 'Cu Florin Bratescu despre *Reflector*'. *Cinema*, August.

Papathanasopoulos, S. (1994) *Deregulating Television (Apeleftherwnontas tin tileorasi)*. Athens, Kastanioti.

Psalidas, M. (1996) Interview for *Tribute to 30 Years of Greek Television*. ET1, 23 February.

Puia, I. (1982) *Relatiile Economice Externe ale Romaniei in Perioda Interbelica*. Bucharest, Editura Academiei Republicii Socialiste Romania.

Rioux, J.-P. and Sirinelli, J.-F. (1998) *Histoire culturelle de la France*, Paris, Seuil.

Securitate Archives (n.d.) File D135/37.

Securitate Archives (1982) *Radiograma* 120, 17 June.

Selejan, A. (1992) *Tradarea Intelectualilor*. Transpres, Sibiu.

Sohn, A.-M. (2001) *Âge tendre et têtes de bois: histoire des jeunes des années 1960*. Paris, Hachette.

Souchon, M. (1978) *Les usages de la télévision*. Paris, INA.

Teodorescu, A. (1998) 'Disguised players waiting in the wings: Romania'. In: *The Development of the Audiovisual Landscape in Central Europe since 1989*. Luton, John Libbey Media.

Valoukos, S. (1998) *Greek Television (1967–1998) (Elliniki Tileorasi (1967–1998))*. Athens, Aigokeros.

Veyrat-Masson, I. (1997) *L'Histoire à la télévision française, 1953–1978*. Thesis, Institut d'Études Politiques de Paris.

4

Searching for an Identity for Television:
Programmes, Genres, Formats

Jérôme Bourdon, with Juan Carlos Ibáñez, Catherine Johnson and Eggo Müller

Introduction

This chapter will not propose a summary of the history of television programmes in Europe, even a sketchy one. It is still too early for such an undertaking, as programme history faces many obstacles, both material and methodological. The chapter will rather suggest a framework for historians of television programmes, especially in a European setting. It will give examples of comparative research through three case studies of genre and format, and will ask whether, and how, certain genres or specific programmes can rightly be called 'European'.

We begin with a few words about access and method. Programmes have long been inaccessible to historians. Most have studied them indirectly, using press coverage (especially the local television listings or guides), testimony or photographs, but rarely by consulting television archives. This situation is slowly changing and access is now possible in many West European countries, though in a range of degrees from free and exhaustive in France (for material since 1992 at least), to partial and expensive (in a number of countries). But programme historians will still overwhelmingly have to rely on the indirect reconstruction of their object. This is crucial for comparative historians as it is very difficult to compare programme content, especially, without actual access. Spontaneous comparisons are often made by witnesses, especially professionals, for example the producers of *Crimewatch UK* claimed that reconstruction was 'less graphic' than in the programme's German model. But those comparisons are connected to value judgements about national television, be it either superiority ('we wouldn't go so low') or inferiority ('we were never able to produce drama like the British did'). This shows that comparison is both interesting and tricky.

But problems of access must not hide methodological problems, which are no less complicated. The first major problem concerns this whole book, but is especially relevant here. Most histories of television have been framed as purely national histories. Not only have they been written mostly on a national basis, but researchers often insist on national specificity without actually clarifying its comparative basis. For example, French researchers would lament the tight political control on television in the 1960s as opposed to freedom elsewhere (but where exactly?, what amount of freedom?). The only major attempt at an 'international' history is framed mostly as a set of national (at best continental) histories (Smith 1998). But reading alongside each other the national histories which all (at least implicitly) insist on national specificities is fascinating, since global similarities are no less striking than celebrated differences, and our case studies will give many examples of this.

In this chapter we are primarily looking for cultural resemblances in Europe. Since the emergence of the European Community as a political entity, there have been many attempts to define 'Europe', especially in terms of a shared culture. Many of these efforts (e.g. Morin, 1986 in French, translated into several European languages) smack of wishful thinking: they are forced attempts by well-meaning intellectuals to accompany what seems a laudable political effort. With economics progressively taking centre stage, the European debate about culture has receded, but still the question remains: what do Europeans have in common (Urrichio 2008)? Interestingly, the most successful answers have centred on high culture, while the idea of a popular European culture remains more elusive. Television, especially public service television, cannot be treated only as a popular medium, but it obviously brings 'the popular' into the debate in a radical manner (Bourdon 2004a). Is there a specificity of a televisual/popular European culture? What is its relation with public service ideologies in different countries? Before we return to this, however, we will discuss our object (programmes) and present our three case studies as a basis for the discussion.

Histories of Programming, 'Programme' and Programmes

A primary and significant issue arises around the very notion of 'programme', the substance of this chapter. It is difficult to write a history of programmes (for example, of major television 'shows') as has long been done (and still is done) for the fine arts or literature, even if considering only their changing series of intrinsic aesthetic characteristics. The essence of programme history is the relationship between the diffusion of a text and a certain social context. Such a history has to take into account the histories of production, of production methods, of technology, and most importantly of audiences who have viewed these programmes, have discussed them, and have been, in one way or another, in the long term or in the short term, and despite all the sociological reservations about the word, 'influenced' by them. Programmes should be studied in their social and political context at the time they were viewed (and viewed again, as repeat broadcasting, once rare, has become a key programming strategy after deregulation). They should also be considered within their schedule: a television programme is inserted into a grid (in French *grille*, in Spanish *palimpsesto*, in Italian *grilla*). Historians, no less than schedulers, should be aware of what was broadcast before, after, at the same time on other channels, and at the same time the next day. The word programme itself gives us a precious clue. In many European languages, 'programmes' first meant the set of shows to be broadcast in the day, or the week, which would later be called the 'schedule'. Its meaning has progressively moved from programme as the systematic arrangement of shows to the shows themselves. Even when we refer to a single show, we continue to assume the whole televisual context by using the word 'programme', and rightly so. Furthermore, programming (in the sense of scheduling) is not only about commissioning or purchasing specific shows, but shows understood within genres: a sitcom for this day and time, an action movie for that evening, and so forth. The notion of genre is crucial here, with all its transnational implications.

To study programming, we can start from a distinction made in a study of European television in 1986 (Chaniac and Bourdon, 1990) between two models of programming, the 'courteous' and the 'competitive'. The courteous model was dominant in Europe until the 1980s, and in it there might be several channels, but they were all public service channels. Competition for ratings was not central, and indeed, ratings were measured through rather uncertain methods (telephone surveys or viewing diaries, for example) and were only one element in the 'mix' of programme evaluation. Television reviewing mattered, as did the opinion of peer-professional groups such as directors or producers. This affected programming. There were, almost from the start, elements of rigid, 'horizontal' programming in 'daytime' (an anachronistic expression because the rigid division of television time belongs to the competitive model). News, especially, started as a regular fixed staple. Some light entertainment programmes were also broadcast in the middle of the day. In France, *Télé-Paris*, an early 'talk show' (also an anachronistic term) despised by drama directors, was broadcast every day for many years at 12 noon because the head of programmes saw this as a kind of advertisement for television. This was not a systematic strategy, but simply followed in the steps of radio and the need to discipline the time of viewing, especially for news. But in the evening, schedules changed from 'horizontal' to 'vertical' programming. This opposition is anachronistic as well, though after deregulation it became widespread. It is inspired by the way programmes are shown on a schedule:

the same show on every day creates a horizontal stripe, while different shows on different days create vertical stripes side by side – even more so when, as often occurred in courteous programming, the same day of the week was not systematically devoted to the same genre. The first Monday of the month, for instance, would be devoted to a major variety show with a certain format, the second Monday to a game show, and so on. For audiences this was not an easy 'rendezvous' to remember, but was more related to the needs of production planning. In addition, programme length could vary, especially for drama (in France, Italy or Spain, for example).

When a second (and sometimes third) channel was added, this did not produce intensive competition. In many cases the added channel was a public service one, either within the same institutional structure (RAI2 in Italy 1961, BBC2 in Britain in 1964, the second ORTF channel in France in 1964), or, much more rarely, outside it (ZDF, the second German channel, joined ARD in 1963). Often 'complementary' programming was adopted, meaning that distinct genres (which assumed different tastes and audiences) were programmed at the same time, especially in prime time. The major exception to this was the UK, although ITV's commercial onslaught on the BBC was curbed by a heavy public service remit, especially for news. In the European context, British programming schedules looked different almost from the start, with programmes on both BBC and ITV starting and finishing at specific times, with standard duration, and specific genres (especially game shows brought by ITV from the US) allotted to certain slots. How much of this was due to competition and how much to relations with US television still remains to be researched. In the UK as well, ratings – still based on viewing diaries, not automated measurement – were used in a systematic manner earlier than in the rest of Europe. The history of British television, however, shows that this did not necessarily correspond with a drop in quality. Indeed the opposite was the case, although competition and ratings have often been blamed in European television history for lowering of quality, especially in the 1980s and 1990s. Professional traditions, and ITV's constraining public service remit, much affected the consequences of competition, which would be more serious and more uniform elsewhere.

By contrast with the courteous model, it is easy to describe the 'competitive' model which took hold in European television after deregulation and the rise of commercial channels. But a caveat is needed, for commercial competition (not only for audiences, but also for advertising revenues) is a key factor in television history because it affects not only programme schedules but every aspect of television: costs, production practices, professional models, working habits, and relations with politicians and the audience. In the area of programming, competition has meant rigid schedules, systematic horizontal programming (or 'stripping') in the daytime, and vertical programming in prime time after the news, with a systematic relation between a genre – or a series – and a specific weekday in each television season. Each day has been divided into specific slots related to certain types of audience age group and gender, and certain genres. A whole jargon (often in English) entered European professional parlance, for example 'prime time', 'daytime', etc. In the so-called 'access prime time', when the audience progressively grows towards the evening, specific strategies have been adopted, with genres like game shows (*Wheel of Fortune* in France in 1986, for example) or a sitcom (*The Cosby Show* on Channel 4 in the UK in the same year) 'stripped' or programmed horizontally across the week. All this is of course related to a certain type of Americanisation, as these examples show. But before defining Americanisation as the import of content and format, we must understand it as the import of professional habits and routines. These changes affected audiences, who have watched more and more television and also divide their days, weeks or months in different ways: the changes are connected to a change in the everyday.

Change, however, does not mean a wholesale transformation, since public service might still offer something specific, simply through professional tradition and also through conscious efforts, often after yielding to the temptation of aping commercial television. This has occurred especially in countries where public service television was weaker. Overall, northern European public service television has resisted commercialisation more effectively than in southern Europe, including France. There were many reasons for this. One reason is institutional stability (as opposed to continuous reforms in the south), another is better financing in the UK and Germany especially, and in consequence of both, strong production bases. Germany and the UK (in this order) remain the strongest fiction producers in Europe today (Bourdon 2004a). This also affects programming, including commercial channels, and German or British viewers are much more likely to watch national fiction (even with 'Americanised' content) than southern viewers. Apart from films, especially in France, variety shows and light entertainment feature strongly on southern Europe's commercial and public service channels.

Our three case studies do not discuss scheduling directly, but it is interesting to place them in that context. The first case study on early television drama shows that it was not only a highly regarded genre, favoured by critics and with aesthetic and sometimes national claims, but also a prime-time genre and often the main event of the evening. However, where production was stronger it diversified into subgenres, some of which could be adapted to daytime, especially in the forms of daily fiction such as soap operas (*Coronation Street*, ITV, 1960–) and the short French, pre-news, 15-minute *feuilletons* that were a national speciality in the early 1960s. By contrast, each of the 'crimewatch shows' discussed in the second case study are or were prime time audience-pullers, despite (or partly because of) their controversial character and association with voyeurism and collaboration with the police. Finally, the third case study on historical documentary offers an interesting example of a genre which, like early drama, had cultural (but only marginally aesthetic) claims and was broadcast in prime time. It almost disappeared in the 1980s before making a comeback in the 1990s and later, but in smaller quantity than before and only exceptionally in prime time, only on some public service channels, and dealt with controversial, very recent history.

The Aesthetics of Early Television Drama in the UK, France and Flanders

In many European countries, particularly those where television started before 1960, early television programming was produced and transmitted live. While liveness has continued as a central aspect of television broadcasting, particularly in factual programming such as news and in light entertainment, within other genres such as drama, live production was superseded with the introduction of recording technologies in the early 1960s. Within the histories of television drama in Europe, therefore, drama produced before 1960 appears to belong to a different order from the programming that came after, an early experiment whose aesthetics have been understood (particularly in the UK) as primitively constrained by the limitations of live studio production. In the UK, until relatively recently, most histories of television drama dismissed examples from before the 1960s as lacking their own aesthetic, borrowing instead from the traditions and tropes of the theatre (Gardner and Wyver, 1983).

Yet more recent scholarship on early television drama in the UK and France suggests that there was much more variety in early television drama, and far richer debate about the aesthetics of television as a medium. In many countries, the debates focused on the question of specificity (in which ways, if at all, is television different from theatre and/or cinema?), and at the same time, of art (is television a new art form?). The debate about specificity involved at least three aspects of television: screen size (especially at a time when definition and image quality were not as good as today), domestic reception, and finally liveness. Screen size and domestic reception, added to economic limitations, led to a debate about the use of close-up, especially close-ups on the human face. Such debates were not of uniform importance and centrality across the different production contexts of European television. In Flanders issues of aesthetics and quality emerged more specifically in relation to questions of national identity and culture than they did in relation to the specificity of television as a medium. Comparing and contrasting the histories of early television drama within three different contexts, France, the UK and Flanders, this section will examine the different ways in which debates formed around early television drama.

Television began in France in 1935 (experimental service) and officially in the UK in 1936 (after an earlier experimental period). Yet in both countries the pre-war service was limited. In France, drama on television before 1950 consisted almost entirely of cinema films (almost one a day until 1949), accompanied by a large number of magazine programmes devoted to cinema. From

1950, drama production was based either on plays or on literary adaptations, with only a small minority of texts written specifically for television. Drama formed a focus for debates about the specificity of the medium at this time, and although the theatre was a major term of reference, cinema exerted a particularly strong influence. The majority of French television directors came from the IDHEC, the national film school, with (in the beginning) little or no training for television, and cinema mattered more to television directors in France than the theatre. Within the French televisual and cultural context, the directors (*réalisateurs* in French) were considered the main authors of television drama, at least until the mid- to late 1970s (Bourdon 1993). Writers played only a minor part, and producers (for television drama) were nonexistent. Within the highly-developed debate at this time about the specificity of television, the focus was on direction (the use of the studio and outside broadcasts, editing, the live and the recorded and so on), with far less debate about the specificities of writing for television. Furthermore, television was growing at a time when cinema was increasing its status within French culture, with (again) the director considered as the author by critical discourses on cinema (*la politique des auteurs*). This affected the terms of television criticism which flourished at this time, and enhanced the emphasis on cinema as a frame of reference.

Within the British context, the frame of reference for early television drama was much more clearly theatre, rather than cinema. As elsewhere, television drama in the pre-war period (1936–9) took three forms: extracts from plays and full adaptations of plays and novels, both broadcast live from the television studios, and live outside broadcasts from theatrical performances in the West End of London. As such, therefore, television was dependent on the theatre for much of its dramatic content. This dependency continued when the television service resumed after the Second World War in 1946. While in the 1950s there began to be an increasing number of original dramas written for television (and an increasing appetite for them from the audience), the strong relationship between theatre and television continued well into the 1970s as the theatrical adaptation formed a central part of British television's dramatic output.

Yet to restrict an understanding of early British television drama to its dependency on the theatre, or early French television drama to its close association with cinema, would be too simple an account of this formative period in the history of television. Within both the French and British contexts, those involved in television production enjoyed significant independence. At the BBC in Britain (particularly before 1939) television was very much seen as an experiment, receiving relatively little funding. Although British television was produced and transmitted under the BBC's public service remit, as Creeber argues (2003: 25), 'because the medium was still generally regarded as an experimental novelty it tended to get away with more "frivolous" entertainment than radio'. This was even more relevant in France where politicians and intellectuals despised the medium. Recent research has demonstrated that within both contexts there was a culture of experimentation within the production of television around which significant debates about television's specificity took place.

Within both the French and UK contexts, liveness was at centre of debates about television's specificity. Videotape was not introduced to the UK until 1958, and to France until 1960, and even then, due to the initial difficulties of editing videotape, many programmes were still shot as if live, in a continuous take. While film was available, 35 mm film was considered too expensive in the 1950s in both France and the UK (although it was used for some prestige productions) and it would take time before professional 16 mm film, first used for documentaries, would be considered of high enough quality for drama. Telerecording (or kine, where a film camera is set up in front of a television screen to record the images as they are broadcast live) was available in the UK from 1947 and in France from 1953, but its use was limited, particularly initially when the quality was low. Later in the 1950s it was sometimes used to show repeats of dramas initially transmitted live, and also for training purposes. As a consequence over the 1930s, 1940s and 1950s, television drama production in France and the UK was largely live.

Many of those working in television drama saw the medium's liveness as the key attribute of television, separating it from cinema. In both the UK and France, champions of television's liveness claimed that it gave television drama a feeling of authenticity and immediacy to viewers. Within the UK, there was a significant group within television drama production at the BBC – which Jacobs (2000) has termed the 'intimate school' – who argued that television's liveness offered audiences the combined benefits of both theatre and cinema. Viewers could watch a skilled actor offer a continuous performance with all the immediacy of a theatre production (and none of the disjunction of film acting, where sequences are shot out of order). At the same time, they could be brought close to the actors in a way not possible in the cinema, making television an ideal medium for exploring emotions and the sensitivity of performance in close-up detail. As a consequence, the intimate school argued that television drama should focus on intimate, small-scale subjects that exploit television's ability to bring the audience close to the character and the actor. Screen size was also a factor here. Early television sets were around 14–17 inches (45–50 cm) wide. This, combined with the domestic location of television which assumed a spectator close to a small screen in a private domestic setting (in contrast with the large, public spaces of cinema and theatre), led many to favour an aesthetic resembling the home, in which the studio is used as a closed space, and the address and tone is intimate. In both France and the UK, the human face was often seen as the main 'object' to be shown by television, and the often-extolled close-up centred on the human face. This extended beyond television drama into other genres, and perhaps offered a unified aesthetic across television's different genres. In particular in the French context, the proximity of the viewers and possibly the presence of other genres and the influence of liveness led to the use of direct address by actors. This technique was used in the adaptation of television plays for drama very early on, and became a systematic way of shooting after the director, Pierre Cardinal, shot a documentary series, *Gros Plan* (1956–61), where famous interviewees had to address the spectator by constantly looking at the camera. Cardinal later shot literary adaptations where all of the actors/characters addressed the spectator in the same way. This technique was taken up, in part, by other directors (Delavaud 2005: 167). The reference to 'the real', to current affairs, in drama, was another direction explored in France, albeit only by a minority of directors, as it required the collaboration of a writer. A live series in six episodes, *Si C'était Vous (If it Were You)*, explored contemporary problems such as housing and birth control through dramatisations (writer: Marcel Moussy, director: Marcel Bluwal, 1957). In the early 1960s another director, Jacques Krier, became famous for the use of non-professional actors and interviews in dramas that were strongly anchored in contemporary daily life in a style reminiscent of that used by Ken Loach and Tony Garnett in the mid-1960s in the UK with *Up the Junction* (1965) and *Cathy Come Home* (1966).

In both France and the UK, however, there were challenges to the schools of thought which defined television's aesthetics through reference to its liveness, intimacy and immediacy. While in France the opponents of live drama gained strength as professional 16 mm film was progressively adopted for drama shooting, in the UK there emerged a significant school of thought in the early to mid-1950s (which Jacobs (2000) terms the 'expansive school') that saw the technical restrictions of live drama production not as limitations but as possibilities that could be exploited for specific dramatic effect. The key proponents of the expansive school were the writer Nigel Kneale and the Austrian-born director Rudolph Cartier, who had trained as a film director. Kneale and Cartier first worked together in 1953 on a six-part television drama serial called *The Quatermass Experiment*, a fantasy about an alien invasion that follows the first manned space flight. This serial was unusual in a number of ways. Original dramas and serial production were both relatively uncommon at this time, as were fantasy dramas, which were largely seen as unsuitable and unpopular on television. However, *The Quatermass Experiment* was also unusual in terms of its visual style. In contrast to the intimate school, it made extensive use of spectacle and crowd scenes, including a sequence in which a huge alien is represented engulfing Poet's Corner in London's Westminster Abbey (Johnson 2005). The serial was a huge success, and Kneale and Cartier went on to collaborate on a number of other dramas, including two more *Quatermass* serials in the 1950s. These programmes demonstrated that live television drama could break out of the confines of intimacy and the close-up, and of the intimate, domestic subject matter associated with it. Cartier was particularly skilled at combining live drama with filmed inserts allowing him to produce sequences (such as a riot scene in *Quatermass II*) which appear to go beyond the boundaries of the studio space. Despite this, and despite both Cartier's and Kneale's assertions that the differences between television and cinema were merely technical ones to be overcome, Cartier also argued that television's liveness and domestic location made it particularly suitable for horror. He claimed that the *Quatermass* serials were much more successful in their television versions than when adapted for the cinema because he was able to exploit the power of the televisual close-up to create fear and horror in the audience (Johnson 2005).

The example of Kneale and Cartier raises a significant difference in early television drama between the French and British contexts. Within the UK the writer was central to debates about the aesthetics of the medium from very early on. In fact in the early 1950s the paucity of television drama scripts was seen as the major difficulty facing drama production in the UK (Johnson 2005). As a consequence the BBC set up a Script Unit specifically for the development of television drama scripts. It was here that Nigel Kneale first gained employment at the BBC, later being appointed as one of its first staff writers, partly as a response to fears that the BBC would lose valuable trained staff with the arrival of the commercial channel ITV in 1955. Yet there is a striking similarity in the terms of the debates about the specificity of television within France and the UK, despite the different ways in which cinema and theatre function as points of reference. Such debates are not uniform across European television in the 1950s, however, and the different context of Flanders offers a point of comparison, inviting us to consider the importance of looking beyond clear national boundaries when considering the history of early television drama.

The case of Flemish television drama points to the need for a different historicisation, in which there was a much greater concern with its role in the formation of national identity. This contrasts with the British case, where in television's early years the role of broadcasting in national formation was largely taken by BBC radio rather than television. Once television became a national medium in the 1950s the role of television in the formation of British national identity was already being redefined by the introduction of ITV, its regional structure offering a challenge to the BBC's apparently London-centric bias. Flemish television began with the establishment of NIR in 1953 as part of a unitary Belgian institution. It gradually became independent by 1960 (and was renamed BRT) alongside the broader emancipation of Flanders and the formation of a federal state (Dhoest 2004b: 398). NIR was modelled on the BBC's ideal of public service broadcasting. It privileged information and education closely linked to nationalism, but was also seen specifically as an instrument of emancipation. As such, while there were strong similarities with the BBC's paternalistic ideal of broadcasting as a form of cultural enlightenment, Flemish broadcasting was seen as primarily responsible for the protection and promotion of the nation's cultural heritage. Dhoest (2004a: 311) argues that the quality of programming was one of the core values of the BRT's project of 'cultural nationalism' and that 'quality was strongly linked to the "national character" and was often judged according to theatrical and literary norms'. However, while those working in Flemish television came from elite artistic backgrounds in theatre and literature, there was also much discussion about the desirability of popular programmes, particularly those that drew on traditions of Flemish popular culture (Dhoest 2004b: 400–1). Although these programmes 'did not fit within the broadcasters' ideal image of television' (Dhoest 2004a: 311), they were popular with viewers and accessed large audiences, hence contributing to the ideal of television as a medium for nation building.

Despite the desire for quality programming, Flemish television drama (particularly serials and series) was frequently criticised by the press for being amateur, theatrical and exaggerated (Dhoest 2004a: 313). As Dhoest argues, some of these criticisms were justified. The financial poverty of Flemish drama production from the 1950s until the 1980s led to restrictions in production (for example, in numbers of characters, settings and costumes) and in genre choices (for example, in the preference for small-scale realism that could be easily located within the studio) (Dhoest 2004b: 402). Most early television directors came from theatre and, as in the UK in the 1930s, the use of theatre actors not used to the demands of television performance hindered quality. However, while over the 1950s British television developed writers skilled in the specifics of writing for television (such as Kneale), within Flemish television there were almost no professional television screenwriters until the late 1980s. Television dramas were largely written by novelists or journalists with little process of adaptation, and there was a lack of original material (Dhoest 2004b: 403–4). Dhoest (2006: 150) notes:

> more televisual forms were explored in single drama, culminating in the TV movies of the 1970s and 1980s, using location shooting and a more dynamic editing style. However, compared to larger countries, this was a very slow evolution, due to the small scale of production: there were little technical means and budgets, and the staff was limited and trained on the job . . . For lack of a 'critical mass', the development of televisual forms (including genres) was a slow process of trial and error, with little room for failures and therefore an inbuilt conservatism.

It is apparent in the French, British and Flemish contexts that the limitations on the production of early television drama had a potential impact on the aesthetic ambition of the medium. In each case there is an early dependence of material from other, more established, art forms (theatre in the UK, cinema in France, literature in Flanders). Yet it is also apparent that these technological and production limitations had different impacts within each context. In the UK, television was initially secondary to the more important project of radio production at the BBC, arguably giving producers the space to experiment with the medium without the fear of failure. In the post-war period, expansion of the television service led to an increased professional-isation of television production, which coincided with the development of training and the Script Unit, which placed a focus on producing skilled staff trained in the specificities of television production. At the same time, the immin-ent arrival of ITV as competition to the BBC's television service placed an increased emphasis on the need for the quality of drama scripts and pro-duction to improve. In France, television's inferior status to cinema, and the independence and recognition enjoyed by directors, allowed directors to experiment in a number of different ways with the formal possibilities of television. By contrast, in the Flemish context, television was an important medium of national emancipation from its inception; leaving 'little room for failure' (Dhoest 2006: 150). While expansion occurred early within the con-text of UK and French television (although the second produced, overall, many fewer hours of drama), this was not the case in Flanders, which struggled with small budgets and limited facilities until the late 1980s. The dependence on classical literature could be seen as a consequence of limited ambition within Flemish television and a lack of interest in creating 'televisual' television drama. Yet it could also be seen as a pragmatic response to the demands on Flemish television to contribute to a broader project of cultural nationalism. Hence, the focus on established literature already understood as 'Flemish' in charac-ter which, aligned with the production limitations of Flemish television, per-haps points less to lack of ambition in television drama, and more towards an understanding of quality television which stems from outside the medium rather than from within it. In terms of a comparative history of the aesthetics of early television drama in Europe the contrasting case of Flanders raises issues about the consequences of examining television programming within certain proscribed national boundaries. While debates about the specificity and aesthetics of television are not absent, they are shaped by the broader national role of television, which shifted the focus from the aesthetics of television drama to its social and cultural role in society.

Further frameworks are therefore relevant for further comparison of the aesthetics of television drama. First, the debate on aesthetics might have been obfuscated by other questions. In a small, relatively fragile 'country' (Flanders is a region and not a country), the debate on the specificity of national culture was stronger than the debate on the specificity of the new medium. It would be interesting to compare Flanders, in that respect, to other regions struggling with similar problems at different times. These could include Basque television in its early days (struggling to revive, in addition to culture, a regional language with a low cultural status), but also Italy, whose 'national' culture is a more recent creation than in other large European countries. Second, whether or not there was a debate on national culture, all countries used drama, to different extents, to transmit 'pre-existing' literary or dramatic works by televised adaptation. In some countries (in the UK in particular; see Bourdon

2004b), this was mostly based on a national corpus. In others, there was a mix of national and what was then called 'universal' literature (in French, *littérature universelle*) which included British (Shakespeare), French (Molière) and German (Goethe) classics. All countries used television (as they had previously used print and cinema) to promote their own classics, however, for example the three televised adaptations of Italy's 'national novel' *I promessi sposi* (The betrothed). Third, even where national culture was self-confident, if not taken for granted (in France or the UK), the debate on aesthetics was most developed but was not and could not be a purely formal debate: it was mixed with political and economic considerations. Comparing television to a richer medium, television professionals had to invent with what was to hand, and aesthetic debates might seem to be rationalisations or denials of economic constraint. However, it would be all too easy to dismiss the whole question of television aesthetics in that way. The very notion of a 'pure' aesthetic debate is problematic, and all art forms have to cope with a number of social and economic constraints. But some succeed in 'purifying' certain activities into art (Becker 1982); some do not. The question thus becomes why this debate has so dramatically receded. Why did television drama not become a new art form? Why has it been everywhere considered as inferior to cinema (or theatre)? These are crucial questions for television in general, but especially for European television.

Aktenzeichen XY . . . Ungelöst and its European Circulation

In the context of a comparative history of television programmes and programming, the European circulation of the German crime-appeal show *Aktenzeichen XY . . . Ungelöst* (*Case XY . . . Unsolved*), broadcast on ZDF since 1967, is a very specific one. Despite its extraordinary ratings in Western Germany, Austria (1968–2003) and the German-speaking part of Switzerland (1969–2003) from the late 1960s on, it took almost twenty years before public broadcasters from non-German speaking countries such as the Dutch AVRO (since 1984), the British BBC (since 1985) or the French TF1 (1993–6) adapted the formula of this popular programme. Since *Aktenzeichen XY . . . Ungelöst* animates its audience to help the police to solve real crimes, the programme raises fundamental legal, social and moral questions. Not surprisingly, it evoked public debates on its democratic legitimacy and moral responsibility in any European country where it was produced, especially since it addressed its audience through a popular aesthetic. On one hand, the programme did not correspond with ideas about the roles and functions of public service broadcasting that were held by cultural and critical elites. On the other hand, programme makers of all producing broadcasters claimed that *Aktenzeichen XY* was an example of ideal democratic programming since it stimulated the audience to participate virtually or actually as citizens in the public domain. Despite these general similarities, a short history of *Aktenzeichen XY*'s European circulation reveals that the cultural meaning of each adaptation depends on the historical context of its production, including specific political circumstances, the development of a country's television culture, the broadcaster's policy and more or less contingent production circumstances. Though the original formula of the programme has not been changed significantly, its cultural significance differs from country to country. Therefore, *Aktenzeichen XY*'s adaptations tell more about the differences between European television cultures than about their similarities.

The history of what today is generally referred to as 'reality crime television' goes back to the earliest visions of television as a technology for the live transmission of picture and sound over long distances. Early speculations exploring the possible functions of a future television system mention the transmission of crime warrants in their lists of the technology's future functions. Not surprisingly, Nazi Germany's television introduced a short crime-appeal programme in 1938 called *Die Kriminalpolizei Warnt!* (*The Criminal Investigation Department Warns!*). The presenter Fritz Schiekg talked on Monday evenings live with police officers about unsolved cases, showed evidence and asked the audience to collaborate with the police (Pinseler 2006, Rüden 1979: 155, Winkler 1994). But the mere 300 or so television sets in Nazi Germany and the few public viewing spaces in Berlin in the late 1930s (Lerg 1967) meant that this crime-appeal programme had merely a symbolic function. Though crime-appeal spots were part of main news programmes in Germany from the late 1950s on (Pinseler 2006), and short crime-appeal programmes like *Police 5* (*LWT* in the UK, 1962–92) were broadcast by some public service channels in Europe from the early 1960s, *Aktenzeichen XY* was the first reality crime show presenting reconstructed real crimes as short filmic narratives. Asking the audience to call in live, it turned the television studio into a kind of police department and reported in a follow-up later in the evening about progress in solving the cases and arresting suspects. The producers of *Aktenzeichen XY* and of its European adaptations have claimed a detection rate of about 50 per cent, but Godfroy and Van der Velden (1984) argue, with respect to the Dutch version, that the detection-rate is actually less than 10 per cent. The one-hour programme was broadcast from October 1967 once a month on Friday evening in prime time. In March 1968, the first Austrian public channel ORF started collaborating with the German programme, and in January 1969 the Swiss public channel SRG joined this co-operation, now also covering Austrian and Swiss cases. An average episode would present three to five cases, often with dramatic reconstructions followed by interviews with senior detectives. As well as the main unsolved cases, a number of crime appeals would be displayed in the form of a warrant. Thanks to the popularity of *Aktenzeichen XY*, its presenter Eduard Zimmermann became a highly controversial representative of West German conservatives' calls for law and order as a reaction to the student protest movement in the late 1960 and early 1970s and its political aftermath. He was notorious for the programme's engagement in prosecuting members of the Red Army Faction (the 'Baader-Meinhof Gang') in the late 1960s, and also for his discrimination against women through its obsession with rape and its long-standing campaign against women hitchhiking (Pinseler 2006: 46).

In the public debate, *Aktenzeichen XY* became a catalyst for more general discussions about the democratic legitimacy and cultural effects of television. In a well-known attack, Claus-Dieter Rath (1985: 200) described the programme as a perverse realisation of Brecht's theory of radio, turning the social arena into a hunting ground, the living room into a hunter's hide. Mixing documentary, fiction and live action, he asserted that the show also mixes the enjoyment of television with the denunciatory activity of a viewer who passes on advice to central office. The programme was accused of blurring the boundaries between fact and fiction, and between information and entertainment, considered as a violation of fundamental journalistic conventions. It was said to hand editorial authority to police and state authorities, violating a fundamental principle of public service television, to stereotype criminals and discriminate against suspects, and disseminate fear and anxiety about crime among the audience, especially children and women (Dobash et al. 1992, 1998; Jermyn 2007). It was accused of profiting from viewers' voyeuristic pleasures, and addressing the national audience as police informers. Critical comments like these accompanied the programme wherever a broadcaster adapted the formula, but with significant differences in hierarchy and weight of the arguments, depending on the historical moment of the introduction of the programme, on the country's particular legal policy and the characteristics of its national television culture.

Since production of formatted television in Europe was not widespread until the 1990s (Malborn & Moran 2006), and since *Aktenzeichen XY* had never been copyrighted as a distinctive format, national television channels were free to create national versions. Though *Aktenzeichen XY* was a major and long-lasting success in West Germany, Austria and Switzerland from the beginning, it took more than 15 years for other West European channels to produce and broadcast a crime-appeal series on a regular basis. The Netherlands, the first non-German-speaking country to adapt it, went through a long period of public and parliamentary debate about the desirability of the programme since it did not correspond with the Dutch climate of mild criminal penalties (Brants 1998). In 1982 the AVRO finally created *Opsporing Verzocht* (*Detection Requested*), which dealt only with low-level crime and used a deliberately neutral style of representation. *Opsporing Verzocht* did not adapt *Aktenzeichen XY*'s most famous feature, its dramatised reconstructions of cases. Despite being dull, decent and dependable, according to the Dutch professor of Jurisprudence Chris Brants (1998: 181), it achieved an average audience share of 25 per cent in the 1980s and still of more than 10 per cent after the introduction of commercial television in the 1990s (Brants 1998: 185). Shaped by the specific Dutch legal climate, by passionate public debates resulting in editorial supervision by state authorities, police and public committees, and by the specific 'non-aligned' ideology of the AVRO, *Opsoring Verzocht* was nevertheless a version of the original formula.

Different to the German original and the Dutch approach, the editors of the British adaptation of *Aktenzeichen XY* claimed a position totally independent from state and police authorities, though *Crimewatch UK* naturally had to collaborate closely with police authorities as well. It seems that a freelance researcher had more or less accidentally come across the show on German television (Ross and Cook 1987: 9), which is interesting in itself since it demonstrates the 'localness' of public service institutions which did not then seek out foreign television programming systematically in order to copy popular shows from abroad (Malborn & Moran 2006). But when the programme was introduced into Britain in 1984 the sociopolitical climate there was completely different to the German and Dutch situation in the late 1960s and early 1970s. In the Thatcherite climate of mid-1980s Britain, the programme corresponded ideologically with the government's policy of reinforcing 'law and order', focusing on the detection and conviction of criminals instead of the social backgrounds of delinquency (Biressi 2001, Jermyn 2007, Kettle 1983, Palmer 2003, Schlesinger & Tumber 1994). Since the BBC and the producers of *Crimewatch UK* managed to promote the conservative approach of the programme as a participatory, community-enforcing contribution to the acclaimed tradition of public service television (Jermyn 2007, Miller 2001), public debate about the programme did not question its legitimacy, as happened in Germany and the Netherlands. Major public concerns rather addressed the supposed dissemination of fear of crime (Gunter 1987, Wober & Gunter 1988). But the BBC version presented cases in a way that distinguished *Crimewatch UK* from other British examples of the crime appeal produced in the early and mid-1990s to emulate its success. *Crimewatch* contained all significant features of its German prototype except *Aktenzeichen XY*'s anti-terrorist appeals, but added interviews with victims and victims' friends and relatives.

It was *Crimewatch UK* that made crime-appeal programmes accessible to the international television market. From the mid-1980s onwards, many public and later also commercial broadcasters created adaptations of the formula all over the world, among others in the US (*America's Most Wanted*, Fox 1984–), Spain, Italy, Hungary, Sweden, Israel, New Zealand and Australia (Pinseler 2006: 55), where it was part of the international boom in reality TV. In this context, the significance of the programme changed. In France, for example, plans for its adaptation began in 1990, but created consternation among television regulators and the judiciary. As a consequence, the show was not commissioned for production at first attempt, and was introduced only in March 1993 as a 'key instrument in TF1's rating strategies' (Dauncey

1998: 201) after the channel's privatisation in 1987. But due to public concern and low ratings, *Témoin No. 1* (*Witness no. 1*) was dropped by December 1996. In Spain, the programme was based on the French version and was launched in 1993 by TVE1 as *Código 1* (*Code 1*). It quickly became one of the top twenty monthly programmes, as in the UK, but evoked strong public opposition and did not last. One of the two original hosts, TVE journalist Arturo Pérez Reverte, quickly left and condemned the exploitation of victims in the programme (Diaz 1994). It might be noted that no southern broadcaster had any successful crime-appeal formula on its schedule for long stretches of time as happened in the UK, Germany and the Nertherlands.

In the public debate in France, the programme was framed as part of the boom of reality TV, or 'trash TV' (*TV poubelle*), and was accused of Americanisation and the dumbing down of French television. According to Hugh Dauncey (1998: 201), the debate in France 'has been wider and more heartfelt [than in Britain] because of traditional French unease at the possibilities of informing'. The programmes' coverage of the Carpentras affair serves as an example that shows how the association between judges and journalists (impossible in the British and the German versions) turned out to be problematic. On 9 May 1990, the desecration of a Jewish cemetery in the southern city of Carpentras shocked the country and was associated with the climate of hate and intolerance encouraged by the rising extreme-right party, the National Front. On 16 September 1995, on the set of the programme, the State Prosecutor of Carpentras announced another lead: young respectable citizens secretly playing games in the cemetery were the real perpetrators. This populist theme, which suited well the needs of the extreme right, was elaborated in further episodes of *Témoin No. 1*. In July 1996, the arrest of the culprits confirmed the connection with the extreme right, and by December 1996 the programme disappeared from the screen.

As this short history of the European circulation of *Aktenzeichen XY Ungelöst* reveals, popular programmes do not automatically and easily travel. Language barriers play a role, despite the institutionalised programme exchange between the European Broadcasting Union (EBU) countries. Furthermore, popular programmes that do not correspond with general conception of public television have been less likely to be adapted. In this period, public debates could still create the cultural power that could delay the introduction of a controversial programme. At the same time, the programme's success shows that there was a demand for popular programming that public service broadcasters have never fully served, developed and exploited. The success of *Aktenzeichen XY* and its European adaptations as 'key forerunners' (Jermyn 2007: 10) of the reality TV movement might help to remind future television historians to address questions of popular television in a more differentiated way. This is a complex history where political, economic, social, juridical, cultural and 'televisual' dimensions of programme history converge. As this glimpse of just one of many popular programmes has shown, a programme that travels is different depending on the context of a national (television) culture, even though its adaptations only slightly vary the formula.

Historical Documentary in France, Spain and Italy

History, in a broad sense, has been central to public service programming. Public service channels have prided themselves on expensive historical drama, that is, fiction located in the past, often adapted from literary sources. Such drama was central for reviewers, and seems to have been important to audiences, especially in Europe where national identities are grounded in history in varying ways. But historical documentaries using the resources of audio-visual archives (at least for twentieth-century subjects) but also documents, reconstructions, imaginary interviews and interviews with historians, were also a major part of public service output, although less publicised and less prestigious than drama.

In the 1970s, televised history went into crisis. Historical drama almost disappeared, with the notable exception of the UK. In the 1980s and 1990s, increased competition and privatisation, which was remarkably brutal in southern Europe (including France), made the crisis deeper. For private channels and for threatened public channels, there was little or no place for history, simply because it drew small audiences at a high cost. Documentaries in general receded, and while they did not disappear they were scheduled later, and rarely in prime time. In France in 1991 (before the birth of the Arte channel), 96 per cent of all documentaries were broadcast between 10.30 p.m. and 6.00 p.m. (Chaniac 2000: 388). Within the documentary genre, historical documentaries had always been a minority and became a rarity. Often, among the two or three public service channels, only one would continue to broadcast documentaries in prime time (France 3 in France, and RAI 3 in Italy, for example). One French scheduler reported that historical documentaries have a smaller audience than social documentaries because they do not address everyone, but only viewers with an interest in history or in the specific topic (Veyrat-Masson 2000: 389). The genre found a refuge on Arte, the European cultural channel, which decisively stimulated production but also turned televised history into a genre for minorities, and also faced the challenge of building a non-national version of history. It focused on contemporary history, especially the Second World War. Between 1992 and 1996, this was the theme of 35 per cent of Arte's historical documentaries, with the largest audience for Nazi 'monsters' like Hitler (Veyrat-Masson 2000: 384), but equating even so to only a modest 2.5 per cent audience share for the channel.

By the mid-1990s, researchers were predicting the 'end of history', at least on the small screen. However, European viewers have recently witnessed a modest revival of history, especially on public service television, while wealthy commercial channels remain decidedly contemporary with only rare forays into the past. These included the French TF1's expensive historical miniseries such as, in 2002, *Napoléon*, starring, among others, Gérard Depardieu and John Malkovitch, which gained a 35 per cent audience share. This resurgence is connected to the soul-searching of troubled nations, and the rise in often controversial debates about the past that might be seen as a global trend. In Europe, however, this return of history has some specificity. Public service television seems still to pride itself on its abilities to put history in the foreground of programming, although this sometimes looks disingenuous. The revival has been more relevant in nations with a highly contested past, divided by civil war or having experienced periods of dictatorship. Public service television has been but one actor among many, since artists, writers, intellectuals and other media have also done their share. The revival has played a more central part in some countries than in others, and this section will discuss Spain, Italy and France.

Undoubtedly, since the early 1990s Spanish and Italian public service channels have produced notable documentary series to confront difficult memories. In Spain, this first wave of historical documentary started in the 1990s on TVE. It reflected the efforts made in the post-Franco era to reach an agreement by a so-called 'pact of oblivion' (1977 Amnesty Act, 1978 Constitution) allowing former enemies to work together under the benevolent leadership of King Juan Carlos, an embodiment of national unity. This was expressed, for example, in *Los Años Vividos* (*The Lived Years*, TVE1, 1992), where famous people of all kinds and opinions recounted the history of Spain in the twentieth century, or in the highly successful *La transición* (*The Transition*, TVE2, 1995), which proposed a consensual version of the end of the Franco dictatorship. Outside television, a much less consensual battle of memories started raging and soon reached the medium. Conservative historians who justified the Francoist attacks on Spanish revolutionary-Bolshevik projects found some legitimacy when the right-wing Popular Party won the 1996 elections. This had an effect on a public television which had never completely cut the umbilical cord that, since the times of the dictatorship, attached it to public authorities. A first documentary series in seven episodes, *Felipe II* (*Philip II*, TVE, 1998), came close to glorifying the authoritarian, Catholic and imperial Spanish past. The same year, several documentaries evoked the colonial past in a lenient if not wholly positive manner. Most ambitious and controversial was *Memoria de España* (*Memory of Spain*, 2004), which began just before the election of the socialist Zapatero, with low audiences. Under the guidance of a conservative historian, this series massively resorted to the archives of TVE to tell a liberal-conservative history of Spain, with a negative view of revolutionary and left-wing movements.

Different or dissident voices were then heard. Left-wing, popular voices claimed that the ferocious character of the Francoist repression had been ignored, while right-wing authors fought back and claimed to expose atrocities committed by the left. One of Zapatero's first initiatives was to pass a controversial

'Law of Historical Memory' (*Ley de la memoria histórica*). On television, those efforts resulted in a new wave of documentaries on TVE2. Some of them exposed, through debates, opposite viewpoints such as *El laberinto español* (*The Spanish Labyrinth*, 2006). The five episodes of *La memoria recobrada* (*The Memory Recovered*, 2006) went back to oral memory, with both ordinary witnesses and also well-known artists and intellectuals linked with the project of the associations for the 'retrieval of historical memory' which aimed to expose the past crimes of Francoism. Today, Spain is still struggling with the past of the Civil War and the dictatorship, with television as an active and changing actor in this.

In Italy, the past is probably a less controversial topic but that may be because the present is even more unstable, with a political system that was imploding in the early 1990s under accusations of corruption, the rise of private television mogul and two-times prime minister Silvio Berlusconi, and the constant sense of a fragile state penetrated by political parties and private interests. Ever since the 1970s, public broadcaster RAI has been subject to *lottizazione*, the direct allotment of channels and executive positions to political parties, and also to the pressure of competition which made it one of the rare public service broadcasters to massively resort to reality programming (*televisione verità*) from the late 1980s, for example on the third channel RAI3. RAI3 has also traditionally been the only channel to systematically promote documentaries. The most controversial topics have been Mussolini and the fascist regime. In 1993, the miniseries *Il Giovane Mussolini* (*Young Mussolini*) created a scandal because it was accused of 'humanising' the dictator. Another documentary, *Combat Film*, created a shock in 1994 – the year when Berlusconi first became prime minister – when it showed the lynching of Mussolini and his wife and the shooting of fascist youth by Allied troops. This seemed more than a coincidence, since some right-wing parties willing to revise the history of fascism were close associates of Berlusconi. In 1998–2000, no less than six different documentaries dealt polemically with Mussolini, with the left again levelling accusations of humanising the dictator. From 1997, history played an important role on RAI3. Regular slots reserved for one-off historical documentaries were created, most importantly *La grande storia in prima sereta* (*The 'Grand' History in Early Prime Time*, 1997–), with audience shares often reaching 8 per cent with some peaks at 15 per cent. Another slot was created in 2000: *Correva l'anno* (*That Was the Year that Was*). This historical magazine programme with a journalistic format was designed for the late evening. A new wave of documentaries approached the fascist past in a different manner, questioning the construction of the Italian Republic which had been associated with a consensual view that Italians repudiated the fascist past after the Second World War. This culminated with *Guerra Civile* (*The Civil War*, 1999), adapted from a successful book by historian Claudio Pavone (1991), who also was the historical supervisor of the series. The very phrase 'civil war' had long been the monopoly of the Italian Right. The documentary exposed the repressed memory of the battles between Italians in 1943–5, the bombing of Rome by Allied forces, and the painful process of the purge of fascists (*depurazione*) which had included summary executions.

This latter theme had long been painful and controversial in France, and at about the same time French television experienced a 'return of history', but it was not focused on specific traumatic periods, as it decisively was for its southern neighbours. It is crucial to remember here that this 'return of history' only rarely reaches mass audiences, since it takes place outside prime time, with the exception of Arte and some rare initiatives on the public channel France 3, while France 2, which has higher audiences, has officially given up on history. Two major topics have been lingering in the French conscience: collaborations with the Nazi occupation, and the Algerian War. The second has recently been linked with France's broader colonial past and the growing discontents and claims of minorities born from immigrant parents (*issues de l'immigration*). This section deals only with the Algerian and colonial past, because it is a more burning topic for French society, while the collaborationist past has been much debated but also officially acknowledged by the then president Jacques Chirac on 15 July 1995.

Ever since the early 1970s, some documentary productions and current affairs programmes have discussed the darker aspects of the Algerian War, notably the use of torture. Approximately every ten years, there has been a new wave of productions and debates which each time evoked a strange feeling that they talked for the first time about things no one wanted to hear before. It is true, however, that television has been slow to tackle the past, and has gradually delved deeper into it and framed it in a more critical manner, moving from regarding repression as an unavoidable part of the war against terrorism (which has a very contemporary relevance) to its darker political, colonial – and racist – significations. 'State memory' has been even slower to follow, and it was only in June 1999 that the French national assembly passed a law referring to 'the Algerian War' instead of 'the events of Algeria' which had been the phrase previously used.

Although current affairs programmes had covered the Algerian war in the early 1960s, but in ways which suited the aims of Gaullist decolonisation, major programmes were produced on the occasion of the tenth anniversary of Algerian independence in 1972. A three-episode series, *L'Algérie des Algériens* (*The Algeria of Algerians*), focused on Algeria itself but without eschewing the harsher side of the conflict, especially images of the French army shooting at French opponents of the independence. Indeed, the French ex-settlers (*repatriés*) had been the focus of much previous coverage of the war. However, it was in cinema that the first major documentary on the war, *La Guerre d'Algérie* by journalist Yves Courrière, was shown. A major turning point for French television was 1981–2. After the Left's accession to power, the Algerian War was very present, especially in debate programmes like *Apostrophes*, but also in news where on anniversaries of events like the massacre of Algerian demonstrators by the French police in Paris on 17 October 1961, it was discussed for the first time. Ten years later, in 1990, the first documentary series bearing the title *La Guerre d'Algérie* was broadcast by FR3 (which would become France 3), first early in the morning then in prime time, but during the low season for French television in the summer. Ironically, the series was British: Peter Batty's five-episode *The Algerian War* had been commissioned by Channel 4 and Belgian TV and broadcast in 1984 on the occasion of the anniversary of the start of the war in 1954. However, one year later in 1991 *Les années algériennes* (*The Algerian Years*, Antenne 2 – later France 2), produced by historian Benjamin Stora, dealt with the competing memories of the war and for the first time explicitly linked the discontent of ethnically North African youth in France with the inability of the country to deal with its colonial past. In 2002, public television financed several series on the war, but not on prime time. A long documentary exposing for the first time the systematic and massive use of torture, Patrick Rotman's *L'ennemi intime* (*The Intimate Enemy*), was an exception, however, and was broadcast in prime time on France 3 and re-broadcast in November 2004.

It is worth mentioning the specific programming policy of the encrypted channel Canal Plus. In 1997 it was the first channel to propose a prime-time series exposing the original history of immigrations as told by the immigrants themselves, and produced by Algerian born Yamina Benguigui: *Mémoires d'immigrés, l'héritage maghrébin* (*Memories of Immigrants, the North African Heritage*). In 2005, it dealt with the 17 October 1961 massacre in a highly praised historical fiction, *Nuit Noire* (*Black Night*). Canal Plus has recently screened many bold political fictions, and paradoxically it is this privately owned channel which is the most audacious. Its historical programming contributes to its image as an original, innovative channel (akin to HBO in the US), but it reaches only minority audiences.

Although the debate is not over, and no doubt other productions will suggest more 'revelations' before long, there is a sense that the major historical facts are known, if not accepted. But television has been following this debate, not leading it, and the same has happened for the larger debate about the colonial past, which is slowly emerging on television. The Algerian past still lingers, with memories competing for recognition: those of former soldiers, Algerian victims and their descendants, Algerian citizens living in France and linking the 'civil war' in the country today with the past war. While 'Arab–Muslim' citizens are now more visible on French television, their presence and integration is still a highly controversial topic which television seems able to evoke only indirectly and with caution. All too often, the vision of people of North African origin is tied up with crime and *insécurité* and feeds spectacle in news programming. During the presidential campaign of 2002, the stress on 'insecurity', with its racist implications, was said to have contributed to the presence of extreme-right wing Jean-Marie Le Pen in the second round of the election. In December 2005, riots in the suburbs were widely covered by television, which was accused of fuelling them. By contrast, the patient work of documentary film-makers has little chance of proposing a different, more nuanced image of those populations. Public service television might here contribute to a better integration of people of Algerian (and North-African) origin, torn between images of past victims of the war, terrorists, or parents of young criminals, and only rarely actors in their own history. It remains to be seen whether other descendants of formerly colonised peoples will be better treated by television, for French channels are preparing several documentaries in 2007 on the history of colonisation.

European Television, European Televisions?

Our case studies lead us towards general questions about European television programmes. These begin from the issue of whether there has been (and still is) a specific relationship between certain genres and European television, especially European public (service) television. All three genres discussed here touch on this debate. While drama (as an art form) and documentary (as a tool for both popularising and problematising recent history) stay close to long-established debates about public service as a cultural tool, *Aktenzeichen/ Crimewatch* signals a new stage in the history of European television. This is its growing ability to produce popular programmes rejected by the cultural establishments, but enjoying high ratings. This prompts the questions of what remains of the relationship with high culture, high European culture, and the public service tradition.

First, the trends at work might be mainly European but they are never solely European, even broadly speaking. In general, whether commercial or public, many national broadcasters tried to appropriate television not only as a new medium but also as a new art form, focusing on drama. A hybrid class of creators excluded from cinema, engineers dreaming of poetry, avant-gardists willing to experiment with technology, entered television to experiment, mostly in drama and especially in live drama, with Shakespeare being a global favourite (televised Shakespeare can be found in most of Europe, but also in Latin America and in Asia). Although with less encouragement from heads of programming, this was true both in public and in commercial television institutions. Live drama with strong aesthetic claims was a very European genre at least where television started early, but it was also present in the USA, though it was discarded more quickly than in Europe. It is hard to find any discernible heritage of these aesthetic researches on today's television screens.

Aktenzeichen was adapted beyond Europe with much success, notably in the USA as *America's Most Wanted*. Its public service claims cannot easily be related to the public service status of commercial television. One should remember here that commercial television has made such claims of fulfilling public service missions, and that crime-appeal programmes were important to these arguments. It would be too easy to dismiss these claims as hypocrisy, and clearly some professionals truly believed in their mission. Beyond the crime-appeal format (and genre), the whole area of reality programming is now an international phenomenon whose roots cannot be traced to any specific geographic location, despite the Dutch origins of *Big Brother* and the Swedish ones of *Survivor*. There is an international professional culture of television formats which it would be unproductive to attach to national context. The relevant question here is to know whether a specific trend of reality programmes can be attached to European tradition(s) of public service. *Aktenzeichen*, in this respect, illustrates a very political, law-and-order version of public service which might have been popular with viewers but has been hard to digest in most countries (or was not adopted, or not for long). Other reality genres might be more interesting here, especially the genres which give an authentic 'voice' to the 'voiceless' with the help of professionals, or genres with pedagogical claims like programmes which try to take viewers back in time (for instance *The Trench* on the BBC, which was based on the experience of soldiers in the First World War). But this is a rather fragile public service claim to extol, as Jon Dovey (2000) has discussed.

Undoubtedly, debates about the national past and difficult memories are plentiful outside Europe, for example in Latin America. However, it is perhaps historical documentary which can make the strongest European claims. It is true that the genre is both too controversial and not quite profitable enough for commercial television (in addition, its market is very national). But it matters. As the French union of multimedia authors' motto puts it, a country without documentaries is like a family without a family photo album. Digging into the controversial past in prime time, in relation to a national, and often painful political historical debate has been done in a variety of countries with some success. To avoid any idealisation, and also the natural sympathy of academic writing for public service television which often prevents trenchant criticism, it is necessary to insist on the major weakness of the genre. In all three countries analysed, especially in Spain, the efforts of television were directly related to the political colour of the parties or coalitions in power, with right-wing and left-wing readings of recent history alternating on television. Yet public television, for all its faults, which include political weakness and a tendency to sensationalise contemporary history, seems able to support historical documentary and to fuel a debate of much social relevance. Moreover, outside Europe or on its borders, it is public stations, even declining ones, which have produced such series. In Israel, the major televised effort to participate in the nation's soul-searching, the series *Tkuma* (*Revival*, 1998) was broadcast on the main public channel.

References

Becker, H. (1982) *Art Worlds*. Berkeley, University of California Press.

Biressi, A. (2001) *Crime, Fear and the Law in True Crime Stories*. Basingstoke, Palgrave Macmillan.

Bourdon, J. (1993) 'Les réalisateurs de télévision: essai sur le déclin d'un groupe professionnel'. *Sociologie du travail* 4, 431–45.

Bourdon, J. (2004a) 'Old and new ghosts. Public service television and the popular: a history'. *European Journal of Cultural Studies* 7:3, 283–304.

Bourdon, J. (2004b) 'Shakespeare, Dallas et le Commissaire: une histoire de la fiction télévisée en Europe'. *Le Temps des Médias* 2, 176–97.

Brants, C. (1998) 'Crime fighting by television in the Netherlands'. In: Fishman, M. and Cavender, G. (eds.) *Entertaining Crime: Television Reality Programmes.* New York, Aldine de Gruyter, pp. 175–91.

Chaniac, R. (2000) *L'offre des programmes et l'écoute des chaînes nationales hertziennes en clair.* Bry-sur-Marne, INA.

Chaniac, R. and Bourdon, J. (1990) 'L'Europe au prime time'. *Médiaspouvoirs* 20, 145–52.

Creeber, G. (2003) 'The origins of public service broadcasting (British television before the war).' In: Hilmes, M. and Jacobs, J. (eds.) *The Television History Book.* London, BFI, pp. 22–5.

Dauncey, H. (1998) '"Témoin No. 1": crime shows on French television'. In: Fishman, M. and Cavender, G. (eds.) *Entertaining Crime: Television Reality Programmes.* New York, Aldine de Gruyter, pp. 193–209.

Delavaud, G. (2005) *L'art de la télévision.* Brussels and Paris, De Boecke and INA.

Dhoest, A. (2004a) 'Quality and/as national identity: press discourse on Flemish period TV drama'. *European Journal of Cultural Studies* 7:3, 305–24.

Dhoest, A. (2004b) 'Negotiating images of the nation: the production of Flemish TV drama, 1953–89'. *Media, Culture & Society* 26:3, 393–408.

Dhoest, A. (2006) 'From theatre play to reality comedy: a history of fictional comedy genres on Flemish television'. *New Review of Film and Television Studies* 4:2, 147–66.

Diaz, L. (1994) *La televisión en España, 1949–1995.* Madrid, Alianza.

Dobash, R. E. et al. (1992) *Women Viewing Violence.* London, British Film Institute.

Dobash, R. E. et al. (1998) 'Rating and reality: the persistence of the reality crime genre'. In: Fishman, M. and Cavender, G. (eds.) *Entertaining Crime: Television Reality Programmes.* New York, Aldine de Gruyter, pp. 37–58.

Dovey, J. (2000) *Freak-Show: First-person Media and Factual Television.* London, Pluto.

Gardner, C. and Wyver, J. (1983) 'The single play: from Reithian reverence to cost-accounting and censorship'. *Screen* 24:4–5, 114–29.

Godfroy, F. and Van der Velden, R. (1984) *Opsporing verkocht: Mensenjacht via de televisie.* Den Bosch, Vereniging van Reklasseringsinstellingen.

Gunter, B. (1987) *Television and the Fear of Crime.* Luton, John Libbey.

Jacobs, J. (2000) *The Intimate Screen: Early British Television Drama.* Oxford, Oxford University Press.

Jermyn, D. (2007) *Crime Watching: Investigating Real Crime TV.* London and New York, I. B. Tauris.

Johnson, C. (2005) *Telefantasy.* London, BFI.

Kettle, M. (1983) 'The drift to law and order'. In: Hall, S. and Jaques, M. (eds.) *The Politics of Thatcherism.* London, Lawrence & Wishart, pp. 216–34.

Lerg, W. B. (1967) 'Zur Entstehung des Fernsehens in Deutschland'. *Rundfunk und Fernsehen* 15, 349–76.

Malborn, J. and Moran, A. (2006) *Understanding the Global TV Format*. Bristol and Portland, Intellect.

Miller, H. (2001) *Crimewatch Solved: The Inside Story*. Basingstoke, Boxtree.

Morin, E. (1986) *Penser l'Europe*. Paris, Gallimard.

Palmer, G. (2003) *Discipline and Liberty: Television and Governance*. Manchester, Manchester University Press.

Pavone, C. (1991) *Una guerra civile: Saggio storico sulla moralità nella Resistenza*. Turin, Bollati-Boringhieri.

Pinseler, J. (2006) *Fahndungssendungen im deutschsprachigen Fernsehen*. Cologne, Herbert von Halem.

Rath, C.-D. (1985) 'The invisible network: television as an institution in everyday life'. In: Drummond, P. and Paterson, R. (eds.) *Television in Transition*. London, BFI, pp. 199–204.

Ross, N. and Cook, S. (1987) *Crimewatch UK*. London, Hodder & Stoughton.

Rüden, P.v. (1979) 'Ablenkung als Programmauftrag: Das NS-Fernsehen – ein Unterhaltungsmedium'. In: Rüden, P.v. (ed.) *Unterhaltungsmedium Fernsehen*. Munich, Fink, pp. 143–63.

Schlesinger, P. and Tumber, H. (1994) ' "Don't have nightmares . . ." '. In: Schlesinger, P. and Tumber, H. (eds.) *Reporting Crime: The Media Politics of Criminal Justice*. Oxford, Clarendon Press, pp. 248–70.

Smith, A. (ed.) (1998) *Television: An International History*. London, Oxford University Press.

Urrichio, W. (ed.) (2008) *We Europeans? Culture, Media, Identities*. Bristol, Intellect.

Veyrat-Masson, I. (2000) *Quand la télévision explore le temps*. Paris, Fayard.

Winkler, K. (1994) *Fernsehen unterm Hakenkreuz: Organisation, Programm, Personal*. Cologne, Weimar and Vienna, Böhlau.

Wober, M. and Gunter, B. (1988) *Violence on Television: What the Viewers Think*. Luton, John Libbey.

5

TV Nations or Global Medium?
European Television between National Institution and Window on the World

*Sonja de Leeuw, with Alexander Dhoest,
Juan Francisco Gutiérrez Lozano,
François Heinderyckx, Anu Koivunen
and Jamie Medhurst*

Introduction

The title of this chapter recalls one of the key metaphors of television: television, seeing at a distance (Gripsrud 1998). It is based upon the technical capacity of television to simultaneously transmit and receive images and sounds of an event that is taking place somewhere in the outside world. Irrespective of the fact that most television programming has for a long time been pre-recorded, the basic notion of television as a window on the world has remained one of the strongest features of the medium. It does not only claim to account for the aesthetic values of television, such as 'realism' (Williams 1974), but also television has been acknowledged as a forceful medium in the process of modernisation. Precisely because it offers the technical possibility of watching across borders, television enables people to literally see beyond their own group, beyond those national borders. Television as seeing at a distance, however, was also feared as a challenge to the notion of national belonging; the expected social disintegration of this process was countered by the formation of national public broadcasting in many European countries, serving the construction of national citizenship. Broadcasting, as the institutionalised form of television, was supposed to bridge the public and the private spheres, bringing an image of the outside world into the home. It made it possible to reach all citizens at once, providing them with centralised information, and thus it became a useful instrument in constructing 'stable communities' (Gripsrud 1998).

Television has played and still plays a crucial role in constructing notions of citizenship and cultural identity. On the one hand it is primarily a national institution, producing identifiable national productions; on the other hand it is a global medium sensitive to global trends and industrial and economic mechanisms, operating independently of geographical boundaries. In this chapter we address this dual orientation that is evident not only in the specific forms of television within national broadcasting contexts, but also in relation to regional and global television flows. We examine examples of programming that point to the tension arising from television's mission to model national identities as well as its essential ability to represent the (unfamiliar) world. The emphasis is on the production-text relationship, with only brief references to reception practices, and on how particular programming practices relate to notions of identity.

We have chosen identity as a central concept here. We do not claim to pronounce upon how exactly how television constructed identities at specific historical moments. We think, however, that in a European comparative context 'identity' is relevant for understanding television's role in national and global practices of cultural production. We use the concept in the ways discussed in the introduction to this book, and with particular reference to social and cultural theories that emphasise that identity is a hybrid and dynamic concept, which is formed in the relationship and interaction between the individual and his or her social and cultural environment (Giddens 1991, Hall 1996). According to Barker (1999: 33), identities are constituted in and through cultural representations with which we identify, and television is the major cultural form for producing and distributing those representations. To put it differently, television as a cultural space can be regarded a site for negotiating identities (even if they are 'imagined'), ranging from locally specific to globally uniform ones. It provides different groups with different identities (local, ethnic, regionally specific) by pointing out relevant differences in relation to something else. On the other hand, television is capable of homogenising differences, mobilising collective experiences into less specific social identities that appeal to a whole nation. As the normative understanding of television is in terms of national broadcasting, we will start there.

National Broadcasting

From the outset, in many European countries broadcasting was devised as a national institution. Legislators quickly intervened in the developing radio landscape to grant monopolies to single broadcasters, who subsequently became the prime site for the development of television. In communist and other authoritarian regimes, television became a 'state' medium, a voice of government and a means to unite the nation-state. But also in democratic regimes, the unifying power of television was quickly identified and acted upon by the establishment of public broadcasters (Newcomb 1997). The BBC is the classic example, as an institution overarching the British regions with the explicit aim 'to make the nation one man' (Cardiff & Scannell 1987). As noted by Van den Bulck (2001: 54), such public broadcasting was the modernist project of a cultural elite aiming to create national culture through a uniform high culture. One of the prime functions of television, then, was to create an 'imagined community' of viewers (see Anderson 1991). This became something constantly to be worked upon, as the notion of national identity is not obvious to every individual citizen.

The project of national unification thus runs through the history of most European countries, but their differing national contexts made for divergent forms and intensities of nationalism. In 'old', established and (allegedly) 'monocultural' nations such as France or the UK, early television addressed the nation as a self-evident entity it claimed simply to represent. In other contexts, divisions within the nation were acknowledged and reflected institutionally. For instance, in the Netherlands ideological differences within the 'pillarised' society were reflected in a nationally regulated system of ideologically differentiated broadcasters. In Belgium, cultural differences between the Dutch-language North (Flanders) and the French-language South led to a division into two increasingly independent public broadcasters. Particularly in Flanders, broadcasting was inspired by a drive to contribute to Flemish national culture. In Finland almost from the outset national broadcasting exhibited co-operation between public and private services, due to specific national historical, political and economic factors. They include the small size of the nation, the tradition of political coalitions and the rapid growth of the post-war economy (Hellman 1996: 91).

Despite these early differences, each of these national broadcasting systems in turn had to deal with evolving notions of 'the national'. In many European nation-states, the second half of the twentieth century saw the (re)emergence of sub-state national movements. National regions sought to be acknowledged and addressed as distinct unities, including in broadcasting. This often led to the establishment of regional offices or separate broadcasting institutions such as in Spain and in the UK. The fiction of self-evident national unity was questioned and the notion of culturally unified and homogeneous nations became untenable.

At another level, national broadcasting was challenged with the arrival of commercial stations. From the 1980s onwards, the television market was liberalised across Europe. This brought about an increase in transmission time that had to be filled without excessive cost. As a result, a vast amount of popular entertainment was bought from the American market, mainly by commercial channels, in order to serve large European audiences. In general, the market shares of public programming decreased. Moreover, European governments decided first and foremost upon economic measures such as deregulation as a means of stimulating greater unity and furthering European economic interests in global markets (McQuail 1996: 112). But even so, domestic programming on domestic channels remains successful across Europe, even within the ever-expanding and increasingly fragmented media landscape.

In the late twentieth century, the cultural and ethnic differences within nations but also within regions or sub-nations had to be acknowledged by public broadcasters. Global movements of people and media content reinforced this process, and as a result national borders were being transgressed with increasing ease and speed. As a result, the notion of national broadcasting, with its assumed specificity in terms of, for example, language, cultural reference points and programme forms, was complicated by European or global cultures and by issues of regional culture. In the global post-modern era national identity has become a problematic concept because of post-colonialism and because societies have become hybrid, exhibiting differences between where you actually are and where you feel you belong (to mention only the increasingly complex relationship between geographic and cultural communities).

There is, however, also another side to the picture. Essentialist notions of identity can be observed in recent debates in Europe. Processes of globalisation and internationalisation and related processes of forced or voluntary migration go hand in hand with an increasing interest in national and regional questions. These issues rose higher on the agenda in 2004 when 15 new countries entered the European Union (EU), and again in 2007 when the membership of another two (Bulgaria and Romania) increased the EU to 27 nations. Despite the constant reproduction of the idea of European citizenship as one complementing national citizenship, European nations could not be prevented from feelings of threat that were expressed after the expansion of the Union. In view of growing European unification, 'national identity' has increasingly become an important topic in many European countries.

In order to explore some of the (changing) relations between the national and the global we now present our three case studies. News is the first, as one of the dominant television genres and an equally dominant player in the global market. It is subject to transnational flows, while at the same time articulating culturally specific characteristics. It is also the most concrete example of the notion of television as a window on the world. We continue with a case study that by definition has a strong national appeal, historical drama, and we show how in three different countries national history was used to reinforce the experience of national identity, while also pointing to the use of culturally established conventions of heritage representation. Finally we turn to a smaller unit within the nation, the region, as it questions the notion of the national; we discuss the extent to which regional television in two countries positions itself within and against the national.

Television News: Transnational Market, Local Outlets

The origins of television news bulletins are closely linked with those of television itself. First a rudimentary visual variation of radio news, they soon developed into a fully-fledged and fundamental genre, which has consistently been given considerable resources and attention ever since. From the start, the main newscast has always been scheduled in the particular time slot between 'access prime time'(in the early evening) and evening prime time. In the pre-remote control era, the news aimed to attract as many viewers as possible, thus gathering an audience very likely to remain on the same channel all evening. The news programme was conceived as an audience builder and accumulator. Traditionally, the airtime of the main evening newscast has been a reliable indicator of the start of the prime-time period in the corresponding country or region, which usually coincides with the time of the evening meal.

Today, in the age of fragmented, volatile, channel-switching audiences, news bulletins are still considered as flagship programmes offered by all general-interest channels. Not only are these programmes still attracting sizeable audiences (much sought-after by advertisers), they also constitute a crucial facet of the broadcaster's identity, particularly with regard to credibility, trust and significance. In comparison with the evolution of television in general, news bulletins have remained remarkably stable in form, across both time and space. The classic model is astoundingly consistent, and consists of alternating cycles with an anchor person reading out a short introduction to a story, followed by an edited report or a live commentary or an interview, in a studio setting of a large desk in front of a green-screen or, more recently, a busy and high-tech newsroom (Heinderyckx 1993). Periodically, each and every broadcaster announces that they are completely reformatting the news, with a brand new set, new structure and new approach. But invariably it turns out that changes are only marginal and cosmetic while narrative structures remain untouched.

The similarity in form and stability in time, combined with the pronounced globalisation of the television industry, would seem to offer a golden opportunity for radical transnationalisation of televised news. Large news corporations could easily supply television channels across the globe with ready-made news bulletins, slightly customised and ready to air. The cost would be reduced and brought under control for stations while providing their audience with news content produced by specialists. Or even more simply: as with other thematic content, general-interest channels could simply discontinue their news on the basis that the audience could turn at any moment to one of many all-news channels. And yet, unlike what happened for other types of content (like game shows or drama), all general-interest channels continue meticulously to produce their own news bulletins, with no plans to give them up.

In the 1980s, when Cable News Network (CNN) was gaining audiences and attention, many thought that a few transnational actors would soon deal with international news, while local outlets would be confined to local news. Such concentration did indeed occur, but most notably in the market of news sources. Although other transnational news channels followed successfully in the footsteps of CNN, most remarkable was the proliferation of national news channels. Concurrently, the most successful transnational broadcasters saw fit to gradually offer different content for different regions of the world, then for specific countries (generally in association with local media). CNN and MTV, to mention but the most emblematic and thematic transnational brands, are now present in a variety of regional and national markets with specific, targeted channels providing strong evidence that there is a future for local outlets, even if they are largely fed with content and concepts developed globally (formats, games, music, shows, workflows, management style, etc.). The early success of CNN did not anticipate the model of transnational television news as much as it proved the viability of the all-news television channels (Chalaby 2002, Heinderyckx 1998).

The launch of Euronews in 1993 could be seen as a reaction to the overwhelming supremacy of US outlets in the media coverage of the first Gulf War of 1991, in particular CNN and its live feeds from within Iraq. The limited resources available in the relatively small newsrooms found in a fragmented European media landscape left European journalists and audiences captive to larger Anglophone news organisations. Euronews was not the first attempt at a European, all-news, public service-led channel, but previous attempts such as Eurikon or Europa TV were short-lived (Baisnée & Marchetti 2000). This time, public broadcasters from France, Spain, Italy and Switzerland joined forces with the European Broadcasting Union, with the support of the European Commission which hoped to stimulate and promote a European public space. Public service media from other countries joined the effort. In 1995, 49 per cent of the shares were sold to Alcatel-Alsthom (which then sold them to British news production company ITN in 1997), marking the beginning of a turn in management style towards that of commercial organisations (Baisnée & Marchetti 2000).

Euronews seemed somewhat improbable. Not only was the channel to provide multilingual news coverage from a central location and with limited budgets, it also proclaimed that it would report the news from a European perspective, in a context where the very notion of a European perspective was as questionable as that of a European identity. Beyond the technical difficulties of the different language variants superimposed on a single video output, Euronews seemed to overlook the lack of a European public sphere, the multidimensional diversity of the targeted audience (Schlesinger 1991, Wolton 1990) and the enduring preference by viewers for a national perspective on news (European Television Task Force 1988). Other transnational channels are less vulnerable to such difficulties because their target audience is much more homogeneous, particularly in the case of the numerous transnational ethnic channels aimed at various diasporas (Chalaby 2002). In spite of these impediments, Euronews established itself and managed to keep the support of its main shareholders (European public service broadcasters) and even to grow by increasing the number of language versions to seven by 2007. Euronews uses footage provided by the partner channels, relying heavily on EBU's Eurovision News exchanges, better known as the EVN (Baisnée & Marchetti 2000, Friedland 1996). The EVN, which started in 1954, is a platform for exchanging footage produced locally, for local use, among partners in other countries should they decide to cover the corresponding stories.

Other transnational all-news channels fall within a tradition that predates global television and aims at providing foreign audiences with the views of a particular culture or country on current affairs. The Cold War and, more recently, the Gulf crises triggered a long string of initiatives to launch 24-hour rolling news channels, each presented as a necessary counterweight to the allegedly biased coverage of other broadcasters. Following up on the long tradition of propaganda and counter-propaganda radio stations, a number of these outlets provide their programmes in languages which are not that of their region of origin. Notorious recent examples include Qatar-based Al-Jazeera's programme in English, the French government-funded France24 in English and Arabic, and US government-funded Al-Hurra in Arabic. The television news landscape now offers a variety of outlets, which proves the interest or even the fascination for television news among private media conglomerates as well as among the public authorities and the audience. As an example, France alone enjoys three national all-news channels (LCI, iTélé and BFM TV), one transnational French-speaking television channel relaying news bulletins from partners and airing their own news (TV5), one pan-European news channel (Euronews in seven languages) and a French all-news channel intended for foreign audiences (France24 in French, English and Arabic).

Yet news bulletins aired on national, general-interest channels still gather by far the largest audiences. The steady preference of viewers for their national or local news bulletin (European Television Task Force 1988) results from the combination of their interest in local stories and their preference for a local framing of international events, a familiar flavour and texture (Heinderyckx 1993, 1998). This is the case even if international stories in particular vary only marginally when based on the same footage provided by scarce international sources (Marchetti 2002). The large number of national and local stories covered by newscasts explains why few topics are covered Europe-wide. Even the proportion of international stories varies greatly among countries (Heinderyckx 1993, 1998).

Europe is also marked by considerable differences in the attitudes of television news audiences. On average, two-thirds of Europeans say they watch the news on television every day (Eurobarometer 65, January 2007), with sizeable differences between heavy viewing countries such as Finland (over 80 per cent), the Netherlands, Denmark, Lithuania, Portugal and Estonia (about 75 per cent) and light TV news-viewing countries such as Austria,

Cyprus, Slovenia and the Czech republic (about 50 per cent). Television also enjoys a fair level of trust, but here again, not homogenously across Europe: a majority of Europeans (53 per cent on average in the 25 EU member countries) say they tend to trust television (Eurobarometer 64, June 2006), which is more than their trust in the press (44 per cent) but less than in radio (63 per cent). Trust in television is highest in Finland, Romania and Estonia (more than 70 per cent), and lowest in Spain, Italy, Greece, Hungary and France (between 40 and 50 per cent).

The emergence and adoption of information and communication technologies and the advent of an information society offering on-line news-rich content, personalised media and participatory features will inevitably have some bearing on television news. Yet, just as satellite television and the global news channels did not overtake national outlets, the World Wide Web and its incantatory claims of global reach beyond boundaries may well be just another means of dissemination serving the reconfigured but still robust national and local news outlets.

Historical Drama: A National Narrative

Despite the great amount of American fiction broadcast in Europe, audiences generally prefer domestically produced fiction, and this has been mainly attributed to recognition, identification and cultural proximity (e.g. Bechelloni 1999: xvi, Buonanno 2000). Domestic drama is deemed to express national specificities and cultural sensibilities, and one particular way of addressing national sentiments is to reconstruct the national past in historical drama. Alongside national language, the sense of having a shared historical ancestry and cultural heritage is a key element in most discourses about nations. Media to a large extent contribute to what Hoskins (2001) calls 'memory devices', the means through which we remember and construct new memories which are by definition artificial. According to Hoskins collective memory has increasingly become mediated, and television in particular is seen as shaping collective memory, producing images continuously.

Throughout Europe, both television and film productions set in the past were an important genre in the twentieth century. Many high-profile, internationally successful and critically acclaimed productions revisited the past, such as the German *Heimat* cycle (1984–2004) or the British *The Forsyte Saga* (1967), *Brideshead Revisited* (1981) and *Pride and Prejudice* (1995). Many other countries have traditions of nationally successful period productions that have not been exported so extensively. Like most historical drama across Europe, these were literary adaptations with a strong high-cultural (theatrical, literary) pedigree, explicitly or implicitly telling stories about the nation. Historical drama often deals with cultural roots and formative moments in national history. Great attention is given to accurate reconstruction of the past, through the use of authentic period props or faithful reproductions. Historical drama is often costume drama, with great stress on elaborate outfits and glamorous surfaces. It often has high production values, which allow for credible and attractive reconstructions of the past, and therefore historical drama is often equated with 'quality drama' (Caughie 2000).

Despite these generic similarities, historical productions across Europe also show important differences, which are related to and confirm the diversity of national and cultural contexts. Historical drama refers to pre-existing discourses about the nation and its history, builds on national literary, theatrical and painterly traditions, and focuses on specific customs and landscapes. Another source of national differences is economic: depending on the size of the internal market (national viewership) and the external market (international sales), budgets may differ considerably (Dhoest 1999). This not only affects production values and the possibilities for elaborate and attractive historical reconstruction (in turn facilitating international sales), it also inevitably influences the kind of images being produced. On a very basic level, it is hard to reconstruct grand national moments like wars on a shoestring budget – which partly explains why smaller regions tend to focus on more intimate, social realist drama. On a deeper level, images only meant for domestic viewing may focus on different aspects of the past than images meant for international viewing. As English-language productions generally travel more easily, British historical drama in particular may tend to 'clean up' images of the past (Nelson 2000). Therefore, Caughie (2000: 209) warns against reading television drama too easily as a product and expression of the national psyche, for it is always both a cultural representation and a tradable good. This may be true in the British context, but in smaller countries, as we discuss below, historical drama seems first and foremost to serve the construction of a (contested) national past.

History and politics in Finnish television drama

History hurts in Finnish television drama. In a country that gained its independence in 1917, narratives set in past centuries are of Swedish (up to 1809) or Russian rule, or literary adaptations of nation-building fiction. The history of the independent Finland includes a bloody civil war of 1918, two lost wars with the neighbouring Soviet Union in 1939–40 and 1941–4, followed by post-war decades of reconstruction and geopolitical tension. In terms of social history, the story of a country with five million people features a nation divided in terms of class, language and region. It is a narrative of a belated and violent economic modernisation since the 1950s. As one consequence, about 250,000 Finns emigrated to Sweden in search of employment and a higher standard of living. Different interpretations of these conflicts and tensions have propelled serious television drama since the late 1960s. Indeed, social and political history has been a popular topic in Finnish literature, television drama and film.

In the 1970s, the terms of the nation were renegotiated. Producing both literary adaptations and drama-documentaries, the four existing 'television theatres' – three public service drama units, one within the commercially funded company – turned towards the national past, engaging in a politics of memory, examining, contesting and rewriting the meanings of modernisation in terms of class, region and gender (Koivunen 2007). A three-part drama serial from 1978, *The Way Life Goes (Elämänmeno)*, illustrates this process of renegotiation. An adaptation of a 1975 prize-winning first novel by Pirkko Saisio, the serial was directed by Åke Lindman, scripted by Saisio and Lindman together, and produced by Channel One Television Theatre within the National Broadcasting Company YLE. *The Way Life Goes* tells the story of the post-war decades from the twin perspectives of Eila and her daughter Marja. The narrative starts in 1946, with a post-war urban restaurant scene where Eila works as a waitress. She meets Reino, a war veteran and the unhappy love of her life, then becomes pregnant but is left alone with the child, Marja. Eila drinks too much, loses jobs, struggles through poverty, marries Alpo, gives birth to two more children and spends her prime working hard in factories at the cost of her health. The story closes at the end of the 1960s as the family moves from a small, inner-city flat to a new suburb of Helsinki. Eila's story is witnessed by her daughter, and contrasts with Marja's narrative of growing up with the legacy of the lost war at a time of rapid modernisation and ideological contradictions.

A costume drama with high production values, *The Way Life Goes* was shot on film and emphasised the visual look of past decades, authenticating its representation with details of décor and popular cultural references. While the aesthetic look of the serial echoes the European heritage cinema of the time, public reception unanimously applauded it as realist in terms of style, themes and address. 'It was just like our life', people told Pirkko Saisio (*Tiedonantaja*, 15 November 1978), and in 1978 the TV listings magazine *Katso* described the serial as a portrait of 'Finnish everyday life'. A narrative of private trauma and survival was received as a powerful document of the post-war Finnish mentality and the generational conflicts of the reconstruction period.

The sense of authenticity attributed to *The Way Life Goes* exhibits what John Caughie (2000: 88) has called a 'rush of the real' and underlay the contemporary critical enthusiasm and high audience ratings of the serial. It contributed to relocating the imaginary Finland of the past, introducing both a new setting and a new subject for the narrative of modernisation. Instead of in Häme, the Southern agricultural landscape, the woman embodying the nation was located in Helsinki and her dialect signalled her Karelian descent and her roots close to the Russian border. Furthermore, instead of the affluent, middle-class parts of Helsinki such as the Töölö of the many family comedies of the 1940s and 1950s, Finland was imaged as Kallio, the inner-city, working-class neighbourhood. This new national landscape was applauded by the public as proof of a heightened sense of the real, matching discourses of realism in Finnish television journalism (Ruoho 2001: 201–4).

All this signalled a remarkable change in the cultural understanding of national history that had obtained since the 1960s when the 40 years of silence around the Civil War ended with Väinö Linna's three-part novel *Under the Northern Star* (*Täällä Pohjantähden alla*, 1959–62). It challenged the official version of Finnish history by introducing the working-class perspective on the war, its background and legacy. The existence of a 'Red Finland' had remained unacknowledged by the political elite until the mid-1960s and the speeches of President Urho Kekkonen. In 1966, left-wing parties won a majority in the Parliament and the first academic study confirming the degree of terror during the Civil War was published: 37,000 people had been killed, almost 27,000 of them on the Red side. Concurrently with the public acknowledgement of working-class experience and leftist interpretations of history, an archival revolution took place. Projects investigating working-class memories were launched and new museums and archives were established.

In television drama, adaptations of books by male working-class authors scored high ratings and attracted critical acclaim. Film director Rauni Mollberg adapted autobiographical novels by Toivo Pekkanen (*Lapsuuteni/My childhood*, TV1, 1967; *Tehtaan varjossa/In the Shadow of the Factory*, TV2, 1969). If Pekkanen's novels brought Kotka, an industrial coastal town east of Helsinki, to the fore, *Moreeni* (TV2, 1972, Jarmo Nieminen) by Lauri Viita made Pispala in Tampere, once the very centre of 'Red Finland', a key locus of Finnish social history. In *The Way Life Goes* the centre of the nation moved to Kallio in Helsinki and, for the first time, the focalisation prioritised women's point of view, articulating their experience of everyday life. While heated debates about the politics of realism and class surrounded the 1975 BBC serial *Days of Hope* (Bennett et al. 1981), in the Finnish public sphere *The Way Life Goes* passed as an image of 'us' without controversy.

In terms of public reception, the character of Eila (played by Ritva Oksanen) was hailed as a monumental homage to working-class women and mothers. In a reviewer's words: 'Men are in the background. The novel and the TV movie pay a beautiful tribute to women in working-class homes, to people who were often forced to struggle under difficult circumstances in the post-war Finnish reality' (*Rakentaja*, 15 November 1978). According to another, 'as a story of a woman's lot, Eila is somehow so familiar and ordinary that she becomes monumental' (*Uusi Suomi*, 1 November 1978). Interestingly, the many affective and identificatory readings of Eila in 1978 reiterated a whole range of celebrated, yet contradictory qualities – hard-working, sacrificing, monumental, dreamy, tough – that since the 1930s were associated with strong matron-mother-figures in peasant melodramas, the Finnish version of the melodramatic heroine (Ang 1990: 87, Koivunen 2003).

While the peasant melodramas and autobiographies of male working-class authors featured male genealogies, *The Way Life Goes* centres on a mother–daughter relationship, contrasting the bitterness and feistiness of Eila with Marja's inwardness and her ideological confusion. Both of them are marked by traumatic experiences. Eila never recovers from the rejection by her lover, and regards her daughter Marja as nervous, underachieving and unfit for the challenges of future life. The daughter is portrayed as cherishing a Freudian family romance fantasy, identifying with Lempi, a friend of Eila and a union activist, and seeking new affiliations in religious circles. Underneath her bitterness Eila, too, is represented as yearning, desiring and sexual. In the end, however, she accepts her lot. As for the daughter's coming-of-age narrative, *The Way Life Goes* ends with Marja still searching for 'her place in the world'.

It was recently revealed that the novel originally featured a lesbian romance which was removed after consultations with the publisher. In the homophobic Finland of the 1970s, a lesbian theme would have overshadowed its reception, it was argued. In retrospect, Saisio – for a long time the only lesbian celebrity in Finland – agreed with her editor's judgement, but saw it as symptomatic of the hope for a great working-class novel in the literary climate of the time. In the 1970s, the national imaginary was being renegotiated in a context where bourgeois culture coincided with Stalinism, a Marxist scientific conception of social life, and strivings for socialist realism (Saisio 2000: 352). Furthermore, the lesbian relationship would also have disturbed the monumental effect of Eila and the identificatory celebration of working-class womanhood that the serial occasioned. A major Finnish women's magazine saw Eila as an image of 'all women's lives' (*Anna*, 24 October 1978), while an article in the TV listings magazine *Katso* described her in 1978 as 'a grand reminder of how difficult it is to be a woman'.

The Way Life Goes is an all-time favourite television drama, and is rerun regularly. In terms of popularity and thematic focus, it echoed two other 1970s literary adaptations: *The Song of Solveig* (*Solveigin laulu*, TV1, 1974, dir. Reima Kekäläinen) and *Maja from the Stormy Island* (*Stormskärs Maja*, RTV, 1976, dir. Åke Lindman), serials which each paraded stories of women's hardships and survival. In the 1970s, these narratives of nation and its modernisation from women's everyday perspectives were counterbalanced by the many literary adaptations of books by male authors (e.g. Veijo Meri, Pentti Haanpää) and drama-documentaries about 'Great Men'. In these, the battles over nationhood and the national past were fought in the name of new historical research and by personifying key political figures. Crucial moments of Finnish political history were dramatised, for instance, in Matti Tapio's serial *The Men of War and Peace* (*Sodan ja rauhan miehet*, TV2, 1978–9). It used documentary footage and dramatised sequences to depict the negotiations preceding the Winter War of 1939–40 and, as it was explicitly called, the Soviet attack on Finland. The serial attracted large audiences, breaking a boundary between high and low cultures, and it also caused public debates underlining the politics of historical narratives and their potential threat to national security. While dramas of social history, such as *The Way Life Goes*, did not challenge foreign policy, they were nevertheless watched and celebrated as political interventions.

The construction of a Flemish identity in television drama

To illustrate the strong interdependence of historical drama and national identity, we will analyse the prototypical Flemish period serial, *Wij, heren van Zichem* (*We, the Lords of Zichem*, BRT, 1969), which was the product of a specific historical interplay of creativity, policy and economic factors. From its beginning in 1953, Belgian television has been divided by language, with a Dutch-language Flemish and a French-language Walloon division within a monopolistic public broadcasting institution. Each operates independently, the Flemish broadcasters in particular driven by (cultural) nationalism – the nation, in this context, not being the Belgian nation-state but the Flemish community. While not overtly supporting political nationalism, the broadcasters have sought to reinforce and stimulate Flemish culture, opposing the strong position of the French language in Belgian cultural life. Both in information and in entertainment, the aim has been to show Flemish culture in all its aspects.

In the 1960s, television drama was produced by the division of dramatic and literary programming within the department of cultural broadcasts, so it fitted in with the overall policy to both reinforce and create a uniform Flemish culture. While there was some room for contemporary and original drama and comedy, the majority of the output consisted of literary and theatrical adaptations, first in single drama and increasingly in serial form. From the mid-1960s, a cycle of period serials was initiated, and a succession of popular productions led to the near-monopoly of this genre. They all shared a few basic characteristics: based on (often well-known) literary sources, they re-created life in Flanders in the first half of the twentieth century, focusing on rural life and peasant characters – to whom they owed the nickname of 'peasant drama'. *Wij, heren van Zichem* was the most successful example of this trend. It was adapted from a series of books by Ernest Claes, one of the most popular and respected Flemish authors at that time. The serial recounts everyday life in the Flemish village of Zichem during the 1920s, over 26 episodes.

Thematically, *Wij, heren van Zichem* is not 'about' Flanders but it does address many themes in Flemish history and society. It presents the chronicle of an age, using a broad range of characters and storylines to evoke a formative period in recent Flemish history. Rather than lecturing about the past, popular types in seemingly everyday situations embody social issues. The ensemble cast allows for the exploration and juxtaposition of divisions and tensions: the stubborn and temperamental rich farmer Coene is opposed to the francophone village baron Alex; conservative village priest Munte confronts the more progressive and socially inclined mother superior Cent; and both representatives of Catholicism in turn clash with the free-thinking liberal Jef the blacksmith. Crucial characteristics of the period are referred to, such as the poverty and misery of rural workers, the central position of Catholicism in everyday life but also its waning power through the rise of socialism and liberalism, and the struggle for emancipation of the lower-class Flemish language against the upper-class French. Strictly speaking *Wij, heren van Zichem* is not a comical series, but the strongly typed characters add a light-hearted tone and make the drama accessible and enjoyable to a broad audience. To this day, it is remembered as the most popular Flemish serial of all time, and some of the characters such as village priest Father Munte are fondly remembered by many older viewers (Dhoest 2005).

The serial echoes an established representation of Flanders as a backward region of hard-working, stubborn and rebellious farmers. It builds upon the mythology of Flemish history as the suppression of and resistance by the Flemish 'folk'. While critically portraying these social issues, *Wij, heren van Zichem* equally offers a nostalgic look back upon a harsh but pure life in the Flemish countryside. The characters are sympathetic and simple country people, slightly rough and each with their faults but ultimately likeable. The poverty, drama and conflict in the foreground are tempered by idyllic imagery of beautiful and unspoilt countryside, authentic farmhouses, old-fashioned village squares and churches. In terms of iconography, *Wij, heren van Zichem* is reminiscent of a folkloric museum: it displays period costumes and interiors and it revives old trades, popular customs and superstitions. As a whole, the serial contributes to the representation of national (popular) history (Dhoest 2003, 2004a). This is reinforced by other national elements, first and foremost the use of Flemish dialects. Officially, the language used in Flanders is Dutch, but to reflect actual language use in the countryside and to stress national specificity, many period serials use dialect that differs from the 'standard' Dutch imported from the Netherlands. While *Wij, heren van Zichem* was successfully broadcast on Dutch television, it had to be subtitled even though both regions officially speak the same language.

Wij, heren van Zichem sparked the (Flemish) national imagination. This is partly due to its strong links with both Flemish high and popular culture. It is based on the work of the popular author Ernest Claes, in particular his evergreen bestseller *De Witte (Whitey)*. This novel about a young blond rascal with a heart of gold is also set in Zichem and had already been adapted into a very successful film in 1934. As noted by Biltereyst and Van Bauwel (2004), both the film and author Claes had links with the German *Heimatkunst* (homeland art), offering an idealised view of the unspoiled rural life of the past. It is telling that Ernest Claes sympathised with the Germans during the Second World War and got into trouble after 1945 for this reason. However, his nostalgic rural image of Flanders was not exceptional and was part of a broad tradition of literary '*Heimat*' novels and theatre plays which inspired much film and television drama from the 1960s until the 1980s. Like much of the literary elite, Claes was culturally very Flemish-minded. In the serial, this is explicitly addressed in the storyline of farmer's son Herman who is involved in nationalist student activity, fighting to be allowed to speak his mother tongue.

While it was presented as an authentic reflection of the Flemish past, *Wij, heren van Zichem* clearly offers a particular representation influenced by the national political and cultural context. It was not explicitly (politically) nationalist, but it did stress the unique cultural and historical roots of Flanders. It contributed to creating a sense of shared culture, by referring to an established author and familiar iconography. While eventually exported to the Netherlands, it is very much an inward-looking representation addressed primarily to Flemish viewers. The budget was limited, which according to the producers partly explains the serial's gritty social realism. This confirms the economic dynamic involved in producing images of the nation, for while fulfilling a similar function of recreating national history, this serial is very unlike the more sumptuous heritage dramas produced throughout Europe (Dhoest 2004b). But at the same time, it repeats many of the supposedly typical national characteristics recurring in nostalgic national histories across Europe, such as bravery or the wholesomeness of country people's folk culture.

Pluralist notions of nationality in Dutch television drama

The specificity of Dutch television drama to a large extent reflects the central concept of pillarised organisation in Dutch broadcasting, which is itself rooted in the history of Dutch society. The history of Dutch broadcasting shows how pluriformity (in the sense of diversity of opinions and beliefs) has always been one of the system's most important and carefully defended characteristics, and television drama in general is one of the most prominent platforms for presenting the different identities of the pillars (de Leeuw 1995). In the 1970s public broadcasting companies started developing prestige series, set in the past, in the city and countryside alike, projecting present-day values and standards on to an historical mirror. These were very popular among audiences, not only because of their nostalgic point of view but also because they stressed aspects of Dutch history and culture as collective experiences. Individual struggles against the social rules of the periods represented in these prestigious series appealed to supposedly shared experiences, values and standards in the traditional target group (the pillar) of the company involved.

To illustrate how the concept of pluriformity informs programming with a strong national appeal, we will discuss Dutch historical drama on a topic that by definition is national in its scope: the Second World War (for the monarchy see de Leeuw 2002). Televised dramas about the Second World War reflect and reinforce changing attitudes towards the national past (de Leeuw 2001). Given the experiences of the Dutch people during the war, when the Netherlands was an occupied country and a large percentage of Jews were killed in German camps, it is no surprise that the Second World War takes up a significant part of feature film and television drama production. Until the

end of the 1980s, historical dramas dealing with the war reflected moral
discussions of right and wrong. Nearly all of them were broadcast in the first
week of May, when several memorial services take place. Evidently, dramatised commemoration was looked upon as a means of consolidating the concept of nationality, of the nation as one unit, for example from a Protestant
point of view at the Protestant broadcasting company where the emphasis was
on human values and individual responsibility rather than the tenets of scrip-
ture. Since the late 1990s, however, some changes can be observed as several
hitherto unnoticed aspects of wartime (such as children's experiences, or the
myth of resistance) have appeared on the screen with changing narrative forms.
We now focus on some of the (mini)series that demonstrate these changes
and that at the same time were acknowledged to contribute to national debates
on history.

The idea of history as construction is dramatised in the three-part serial
The Partisans (Catholic Broadcasting Company/KRO, 1995). It deals with a
little-known incident that took place in autumn 1944 in the resistance movement in one of the southern Catholic provinces of the Netherlands. A little
group of inexperienced partisans by accident gets hold of a group of more
than thirty German soldiers, disarms them and holds them captive, waiting
for the Allies who are about to liberate the area. But the Allies are delayed,
having been defeated in the Battle of Arnhem, and as a consequence the Dutch
partisans and the Germans are forced to live together for more than two months.
The harsh circumstances of their wanderings blur the distinction between cap-
tives and captors, and between right and wrong. Moral dilemmas are strongly
felt, and include discussions about whether to execute prisoners who are in
the end killed. This story of a failure does not offer narrative closure; it rather
questions a final narrativisation of history by linking past to present, jumping
backwards and forwards in time and connecting what must have happened to
how people recollect it. In order to realise this concept of history as construction,
the scriptwriter presents two fictional worlds, one situated in the past, telling
the story of the hostages in 1944, and one set in present, half a century later.
In the present we follow a local radio reporter, who sets out on a quest for
this local history. It soon becomes apparent that the memories of five sur-
vivors are inconsistent. The experiences of the radio reporter, being a professional seeker for truth, run parallel to the experiences of one of the main
characters, a man from the north of Holland who at the time joined the resistance movement in the south and later became a judge (which represents another
way of searching for truth). The questions that occupy his mind (for example
about the execution, or about the line between terrorism and anti-terrorism)
also become questions for the viewer. The judge's eventual recollections of
the incident, when he finally consents to meet the reporter and tell his story,
help to bring about a reworking of the past. He admits that in fact it was a
senseless undertaking; and above all this holds true for the execution of two
Germans and the death of one of the resistance fighters.

After fifty years myth has been unmasked, and history is presented as only existing in the minds of people. This is a very general message, but the regional setting, foregrounded by the use of dialect as the main language in the serial, provides a specific context for a particular part of Dutch Catholic history. The serial refers implicitly to the myth of the absence of Catholics in the resistance movement, the dominant view in Dutch history (and beyond) for a long time. *The Partisans*, recounting a bizarre story, reveals the myth of Catholics as mere bystanders in the Second World War and at the same time it does not replace one myth with another. More than anything else this drama discusses the construction of memory. In its narrative construction the past is commented upon as a domain of various truths and thus of various memories.

What is most striking in 1990s television drama production, however, is the indirectness of representing the Second World War in epic series that deal with history. This indicates a new tendency in the period, namely the chronicle which portrays history as décor and simultaneously as a process of change (de Leeuw, 1998). In relation to continuities and breaks, it is also striking that the stories in these series are all set after the war, whether in the city or in the countryside (*Bij Nader Inzien/In Retrospect*, VPRO; *De zomer van '45/The Summer of 1945*, NCRV; *Tijd van Leven/Time to Live*, KRO). In the 1990s regional settings returned, having been almost absent in the history of Dutch television fiction about contemporary or historical subjects (including the Second World War). By using regional settings broadcasters pointed at cultural roots and cultural differences alike, and the use of dialect underscored this.

In *In Retrospect* (1991) the years of restoration after the war are reflected on in the present, forty years later. This six-part series set a new standard for television drama production in the Netherlands. It was broadcast by a company traditionally rooted in liberal Protestantism, VPRO, which took up a progressive stance at the end of the 1960s. As a result of its deeply rooted interest in avant-garde and advanced representational strategies, this broadcasting company aims at exploring in television drama the relationship between fiction and reality, and experimenting with new dramatic forms. *In Retrospect* concentrates on the experiences of six classmates who form a group after the war in Amsterdam and swear to be friends forever. In 1949 they lose sight of each other, but are brought together by the suicide of one of them, forty years later. The sequences set in the past are based on a Dutch novel, while the present-day scenes are originally developed. Each episode is dedicated to one of the friends, bringing them all together in the last episode where they all attend the funeral of their classmate. Each episode starts in the present time, introducing one of the friends' personal life until the moment he or she receives the farewell letter from their friend, who committed suicide after his wife died. *In Retrospect* is about lost ideals, about friendship that turns out to be based on false expectations and is unmasked as an illusion. Like *The*

Partisans, the series is unconventional in the way it jumps backwards and forwards between past and present. The roots of life in the present are made visible in the past, although unrecognised by the characters, and in lighting, camerawork, acting and style the two worlds are completely different, though related.

Overall, the series narrative illustrates how post-war Dutch values and standards determined the late twentieth-century mentality of a group that was looked upon as the hope of the nation. In this respect, the indifference shown in the series towards the Jewish character, David, is striking and especially the lack of attention given to his war experience hiding from the Germans. Only in one scene set in the past, where he is playing the piano as he often does, is there a brief reference to his background. In a way this reflects the continuing lack of attention to the experiences of returned Jews in the years after the war, but in the series this is not evident as an omission. David is one of the characters who seem to have failed to establish meaningful personal relationships, and he hides in a twilight world of drugs and alcohol befitting his life as an art trader. The Second World War, it seems, has simply become part of the continuum of his life.

Lack of attention to the experiences of returned Dutch Jews, and even more so the incapability and impossibility of speaking about these experiences, is dramatised in a very subtle way in one of the episodes of a ten-part series, *Time to Live*, made by the Catholic broadcasting company in 1996. It asks the Netherlands to acknowledge that the nation has neglected an essential part of collective history that still has to be turned into collective memory. For the first time in Dutch television drama post-war history is represented as a chronicle, situated in a little Catholic community in eastern Holland between 1945 and 1985. Life in the small village is framed not by big historical events, but by small, everyday happenings. Through the stories of three generations the series demonstrates how the village community is slowly opened up to the outside world. Major historical events are reflected in village community life only after some time, or rather are summarised within the margins of the story. As the proprietor of the local café puts it: 'It looks like the five years of war have not touched the village.' The son of the Jewish smith returns home, smarting from the loss of the rest of his family. He finds his father's business already taken over by the locals and encounters only insensibility and a sense of shame that keeps his former neighbours from communicating with him. He leaves for Israel. These dramatic actions take place in relatively silent scenes. The series not only tries to stay away from major historical events, it also avoids strong dramatic moments and in doing so it follows a narrative strategy in which climaxes take place between the episodes instead of within them. It focuses on family history, framed by the history of the region, and in doing so the series investigates the relationship between individual and community in a period of economic, social and cultural changes. In this respect the series is indebted to the German epic *Heimat*, since *Time to Live* writes the history of its characters' attitudes, and mainly deals with family life. We see how change touches the characters and how they become insecure as a result, as well as the efforts they make to find their way in modern times. Modernity is embraced, while the past is cherished. Sense of community is a central issue in this series, albeit at the expense of individual happiness, as in the case of the Jewish character. The community is presented as a place that provides memory and thus an identity that is understood as 'home' (Morley & Robins 1995: 85–104).

Television and Regionalisation

The case studies on historical fiction demonstrate the extent to which the notion of the national was expressed in terms of the regional (in setting, dialect and topic). The issue of language and regional culture in general have complicated the conceptualisation of television as a national medium. In this section we illustrate how the regional as a specific articulation of the local should be read in the context of the national and the global (Barker 1999: 41–4).

Television in Andalusia

Regular television broadcasting began in Spain in 1956. Throughout the years of the Francoist dictatorship (1939–75) Televisión Española (TVE) was characterised by its centralist, monopolistic and propagandistic character, and the spread towards other Spanish regions was only undertaken gradually. The first regional expansion was into Catalonia, to which television broadcasting was extended in 1959 in order to boost connections with the Eurovision network (Baget Herms 1993). The arrival of television in Andalusia took place in stages, beginning in 1961. Its evolution developed parallel to national economic growth, which was driven by industrial development and the expansion of the tourist industry nationwide during that period. However, the moment of the beginning of television broadcasting in the region was marked by an essentially agrarian economy, a high level of illiteracy and inequalities in labour and the social system (Gutiérrez Lozano 2006). In addition, in the late 1960s, a rural exodus and outward migration were the most significant demographic phenomena in the region.

Despite these backward social and economic landscapes, Francoist national television used elements of collective *alegre* ('happy') imagery including *flamenco*, *copla*, bullfighting and religious celebrations in order to extol the so-called 'typical Spanish' national character. Andalusian reality did not arrive in regional broadcasting until the advent of democracy in the early 1980s. But even in this new sociopolitical context, many of the stereotypes related to the imagery of the 'typically Spanish' persisted in the context of regional programming of national television, and continued even with the arrival of autonomous regional television broadcasting, which developed in the late 1980s. The reproduction of national stereotypes in regional programming is very conspicuous.

Notwithstanding its centralist nature, TVE developed a number of production centres across the various regions of Spain during the last years of the dictatorship. The most important of these were in Catalonia and the Canary Islands, which were able to independently produce and broadcast feature programmes. Other centres, among them the one in Andalusia which was created in Seville in 1971, functioned as simple transmitters of information (Palacio 2001). With the arrival of democracy in 1975, TVE decided to create a brief daily simultaneous regional news programme, dependent on each regional centre. In Andalusia, this new type of programme was called *Telesur*. While the process of decentralisation of power was being consolidated nationally, notably with the creation of the so-called 'political autonomies', regional programmes increased their broadcasting time and began to diversify their themes. However, in the case of *Telesur*, clichés predominated again, with regional sports, bullfighting and flamenco programming. In 1980, the legal framework for Radio Televisión Española (RTVE) was approved, allowing even more space for regional content. Also, the new regional governments created self-managed channels run from within their autonomous administration. The first ones to appear, breaking up RTVE's monopoly, were situated in the regions that have their own language (not in Andalusia): Euskal Telebista in the Basque Country (1982), TV3 in Catalonia (1984) and TVG in Galicia (1985) (Bustamante 2006, Maxwell 1994).

Radio Television of Andalusia (RTVA) opened its doors as a public entity in 1989. Since then, Canal Sur (the brand name for RTVA) has become the first medium to reach the entirety of the Andalusian autonomous territory. Beginning in 2008, the conversion to a digital television system will add two private channels in Andalusia, a territory that records the highest levels of television consumption in all of Spain (227 daily minutes in 2004) and the largest number of local television stations in the country (283 stations in 2002, 31 per cent of the total). The evolution of Canal Sur, however, caused controversy. With the arrival of commercial television at the beginning of the 1990s, competition for advertising increased and, consequently, programme quality went down as entertainment programmes boomed. To counter that trend, a second regional channel was created in Andalusia, Canal 2 Andalucía, focusing on cultural and educational programmes aimed at a younger audience. Also, the channel Andalucía Televisión was created, broadcasting via satellite and on-line, and offering the best of both channels to Andalusians living abroad; an example of regional transnational television. Currently, the most viewed programmes on RTVA are the news, magazine programmes and entertainment (music and comedy). Provincial news has reached very high rating levels as compared to other news programming broadcast on national channels since 1987. The same may be said for the soap opera *Arrayán*, where the actors retain their local particularities.

Despite its great regional appeal, the most significant criticism of the autonomous channel is that it keeps broadcasting a traditional and backward image of Andalusian society that does not correspond with the economic, social and political accomplishments of the region. The main examples of such an image would be, again, the numerous music programmes focusing on *copla* and flamenco, the popular folk singers and Andalusian comedians, and the widespread broadcast of popular traditions which are sometimes linked to religion (Holy Week, the El Rocío pilgrimage, bullfighting, and the *ferias* or local festivals). In past years, the most famous and controversial programme has been an evening talk-show, *Punto y Medio*, featuring people aged over 55 who search for a partner live on television. This talk show, which went into great detail about its participants, was broadcast from 4.00 p.m. until 6.00 p.m. and reached a peak audience share of 40 per cent. However, despite the polite manners of its host, critics argued that through the experience of its participants the programme communicated a conservative image of Andalusia. The phenomenon might be a consequence of the strong popular cultural roots that are being preserved among the older population, as well as among Andalusian people living abroad.

Although Canal 2 Andalucía might attempt to reform and rejuvenate the schedules of regional public broadcasting, the backward image of Andalusia can still be found in some of RTVA's programmes. Also, stereotypes of Andalusians such as supposed predilections for partying, laziness and having a strong sense of humour are current on national television. The Andalusian Parliament, for instance, presented a formal complaint in 2005 to public and private national television concerning the treatment that the region received through the characters in their fiction productions (*Boletín Oficial del Parlamento de Andalucía*, 2005). RTVA will have to confront its future challenges without forgetting that important older part of its audience (one of its main target groups). Among these challenges will be the regeneration of the collective imagination of Andalusia, one that would integrate the values of modernisation and avoid the broadcasting of stereotypes and social landscapes related to other periods. This is a challenge recognised by many of the political actors in charge of programming content.

Television in Wales

'A history of media', according to Colin Seymour-Ure (1996: 271), 'could easily slip into being a history of society as a whole.' This is certainly true in Wales where the broadcast media, in particular, are perceived to have had a central role in the creation and maintenance of a national consciousness. This notion of broadcasting as an emblem of national consciousness has always been a key characteristic of the campaign for Welsh broadcasting. Much of the writing on the history of broadcasting in Wales portrays the campaign as a struggle or battle against the forces of Anglicisation (see for example, Talfan Davies 1972).

In addition, however, there are other issues which characterise this 'battle' for Welsh broadcasting. First is the lack of consensus over the best way forward in terms of securing a broadcasting service for Wales which came to the fore, in particular, following the advent of television as a mass medium in the mid-1950s but which was also a feature of the campaign for a Welsh Fourth Channel in the 1970s. Second is the technological issue, whereby transmitters, by virtue of their location, served both English and Welsh audiences, thereby contributing to debates over the impact of radio and television on the language and culture of Wales. The third characteristic is the importance of developments in Welsh broadcasting in the wider context of UK politics and the numerous government-appointed committees of enquiry into broadcasting which proliferated in the twentieth century. The campaign for Welsh broadcasting also resonates with other areas of Welsh life such as education, publishing and cultural activities. That is, a community which sees itself as being under threat from an increasing tide of Anglo-American culture (in all its forms) resists and creates structures whereby the tide can be stemmed but also where there exists a sense of ownership and control from within the community itself (see Hechter 1975). Furthermore, the words of Jonathan Coe (1982: 54–5) need to be borne in mind: 'It is often said by broadcasters – or rather by the administrators of broadcasting – that Wales is a broadcaster's nightmare . . . broadcasting, more than any other sphere of public life, has been the focal point of political and linguistic conflict.'

In television terms, Wales has always been – in a phrase coined by Lord Hill, Chairman of the regulatory Independent Television Authority from 1963 until 1967 – 'an awkward area'. The situation was summed up in the 1969–70 *Annual Report* of the BBC's Broadcasting Council for Wales (1970):

> The major problem remains: that of serving a country with two languages. The problem continues to be not so much one of providing programmes in two languages but rather one of assessing the needs of Wales as a whole. There are varying views on the extent to which, for broadcasting purposes, Wales can be considered an entity. Some people, indeed, see Wales as an uneasy alliance of two cultures, two nations, with language as a divisive factor.

The language issue dominated debates on broadcasting during the 1970s, and opinion was polarised between those who complained of being deprived of national (i.e. 'British') network programmes because of the policy of broadcasting Welsh-language programmes as 'opt-outs' from UK-wide programming at various points during the day, and those who argued that scant regard was paid to the demands for increased Welsh-language broadcasting, particularly in 'good' viewing hours. The turning point came in 1974 with the publication of the government-appointed Crawford Committee Report on Broadcasting which recommended that the fourth channel (which was now technically possible) should, in Wales, 'be allotted as soon as possible to a separate service in which Welsh language programmes should be given priority' (*Report of the Committee on Broadcasting Coverage* 1974: 42). This ultimately led to the establishment in 1982 of the Welsh Fourth Channel, S4C, under the terms of the 1980 and 1981 Broadcasting Acts. Since that time, the channel has been at the forefront of Welsh-language developments and its efforts to preserve, promote and develop the indigenous language and culture of Wales have been praised. Its remit to cater for all shades of opinion and background within the Welsh-language audience has provided a valuable forum for debate and reflection. At the same time, the fact that it has to cater for all tastes (as the only Welsh-language service) means that it often finds difficulty in pleasing all the people all of the time. An example of this was the Welsh-language drama set in Cardiff, *Caerdydd* (the Welsh name for the capital city). Language purists complained of the excessive (as they saw it) use of English in a Welsh-language programme on S4C. However, the progressive audience applauded the programme makers for a more accurate and realistic representation of a bilingual city.

In structural and geographical terms, the commercial (advertising-funded) broadcaster, ITV Wales, is part of a larger concern – ITV plc – and this has led to fears of a loss of identity in terms of its relationship to Wales. Likewise, BBC Wales is still part of the larger 'British' corporation. Also, in terms of the audience, there are still homes which turn their aerials to pick up English-based ITV companies and BBC regions, for largely historical reasons. The infrastructure for a coherent print-based media is also absent. The so-called 'national newspaper of Wales', the *Western Mail*, has a solid readership base in south Wales, whilst the north Wales edition of the *Liverpool Daily Post* circulates widely in the north of the country. Interestingly, this north–south divide manifests itself in terms of the representation of Wales on the television screen. Welsh broadcasters have often been accused of a south Wales bias in many aspects of their programming. The accusation has not only been levelled at news programming (for paying undue attention to the capital city, Cardiff, and its environs) but also drama. BBC Wales's English-language serial, *Belonging*, and the Welsh-language daily soap opera, *Pobol y Cwm*, are set in the south Wales valleys and the south-west valleys, respectively and, in the past, have led to complaints of ignoring north Wales. More recently, Welsh-language dramas have instead been set in northern towns such as Caernarfon and Bangor, but an attempt to answer the needs of the whole of the Welsh population, in both languages, appears to be an impossible task.

There is no doubt that television in Wales has a role to play in the creation and maintenance of the sense of belonging. BBC Wales (and to a lesser extent ITV Wales) have been seen as visible signs of Welsh nationhood alongside institutions such as the National Assembly for Wales, the University of Wales, the National Library and National Museum and the National Eisteddfod arts festival. All broadcasters underline the 'national' (as opposed to the 'regional') nature of the television services. What have been less successful are the efforts of the Welsh broadcasters to gain a foothold in the UK-wide network services. Welsh output remains minimal on both BBC and ITV UK networks although the BBC Wales presence has recently been bolstered by the fact that the award-winning science fiction series *Doctor Who*, shown nationally in the UK, is produced in Cardiff by BBC Wales. There is, however, nothing inherently 'Welsh' about the series! At the same time, nevertheless, the internet and other electronic methods of communication have been seen as a threat to Welsh-language and Welsh-interest broadcasting, by consolidating and strengthening a global hegemony of Anglo-American culture; Kevin Williams (1996: 29) goes so far as to suggest that technological developments in the converging area of telecommunications may even 'kick away the chair of national identity'.

Broadcasting, from the outset, has been one of the key focal points for debates surrounding national identity and national consciousness in the 'awkward' area of Wales. In an age of increasing globalisation, the arguments are unlikely to disappear.

The National and the Global, but What about Europe?

The focus of this chapter was on the position of European television within national and global communication spaces. Bearing in mind the arguments of Morley and Robins (1995: 98), we will briefly address the question how European it is after all. An easy answer would be 'not very much'. As our case studies reveal, national orientation has been and still is dominant, though intertwined with the regional and the transnational. There have indeed been national ways of representing history, and we might argue that as such they are also very much European. As Morley and Robins (1995: 91) put it: 'it is a question of recognising the role of the stories we tell ourselves about our past in constructing our identities in the present . . . Identity is a question of memory, and memories of "home" in particular.' These memories are being created through news production; they are preserved as signs of an autonomous culture including language (as the use of dialect or a second language illustrates) and they are reproduced in narratives.

Historical fiction in Europe offers a diversity of stories serving the production of a shared past that enables the experience of 'home'. Its cultural heritage represents both collective memory in the sense that it represents 'the nation' and sub-cultural identities in the sense that it addresses the specific needs of diverse groups in society (in Finland and in the Netherlands) or a specific region (Flanders and the Netherlands). Even more so, as far as the latter is concerned, the idea of the national is expressed in the regional.

The national has not only been renegotiated within the smaller territories of regions that provide for senses of belonging; conversely, regional identity has become an articulation of national identity (Flanders, Spain/Andalusia and the UK/Wales). Regional news is not only more widely watched then national news; national news itself (through local outlets) is preferred over international news channels. News in particular is an example of how, in globalised culture, transnational programming is being adapted to the national culture. International content (such as news) apparently needs to be locally framed to serve the needs of its audiences.

What has become evident is the dominance of the national political and cultural context that informs the signifying practices of television in Europe. As a result we observe a fragmented European space, which, as is being increasingly argued, could also be read as a wealth of cultural diversity; in the end this constitutes European culture as unity in diversity.

References

Anderson, B. (1991) *Imagined Communities: Reflections on the Origin and Spread of Nationalism.* London, Verso.

Ang, I. (1990) 'Melodramatic identifications: television fiction and women's fantasy'. In: Brown, M. E. (ed.) *Television and Women's Culture: The Politics of the Popular.* London, Sage, pp. 75–88.

Baget Herms, J. M. (1993) *Historia de la Televisión en España 1956–75.* Barcelona, Feed-Back.

Baisnée, O. and Marchetti, D. (2000) 'Euronews, un laboratoire de la production de l'information "européenne"'. *Cultures et conflits* 38–9, 121–52.

Barker, C. (1999) *Television, Globalization and Cultural Identities.* Buckingham, Open University Press.

Bechelloni, G. (1999) 'Introduction'. In: Buonanno, M. (ed.) *Shifting Landscapes: Television Fiction in Europe.* Luton, University of Luton Press, pp. xv–xix.

Bennett, T. et al. (eds.) (1981) *Popular Television and Film.* London, Open University Press/BFI.

Biltereyst, D. and Van Bauwel, S. (2004) 'De Witte/Whitey'. In: Mathijs, E. (ed.) *The Cinema of the Low Countries.* London, Wallflower, pp. 49–58.

Boletín Oficial del Parlamento de Andalucía (2005), no. 211, Eighth Legislature, 3 June, pp. 12.869–12.874.

Broadcasting Council for Wales (1970) *Annual Report 1969–70.* London, BBC.

Buonanno, M. (2000) 'A comparative overview'. In: Buonanno, M. (ed.) *Continuity and Change: Television Fiction in Europe.* Luton, University of Luton Press, pp. 7–27.

Bustamante, E. (2006) *Radio y televisión en España: Historia de una asignatura pendiente de la democracia.* Barcelona, Gedisa.

Cardiff, D. and Scannell, P. (1987) 'Broadcasting and national unity'. In: Curran, J., Smith, A. and Wingate, P. (eds.) *Impact and Influences: Essays on Media Power in the Twentieth Century.* London, Methuen, pp. 157–73.

Caughie, J. (2000) *Television Drama: Realism, Modernism and British Culture.* Oxford, Oxford University Press.

Chalaby, J. (2002) 'Transnational television in Europe: the role of pan-European channels'. *European Journal of Communication* 17:2, 183–203.

Coe, J. (1982) 'Sianel Pedwar Cymru: fighting for a future'. In: Blanchard, S. and Morley, D. (eds.) *What's this Channel Fo(u)r? An Alternative Report.* London, Comedia, pp. 54–61.

de Leeuw, S. (1995) *Televisiedrama: podium voor identiteit: Een onderzoek naar de relatie tussen omroepidentiteit en Nederlands televisiedrama 1969–1988.* Amsterdam, Otto Cramwinckel.

de Leeuw, S. (1998) 'Omzien in wisselend perspectief. Geschiedenis in het Nederlands televisiedrama'. *Tijdschrift voor Mediageschiedenis* 1, 47–69.

de Leeuw, S. (2001) 'Television drama: narrative and identity'. Proceedings of the ISSEI 1998 Conference 'Twentieth Century European Narratives: Tradition and Innovation'. ISSEI Haifa University (CD-ROM).

de Leeuw, S. (2002) 'National identity and the Dutch monarchy in historical fiction: revisioning "the family on the throne"'. In: Brügger, N. and Kolstrup, S. (eds.) *Media History: Theories, Methods, Analysis.* Aarhus, Aarhus University Press, pp. 175–93.

Dhoest, A. (1999) 'Poorly imaging Flanders: economic determinants in Flemish television drama supply'. *Communications: The European Journal of Communication Research* 24:4, 423–41.

Dhoest, A. (2003) 'Reconstructing Flanders: the representation of the nation in Flemish period drama'. *Communications: The European Journal of Communication Research* 28, 253–74.

Dhoest, A. (2004a) 'Negotiating images of the nation: the production of Flemish TV drama, 1953–1989'. *Media, Culture & Society* 26:3, 393–408.

Dhoest, A. (2004b) '*Zichem* versus *Brideshead*: the construction of national identity in Flemish and British period drama'. *Film & History*, 2003 CD-ROM Annual.

Dhoest, A. (2005) 'Nostalgie en collectief geheugen. Kijkersherinneringen aan Vlaamse tv-fictie'. *Tijdschrift voor Mediageschiedenis* 8:1, 41–62.

European Television Task Force (1988) *Europe 2000: What Kind of Television?* Manchester, European Institute for the Media.

Friedland, L. A. (1996) 'World television news: an analytical map'. *International Communication Gazette* 57:1, 53–71.

Giddens, A. (1991) *Modernity and Self-identity: Self and Society in the Late Modern Age.* Cambridge, Polity Press.

Gripsrud, J. (1998) 'Television, broadcasting, flow: key metaphors in TV theory'. In: Geraghty, C. and Lusted, D. (eds.) *The Television Studies Book.* London, Arnold, pp. 17–32.

Gutiérrez Lozano, J. F. (2006) *La televisión en el recuerdo: La recepción de un mundo en blanco y negro en Andalucía.* Málaga, RTVA/University of Málaga.

Hall, S. (1996) 'Introduction: who needs "identity"?' In: Hall, S. and de Guy, P. (eds.) *Questions of Cultural Identity.* London, Sage, pp. 1–17.

Hechter, M. (1975) *Internal Colonialism: The Celtic Fringe in British National Development, 1536–1966.* Berkeley, University of California Press.

Heinderyckx, F. (1993) 'Television news programmes in Western Europe: a comparative study'. *European Journal of Communication* 8:4, 425–50.

Heinderyckx, F. (1998) *L'Europe des médias*. Brussels, Editions de l'Université de Bruxelles.

Hellman, H. (1996) 'The formation of television in Finland: a case in pragmatist media policy'. In: Bondebjerg, I. and Bono, F. (eds.) *Television in Scandinavia: History, Politics and Aesthetics*. Luton, University of Luton Press, pp. 91–111.

Hoskins, A. (2001) 'New memory: mediating history'. *Historical Journal of Film, Radio and Television* 21:4, 333–46.

Koivunen, A. (2003) *Performative Histories, Foundational Fictions: Gender and Sexuality in Niskavuori Films*, Studia Fennica Historica. Helsinki, Finnish Literature Society, pp. 247–63.

Koivunen, A. (2007) 'Koko kansan teatteri? Televisioteatterit Suomessa 1960–luvulta 1980–luvulle'. In: Wiio, J. (ed.) *Television viisi vuosikymmentä; Suomalainen televisio ja sen ohjelmat 1950–luvulta digiaikaan*. Helsinki, Finnish Literature Society.

Marchetti, D. (2002) 'L'internationale des images'. *Actes de la recherche en sciences sociales* 145:5, 71–83.

Maxwell, R. (1994) *The Spectacle of Democracy: Spanish Television, Nationalism and Political Transition*. Minneapolis, University of Minnesota Press.

McQuail, D. (1996) 'Transatlantic TV flow: another look at cultural cost-accounting'. In: van Hemel, A., Mommaas, H. and Smithuijsen, C. (eds.) *Trading Culture. GATT, European Cultural Policies and the Transatlantic Market*. Amsterdam, Boekman Foundation, pp. 111–25.

Morley, D. and Robins, K. (1995) *Spaces of Identity: Global Media, Electronic Landscapes and Cultural Boundaries*. London, Routledge.

Nelson, R. (2000) 'Framing "the real": *Oranges, Middlemarch, X-Files*'. In: Buscombe, E. (ed.) *British Television: A Reader*. Oxford, Oxford University Press, pp. 265–77.

Newcomb, H. (1997) 'National identity/national industry: television in the new media contexts'. In: Bechelloni, G. and Buonanno, M. (eds.) *Television Fiction and Identities: America, Europe, Nations*. Naples, Ipermedium, pp. 3–19.

Palacio, M. (2001) *Historia de la televisión en España*. Barcelona, Gedisa.

Report of the Committee on Broadcasting Coverage (1974) Cmnd 5774. London, HMSO.

Ruoho, I. (2001) *Utility Drama: Making of and Talking about the Serial Drama in Finland*. Tampere, Tampere University Press.

Saisio, P. (2000) 'Miten kirjani ovat syntyneet'. In: Haavikko, R. (ed.) *Miten kirjani ovat syntyneet 4*. Helsinki, WSOY, pp. 336–69.

Schlesinger, P. (1991) *Media, State and Nation: Political Violence and Collective Identities*. London, Sage.

Seymour-Ure, S. (1996) *The British Press and Broadcasting since 1945* (2nd edn). Oxford, Blackwell.

Talfan Davies, A. (1972) *Darlledu a'r Genedl*. London, BBC.

Van den Bulck, H. (2001) 'Public service television and national identity as a project of modernity: the example of Flemish television'. *Media, Culture & Society* 23:1, 53–69.

Williams, K. (1996) 'All wired up and nowhere to go', *Planet* 115, 29.

Williams, R. (1974) *Television, Technology and Cultural Form*. Oxford, Oxford University Press.

Wolton, D. (1990) *Éloge du grand public: une théorie critique de la télévision*. Paris, Flammarion.

6

American Television:
Point of Reference or European Nightmare?

*Ib Bondebjerg, with Tomasz Goban-Klas,
Michele Hilmes, Dana Mustata,
Helle Strandgaard-Jensen, Isabelle
Veyrat-Masson and Susanne Vollberg*

To a very large degree the USA has acted as both the hated and the celebrated 'other' in European media and culture in general. Especially in relation to the flow of television fiction and films, but also in entertainment programmes and talk shows, the USA has been very dominant on European television screens both in terms of the actual number of programmes and in the formats and genres that have been adopted, integrated and transformed. However, if we examine news and factual programmes, cultural programmes and programmes for children and young people the American influence or dominance is not nearly as strong.

The forms of American influence on European screens have changed historically and varied with national history. From the start, British television had a very privileged collaboration with US television, but in most countries with a strong public service tradition or a monopoly there were strong attempts to limit American dominance. Eastern Europe, of course, also has a special history in relation to US television and American culture in general. After communism took over and the Cold War became normalised, communist governments tried to ban American programmes, but they still had a strong influence in some countries, and after 1989 it is appropriate to talk about an American cultural invasion of these countries.

But even though European public service channels, at least, have tried to develop domestic programming to counterbalance US fiction programmes, in the areas seen as central to national cultural quality and identity such as arts programmes, factual programming and programmes for children and youth audiences, audiences have favoured American programmes as well. For viewers this has not been a choice between alternatives, but a matter of having both together. As the dominance of public service channels diminished during the 1980s and 1990s and commercial competition set in, American programmes and formats were among the most competitive and popular in the market. In all European countries there is a clear pattern of preference for national programmes in many genres, but for fiction and entertainment it is very clear that US products dominate quantitatively and are very popular. From the beginning of television and even before television this has provoked debate and caused alarm among cultural elites. But the history of the American cultural 'invasion' of Europe is a story that can be told in many ways: Western and Eastern Europe have different storylines, and at particular times in television history this cultural conflict has been more or less vigorous. Within Europe there are also national differences, with France being the culturally most aggressively anti-American nation.

'Americanisation'? Popular Culture, Cultural Wars and Globalisation

Long before television, from very early in the twentieth century, conservatives and the cultural left have shared fear and criticism of American cultural influence on Europe. But in the post-war period, American dollars (through the Marshall plans for reconstruction), American cinema, cartoons, and icons of modernity from jeans to milk shakes and Coca-Cola arrived on a massive scale all over Europe. There was both a European popular fascination with America and an intellectual fear of cultural levelling-down and threats to national culture. The rise of television to become the primary popular medium during the 1950s and 1960s increased this fear and the cultural gap between the cultural elite and the general public all over Europe. Tony Judt (2005: 220) quotes a French radical cultural critic remarking in *Le Monde* that America's chief gift to the world has been 'that even in the land of Stendhal the phallus is on its way to becoming God', and from an opposite political perspective the Christian, conservative editor of *Esprit* who wrote: 'We have from the outset warned of the dangers posed to our national well-being by an American culture, which attack the very roots of the mental and moral cohesion of the people of Europe' (Judt 2005: 221).

Quotes like this could be found all over post-war Europe, both in the west and in Soviet-dominated communist Europe, where the fight against all things American was of course very strong for political reasons as well. The liberators and economic helpers of Europe were seen as a threat to national culture, and anxiety was caused especially by the fact that children and young people seemed to embrace American culture and see it as a kind of liberation from a paternalistic national culture. American films, film stars, music and consumer goods represented modernity and a new age after war, poverty and depression. Tony Judt (2005: 221) notes for instance that between 1947 and 1950 the Coca-Cola company managed to establish plants in almost every

European country, and in 1950, when around 250 million bottles were sold in France, this again united the nation's intellectuals from right to left against this 'Coca-Colonisation'.

Television and the construction of nation-states

Television in the post-war societies of Western Europe was, among other roles, to act as an instrument to create a more homogenised national public sphere through both national news and factual programming and through drama and fiction. The first BBC Director-General, John Reith, is well known for his strong paternalistic public service philosophy: television was not dedicated to popular entertainment, but aimed to elevate citizens to a higher level of culture and information; in short, television should produce national citizens. In each European country we can localise trends in fictional and factual programming that helped to develop this feeling of a national 'imagined community'. But at the same time national television, whether public service or commercial, faced a growing globalisation and Europeanisation of the national space in which American culture was one important factor, but where increasing multicultural developments inside the national space and in the European space as a whole also created challenges to the hegemony of one, national culture. This was clearly reflected in news and factual programming, but also in fiction and in the growing interaction between national programmes and formats and global (not just American) trends and formats.

But as we shall see, the 'cultural war' with America, expressed strongly in post-war debates on culture and popular culture in general, was actually more of an ideological cover for a very direct influence, import–export trade and close collaboration between Europe and the USA in television. What seemed historically to develop as a contest between nations can more correctly be seen as an internal, national contest between high and popular cultural forms. In strong public service cultures both fictional and factual programming in the early years of television were very much oriented to national high cultural aspirations and had a very educational tone. This national conflict between high and popular culture had nothing to do with American culture as such. But US strength in producing and exporting popular genres influenced the national balance: in many ways American culture was seen as the equivalent of popular culture, whereas in fact popular culture was both a national and global phenomenon. The cultural war with America was therefore an indicator of the processes of modernisation and globalisation of post-war Europe in which television was one increasingly important aspect.

Americanisation, Europeanisation and globalisation

American influence in Europe is clearly not just a story of unwanted, cultural 'invasion', but also of liberation and modernisation of old, European cultures that were not sufficiently able to integrate globalisation and new mainstream popular cultures such as those of young people. American entertainment genres such as quiz shows and talk shows were popular with large groups among the audiences of national television in Europe, no matter whether they were 'the real thing' or adapted national versions. In fact viewers often preferred the national version, they had no worries about the levelling down of culture and Americanisation was not understood negatively.

But among intellectuals of different orientations this development and even the very existence of television was a sign of decay. In Denmark, for instance, a group of intellectuals published the book *Midt i en Quiz-tid* (In *Quiz-Time*; Svendsen 1958) where television entertainment programmes and American-influenced popular culture in general were called 'the new plague'. Dick Hebdige (1988) has traced similar metaphors for American influence and popular culture in the UK between 1935 and 1962, in relation to youth cultures, among other things. He reminds us of the attitude of left-wing intellectuals like Raymond Williams and Richard Hoggart, where the latter's inspiring book on post-war working class culture, *The Uses of Literacy* (1958), used the American term 'candyfloss' to metaphorically attack the new consumer and media culture.

But the tendency in both early television culture and even today to blame the Americans all too often underestimates on the one hand how much American television culture has inspired European television cultures, and on the other hand that many of the problems television in Europe has had in meeting the needs of a broad audience are caused by the lack of European collaboration. With the development of the European Union and the stronger emphasis on one European market without frontiers, a potential audience of about 550 million people is open to stronger film and television co-production across national borders. But apart from the long-standing EBU co-operation in news exchange, the Eurovision Song Contest and football, there is not much to indicate a more Europeanised audiovisual space. The latest figures from the so called Eurofiction project (Buonanno 2000) list a sample week of fiction by national origin in spring 1998. The figures (see table 6.1) show a large difference between the profiles of the five biggest European countries if we calculate national, European or American content in prime time as a percentage of total fiction output.

Prime time seems to be very national, and then American, apart from in Southern Europe, where American dominance is much greater. But in all European nations there is not much room for products or co-productions from other European countries. So blaming the Americans is closing the eyes to Europe's own problems, to the process of globalisation in general and the trend since 1990 towards a global, digitalised space in which individual television nations in Europe will have to find their place. In 1973 Raymond Williams spent time in the USA and he published a classic study (Williams 1974) in which he tried to define a clear difference between a European model of programming and an American model. This difference has gradually disappeared

Table 6.1   Television Fiction Output in Prime-time, by Origin (%)

	National	*European*	*American*
England	89	0	11
Germany	69	0	31
France	47	18	35
Spain	50	0	50
Italy	17	19	64

Source: Bunonnano 2000: 23.

with the development of a mixture of commercial and public service stations in all European nations.

There is still quite a difference in profile between the most commercially oriented channels and the most public service-oriented channels. But this is not a unique European situation. In American television not only PBS channels but also increasingly pay channels like HBO have a quite different profile compared with the big networks. To see American influence on European television as Americanisation – understood just negatively – is to forget that globalisation is never just a hostile one-way dominance, but also a negotiated 'glocalisation', where cultural forms meet and meld into new forms. American television is not an ideal reference point for European television, but it is certainly not a European nightmare either. The tendency to blame everything on the Americans is to overlook the many problems in Europe that are national or European, and to forget that if American television programmes and films have been popular in Europe it is probably because they are in many cases high in quality and have fulfilled a demand for a large European audience that national stations have not been able to meet.

The European Imaginary and the American Challenge: Television Fiction between the National and the Global

Fiction on television is closely linked to notions of national identity, since drama has the potential to express the 'imagination' of a nation and its history. Successful European mini-series like the British *A Family at War* (1970–2) about the life of a family during the Second World War, the Danish *Matador* (1978–81), a multi-plot story of life in provincial Denmark between 1930 and 1945, the American *North and South* (1989) about the American Civil War, the French *Les Collonnes des Ciels* (1984) about life in medieval France, or the German *Heimat* (1984) centring on the life of a German family from 1919 to 1984, all indicate that serial, historical family narratives can capture a broad national and sometimes global audience. Many series have also caused deep controversy and debate, and this goes for both European and American products. Many series, especially in Europe, were based on literary classics from either high or more popular culture, and there is an equivalent American phenomenon that is often called 'novels for television' (Bondebjerg 1993). In France, for instance, popular classics like Victor Hugo's *Les Misérables* (1985) gathered most of the national audience, in Germany both Thomas Mann's *Buddenbrooks* (1979–80) and the more controversial *Berlin Alexanderplatz* (1980), made by the film director Reiner Werner Fassbinder and based on Alfred Döblin's novel, had both a large national and European audience. Swedish television has also produced several international hits, for instance Jan Troells's *Udvandrerne* (1971), and *Hemsøboerne* (1966), based on August Strindberg's novel.

What these American and European series have in common is the ability not only to capture and express the imagination of a nation, but often also to touch upon strong conflicts in the past that still have implications for the present. Many series have therefore also created a debate, which in the case of American series being broadcast in Europe also very often triggered not just discussions about content, but also form and aesthetics in such a way that a 'cultural war' was again put on the agenda. Two of the most popular world-wide successes, the American series *Holocaust* (1978) and *Roots* (1977), are clear examples of this, and the controversies and kinds of debate they created when they were broadcast in Europe (and in the case of *Holocaust*, especially in Germany) tell an interesting story of American–European relations in tele-vision. *Holocaust* addressed the sensitive European phenomenon of the exter-mination of the Jews in the Second World War, but *Roots*, the globally most watched historical serial ever, addressed American racial questions that also fascinated a European audience, but its form was heavily criticised by the cultural elite. The question of Americanisation of European television was certainly also put on the agenda by the breakthrough of the prime-time soap series *Dallas* (1978) and *Dynasty* (1981), mainly because these series came at a time where European television was starting to undergo major shifts towards a more commercial and competitive television culture. *Dallas* and *Dynasty* signalled for some the ultimate doom of European public service and quality television.

From Holocaust *to* Heimat: *the power of popular American agenda-setting*

'Popular melodrama makes us feel in the midst of our everyday life the con-tours of abyss, it makes us feel that we live in the middle of these forces and they among us' (Brooks 1976: 205). In these words, Peter Brooks moves between the tragedy of high culture and the melodrama of popular culture, aesthetic forms that for him are connected. Melodrama is often seen as a particularly strong form in American television, and often looked upon with contempt by European critics. 'They claim that TV-films and mini-series are excessively sentimental, constructed and unrealistic, focusing too much on sickness and grotesque crime. But would they also mock Puccini's *La Bohème* because of its heroine suffering from tuberculosis, or Thomas Mann's *Der Zauberberg*, because it uses a sanatorium as a setting?' (Jarvik & Strickland 1988: 43). The latter quotation demonstrates the American defence against the European high-culture position.

The two positions are classical, frozen and antagonistic poles in the ritual culture wars between Europe and the USA which have been played out so many times in history that they seem impossible to overcome. But Peter Brooks certainly has a point, which was clearly demonstrated in 1979 when *Holocaust* was shown in Germany, and clearly managed what hours of documentary films and information had not: to make Germans feel and live through the horrors of everyday life in Nazi Germany, not least the brutal crimes against the Jews. Leading German and American critics and even the internationally known Jewish intellectual Eli Wiesel spoke against the melodramatisation and trivialisation of both Jewish and German history, 'history as soap opera' (Bondebjerg 1993: 309, Kaes 1989: 28). But many of these critics, for instance Sabina Lietzmann from the influential newspaper *Frankfurter Allgemeine Zeitung*, gradually changed their view as they saw the tremendous reaction among the German audience, and the very broad debate about history and personal memory that was triggered by the series. 'We still consider a good, objective documentary film the best instrument for information, when we know that for "ordinary" people this TV-serial meant that a mass audience was irresistibly drawn towards watching and compassion . . . *Holocaust* serves a purpose, no matter how much our taste and critical purity revolts against it' (Lietzmann, quoted in Kaes 1989: 33).

In Denmark the head of the drama department at DR, the only television station at that time, publicly announced that *Holocaust* would not be broadcast because it did not live up to the artistic standards set by the channel. A public storm followed in which Danish viewers demanded to see *Holocaust*, supported by many newspaper editorials, and where the tabloids especially talked about 'the paternalism of television' and its leaders (Bondebjerg 1993: 313). The serial was broadcast shortly afterwards, overseen not by the drama department but by the culture department, and carefully accompanied by discussions among experts after each episode. Viewing figures for *Holocaust* in Denmark were extremely high, although not as high as the figures for the national serial *Matador* which had started the year before. Intellectual voices, on the other hand, were extremely critical. But one critic, Jens Kistrup, from the conservative *Berlingske Tidende*, touched a raw nerve when he wrote on 6 March 1979: '*Holocaust* enters a media situation – or a civilization – which has created a fateful, even perilous gap between to enlighten and to entertain' (Bondebjerg 1993: 317).

This seemed to be the kind of gap the Americans were good at crossing, but one in which European creators and intellectuals were met with hostility. In Germany, audience reactions seemed to confirm that American melodrama was able to initiate real changes in the historical mentality of the generations that were part of what happened or had experienced it as children. But *Holocaust* was also the direct inspiration for the German director Edgar Reitz to begin the huge 11-part serial *Heimat*, broadcast in Germany in 1984 with just as big an audience as *Holocaust*, and which subsequently was screened success-fully in several European countries. In 1979, just after *Holocaust*, Reitz said: 'Authors all over the world are trying to take possession of their history, but very often find that it is torn out of their hands. The most serious act of expro-priation occurs when people are deprived of their history. With *Holocaust*, the Americans have taken away our history' (Bondebjerg 2005: 207). The clash between *Holocaust* and *Heimat* is a very prototypical case of the aesthetic and cultural clash between what is considered typically American popular culture, and what is considered a higher and more authentic form of European art television.

Heimat is an evident and important piece of European television art and the narrative and aesthetic strategy is very different from melodrama. But when cultural stereotypes are mobilised it is often overlooked that Europeans also make popular, melodramatic television and that Americans also have an in-dependent art cinema and television production culture. But nevertheless *Heimat* has a quite different approach to history: Reitz wanted to build a 'history from below' out of everyday structures of memory. Even though he also used the family as a narrative centre from which large-scale history is seen, he made room for a much slower than usual time structure, and a much more symbolic play with memory. The daring aspect of *Heimat* is that Reitz tries to illustrate the long course of German history from 1919 to 1984 and that he does this through everyday life and without going deeply into those parts of German history where larger moral issues become crucial. The Nazi period is portrayed without the normative and moral dichotomies built into *Holocaust*, which of course was criticised, but it is not hidden, it is just seen as a problematic but integrated part of longer structures in everyday life that are more important in the terms established for the serial. The controversy over *Holocaust* and *Heimat* is one good example of real difference between European and American television, but also of stereotypes that get in the way of a more neutral explanation (Elsaesser 1989, Hansen 1985, Kaes 1989).

Close encounters of a special kind: UK–US relationships in television drama

If the comparison of *Holocaust* with *Heimat* shows the tensions between an American way of storytelling and European narratives, there is, however, ample evidence in television history of other kinds of relations where America has learned from Europe and Europe has adopted formats and been directly inspired by American television. The UK–US relationship is a very special case because of the sharing of language and because of the early development of a duopoly of public service and commercial television, a duopoly that came much later in other European countries, for instance in Scandinavia.

Britain was the first European nation to form, in 1922, a non-commercial, state-supported public service broadcasting system, in part as an early response to fears of Americanisation of popular culture. Yet when the BBC democratised during the Second World War and when commercial television debuted in 1955, the USA served as a constant source of programme ideas and popularising techniques (Camporesi 2000, Hilmes 2003). Conversely, due to the strong residual influence of British culture in America, US regulators and reformers constantly looked to the British model as they struggled to shape and control the rapidly expanding commercial sphere of US radio and television. American notions of 'quality' and prestige in broadcasting have always been closely linked to British styles and genres, and British–American co-productions and the transnational flow of talent have contributed greatly to television drama in particular, on both sides of the Atlantic. The fact that each is the other's single largest market for exported programming (Steemers 2004) supports a strong flow of continued influence today.

During the early period of radio, though British and American broadcasters and regulators frequently used the example of the other to uphold their own system and distance themselves from their opposites across the Atlantic, a pattern of co-operation and influence quickly emerged. A system of transnational short-wave exchange developed in the early 1930s; NBC and CBS, the two major American networks, placed representatives in London to book special speakers and to cover important European events, and the BBC responded with an American representative to co-ordinate programmes in both the USA and Canada. As war approached, the BBC began to adopt programme forms and practices previously resisted as 'too American', such as regular scheduling, audience research and popular genres often based on US models, such as quiz shows, comedy-variety programmes and serial dramas.

For instance, the first BBC radio serial drama *Front Line Family* originated as a propaganda vehicle for the North American Service in 1941, inspired by US and French Canadian soap operas. It became one of the most popular programmes on the entire BBC Overseas Service and a mainstay of the Light Programme after the war (retitled as *The Robinsons*), leading to other serial dramas such as *Mrs. Dale's Diary* and *The Archers*, and eventually to such staples of British television culture as *Coronation Street* and *EastEnders* (Hilmes 2007). This programme also marked the recognition of women as a part of the audience with particular interests and needs, an audience that American commercial broadcasters had sought out eagerly since the 1920s but that most public service broadcasters preferred to subsume under the notion of the general public until wartime cast women as important defenders of home-front morale. On the US side, reforms brought about by the passage of the Communications Act of 1934 mandated that the networks provide public service programming, and they quickly turned to the BBC for models of serious music, advanced drama and educational programmes.

British gritty realism and Hollywood glamour: distinction and import

Television brought a new arena of mutual influence and exchange, particularly as commercial television ushered in another wave of popularisation and competition for audiences in Britain, and US networks struggled to compete in a rapidly expanding market. Both ITV and the BBC used American imports (within quota limits) to provide relatively inexpensive programmes with wide audience appeal that allowed them to focus funding on more prestigious factual and cultural programming. Some of these, like *I Love Lucy* and *Dragnet*, would go on to influence British domestic comedy-drama and police programmes even as Britain developed its own distinctively different focus and styles, notably an emphasis on 'gritty realism' that contrasted with Hollywood's glamour and slickness.

In the 1950s and 1960s some British producers tried for a 'mid-Atlantic' type of programme that appealed to both British and American audiences, seen in such shows as *The Avengers, The Saint, The Adventures of Robin Hood, Danger Man, The Prisoner* and even *The Engelbert Humperdinck Show* (Sellers 2006). British networks continued to feature numerous American television dramas through the 1970s and 1980s, though they tended to focus on the 'cheap, slick, escapist' formulaic material that British networks did not wish to commission themselves (Lealand 1984), rather than other types of US programme that would not have fitted this model. Though American networks aired relatively few direct British imports in the 1970s and 1980s, many adaptations from British series became important hits, such as *All In the Family* (from *Till Death Us Do Part*), *Sanford and Son* (from *Steptoe and Son*) and *Three's Company* (from *Man About the House*) (Miller 2000).

However, it was the USA's nascent Public Broadcasting Service that most consistently brought British programming to the American public starting in 1968, and both the factual and fictional forms experienced there would have a profound effect on television in both nations. Most notable was the import of British mini-series and serials such as *The Forsyte Saga, Upstairs Downstairs, I Claudius* and other literary adaptations and historical dramas that aired on PBS's *Masterpiece Theatre* (hosted by Alistair Cooke, a British-born, naturalised American with a long career in transatlantic broadcasting). Though serial drama had long been a staple of the American daytime schedule, it was the success of British drama on PBS that made it respectable prime-time fare.

Not only did a boom in US mini-series and made-for-TV movies grow out of this context – with more highbrow programmes such as *Beacon Hill* and

The Adams Chronicles quickly morphing into popular successes such as *Roots, Rich Man Poor Man*, and eventually *Dallas* – so did other British-inflected formats like the laugh track-free 'dramedy' (*Frank's Place, Hooperman, The Days and Nights of Molly Dodd*) and the mix of music and drama in Stephen Bochco's *Cop Rock* (influenced by Dennis Potter's *Pennies From Heaven* and *The Singing Detective*) and the recent *Viva Laughlin* (a version of the BBC's *Viva Blackpool*). US pay-cable channels such as HBO and Showtime would eventually bring the phenomenon back full circle in the late 1990s, mixing the mini-series format with the emphasis on the 'producer-*auteur*' model of production long employed in British television to spark a golden age of television drama in the USA, eagerly imported (and hailed as 'quality drama') by nations around the world: *The Sopranos, Sex and the City* and *Six Feet Under*, for example. Some of these, such as *Rome* and *The Tudors*, are US/BBC co-productions; US co-production has represented an important source of funding for British drama since the 1960s. Meanwhile, PBS and various cable channels continue to import hundreds of hours of British programming each year, even as the cable channel BBC America competes directly for US audiences.

Though the runaway global success of *Dallas* may have sparked a new wave of Americanisation fears across Europe in the 1980s, its roots can be traced not to some kind of 'essential' American culture but to a tangled path that criss-crosses national borders. The same is true, of course, of the reality-show format that has transformed prime-time schedules around the world since the early 1990s. In so far as European nations resisted the 'denationalising' influence of American broadcasting by defining their own national televisual culture in opposition to the popular commercial forms of American television, many backed themselves into a corner in which national culture meant only elite culture, excluding large sections of the population from this national address. This gave an advantage to US imports which has been challenged only recently by an upsurge in European popular television with a potential to transcend the national – from the *Eurovision Song Contest* to *Big Brother* and *The Office*, in all their variations. Meanwhile, British drama and dramatic talent have permeated every aspect of US television; not only has it become standard practice to include British characters in US dramatic casts (perhaps in view of the export market), but British actors play American lead characters in six new major series debuting in autumn 2007.

French television culture and the cultural war against Americanisation

The UK–US case demonstrates very close relations of learning and importing from each other, although we also see a clear form of distinction between British public service culture and mainstream American popular culture. UK imports of US programmes to a large degree functioned as a clear division of labour: UK products were either high-culture experimental or more realist popular programmes, whereas US imports satisfied a need for popular culture for the large, mainstream audience. US products were imported to fill the schedule with things that the British public service channels did not want to produce. But a more hostile cultural attitude to American television and culture in general is often found in other European countries, even though they have the same pattern of import of American programmes and are also in many cases influenced by American formats. In Europe, France is without doubt among the European nations with the strongest cultural opposition to American influence and many of the strongest critiques of modern popular culture and Americanisation are French.

France is one of the most productive nations when it comes to both national films and television fiction. Nevertheless some of the same controversies have been debated in France, and especially around the time of the global breakthrough of the prime-time soap *Dallas* in the 1980s, this debate was intense. As in all other European countries, television fiction after 1945 was strongly influenced by national identity and in France by a special need to rebuild a nation split after the war. The pioneers of French television mainly used drama to achieve these goals: classical literature adapted for television in serial forms and single plays were used to elevate the taste of the population and to construct a national identity based very much on elite culture. Gilles Delavaud (2005) analyses French television drama between 1950 and 1965 and points to the very strong connection with theatre in this early period. In Britain, Scandinavia and other parts of Europe, and even in early American television culture, we see the same tendency. The move towards television films and serials is a later phenomenon, since in the beginning television fiction was seen as a form for the broadcasting of adapted literature and theatre, but the debate on how to do this reflected the conflict between television as a mass medium and the norms of the established culture.

Early French television drama covered both classical and contemporary French and European theatre, but also many American plays. But interestingly enough more popular formats were also developed during the 1950s: boulevard theatre, musicals and even police series, melodramas and novels adapted for television, for example the police series *Enquêtes de l'inspecteur Grégoire* or *Le Chevalier de Maison-Rouge* after Dumas's novel (Delavaud 2005). As well as fictional programmes, historical and more broadly educational programmes were used to construct this televisual form of strong national identity, for instance the series *La Caméra explore le temps* (Stellio Lorenzi, Alain Decaux et André Castelot, 1957–66). These programmes did much to address national unity but also the role of internal conflicts such as the French Revolution and its consequences, Napoleon's Empire, the Commune and so on. Even the new president General De Gaulle (1958–69) interpreted some of these programmes as a little too centripetal and conservative.

American challenge – American influence

But it was also in the 1950s that the first American programmes appeared in France, in the form of series like *The Untouchables*, *Dead or Alive* or *Zorro*, for example. The programmes did not meet strong resistance among the French public, on the contrary some of the first French television series were made with strong influence from the American tradition, as can be seen in the very popular *Thierry la fronde* (1964), a kind of French superhero who is always fighting for a good cause.

The big change in French television culture came in 1974, when a new audiovisual reform divided the ORTF (Office de la radio-télévision française) into seven companies. The three new public service channels (RF1, RF2, RF3) resulting from this split introduced competition between public service stations. Competition and the increase of broadcasting time meant an increase in foreign programmes, because buying foreign programmes was much cheaper than investing in more ambitious French productions. From 1974 to 1987 there was no real investment in alternative, more prestigious French productions, so television fiction in this period was heavily dominated by American and British traditions and products, like *Colombo*, *Star Trek*, *The Fugitive*, *Kojak*, and *Starsky and Hutch*.

The American challenge to French dominance in cinema and also in television fiction was so strong in this period that cultural and political reactions started dominating public debate. Perhaps it was the worldwide and also tremendous French success of *Dallas* in 1981 that sparked the cultural war. One French reaction was to fight back in prime time with *Châteauvallon* (1985) which, however, completely failed to win the audience. The commercial competition increased in 1985 with two new private channels, La Cinq and the music channel TV6. La Cinq started by buying a huge amount of previously broadcast programmes, in particular American series. After a real success due to curiosity, the popularity of American popular culture and the weakness of its competitors, financial problems drove La Cinq to bankruptcy. Reactions to the whole situation and what was seen as American dominance were strong and came from both the cultural milieu and at the political level. Especially strong was the reaction of the socialist Minister of Culture, Jack Lang, at the UNESCO Conference in Mexico in April 1982, where he denounced the hegemony of the USA (though without stating the name of the country).

But perhaps more important was the affirmation of a 'French cultural exception'. The main principle of this was that culture cannot be considered a free-trade good like any other, and the consequence was the acceptance – under American protest – of a shared European notion that each nation has a certain right to protect and support its national culture. France, like many other European countries, had national support for its film industry and a public service remit for television. For France it was important to get this recognised and thus not only to go against the American conception of free trade in the cultural field, but also against the tendency in European television policy to demand 'television without frontiers'. France – and eventually also the EU – adopted this attitude, and also a certain quota for national and European television products.

Competition and serialisation: national and American fiction head to head

The audiovisual reform of 1982 and the emergence of private channels created a new television culture with a combination of commercial and service public channels. The number of broadcasting hours grew rapidly and created an enormous need for products to fill the many channels and hours. TF1 was privatised in 1987 and competition between the old and new channels meant that American imports of fiction went up, and also that national production learned from American formats to create national series in crime, soap opera and comedy form. The figures speak for themselves. In 1984 French television as a whole broadcast 11,000 hours of programming, while in 1987 total hours rose to 44,000. For fiction the figures were even more staggering: 1,200 hours in 1983 and 12,000 hours in 1989 (Cajueiro, Chaniac & Jézéguel 2000: 31).

With the privatisation of TF1 and the new commercial station La Cinq, fiction production in the 1980s was very much dominated by imported American series and French imitations. But the fall of La Cinq in 1992 triggered a change in production and programming in France, with a greater emphasis on national fiction and prestige production on many channels. Also TF1 decided to 'go French' and European after its first more commercial period. In this connection too, Arte – the joint French–German cultural channel – can be seen as a cross-national attempt to address a culturally elite audience by focusing on European programmes. During the 1990s French films and television fiction began to get better ratings. At the end of the 1990s and the beginning of the 2000s, the American 'threat' to French cultural identity seemed to have disappeared. French production dominated prime time and American productions (still very numerous) were mostly confined to the afternoon or night-time, and to cable channels.

One of the strategies adopted by TF1 was a return to the grand, historical costume drama, based on popular literature. The mini-series *Le Comte de Monte Cristo*, based on Dumas's novel and with Gerard Départdieu in the leading role, was a major success with an audience share of 54 per cent. But overall the figures from 1998 show that even though American fiction has strong influence on French and European television fiction and that American series circulate somewhere on the schedules every week, national fiction is completely dominant in the top ten list (and even the top 20): there are simply no other fiction programmes other than French ones, and TF1 is very dominant (see table 6.2).

Table 6.2 Top Ten Television Fiction Programmes in France, 1998

No.	Title	Date	Channel	Genre	Rating (millions)	Share (%)
1	*Le Comte de Monte Cristo*	28/9	TF1	Drama	24.5	54.0
2	*Un amour de cousine*	21/12	TF1	Comedy	24.2	50.5
3	*Julie Lescaut*	26/11	TF1	Action – crime	22.2	50.1
4	*Navarro*	23/4	TF1	Action – crime	20.6	51.2
5	*Une femme d'honneur*	5/3	TF1	Action – crime	19.9	45.2
6	*Weekend*	2/3	TF1	Comedy	19.0	43.1
7	*Les cordiers*	2/4	TF1	Action – crime	18.7	41.7
8	*Joséphine: profession ange gardien*	7/12	TF1	Comedy	17.5	36.7
9	*Pour mon fils*	6/4	TF1	Drama	17.4	37.8
10	*Bébé boum*	9/2	TF1	Drama	16.7	37.1

Source: Cajueiro, Chaniac and Jézequel, 2000: 41.

Looking at these programmes, however, it is quite obvious that although three national dramas (ranked 1, 9 and 10) have a national profile, the others are very much programmes with both a national profile and some American inspiration. American genre traditions are clearly important models, even though the results are seen by the audience as national productions. These French developments are not unique, since even in small European countries like Denmark and the Netherlands a new wave of national genre fiction for television developed, with a clear American genre inspiration combined with national content and an aesthetic based on the inclusion of everyday social realism and psychological conflicts. Denmark, for instance, won an Emmy two years in a row with, first, a romantic comedy series *Nikolaj & Julie* and, after that, a very professional crime series, *Unit One*, with a strong national and psychological touch. After the success of French series on commercial channels and on service public channels one might conclude that the danger of being flooded by American culture had disappeared. But around 2005 we see new trends again, not least through the new generation of quality American series on French prime-time television such as *Desperate Housewives, Sex and the City, Prison Break, Lost, Six Feet Under* and *Grey's Anatomy*, for instance. Also the Americans have learned that it is not always an appeal to the lowest common denominator and a broad family audience that is most successful. Quality pays off in programmes addressed to culturally oriented segments of both the American and European audience.

Rock 'n' Roll, Youth Culture and the Cultural Establishment

The turns of this historical narrative often repeat themselves, and the story of the arrival of jazz on the European continent in the late 1920s and early 1930s was largely repeated in the 1950s when American rock'n roll and, later, beat music knocked at the door of an emerging European public service culture. Even in the UK where commercial television had been introduced in 1954, broadcasting national popular music and the by now accepted jazz, there was no broadcast or even mention of Elvis Presley's first major breakthrough with 'Heartbreak Hotel' in 1956 (Hebdige 1988: 55). And if a mention of American rock music found its way into the press, and it did quite often from 1956 onwards, the tone might be as it was in the prominent music magazine *Melody Maker*, where a comment in that year was:

> Come the day of judgement, there are a number of things for which the American music industry . . . will find itself answerable for to St. Peter. It wouldn't surprise me if near the top of the list is Rock-and Roll . . . Viewed as a social phenomenon . . . Rock and Roll . . . is one of the most terrifying things to have ever happened to popular music . . . the antithesis of all that jazz has been striving for over the years – in other words good taste and musical integrity. (Hebdige 1988: 55)

If Elvis was neglected or criticised in the 1950s it is worth mentioning that it was also Elvis and his *Aloha from Hawaii Show* that comprised the first global live satellite transmission on 14 January 1973. In less than 20 years, controversial youth culture had become part of the global mainstream.

Rock'n roll hit Denmark in 1956 also, and was widely commented on in the press, mostly negatively and in connection with a wider moral concern about the post-war young generations that were developing a new youth culture very much inspired by American film, music and lifestyle. One prominent example was the opening of the Bill Haley film *Rock Around the Clock* in Copenhagen in 1957, which caused riots between police and young fans in the city centre that were widely discussed in the press and increased concern about the young generation. The established public service radio and television stations in most of Europe did the same as Danish radio: they ignored this music as long as they could. But through gramophones and via Radio Luxembourg, for instance, the young could defy the monopoly of television and radio. The pressure in the national media against this supposed Americanisation and lowering of cultural standards could not be sustained in the long run. In the UK, Denmark and all the other European nations a national rock'n roll culture was soon developed and in Denmark, for instance, regular pop programmes found their way on to both radio and television in the early 1960s.

In Denmark this came in the form of *Pladeparade* (1960), with a host introducing artists who performed to recorded music. In the UK one of the first
programmes was *Juke Box Jury*. The 1960s in all of Europe saw the breakthrough of beat and rock'n roll as a global mainstream culture that had both
a UK and a US centre, but was spreading to all countries which then developed their own national versions of the global mainstream. Music culture on
television, from its very early variants to its dominant forms in the 1990s with
the MTV channel, is therefore a very good example of how Americanisation
and globalisation turned into 'glocalisation'. In the very narrow and closed
European public service cultures of the early 1950s, American pop music first
seemed like an American invasion against which the older generations and the
cultural gatekeepers protested. But young audiences quickly adopted this new
global culture and made it their own, with both American and local idols,
and within a very few years the national media had to give space to the new
phenomenon.

This created great cultural debate in many countries and the American
'invasion' clearly exposed national gaps between popular culture and the
established culture. The national public service cultures only gradually made
room for entertainment and a broader variety of national and international
popular culture: aims for cultural education were interpreted in such a way
that forms of high culture dominated over popular culture. Globalisation and
the transformation of public service monopolies changed that situation. But
globalisation does not necessarily lead to homogenisation, as we have already
seen in the case of television fiction. *The Eurovision Song Contest* has since the
1950s been a mirror of Europe's response to global music trends, and it is
also interesting to note that originally global music channels like MTV have
had to regionalise, resulting for instance in the MTV Europe channel.

The Disneyfication of Europe? Disney, *Sesame Street* and European Children's Programmes

Since the 1930s Disney has been developing films, television programmes and
cartoons based on figures known to almost every child. After Coca-Cola, Disney
is the world's best-known brand (Drotner 2003: 7). In many countries the
Disney Channel is very popular, and even before cable television the regular
screening of Disney shows, with all their popular figures, had a ritual function in many families. In Denmark, for instance, *Disney Show* is broadcast every
Friday at 7.00 p.m. and begins the weekend for Danish families, and since
the late 1950s Disney's Christmas show has been a highlight both in cinema
and on television. From early on the Disneyfication of Europe has been met
with just as much scepticism as other forms of Americanisation, but when
in 2001 Janet Wasko published her 18-country comparative study of the reception of Disney the majority of respondents did view Disney as American, but

it was humour and fantasy that were identified as the most central features (Drotner 2003: 15).

It is to be expected that the anxiety over Americanisation is strong in connection with children, and that European television channels, especially public service channels, feel a strong obligation to educate and entertain the child audience. In early European television culture, television for smaller children was not defined in relation to school education. Television for children aimed to connect with their creative play world, to stimulate their creativity and encourage them to discover the world in a playful, experimental way (Christensen 2006: 66–7), and the BBC's *Andy Pandy* (1956–8) is a good example of this. But early European television for children was nevertheless oriented towards a concept of playful education. Children were not imagined to be at school, except in those programmes directly targeted at schoolchildren, but it was often schoolteachers who made the programmes in the early period, and this could be seen and felt.

As a kind of counter-programming to this playful education, fictional programmes for children were often American in the early period, like *Lassie*, *Stan and Laurel* or Disney films and cartoons. In Scandinavian and British television the expansion in nationally produced children's fiction programmes is impressive, however. Series based on Astrid Lindgren's *Pipi Langstrømpe* (*Pippi Longstocking*) or *Emil fra Lønneberg* (*Emil from Maple Hills*), for instance, clearly express a concept of childhood where the child is much more central and where the child's rebellion against grown-up norms is celebrated. The British–American *The Muppet Show* can be seen as a puppet version of this kind of anarchic children's world, with much physical activity and slapstick comedy. In 2004 this programme was bought by Disney, which indicates that American and European trends in this area can meet and fertilise each other. The case of *Sesame Street* and Scandinavian and European public service stations' reactions to it, however, illustrates cultural differences.

Sesame Street and the American–European concept of TV for children

When the head of the pre-school section in Danish Radio, Jimmy Stahr, came home from a visit to Children's Television Workshop (CTW) in the USA in 1972, he brought a sample of *Sesame Street* with him, though he had already made up his mind that DR should not buy the programme (Rigsarkivet, archive no. 1187, B&U-afleveringen, 'Udsendelser' package no. 28, henceforth RA 1187). On the other hand Stahr was fascinated by the show; not by its content, which he found to be too narrowly focused on stimulating children's intellectual skills, but by the huge budgets, the enormous preparations that went into the show and especially the puppets. He liked the frog Kermit so much that he suggested that the Danish pre-school programme *Legestue* (*Play Room*) should have its own frog, Kaj, a jazz-frog (Vemmer 2006: 146). This simultaneous rejection of and fascination with *Sesame Street* illustrates the ambivalent attitude towards American programmes for children in Denmark in the early 1970s, and the attitude to this particular programme also indicates some of the ambivalence around cartoons and Disney.

One of the founding ideas of DR's Children's department was that the programme makers should act as the spokespeople for children. Programmes would not focus on education, but on the everyday lives of children (Jensen 2007, Vemmer 1970). The attempt to be child-centred, a growing interest in viewers, and discussions about how and to what extent their wishes should be met, are all important factors in understanding DR's ambiguous attitude towards *Sesame Street*. In *Sesame Street* the Danish producers saw a programme which was very popular among children, parents, educators and producers, but on the other hand the programme embodied a host of things from which the department disassociated themselves. Thus *Sesame Street* challenged DR's way of making and thinking of children's television. To a large extent the dilemmas and challenges which *Sesame Street* presented to DR can also be said to apply to SVT, NRK and BBC's attitudes towards *Sesame Street* in Sweden, Norway and Britain, though SVT and NRK were more positive than DR and BBC (Bakøy 1999: 290–1, Buckingham et al. 1999: 35, Jensen 2007, Rydin 2000: 195–6).

Sesame Street was intended mainly for an audience of disadvantaged children, although its creators also believed it had the potential to challenge what they perceived as decreasing standards in children's television as a whole (Morrow 2006: 47). The programme premiered in November 1969 and became a huge success in the USA and also among producers in other countries. Until 1973 it was only possible to buy the programme as a whole, which West Germany for instance did with *Sesamstrasse*, but after 1973 it was also possible to buy a selection of items from the programme for use in other (national) frameworks. This fragmented model was called *Open Sesame* (RA 1187). Denmark, Sweden and Norway offered to buy *Sesame Street* in 1971 (though that date is uncertain) and *Open Sesame* in 1973 (Bakøy 1999, RA 1187, Rydin 2000). Reports from DR's children's department about *Sesame Street* reveal what the producers saw as the major differences between American and Danish children's and television cultures, and how they regarded American children's television as on the one hand a role model and on the other a frightening version of what the (commercial) future for children's television might be like.

In contrast to *Sesame Street*, the Danish *Legestue* was inspired by the British *Play School*. These Danish and British programmes' child-centred values were based on a notion of two-way involvement, to stimulate the child in ways that made him or her engage with society. Thus *Legestue* was based on the notions of the child as an active citizen and childhood as a critical source in society, ideas rooted in a progressive and romantic pedagogical tradition. *Sesame Street* was seen as a step backwards to a time where children's culture was (only) focused on stimulating children in terms of education. From the child-centred perspective *Sesame Street* lacked respect for children as individuals who had the right to programmes which stimulated both social and emotional skills, and challenged their imagination and creativity.

The BBC also decided not to buy *Sesame Street* (Buckingham et al. 1999: 35). The head of the BBC Children's Department, Monica Sims, like the producers in Denmark, saw the lack of a social context as an aspect which made the programmes authoritarian and pacifying. In the understanding of the child as an active and critical citizen the function of children's culture and public service television were connected. The pacifying effect which *Sesame Street* was believed to have, because of its one-way communication (talking to, not with the children) and its detached education, was thus one of the worst aspects of the programme from a Danish and British child-centred and public service television perspective (Buckingham et al. 1999, Jensen 2007).

What the Danish producers perceived as authoritarian undertones and pacifying effects in *Sesame Street* was not only connected to the content of the programme, but also very much to its commercial style. Because it was commercial, smooth and professional, the style was seen as alluring to children, and thus considered dangerous because it introduced an aesthetic universe of commercials, which was believed to have a strong habit-forming effect (RA 1187). The Danish producers dreaded the commercial style of *Sesame Street* as an unavoidable future for Danish television and they feared that if *Sesame Street* was shown in Denmark, it would be the beginning of the end of the Danish way of making children's television, because children – and perhaps also their parents – would be attracted by the commercial style and therefore demand more of it (Jensen 2007, RA 1187).

Still, even though there were several objections to the style of *Sesame Street* there is no doubt that the producers of pre-school programmes in Scandinavia were also fascinated by it. Both SVT and NRK did start to make programmes with direct educational aims, although neither the Swedish programme *Fem myror är fler än fyra elefanter* (*Five Ants are More than Four Elephants*) nor the Norwegian *Så rart* (*So Odd*) adapted the commercial style of *Sesame Street* (Bakøy 1999: 290–1, Rydin 2000: 196). The perception of television as a means to overcome class and information barriers was certainly inspired by *Sesame Street*, though it was used in a more politically and socially engaged way in Scandinavian than in the USA.

Ideological Enemies and Cultural Heroes: American Culture and Television in Eastern Europe

Research on television under communism in Eastern Europe is not yet well developed and there may be a tendency to look at the situation in this region as if it were similar in all countries because of Soviet dominance. However there are very clear differences between, for instance, the GDR with the proximity of its western half to capitalist West Germany and the very special status of Berlin; Poland, with its long tradition of autonomy, a strong Catholic Church and a rich, venerable culture and the more undeveloped Romania. Each of these countries adopted different strategies towards America and American culture under communism, and audiences had very different access to American television and culture in general. The very restricted relations with American culture were differently handled politically, but changed almost overnight after 1989 when Eastern Europe moved from state control to a free-market economy. This transition was not necessarily positive, since many areas of public life and communication were suddenly bought into by multinational and American companies. Entities once seen as official cultural enemies and secret cultural heroes in a dark communist reality were suddenly there as economic invaders and conquerors.

Between East and West: Television in the GDR

In the nearly forty years of its existence, television in the German Democratic Republic (GDR) was influenced by the different relationships of the regime, with Western enemies and Eastern friends. The television systems of both the GDR and of the Federal Republic of Germany (FRG) were characterised by reaction and counter-reaction to each other and their regional neighbours. In its own programme planning GDR television tried to react strategically to the structures of Western television (Dittmar 2004) and learn from its enemy. The look to the West was omnipresent for the audience as well as for the leaders of socialist television. But the political leadership was also highly interested in conveying central political-ideological images to influence people's behaviour.

But political relationships between the GDR and the USSR also had a great influence over programming. GDR television was in tension between politically decreed images of friends and enemies: the persistently emphasised fraternal friendship with the Soviet Union and the enmity with West Germany and America. But the majority of viewers rejected Soviet telecasts, while American films and serials broadcast on West German television were very popular. The people in charge of the television schedule were in a dilemma, since they were forced to make programmes that reflected the policies of the SED (the United Socialist Party of East Germany) and at the same time to keep viewers away from FRG television by offering attractive entertainment (Dittmar & Volberg 2003, 2004, 2007).

The proximity of GDR television to the Soviet Union already loomed on the opening day of the official test programme. The leadership chose the 73rd birthday of Stalin on 21 December 1952 as the foundation day of the new medium. The first television set available in GDR was called the 'Leningrad', and the first day of television programming closed with the Soviet documentary film *Stalingrad*. In January 1956 regular broadcasting started under the name Deutscher Fernsehfunk (DFF), and by the beginning of the 1960s, when one million sets had been sold, television in the GDR had developed into a mass medium. From the late 1960s viewers living close enough to Western transmitters had a pleasing choice of programmes, and after 1969 viewers could choose between at least five channels.

Viewers officially had the freedom to choose between different programmes on GDR channels, but not to switch to the Western channels. But viewers of West German programmes preferred American serials and films. The Communist Party, on the other hand, kept emphasising that co-operation with the Soviet Union was strongly linked to the role of GDR television in the greater struggle against Western enemies. The DFF 2 channel, for instance, was based on Soviet films and documentaries, for example the programme slot *Für Freunde der russischen Sprache* (*For Friends of the Russian Language*), shown first once a week and from October 1973 twice a week. But viewers overwhelmingly rejected the programme.

At the beginning of the 1980s GDR television lagged more and more behind developments in the West. The West German media landscape changed with the introduction of the so-called 'dual system' of public and commercial networks. 'Television as entertainment' became increasingly important, and GDR television had to be reformed. The most important element in the reform was the internationalisation of DFF 1 and DFF 2 through much increased import of American and West European films and programmes, and a much stronger emphasis on entertainment in prime time. Fiction and films, above all from the USA, West Germany, France and Britain, dominated, while the number of Soviet programmes was seriously reduced.

Even before 1989 American programmes thus influenced GDR television, first of all through West German television. But it also developed a television culture of its own, which was not as politically exploited as news and factual programmes, and included cultural programmes, entertainment and programmes for children. Official anti-Americanism and support for the GDR/ Soviet friendship was not firmly rooted among the viewers. The GDR's viewers negotiated a curious zigzag course, trying to avoid the more propagandistic parts of the television schedule. After the fall of the Berlin Wall in 1989 the television system in East Germany changed rapidly, and the *Abwicklung* (restructuring) of GDR television led to the establishment of three new broadcasting corporations in January 1992, and the newly formed East German states were incorporated in the media system of the FRG.

From forbidden fruit to overabundance: American influence on Polish TV

In Poland, as in many European countries, until the communist takeover the cinema was strongly dominated by American films, sometimes so much that national quota systems were introduced to protect national film production. But the period of intensive US import of films was brought to an immediate halt in the early 1950s when the Stalinist Soviet Union imposed a strict 'social realism' cultural policy on all its satellite states. In the Stalinist era between 1948 and 1958, only one US film was screened: *The Adventures of Martin Eden* (1942), a story of a sailor who, as a member of a trade union, fights against the capitalist system. In addition, US jazz, country music and especially popular boogie-woogie were blacklisted.

After the first peaceful Polish revolt against the Communist regime in October 1956, cultural policy was changed and imports of foreign books, records and films were allowed. To a certain degree, the government supported this reopening of relations with Western culture. French, Italian, British and even Hollywood films began to be shown. However, foreign films screened in Poland were selected by a state commission composed of a highly educated group of liberal filmmakers, writers and academics, together with a few party apparatchiks.

The situation changed with the advent of colour television in the 1970s. An even more liberal cultural policy of the communist government, together with the inability of state television to provide enough quality programming for two state channels, brought such mini-series as *Washington Behind Closed Doors* or *Dynasty* into Polish homes and strengthened the image of America as a free, democratic and rich country. This was in accordance with common knowledge and imagination, but strongly differed from traditional communist propaganda. The power of these images was seen during the 1980s, when the revolting Polish workers and intellectuals frequently referred to democratic procedures (for example, Congress hearings) or living standards 'in the West', by which they meant the wealthy ranches and shopping malls of Dallas.

After the fall of the Communist regime a new law in 1994 allowed private, commercial television stations to operate. After this breakthrough, the audio-visual media became flooded with American music, films and television miniseries. These productions were professionally made, appealing to viewers, and most importantly cheap to buy. The first Polish commercial television station was Polsat, but due to its huge amount of American programming it is often referred to as 'Amsat'. In the sphere of films, the same happened. Occasionally, Polish productions based on Polish classical literature beat American blockbusters in audience size. However, the only means of watching Polish films regularly is the satellite and cable channel Kino Polska. Cable and dish owners have access to European movie channels, and both satellite and cable channels also broadcast US films and European classics, with some new productions co-produced with HBO.

After 1989 Polish viewers and moviegoers have been strongly influenced by US productions, which – if we accept George Gerbner's (Gerbner & Ross 1976) 'cultivation theory' – thus become the basic form of acculturation. This is also clearly seen in television commercials, where the US way of life appears in Polish advertising. America has, since the late nineteenth century, functioned as a paradise in the minds of Poles. Letters from the first immigrants, journalistic reporting and, since then, films and television mini-series especially, have sustained this image of America in the collective imagination. The commercials that have been flooding the Polish market since the 1990s exploit that mythical image for market purposes (Szymkowska-Bartyzel 2006).

A special kind of relation: Romania and American culture

From 1956 until 1989, Romanian public television was a medium dedicated to socialist propaganda and state control. As the only broadcaster in the market, with one main channel and a temporary second one between 1968–85, it was placed under the supervision of the State Secretariat of Press and Propaganda and was ultimately at the disposal of the dictator Nicolae Ceauşescu and monitored by the Securitate (communist secret service). Despite the state's propagandistic uses of television, American influences on the screen were not absent. However, they were ideologically and politically filtered so as to build upon socialist ideology.

An examination of the magazine *Cinema* (published in Bucharest) shows that while the dominant topics on television were social investigation, history, folk culture, sports events, national scientific achievements or socialist education, genres such as variety entertainment, television drama, news, cultural, educational and scientific magazines, historical films and melodrama abounded on the screen (*Cinema* 1972: 38). Entertainment on communist Romanian television was seen as a means of maintaining peace and pleasing the socialist citizen, as documents in the Securitate archive reveal (Securitate Archives [henceforth SA] D135/7: 105). It consisted primarily of Saturday night musical variety shows, the Sunday afternoon family magazine, Sunday night films and Wednesday night *Telecinemateca*. The imported series *Daktari, Kojak, Mannix, Bewitched* and *Lost in Space* were all broadcast in the early 1970s and most of them were part of the programme *Album Duminical* – a Sunday afternoon family magazine. However, the airing of American series in communist Romania was put at the service of the Party's interests. At the end of the 1960s and early 1970s such liberalised television content, together with the growing sales of television sets from 25,000 in 1960 to 395,000 in 1975 (Deletant 1999: 113) and the boom in house building in 1966–70, was aimed at the domestication of television (Ceauşescu 1971). The domestication process was successful and in the 1970s, on Saturday evenings between 8.00 p.m. and 9.00 p.m. when Western drama was aired, the streets of Bucharest were deserted.

More importantly, however, such American television content was part of Ceauşescu's effort to assert the country's autonomy from the Soviet Union. The goal was to attract new Party members with the legitimising of anti-Russian feeling, by making censorship milder and easier to negotiate with (Schopflin 1983: 166). The broadcasting of American content on Romanian television played a double role in the politics of the communist regime. First, television became an accepted social apparatus within the private household, a foundation on which the future ideological functions of Romanian television were to be built. And secondly, by means of liberalised television content, among other factors, Ceaușescu asserted independence from the Soviet Union and gained Western approval.

The concession of American content on television was politically managed to consolidate the specific Romanian version of socialism. It was the efficiency of American production techniques and American 'scientific' management that made America a utopia for countries with Marxist ideologies. The desire for America's efficient modes of production was adapted into the Romanian context in terms of privileged economic relations with the USA, but also in terms of an ideology that prioritised work versus leisure and productivity over consumerism. American impact was thus tempered by an adaptation to Romania's political interests.

The liberalisation of television content in the 1960s and early 1970s contributed to Romania's separation from the Soviet Union and US approval. During Ceaușescu's visit to the USA in 1972, Richard Nixon was quoted in the Romanian press: 'We admire [the president of Romania]. We admire his people for their faith in their independence, in their sovereignty and for their decision to defend that' (translated from *Cinema* 1973: 3). Ceaușescu's meeting with Nixon was eulogised as a wise initiative to join in with world affairs and therefore enhance national development. Romania's orientation towards the USA in 1975 gave the country most favoured nation status in the US (Mastny 1986: 250). And for communist Romania, this meant the possibility to acquire modern Western technology and become an integral participant in world affairs.

The opening-up towards the USA was tailored according to particular national interests. The television programme *Apollo* – named after the American Space Program – underlined Romania's acquaintance with global technological developments, while at the same time its programme maker was criticised by the Securitate for overpraising the achievements of American science (SA D135/1, Annexe 2, no. 156: 2). The openness towards America occurred only to the extent to which it promoted the Romanian socialist nation. When Alyce Finell, manager of the American ABC network, was allowed to visit the Romanian television studios her visit was closely planned and watched. The notes submitted to the Securitate about her visit reproached her inconvenient curiosity at the presence of armed forces within the television building (SA D135/1, Note 100/0047180, 30 October 1982, no. 388: 2).

The desire for efficient modes of production, adopted from American ideology, was translated into a prioritising of work over leisure and production over consumption, which led to a decrease in broadcasting hours in the 1980s and a reduction in entertainment within television programming. During 1968–74 the main television channel broadcast around 10–11 hours per day. In the mid-1980s, broadcasting time had been cut to 4–5 hours per day at weekends and two hours on weekdays. Saturday and Sunday night films were now heavily cut due to the lack of broadcast time. *Dallas*, broadcast on Saturday evenings in the early 1980s, was significantly censored and shortened. In the 1980s television had become primarily an informative and educational medium meant to energise the masses in their working lives (Deletant 1999: 125–6). Entertainment was seen as necessary only in so far as it kept the population satisfied and reduced the risk of dissatisfaction.

The desire for all things American after the fall of communism in 1989 was even more significant since it represented an aesthetic and ideological opposition to the newly abolished oppressive rule. Until 1994, when the first national private networks appeared in Romania, state television remained the only national broadcaster. The overnight rise in broadcasting hours from a maximum of 4–5 hours per day in 1989 to 24 hours found the institution lacking the necessary production resources. Consequently, imported entertainment and films dominated television programming, at the expense of news or national productions. Early in the 1990s American series such as *Dallas, Bonanza, Beverly Hills 90210, Santa Barbara, Twin Peaks, Star Trek* or *The Twilight Zone* presented audiences of public television with diverse, uncensored Western content. American music videos could be requested by viewers, in another new development for state television.

Yet the dominance of American imports on state television concealed the lack of local production resources as well as the lack of legitimacy of television personnel. Being the only national broadcaster in the market until 1994, the Americanisation of content led to the institutional derailment of public television. The public broadcaster was severely criticised in the press for its poor performance, though a discussion of what the performance of public service television ought to entail never took place. In the six years after the revolution, state television had six general directors, and the editors in the news department changed constantly. The lack of identity of post-revolutionary public television facilitated state interference in the institution. In 1996, during the presidential elections, state television had an overtly partisan position favouring the ruling party, even though it lost the elections. The Americanisation of content served to conceal the ongoing political manoeuvring in state television, a situation resembling that during the communist regime. It seemed as if, once again, entertainment was designed to keep the citizen satisfied and prevent popular criticism of state power.

With the rise of ProTV – a private network in an American consortium and primarily owned by Central Media Enterprises, the public broadcaster gradually lost significant audience ratings. By 1997, ratings placed public service television third in order of preference with 46 per cent of the audience, while ProTV was on top with 62 per cent (Coman 2004: 30). The subsequent competition for ratings led state television to operate increasingly in the same ways as commercial channels, culminating in September 2002 with the change in time slot of the main news bulletin from 8.00 p.m. to 7.00 p.m., just like the private networks (Stavre, 2004: 59). Interestingly, the decision was not based on any market research and underlined the ease with which state television altered its public identity.

The long-term lack of public identity for post-communist state television speaks of the extent to which the rapid post-1989 Americanisation of content occurred within an inadequate local institutional environment. While such programmes pleased the public and alluded to the democratic values of America, they concealed the lack of production resources and of consolidated management within state television. All these factors facilitated continuity in political control of the institution even after the 1989 revolution. By contrast, the American-owned ProTV distinguished itself mainly by the local adaptation of American imports. During the communist regime, American influences on state television were carefully controlled and exploited for national political reasons, but in the period after 1989, the uncontrolled Americanisation of content within an unconsolidated institutional environment delivered public television up for political interference.

True Love, Co-operation and Global War

The very popular Danish writer, Dan Turèll (born 1946) once wrote: 'I am American-Danish. And a very large part of my generation is American Danish ...We did not meet Marguerite Viby [a popular Danish movie star] at Cassiopeia, but Elvis Presley at Heartbreak Hotel . . . for us it was not sausages, but hot dogs, not soda water, but milk shakes. No grand love, but *True Love, True Love*' (in *Politiken* 5:1, 1976, quoted from Barlyng & Schou 1996: 324). Many people of the post-war generations in both Western and Eastern Europe can assent to this, although their societies and television cultures gave them different kinds of access to 'the American way of life' and those strong images connected to the American lifestyle, namely commercials, films and television series. There is no question about the enormous influence of American culture (including audiovisual culture) on Europe since 1945 – and even before that.

However, it must also be noted that national dominance in both fiction, children's programmes, news and documentaries is very strong. In many countries American fiction cannot compete with national products, but especially in the smaller European countries there is not enough national production to meet the demand, and here American products come in handy. It must also be noted that there is a European tradition that is very different from American mainstream production: the German *Heimat* or the British *The Singing Detective* are good examples. The same can be said about the more anti-authoritarian and creative forms of children's programmes. Mutual inspiration and co-operation is more important in some periods than others. But certainly American series taught the Europeans many a lesson on how to reach an audience, and in many European countries both public service and commercial channels have managed to create a national tradition in, for instance, crime fiction, soap opera and comedy. The British way of combining gritty realism and soap forms in the long running *Coronation Street* is a good example, and crime fiction has a particularly strong position in both Britain, France, Germany, Italy and the Scandinavian countries.

The American–European relationship in television is not a cold war, it is rather a hot war, a war where true love and anxiety over independence and excessive dominance are combined. In the history of European television it has sometimes been too easy to blame the Americans. Many of the developments in European television have not been caused by American dominance, but by internal struggles between popular culture and high culture within the nation-states of Europe. The decision to create commercial alternatives to public service was not influenced by America, but was a result of globalisation in general and of political decisions. With the development of the European Union and a more coherent audiovisual policy a framework for a broader European market is basically present. However Europeans do not watch television from other European countries in very large numbers. This is clearly not the fault of American television. If there are problems in European television in the age of globalisation, perhaps it is time to look at Europe with a more critical perspective instead of attacking the Americans.

References

Bakøy, Eva (1999) *Med fjernsyn i barnets tjeneste: NRK-fjernsynets programvirksomhet for barn på 60- og 70-tallet.* PhD thesis, NTNU Trondheim.

Barlyng, M. and Schou, S. (eds.) (1996) *Københavnerromaner: Urbanitet & Æstetik.* Copenhagen, Borgen.

Bondebjerg, I. (1993) *Elektroniske fiktioner: Tv som fortællende medie.* Copenhagen, Borgens forlag.

Bondebjerg, I. (2005) 'European art television and the American challenge'. *Northern Lights. Film and Media Studies Yearbook* 4, 205–37.

Brooks, P. (1976) *The Melodramatic Imagination.* New York, Yale University Press.

Buonanno, M. (ed.) (2000) *Continuity and Change: Television Fiction in Europe.* Luton, University of Luton Press.

Buckingham, D. et al. (1999) *Children's Television in Britain.* London, BFI.

Cajueiro, M. A., Chaniac, R. and Jézéguel, J.-P. (2000) 'Towards a diversification: French TV fiction in 1998'. In: Buonanno, M. (ed.) *Continuity and Change. Television Fiction in Europe.* Luton, University of Luton Press, pp. 29–46.

Camporesi, V. (2000) *Mass Culture and National Traditions: The BBC and American Broadcasting 1922–1954.* Fucecchio, European Press Academic Publishing.

Ceauşescu, N. (1971) *Romania pe drumul contruirii societatii socialiste multilateral dezvoltate.* Bucharest, Editura Politica.

Christensen, C. L. (2006) 'Børne- og Ungdoms-tv'. In: Hjarvard, S. (ed.) *Dansk tv's historie.* Copenhagen, Forlaget Samfundslitteratur, pp. 65–105.

Cinema (1972) 5:10 (issue 113), May.

Cinema (1973) 12:11 (issue 132), December.

Coman, M. (2004) *Media in Romania (1990–2001): A Source Book*. Bochum, Projekt.

Delavaud, G. (ed.) (2005) *Télévision: la part de l'art*. Paris, Harmattan.

Deletant, D. (1999) *Romania under Communist Rule*. Iasi, Centre for Romanian Studies.

Dittmar, C. (2004) 'GDR television in competition with West German programming'. *Historical Journal of Film Radio and Television* 24:3, 327–43.

Dittmar, C. and Vollberg, S. (eds.) (2003) *Die Überwindung der Langeweile? Zur Programmentwicklung des DDR-Fernsehens 1986 bis 1974*. Leipzig, Leipziger Universitätsverlag.

Dittmar, C. and Vollberg, S. (eds.) (2004) *Alternativen im DDR-Fernsehen? Die Programmentwicklung 1981 bis 1985*. Leipzig, Leipziger Universitätsverlag.

Dittmar, C. and Vollberg, S. (eds.) (2007) *Zwischen Experiment und Etablierung: Die Programmentwicklung des DDR-Fernsehens 1958 bis 1963*. Leipzig, Leipziger Universitätsverlag.

Drotner, K. (2003) *Disney i Danmark: at vokse op med en global mediegigant*. Copenhagen, Høst & Søn.

Elsaesser, T. (1989) *New German Cinema. A History*. London, Macmillan.

Gerbner, G. and Gross, L. (1976) 'Living with television'. *Journal of Communication* 26, 173–99.

Hansen, M. (1985) 'Dossier on *Heimat*'. *New German Critique*, Special Issue on *Heimat*.

Hebdige, D. (1988) *Hiding in the Light: On Images and Things*. London, Routledge.

Hilmes, M. (2003) 'British quality, American chaos: historical dualisms and what they leave out'. *Radio Journal* 1:1, 13–27.

Hilmes, M. (2007) '*Front Line Family*: women's culture comes to the BBC'. *Media, Culture & Society* 29:1, 5–29.

Hoggart, R. (1958) *The Uses of Literacy*. London, Chatto & Windus.

Jarvik, L. and Strickland, N. B. (1988) 'TV movies: better than the real thing'. *American Film*, December.

Jensen, H. Strandgaard (2007) *Tv til børn: En analyse af Danmarks Radios Børne- og Ungdomsafdelings programmer og programpolitik fra 1968 til 1972*. MA thesis, Department of Culture and Identity, Roskilde University.

Judt, T. (2005) *Postwar: A History of Europe since 1945*. New York, Penguin.

Kaes, A. (1989) *From Hitler to* Heimat: *The Return of History as Film*. Cambridge, MA, Harvard University Press.

Lealand, G. (1984) *American Television Programmes on British Screens*. London, Broadcasting Research Unit.

Mastny, V. (ed.) (1986) *Soviet/East European Survey, 1984–1985: Selected Research and Analysis from Radio Free Europe/Radio Liberty*. Durham, NC, Duke University Press.

Miller, J. S. (2000) *Something Completely Different: British Television and American Culture*. Minneapolis, University of Minnesota Press.

Morrow, R. W. (2006) *Sesame Street and the Reform of Children's Television*. Baltimore, MD, Johns Hopkins University Press.

Rigsarkivet (State Archive, Denmark) (RA). Archive number: 1187. Documents deposited by Danmarks Radio, Børne- & Ungdomsafdelingen (B&U), (Denmarks

Radio, The Children and Youth department), 'Udsendelser' package no. 28, 'Småbørnssektionen' package no. 1.

Rydin, I. (2000) *Barnens roster: Program för barn i Sveriges radio och television 1925–1999*, Stiftelsen Etermedierne i Sverige, no. 15. Värnamo, Fälth & Hässler.

Schopflin, G. (1983) *Censorship and Political Communication*. Londen, Frances Pinter.

Securitate Archives, file D 135/1, Annexe 2, no. 156. Bucharest, CNSAS.

Securitate Archives, file D 135/1, Note 100/0047180, 30 October 1982, no. 388. Bucharest, CNSAS.

Securitate Archives, file D 135/7. Bucharest, CNSAS.

Sellers, R. (2006) *Cult TV: The Golden Age of ITC*. London, Plexus.

Stavre, I. (2004) *Reconstructia societatii romanesti prin audiovisual*. Bucharest, Nemira.

Steemers, J. (2004) *Selling Television: British Television in the Global Marketplace*. London, BFI.

Svendsen, W. (1958) *Midt i en Quiz-tid*. Gyldendal.

Szymkowska-Bartyzel, J. (2006) *Amerykañski mit, polski konsument czyli reklamowe oblicza Ameryki*. Kraków, Wydawnictwo Uniwersytetu Jagielloñskiego.

Vemmer, M. (2006) *Fjernsyn for dig*. Copenhagen, Nordisk Forlag/DR.

Wasko, J. (2001) *Understanding Disney: The Manufacture of Fantasy*. Cambridge, Polity Press.

Williams, R. (1974) *Television: Technology and Cultural Form*. London, Fontana.

7

European Television Events and Euro-visions:
Tensions between the Ordinary and the Extraordinary

Rob Turnock, with Alexander Hecht, Dana Mustata, Mari Pajala and Alison Preston

Introduction

Events on television have a complex relationship to our understanding of how the medium operates. They raise questions about the temporal arrangements of broadcasting, about the relationship between the ordinary and the extraordinary, about everyday life and historical change, about media production and consumption practices, and about the relationship between the media and political participation and community. Events can also allow us to make comparisons across borders because they often have national, international and historical dimensions. Events on television such as cultural and sporting competitions, revolutions, civil wars or the death of public figures can carry across Europe and beyond, and can often form the basis of common experience and collective memory. So events can make useful points of comparison because they relate to forms of television programming and historical experiences that are at least in some way shared across more international perspectives. Indeed, it is likely that many of the case studies in this chapter, which draw on shared programming phenomena, historical events and experiences, will be familiar to a wide range of readers. The discussion of these case studies will, however, be of a critical kind, and they do not offer easy answers to the types of questions that arise when looking at televised events in the European context.

In much analysis of television events, emphasis has been placed on their extraordinary nature. Perhaps the most influential view of this has been

Dayan and Katz's (1992) analysis of 'media events'. They argued that these are a specific genre of planned programmes that are based on interruption, dominate the schedules and proclaim 'time out' from ordinary and routine television. They are broadcast live and they galvanise large audiences. Importantly, they are organised by agencies outside the television institution itself, such as sporting bodies, national agencies and governments. Dayan and Katz include in their analysis major historical events such as the Apollo 11 Moon landing in 1969, the coronation of Queen Elizabeth II in 1953 and the funerals of John F. Kennedy in 1963 and Winston Churchill in 1965. Such events can mark rites of passage (including weddings and funerals) for a public figure and can form the closure to a period of 'liminality' (Turner 1969) or social drama (Turner 1982). Dominating the media, these events attract large audience ratings which are then read as loyalty to and legitimation for the values being expressed by the event organisers. In events such as sports championships or state ceremonies, the crowds in attendance vicariously stand in for the viewer at home, and the participation of the collective crowd in public space connects directly to the mass audience in the private sphere. Media events can also mark and contribute to periods of historical change, and they include the example of President Anwar Sadat of Egypt making an extraordinary visit to Jerusalem in 1977, which was a profound development in Middle Eastern politics, and the visit of Pope John Paul II to Poland in 1979, symbolically marking the relaxation of religious strictures there.

Yet beyond Dayan and Katz's media events there are other unexpected and potentially catastrophic events that not only disrupt the schedules and attract large audiences but that impact on national and even international discourses, and that can also mark profound historical paradigm shifts. Tamar Liebes (1998) has developed the term 'disaster marathons' to explore the kinds of live and rolling news coverage that follow major disasters or terrorist attacks such as a series of bus bombings in Israel in March 1996. Liebes warned that the coverage of such attacks could have dangerous political consequences as it could prompt media-harried politicians into making hasty and reactionary policy statements and decisions. A very recent example of this might be the terrorist attacks in the United States on 11 September 2001. This event not only dominated the media at the time of the attack and its aftermath, but impacted on discourses about the Middle East, Islam and terrorism. It had profound impacts on US and Western European governmental policy, and has led to conflicts and invasions that may alter the long-term stability of a whole region. It should therefore be asked to what extent the television and other media coverage of the terrorist attacks dominated and controlled the political discourses that followed. If the first Gulf War was a media war (or even a simulacrum of a war; see Baudrillard 1995), the invasions of Afghanistan and Iraq could be understood as extensions of the same media narrative that began in New York in 2001. Significantly here, the media events that Dayan and Katz discuss, such as funerals and memorials, are often emotionally charged and respond to or mitigate trauma or disaster. So the television coverage in the wake of Kennedy's death was not a media event, but his funeral was. So too, as we shall see, was the death and funeral of Diana, Princess of Wales in 1997.

What major events such as the Moon landing, the funeral of Diana, and the terrorist attacks in New York can also promote is an ideology of 'liveness'. While the transmission of television is an active and ongoing process, much of television programming relies on pre-recorded programmes – even if many of those programmes such as game and talk shows have a live in-the-moment feel, which relies on certain modes of address to the audience (Bourdon 2000, Ellis 2000). Media events and the disastrous, however, particularly emphasise television's ability to exist in real time and in the moment. As Mary Anne Doane has argued (1990: 238), the catastrophic event cuts through the banal and commercial routines of broadcasting and 'corroborates television's access to the momentary, the discontinuous and the real'. For Doane, catastrophic events also implicate the viewer – 'we' are all under threat at this moment: the plane crash demonstrates the fragility of modernity, things go wrong and fail, an aeroplane might fall on *our* city.

Yet such discussion so far has suggested that media events, disasters and catastrophes are distinct and separate from ordinary and everyday television. The situation is, however, much more complex because daily television schedules are made up of a stream of different kinds of events and happenings. Most of the time these events are routine or habitual, part of the 'flow' of television (Williams 1990) and the experience of everyday life (Silverstone 1994). The day-to-day production, scheduling and transmission of television involve the staging of small and localised events or occasions, or large broadcasting events that generate a sense of national interest, concern and involvement. Some of these events are organised by non-television institutions, although – as in the case of politics and sport – television has often played an increasing role in their staging. Yet many of the events are set up and organised by television itself. Quiz and game shows, chat shows and magazine programmes have all been staged in some way for the cameras, and involve performance, action, organisation and management. Dramas also are staged and involve performative events – even if this is in a small studio or on location in front of a small camera crew. These events and occasions are usually pre-planned. Even television news programmes are pre-planned and routinised. Much of what appears in the news is based on the daily newsgathering practices of professional journalists, and closely tied to the calendars of national and public institutions, the courts, governments and civil service departments. The serial nature of the news and the recurring cast of politicians, journalists and celebrities have led John Ellis (1982) to suggest that news has much in common with soap opera. Television can also contain and domesticate the disastrous and catastrophic. Wars, famine and flood are usually scheduled and contained within a confined news slot, before making way for the weather and a game or chat show. Even stories of 'communities under threat' are a constant staple of television news (Langer 1998). Of course, for participants and spectators of sporting events, and for the ordinary members of the public who appear on a quiz show or who are the subjects or victims in news stories, these occasions can be special, remarkable, frightening or life-changing experiences. These events are nonetheless part of the steady flow of television.

It is such an interplay between routine schedules and the distressing and threatening images that television brings into the home that has led Roger Silverstone (1994: 165) to discuss the medium in terms of 'security and anxiety'. Drawing on the work of the sociologist Anthony Giddens, Silverstone argued that television can contribute to our sense of ontological security – a trust in the routines and habits of everyday life. This security is partly constructed and sustained through the familiar patterns of scheduling which are themselves attuned to individual habits of work and play. Television itself is also attuned to the calendar of national life, such as large annual sporting events or championships, music festivals or seasonal festivities such as Easter or Christmas. Indeed, radio and television broadcasting have now become constitutive of those events and part of the national experience (Scannell 1996). The Queen's Speech has long been associated with Christmas Day in the UK and a Freddy Frinton comedy is shown in Germany at every New Year. These are key events in television's calendar and they constitute what have been described as 'invented traditions' (Hobsbawm & Ranger 1983). Further important occasions in the cycle of programming are international events such as the Eurovision Song Contest, held every year, and the soccer World Cup and Olympic Games, which are both staged every four years. So there is a tension here between the extraordinary and the ordinary. Dayan and Katz include sporting events such as the Olympic Games in their category of media events because they cause disruption and interruption to the television schedules and to social life. Yet while the Olympics are a major international sporting event and dominate the schedules, they are an anticipated and planned part of the broadcast calendar. Sports programmes that cover the Olympics today do not constitute an interruption to the schedules but are part of them.

What may transcend this complex interaction between the apparently ordinary and extraordinary is the sense in which, at a national level, the small and large events, and the broadcasting of routine television, disasters and media events can all invoke, articulate and be constitutive of the 'imagined community' (Anderson 1991). For Benedict Anderson, the act of reading the national newspaper every morning implies a shared activity and moment of synchronicity. Television also provides a sense of togetherness in routine viewing – a sense of shared patterns and habits. Yet during disasters and media events there is also a sense of shared viewership of something that is happening now, live in real time, which has an impact on everyone viewing. The rhetoric of the disaster and the media event is about shared experience and community. It is this apparent sense of community that allows the individual to 'imagine' a connection with other members of the same nation. This points to another key tension. Dayan and Katz have argued that media events attract large audiences who thus prove their loyalty to core values. Yet as we shall see, audiences are not necessarily uniformly accepting of the values expressed in the media-event texts. This becomes even further complicated if the idea that the audience at the scene of the public event both stands in for and connects directly with the audience at home. The examples to be explored here will clearly show distinctions between public behaviour and private viewing. So a key question is the extent to which events can unite or divide and fragment television audiences. This issue becomes particularly acute when one considers such events in a 'European' context. Can there be events that unite people in Europe? Or are there complex levels of cohesion or fragmentation that transcend national boundaries?

The case studies in this chapter will not be able to answer all of these questions, but they articulate in concrete terms the kinds of tensions that permeate televised events. They constitute a number of different kinds of event – the media event, the disaster marathon, the news event and the television event (including television *about* events). The studies touch in particular on issues relating to liveness and recorded programming, the tension between ordinary and extraordinary events and the issue of whether the representation of events is cohesive or divisive. As well as reflecting different kinds of event, in different periods in different countries, the case studies demonstrate different disciplinary and methodological approaches to the subject matter, using a range of research and analytical techniques including archival research, opinion polls and survey questions, comparative content analysis and textual analysis. The chapter adopts a chronological approach, starting in the earlier period of television that John Ellis (2000) has described as the 'era of scarcity'. It will come up to what Ellis calls the emerging era of 'plenty' at the end of the last decade, with all the expansion of broadcasting systems and emerging technologies that this involves.

The Eurovision Song Contest in the 1960s and Finnish Television Culture

The Eurovision Song Contest (ESC) is an exceptional programme in the history of European television: an international broadcast that has been a part of television schedules for more than 50 years, from the early years of television to the present. The European Broadcasting Union founded the contest in 1956 as a flagship programme for its Eurovision network. The ESC is a typical television event: the competition was set up specifically for television, it is broadcast live and it has attracted a great deal of attention in the media. This case study focuses on the ESC in the context of 1960s television culture in Finland, investigating the significance of the contest at the time of television's popularisation as a medium and how the programme both encouraged and questioned a sense of national and European community. The Finnish Broadcasting Company YLE first took part in the ESC in 1961. During the 1960s television quickly became an essential part of the Finnish media landscape. As part of this, the ESC developed into a highly visible feature of Finnish popular culture, as Finnish press and magazine coverage (some of it collected in YLE's archives) shows.

Television came to Finland relatively late. The large geographical area of the country, combined with a small population (about 4.5 million in 1960), made television seem a difficult and expensive undertaking. During the first half of the 1950s YLE proceeded very hesitantly in its plans for television. In the end the first regular broadcasts were started in 1956 by a private society affiliated with the University of Technology in Helsinki. YLE finally began regular broadcasting in 1958 (Salokangas 1996: 109–22). After this slow start, television spread much more rapidly than had been predicted. By the end of 1962, 90 per cent of the population had access to television broadcasts, although the northern half of the country was still outside their reach. The first broadcasting stations were built in Lapland in 1964 and by the end of the decade the number of television licences in Finland had reached one million (Salokangas 1996: 123–6; *Yleisradion vuosikertomus* 1964: 1969–70).

International television events such as the ESC were important for popularising the new medium. Programme exchange through Eurovision enabled broadcasters in small countries to benefit from the larger resources in wealthier countries. Accordingly, the opinion at YLE was that television would not really break through without the variety and special attractions provided by Eurovision, which the company joined in 1959. Eurovision became an important source of everyday news material, but it also brought special television events, such as major international sports competitions, to Finnish screens (Salokangas 1996: 125–6; Noam 1991: 291–2). The ESC quickly became one of the most prominent programmes in the annual television calendar. The contest functioned as a television spectacular that attracted people to the medium (Parks 2001: 335). As an international programme that was broadcast live from a different European city each year, the ESC showcased the qualities that were seen as television's special characteristics: liveness and the 'ability to bring "another world" into the home' (Spigel 1992: 102). With its festive locations, grand orchestra and some internationally well-known stars, the ESC stood out from everyday Finnish programming as a glamorous and expensive television spectacle.

The ESC was a paradigmatic television event for television's 'era of scarcity', when there were few channels and relatively little programming. John Ellis (2000: 43–51) argues that European television during this era functioned as an influential force for social integration and played an important part in constructing a sense of national community. When there were only one or two channels and most homes had a television set, a large part of the population could follow the same programme. Television offered shared experiences and provided material for everyday conversation. In Finland, the ESC was seen as a television programme that produced a particularly strong response from the audience. The newspaper *Turun Sanomat* summed up its position on 24 September 1965 by describing the contest as 'apparently the most watched and talked about – at the same time the most controversial – programme during the whole era of television'. From the beginning, the contest attracted a great deal of attention in the Finnish media.

The ESC's status in Finnish television culture was supported by its regular annual rhythm. Paddy Scannell (1996: 153–6) suggests that radio, and later television, created a new 'annual calendar of events' by making different kinds of live events accessible to a wider audience than had been possible before. The ESC soon had an apparently stable place in the annual television calendar as a sign of spring, as the city of Vaasa's newspaper reported on 7 March 1966: 'This competition has already become a tradition . . . The contest has received a very enthusiastic welcome and apparently it has been the most widely watched and at the same time the most controversial programme on television. In a way it also marks the beginning of spring.' The ESC was at once an exceptional television event and such a regular feature of the annual television calendar that it soon developed an air of tradition.

The ESC encouraged a sense of national community; a feeling that all over the country people sat in front of the television at the same time to see how well the Finnish entry fared. At the same time, the programme drew attention to differences within Finland. The choice of the Finnish entry was in some cases followed by great controversy. How Finland should be represented abroad and who – musical experts or 'ordinary' people – were qualified to make this choice were questions that were disputed time and time again (Pajala 2006: 164–99). The ESC became an arena for struggles over national representation and authority in the field of popular culture. The discussions around the ESC made it clear that there was no unanimous national community.

Like other forms of communication technology before it, television in its early years inspired utopian hopes that it would increase understanding and advance peaceful co-operation across geographical distance (Marvin 1988: 192–4, Spigel 2001: 34–5). The ESC could also be framed as an occasion for positive international co-operation. At the end of the 1963 ESC in London, the BBC's Stuart Hood gave a little speech on the wonder of international broadcasts, finishing with the thought: 'Perhaps like me, you too have been happy to think that for once we were able to enjoy the achievements of modern science without the chill of fear that so often accompanies the miracles of technology today.' Such solemn words were rarely linked to Eurovision in Finnish media, but the feeling of being part of a huge international audience was one of the attractions of the contest. The newspaper *Keskipohjanmaa* noted on 21 March 1962: 'It was said that about 60 million souls saw Sunday's ESC in Luxembourg on television. It was uplifting to feel that you were one of these souls.' The press regularly commented on the estimated number of viewers, which was constantly rising as new geographical areas came within the reach of Eurovision. By 1968 it was said by the *Turun Sanomat* newspaper (6 April) that the ESC had 200 million viewers in Europe, Asia and Africa. The development of the contest was described as a narrative of apparently limitless growth and expansion.

The ESC did not, however, offer an uncomplicated sense of belonging to an international community. Even the simple fact that Finland is in a different time zone from most other participating countries contributed to the feeling of being slightly apart. In the 1960s the ESC began on Finnish television at 11.00 p.m. This made the contest stand out in the television schedules, as there were rarely programmes that began so late. In the press it was often remarked that viewers were forced to change their daily rhythm in order to watch the ESC, as the *Uusi Suomi* newspaper commented on 11 April 1967: 'But even though we are talking about a recurring annual source of upset, people are always willing to sacrifice their night's sleep in order to enjoy it!' The ESC had been placed in television schedules as a live event for an international audience to watch at the same time, but the fact that it was broadcast so late drew attention to the distance between Finland and Western Europe.

A more acute sense of difference grew out of the perception that Finnish songs did not have much success in the international competition. The ESC drew attention to cultural and political differences among the participating countries and in the Finnish press coverage of the programme in the early 1960s there was much discussion on the variety of musical tastes in Europe. It was commonly thought that the French *chanson* style dominated the ESC and that the kind of songs that were popular in Northern Europe had little chance of winning. By the late 1960s the voting was interpreted less as an expression of musical taste and more as an illustration of alliances among countries. For example when the Nordic countries favoured each other blatantly in the 1966 contest, the Finnish press described this as a successful political manoeuvre against the dominance of the French 'bloc'. The language of politics was now used to make sense of the contest (Pajala 2006: 134–8).

Politically, Finland's position in relation to the community constructed in early Eurovision was ambiguous. The ESC was one example of the increasingly active community-building among West European countries after the Second World War and at this point, Finland did not unambiguously belong to the West. Finnish foreign policy relied on the ideal of neutrality and represented the country as a kind of borderland between West and East. Finland had close relations with the Soviet Union but also gradually joined many West European organisations and collaborations (Harle & Moisio 2000: 183–91). This in-between position was also taken up by Finnish television. YLE was a member of both Eurovision and its East European equivalent Intervision (Salokangas 1996: 126). The Nordvision network, a local branch of Eurovision, was used for programme exchange among the Nordic countries, and between 1963 and 1968 there were annual Nordvision programmes in which singers from Sweden, Norway, Denmark and Finland performed songs from their countries' Eurovision preliminaries. Emphasising the connections between Nordic countries was a way of attaching Finland to the West and accordingly, in the press coverage of the ESC a great deal of attention was given to the Nordic entries. However, the sense of a Nordic community was undermined since Swedish juries did not award a single point to Finnish songs during the 1960s, which greatly frustrated many Finnish commentators (Pajala 2006: 132–4). The failure to appeal to Western neighbours complicated the common presumption that cultural and political ties connected Finland to the Nordic community.

During television's era of scarcity, the ESC was one of the biggest television events in Finland. Until the mid-1980s it was regularly one of the most widely watched programmes of the year along with national beauty pageants and song contests (Pajala 2006: 58–9, 362–3.). In the current television environment there are so many channels and programmes to choose from that a television event like the ESC no longer has such a special position. Still, the contest and the sense of a European community it promises have not lost their appeal. This is apparent in the enthusiasm with which new countries from Eastern Europe have joined the competition. In many ways the ESC is now larger than ever: there are more participants than before and a semi-final has been added to accommodate them all. In Finland interest in the programme has varied but it has never faded completely. Paradoxically, the poor results of the Finnish entries have contributed to the cultural significance of the ESC: the contest became material for a melodramatic narrative of national difference where Finland time and again attempts to succeed in Europe but keeps failing (Pajala 2007). The first Finnish victory by Lordi in 2006 was greeted with huge enthusiasm in the media and their homecoming party became the largest public event in the history of Helsinki. A television event like the ESC still has the power to address a national audience.

Holocaust: Educating the Audience

Holocaust was a four-part, nine-and-a-half-hour US television mini-series first shown on NBC from 16 to 19 April 1978. The series followed two German families through the years before and during the Second World War, the Jewish Weiss family and the Nazi Dorf family. There were positive reviews for the series after it was first shown in the United States, plaudits for cast members such as Meryl Streep and Ian Holm, and the tie-in novel by the series scriptwriter Gerald Green became an overnight bestseller. Yet there were also criticisms, both on its first transmission and its second transmission the following year. The Holocaust survivor Elie Wiesel described the series in the *New York Times* (16 April 1978) as 'untrue, offensive and cheap', while others criticised it for depicting the fate of the Jewish people as a family melodrama (Morey 2004). Despite the criticisms, NBC went on to claim that after the second transmission of the series in 1979 as many as 220 million people had seen the series in the United States and Western Europe.

The impact of the series in West Germany and Austria was stunning. Around 15 million people (Morey 2004), half the adult population, watched part or all of it in West Germany when it was screened on the nights of 22–26 January 1979. The series, shown on the third regional network, ARD, had provoked a storm of controversy in the press in the weeks before transmission, with many expressing unhappiness at its planned screening. The reason was that the extent of Germans' and Austrians' involvement in the crimes committed by the Nazi regime was rarely on the agenda of politicians, historians or journalists at that time. There was much discomfort about the treatment of the subject matter, on the one hand, with criticism on the other that the programme was being shown on a regional rather than national network. Karl-Otto Saur (1979: 21) asked in his commentary in the daily newspaper *Süddeutsche Zeitung* whether *Holocaust* was anything more than 'a cornflakes melodrama', and criticised the decision of the ARD to choose the regional network for the broadcast instead of scheduling it on the main nationwide channel, which is jointly run by all the ARD networks. He alleged that the head of television in the Bavarian region, Helmut Oeller, was heavily against a screening on the main channel.

Polls conducted in West Germany before, during and after transmission showed that television had a profound impact on how people viewed these events. A report in *Variety* (quoted in Morey 2004: 1112) claimed: '70 per cent of those in the 14–19 age group declared that they had learned more from the shows about the horrors of the Nazi regime than they had learned in all their years of studying West German history'. So strong was the reaction to the transmission that the German Society of Language later chose 'holocaust' as the 'Word of the Year 1979'. *Holocaust* also triggered the question of how history should be taught, and some observers claimed that 'reading history' was obviously no longer enough to get people interested whereas moving images could tell so much more. The German news magazine *Der Spiegel* (29 January 1979: 22) proclaimed a 'Black Friday for historians'. West-German newspapers and magazines changed the tone of their coverage as apparent audience acceptance grew. The mainly negative commentaries published early in the broadcast were followed by articles stressing the necessity of a discussion about the Nazi past in Germany. As Countess Dönhoff, the *grande dame* of the German press and editor of *Die Zeit* observed: 'People are agitated, shocked and all of a sudden they want to know' (2 February 1979: 1). The series not only had a significant impact on how the event was seen and understood but also on attitudes to those involved. 'Such was the public response that the West German government promptly cancelled the statute of limitations for Nazi war crimes, formally scheduled to expire at the end of 1979' (Morey 2004: 1112).

In East Germany (the GDR) *Holocaust* and other West German programmes could only be received near the border and in East Berlin. It was
in the GDR capital where the West German newspaper *Die Zeit* conducted
a small survey among people on the street (2 February 1979: 12). Some respondents argued that the way the Holocaust was presented was biased, considering that communists and Jehovah's Witnesses had also been systematically
persecuted by the Nazi regime. Others claimed to be shocked by the apparent lack of knowledge of their West German neighbours about the history of
the Holocaust. The political leadership and the major newspapers all ignored
the discussion going in West Germany. The GDR had no official history before
1949 and so the political elite left the discussion about the crimes of the Nazi
regime to their West German counterparts. Furthermore, *Holocaust* had been
produced in the United States and was thus seen as the result of commercially minded broadcasting that profited from human tragedy. Interestingly,
many viewers in the United States had also felt uncomfortable with the juxtaposition of the grim and serious subject matter of the series alongside jaunty
and upbeat television advertisements (Morey 2004).

In Austria, 1978 had seen several events commemorating 40 years of the
Anschluss (the union of Austria with the Third Reich). Slowly the Austrian
public seemed ready to face their past. Many Austrians had been involved in
Nazi crimes, however the political consensus after 1945 was that Austria was
the first victim of the Nazi aggression, and the past was rarely discussed since
many former members of the NSDAP (the Austrian Nazi party) had rejoined
public life after the war. When the first Labour government was appointed in
1970 former NSDAP members were nominated as ministers even while the
Austrian prime minister was Jewish. By the end of the 1970s, however, a new
generation of critical intellectuals started to ask questions about their parents'
past. The political common ground on Austria's past was challenged and the
judgement of the 1938–45 period started to change. Against this background
the Austrian public channel ORF decided to air *Holocaust* on four consecut-
ive evenings, 1–4 March 1977, on its second channel. Audience ratings for
the series were very high: 61 per cent of Austrians aged over 14 watched at
least one of the episodes (Diem 1980). By that time the ORF had the monopoly of terrestrial television in Austria, but on all evenings when the episodes
were broadcast there was fierce competition from popular entertainment
programmes on the first channel. Nevertheless, on Friday 2 March the second
episode reached an audience of 2.8 million, against the first channel's
831,000 for the *Wencke-Myhre-Show*. Next day the numbers were also impressive, with 2.2 million for *Holocaust* compared to 1.7 million watching the live
Saturday night staple, the Rudi Carell show *Am laufenden Band*.

In parallel to the broadcast of *Holocaust* the ORF started extensive research
into the audience reception of the series. The new department for media
research's survey included a phone poll right after the broadcast of the fourth
episode, an in-depth audience rating and the analysis of incoming phone calls

and letters (Diem 1980). The telephone poll was unequivocal: 87 per cent were positive about the series, 92 per cent said it was 'authentic' and 85 per cent thought it 'exciting'. Most of the audience was young, urban and wealthy. Students, the self-employed and freelance workers watched the series far more than retired people or farmers. It is an important fact that the generation that had lived through the Nazi period were less interested in *Holocaust* than their children and grandchildren who were beginning to ask inconvenient questions about the past.

What is interesting here is the different responses that the series provoked among different countries and groups. In the United States there were questions about authenticity, quality and taste – it was a fictional script in a melodramatic form, shown on a commercial and entertainment-based network. In West Germany and Austria the transmission of the series itself took on an event-like quality, dominating public discourses in the press, in government and about education. While there were inevitably anxieties around the nature of the US-produced programme, there were also generational anxieties about how the events depicted should be understood and about the complicity of an older generation. What is also notable is the division between West and East German attitudes to the same events, on ideological and geopolitical lines.

Media Events and Revolution in Romania

Within their typology of media events, Dayan and Katz (1992) claim that a successful media event is bound to produce large audiences. In their conceptualisation moreover, certain media events, even though rare, can effect change (Dayan and Katz 1995: 99). Yet the extent to which media events can be considered successful or effective in terms of large audiences or change is problematic. This is in part because a discussion of media texts cannot necessarily account for either viewing practices or changes in social processes. In order to illustrate possible limitations of Dayan's and Katz's construction of media events two different case studies will be explored here, both from the context of television during the rule of the Romanian dictator Nicolae Ceauşescu. These are the broadcast of national-day parades in communist Romania, which despite their textual construction as media events failed to attract significant audiences, and the live broadcast of the 1989 Romanian revolution, which served as a platform for preserving continuities with the communist regime.

National-day parades in communist Romania took place every year on 23 August and were the subject of grandiose television events. They managed to mobilise an entire nation on to the streets, and yet failed to generate desired audience responses. Within the context of totalitarian rule, a successful media event that placed power at its centre could, in this instance, only alienate audiences from the event itself. The event consisted primarily of street marches, performances and collective chanting. All participants in the event were grouped together according to their community and social affiliations, and these were distinguished by the wearing of specific uniforms and the carrying of banners. The mass parades were manufactured to symbolise national communion: the marching of millions of people was synchronised; the performances were carried out collectively; the uniforms visually strengthened the sense of affiliation and community; the chanting in unison spoke of unified support for the nation. The television coverage of the event would often show a bird's-eye view of the participants, where individuals were depersonalised and represented by the colour of their uniforms, became moving elements in synchronised choreography or gestured and chanted collectively. When shot from above, pictures of the event would show a mass of moving banners. Since most of these banners were magnified portraits of the dictatorial couple, it appeared as if the national community was mistaken for and reduced to the recurrent images of Nicolae and Elena Ceauşescu. Among such banners, there were others that spoke of the nation, as coverage on *Album Duminical (Sunday Magazine)* on 28 August 1989 showed: 'Long live socialism. The most just and advanced society', 'Let the interference of imperialist circles into the internal affairs of states stop!', 'Romania has economic and diplomatic relations with over 155 countries', 'May Ceauşescu be re-elected', 'Long live Ceauşescu', 'Long live Romania'. Such proclamations asserted a strong sense of the nation, proud of its ideology, supportive of its leader, delineated from the outside world and foreign elements, and yet entertaining international aspirations. The broadcast of the events favoured panoramic shots, in which individuals were transformed into a compact mass representing the community and nation.

There was a large discrepancy between the bird's-eye view of the thoroughly homogeneous and synchronised masses and the lack of close-ups on members of the crowds presenting rigid, unenthusiastic and tired faces. This discrepancy paralleled the discrepancy between the nation and the individual, between the public performance of the citizen and his or her private, intimate behaviour. There is a distinction, especially in a totalitarian regime, between an individual's performance within the public sphere and his or her actions and demeanour within the private sphere. Despite the widespread participation of the nation in the street parades, the national-day event did not generate sizeable audiences within the domestic space. In socialist Romania, home represented a refuge from social duties, where attitudes against the regime could be formed. It was the space where people tuned in secretly to Radio Free Europe and where overtly propagandistic television content was mocked. Viewing television was mostly an activity that was performed within families and behind closed doors. The highly ideological nature of television content most often triggered adverse reactions in the audience, whose privacy at home allowed them the choice to turn away from and deny the regime. This is something that the authorities and state broadcaster were aware of, as papers in the secret police (Securitate) archives show:

Television programming of a highly propagandistic nature . . . without having the desired impact, on the contrary has achieved adverse reactions in the audience due to an objective, scientific fact: the inhibition and the need for protection that is triggered in the viewer who feels himself exploited by such content. It is such programming that best succeeded in pushing audiences away from Romanian Radiotelevision. (Securitate Archives, File D 135/7, Note 105, p. 6)

It was the strict separation between the public and private realms that sustained ambivalent and often paradoxical behaviour among the population. Public space constituted the locus for social and national participation, whereas the private sphere housed contestation and deliberation. It was the active participation in the public domain correlated to the lack of consent occurring in the private space that characterised the reception of ceremonial media events in socialist Romania.

However, the target audience for such events was not really the population at large, but rather the dictatorial couple. It was not sizeable audiences that legitimised the success of a media event, but rather the viewing satisfaction of the Ceauşescus. A successful media event implied a high participation of the nation in front of the cameras, rather than behind their television sets; it implied ceremonial, heroic and eulogistic portrayals of the idealised Ceauşescus being greeted by a euphoric nation. It was their cult of personality and their sense of power that a successful media event had to reinforce. Whereas in the streets the nation celebrated the regime and its ideology, in private individuals celebrated 23 August as a day of no work in a society with a six-day working week, and with feasts of meatballs and Pepsi-Cola in a world where such products were rare. The pleasure of the audience in such moments of socialist abnormality contrasted heavily with the public's unwilling participation in the street parades, and this outlined even further the conflictual gap between the population and Ceauşescu regime. For Dayan and Katz (1992), media events seamlessly integrate the core values of the event itself with the active approval and participation of the audience present there, and the expression of loyalty by the large audience watching at home. Within the specific historical context of national-day parades in Romania, however, Dayan and Katz's typology of media events fails to account for viewing practices and fails to connect the event to the textual and production strategies through which its 'success' was validated. The coverage deliberately avoided showing the discrepancies between what the dictatorial couple wanted to see (from afar) and the demeanour of the public's performances in the street (by avoiding close-up) or the unseen private experiences of the audience at home.

Another major limitation of Dayan's and Katz's conceptualisation of media events is their claim that a media text, such as the live broadcasts of the collapse of communism in Eastern Europe, can be considered as an expression of change. Far from asserting change, the live broadcast of the 1989 Romanian revolution was ambivalent in its effects by preserving continuities with the old regime under the disguise of the formal changes evident in the text's aesthetics. Change was made visible by the 'tele-revolution' (Ratesh 1991), through several formal and textual means. One was the apparent immediacy and transparency of the live broadcasts, which contrasted sharply with the institution's formerly pre-planned broadcasting. Soon after the escape of the Ceauşescus, the newly renamed Free Romanian Television switched to live broadcasts alternating between events in the streets and Studio 4. Key actors in the revolution appeared in front of the camera in the programme *Prima ora emisie (The Early Morning Show)* on 22 December 1989, looking nervous, tired, unshaven and wearing shabby clothes, contrasting with the manufactured and over-elaborate appearances that had previously dominated television content.

The broadcasting of the revolution was itself very dramatic, with action taking place around the television studios on 22 and 23 December 1989. This heightened a sense of difference and conflict between the apparently new regime and the old dictatorial one. It also heightened a state of tension and sense of panic as the television broadcaster claimed to be under attack from people they identified as terrorists or members of the Securitate and Militia. In the ensuing drama on the night of 22 December, shooting took place in and around the television building, as this translated extract from the transcript suggests:

> *Hysterical voice from off*: '. . . they're shooting from there, . . . from the right . . .'
> *Voice from off*: '. . . they're shooting from the left. . .'
> *Hoarse voice from off*: 'Don't shoot, they are our people. . .'
> *Voice from off*: '. . . they are the Securitate'.
> *Hoarse voice from off*: 'They are not the Securitate. They are our people.' (Tatulici 1990: 126)

Another important break with the past was the creation of an active, participant viewer, different from the apparently submissive viewer of the communist regime. Viewers were repeatedly called upon to participate in the defence of the television broadcasting institution: 'There are 2,000 terrorists approaching the television building . . . the population should come outside . . . help us, come help us' (Tatulici 1990: 65). Television also became the platform where viewers could directly participate in the revolution: they were called upon to track down the black car, registration 2-DB-305, in which Ceauşescu was allegedly last seen (Tatulici 1990: 53); they were exhorted to make a telephone call to Ion Iliescu (subsequently interim leader and then the first democratically elected president) and ask him to come to Studio 4. Had Iliescu gone on TV one hour later, the revolution would have failed (Dinescu, in Ratesh 1991: 52). Viewers were also called upon to participate in the formation of the new state when Iliescu announced, on live television, the formation of the National Salvation Front.

The dramatic climax to the revolution was when Nicolae and Elena Ceauşescu were caught, prosecuted and shot. The images of their dead bodies, transmitted on 25 December 1989, marked the end of the old regime. The formation of the new state was performed on air as the National Salvation Front (NSF) proclaimed the introduction of democratic structures in front of the television cameras. The new power structure was (re)presented as the direct offspring of the revolution itself, and deliberated upon in the public space of national television. However, the changes asserted by these televisual representations in fact obscured numerous continuities with the old regime and the perpetuation of communist elements in the apparently new democratic era. Upon the formation of the NSF, it seemed that an authentic and democratic public sphere had arisen. Intellectuals constituting the group of revolutionaries within Studio 4 emerged from the civil sphere, opposed the old regime and publicly debated the future of Romania. But the apparently democratic public sphere soon transformed into the sphere of the new state power when the provisional NSF government was elected in 1990. Iliescu, the main character in the tele-revolution, became president of Romania. Iliescu himself had had a promising career in the Communist Party, and 'for years his name had been mentioned as a likely successor to Ceaușescu at the top of the party and the country, in the event of the collapse of the latter's rule' (Ratesh 1991: 49). The free elections of May 1990 were a form of democratic structure that nevertheless reinforced one-party dominance. With no proper opposition yet formed, the NSF won the 1990 elections with a two-thirds majority (Szajkowski 1991: 224), but there were protests against Iliescu and his government. By means of televised appearances, Iliescu disseminated the image of protesters as hooligans and persuaded thousands of miners to come to the rescue. The protests degenerated into bloody conflict, and another attack on the television headquarters took place, broadcast live. Attacks also took place at the editorial offices of *Romania Libera*, an independent daily which criticised Iliescu's instigation of violence and the democratic crisis he had brought (Berry 2004: 42). These events confirmed that Iliescu would brook no opposition and that independent press organisations were considered a threat. The heroic role attributed to the miners in contrast with the denigration of intellectuals during this period was reminiscent of communist social hierarchies. Yet most of all, the June riots showed the submissive relationship of national television to the new state power, in continuity with the communist regime.

Television News and the Domestic Refraction of Distant Events: The 1990s Bosnian War

By 2007 it was 25 years since the widespread use of electronic newsgathering (ENG) began to enable news to be gathered and replicated more quickly than had previously been possible (MacGregor 1997, McNair 2003, Preston 1991, 2000). During the 1980s and early 1990s the news industry developed rapidly, moving in the UK from the vertically integrated duopoly of the BBC

and ITN to a landscape in which there were a number of providers and outlets, including 24-hour news channels (Boyd-Barrett 1996, Preston 2000).
CNN began transmissions in Europe in 1985, but had been forced initially
to narrowcast to hotels because of rights issues, and in 1989 Sky News began
broadcasting in the UK. In 1998 there were ten television news outlets available to UK audiences, comprising BBC, ITN, Channel 4 and Channel 5, and
the 24-hour news channels of Sky News, BBC News 24, CNN International
and Euronews. News was also carried by the two business channels Bloomberg
and CNBC.

Over that 25-year period, time delay as an inevitable or inherent element
in foreign news production and dissemination had disappeared, and news reporting from other countries could be as instantaneous as from the studio (and
indeed, the 'studio' could move to the news event). This trend was largely
complete by the early 1990s: journalists and executives at this time were concerned with the imperative of immediacy, and the limitations that they felt
this placed upon their capacity to conduct 'considered' journalism. The Gulf
War of 1991 was a particular example of this (MacGregor 1997, Preston 1991,
Taylor 1992). Developments in television news journalism in that period have
given rise to a number of concerns voiced by both journalists and academics
– that there is an overemphasis on the need for 'live' reporting; that the need
for 'new' news squeezes out the possibility of reporting 'routine' news; and
that the need for visual representation means that news events without such
footage go unreported (MacGregor 1997, Paterson 1996). The reporting of
the war in Bosnia in the early 1990s is an important and resonant example
of how what was 'foreign' news was refracted to domestic audiences over a
number of years, during periods of crisis and also periods where there was
little 'new' news. It clearly illustrates how most television news output tends
towards what can be readily assimilated by domestic audiences, which is in
itself an almost tautologous statement since a fundamental purpose of journalism is to explain events in a way that can be commonly understood.

An international content analysis carried out in 1994 looking at the
Bosnian war provides rich historical data for understanding how news is refracted to its audiences, across a range of countries (Gow, Paterson & Preston
1996). As part of a programme of work instigated by the British Film Institute in 1994, the evening television news output from 13 countries was
separately analysed for the week of 16–21 May 1994. Those countries were
Algeria, Austria, Croatia, France, Greece, Italy, Macedonia, Russia, Serbia,
Slovenia, Turkey, the UK and the USA. In addition, the evening news output
from Euronews, CNN International and Sky News was monitored. This
output was considered alongside the items about Bosnia disseminated by the
Reuters news agency World News during the week. The results – what was
shown on screen in different countries and what was not shown – show the
specificity of certain domestic agendas, and how news was framed according
to sociopolitical and cultural norms.

The week of analysis was not a major one for the prosecution of the war, but rather contained a series of smaller events, set out in table 7.1, which also shows which countries reported which stories. The content analysis shows that the type of news from Bosnia broadcast during this 'non-crisis' week by different countries was strongly aligned to the domestic news values of each country. There were a number of ways in which this domestication occurred. First, through the selection of which stories to cover. The coverage in France during the week in question was particularly illustrative of how news outlets tend to focus on stories with direct domestic resonance. The three main stories that the French television news bulletins covered were an electoral campaign by the French film-maker and intellectual Bernard-Henri Levy in support of Bosnia, the release of French aid workers by the Serbs and a decision to withdraw some French troops from Bosnia. While there were some smaller, additional stories reported, relating to daily bombings, diplomatic developments and fighting, Taranger (1996: 133) notes: 'Bosnia at times almost seemed to disappear from view as the French focus of interest fell, for example, on the emotion of the families of the hostages, or on the French electoral campaign . . . This ethnocentrism cannot be considered as exceptional however; it is arguably a general feature of TV news.'

Secondly, domestication occurred through the use of language and tone to convey affiliation to either Serbs or Bosnians, according to the political-cultural stance of the country. As Tsagarousianou (1996) describes, the tone and positioning of a Greek report on the ANT1 channel about the (Muslim) Bosnian Prime Minister's participation in the *hadj* (pilgrimage) to Mecca worked as a means of furthering suspicion about Bosnian Muslims, through juxtaposing a description of the event with the news that the Bosnian Muslim spiritual leader had refused to meet the senior Serbian cleric. The *hadj* event was newsworthy because of 'the "proof" it provided regarding the "Islamic" character of the Republic of Bosnia-Herzegovina' (Tsagarousianou 1996: 139). The Russian channel Ostankino, in its report of the event, emphasised the generosity of the Serbs in allowing the air flight from Bosnia to Mecca in Saudi Arabia to take place. The Turkish channel TGRT described the story in positive terms, noting how the UN had finally agreed to give protection to the Bosnian pilgrims.

Thirdly, domestication was evident in the selection of visual images and narratives to underpin the dominant domestic interpretation of events or norms. In Algeria, the footage shown of Bosnian Muslims was nearly all that of traditional Islamic modes of dress and behaviour: all-male public spaces and all women wearing the veil (Khandriche 1996: 126). This type of portrayal fitted Algerian understanding of Muslim activity. In contrast, other, non-Muslim, countries portrayed the Bosnians quite differently, as Western 'people like us'. For example, one of the very few reports on American television during the week of analysis juxtaposed the lives of American and Bosnian children (Babbili 1996).

Table 7.1 International Content Analysis of the Reporting of the Bosnian War, 1994

	Reuters	CNNI	Euronews	Sky News	Algeria	Austria	Croatia	France	Greece	Italy	Maced.	Russia	Serbia	Slovenia	Turkey	UK	USA
Bosnian Muslim attack on Swedish convoy	*	*	*				A							A			
Clashes between Bosnian Serbs and Muslims near Tuzla	*	*	*	*		*	*	*	*	*		*	*	*	*		
Meeting between Serb President Milošević and Russian Special Envoy	*	*	*	*			*			*		*	*	*	*		
EU ministers meeting in Brussels to discuss Geneva peace plan		*					*	*	*			*		*	*		
French 'List for Sarajevo' development				*					*						*		
Serb shelling of hotel in Tuzla	*	*	*				*	*	*			*	*		*	*	
Hadj to Mecca by Muslims from Sarajevo	*	*	*		*		*					*	*		*	*	
Meeting of Russian and Serbian Orthodox church leaders	*		*				*		*			*	*	*			
British foreign minister threatens to withdraw British troops						*	*					*	*	*	*	*	
French aid workers freed by Serbs		*	*		*			*				*	*	*	*		
Meeting between Bosnian Serb leader Radovan Karadžić, Lord Owen and Thorvald Stoltenberg	*		*				*					*		*			
UN plane lands safely at Tuzla airport	*		*				*					*	*	*	*	*	*
French aid workers reunited with families			*					*				*					
Heavy shelling on route between Bosnian cities of Sarajevo and Tuzla		*													*		
British army officer apologises to Serb soldiers	*			*			*									*	
Opening-up of Croat and Muslim sectors in Mostar	*		*														
Sarajevo ceasefire lasts 100 days	*			*			*					*				*	

Note: A Both Croat and Slovenian television said that the attack was carried out by Bosnian Serbs.

Source: Preston 1996: 120.

The main illustration of the domestic appropriation of news from the week under analysis is that of a shelling of a hotel in the Bosnian city of Tuzla (Preston 1996). The Reuters television news agency distributed footage about the shelling on its World News feed, and its footage was used by a number of broadcasters – CNN International, MTV (Macedonia), Algerian state television, Show TV (Turkey), Croatian television, Slovenian television, Arte (France) and Megachannel (Greece). The same footage was used by most of these: a close-up in the hotel of a red telephone surrounded by debris, and jerky footage of the actual explosion. However, channels were less unanimous over the context and explanation for the bombing, reflecting each country's relationship with the war.

The Reuters Television text apportioned responsibility to the Serbs for the attack, albeit with some caution: 'Three tank shells, thought to be fired from Serb positions, hit the centre of Tuzla late on Sunday evening, two of them slamming into the city's main hotel.' Croatian, Slovenian, Turkish and French bulletins concurred and described the Serbs as perpetrators, for example Show TV (Turkey): 'In the Serbian artillery attack mounted against Tuzla, by chance no one was injured.' CNN International and Algerian TV reported the attack as a neutral event, without agency. CNN described the shelling almost as a natural phenomenon: 'Tank shells began falling last evening. Two struck the city's main hotel but caused no casualties, according to UN officials.' Algerian television news was similar in tone: 'the situation continues to be tense in Tuzla, where three shells fell on the town, on the central hotel'. However, while Megachannel in Greece and the Macedonian channel MTV reported the shelling itself as a neutral attack, by the position of the item within the bulletin they gave an impression that the shelling had been carried out by Muslims. Megachannel's newsreader announced at the start of its item: 'The situation worsens as Izetbegović's generals escalate their attacks against the Serbs, especially in Tuzla.' The bulletin then reported on a meeting in Belgrade between the Russian Special Envoy and the Serbian President. After this the anchor read: 'Clashes in Tuzla. A bomb fell on a hotel yesterday morning, wounding four.' Similarly, Macedonian MTV positioned its neutral report of the shelling after news of a Bosnian army attack on a UN convoy, implicating Bosnian agency in the Tuzla attack.

This tracking of a single news event across different countries clearly illustrates two key factors about the reporting of foreign news. First, that while there is increasing homogenisation of news footage and news sources, the refraction of news 'product' through individual nations' news outlets can remain distinct and particular. The war in Bosnia was a very different event for each of the countries analysed, and consequently, despite showing common footage at various points during the week, the messages that arose from it were quite distinct. This counters Hallin and Mancini's (1991) view that journalists covering an international event tend towards a 'global' framework rather than addressing particular national audiences. Secondly, the priority given to domestic dimensions of the war is an outcome of one of the fundamental purposes of television news: to act as a form of social cohesion. As Schudson (2005: 184) notes, 'journalists at mainstream publications everywhere accommodate to the political culture of the regime in which they operate'. In times of crisis or war, this accommodation is accentuated. As Turkovic (1996: 77) describes, during the war in Croatia, the peacetime norm of impartiality was not only dented, but replaced: 'The basic norm which governs the peacetime news programme – the norm of impartiality – is not just "loosened" in the case of the wartime news programme, and so permitting some degree of propagandistic manipulation, but is changed altogether into its opposite, the norm of partiality, that is partiality to "our cause".' For countries very close to or involved in the conflict, this norm of partiality in television news was present. For others, the norm of impartiality remained intact (although it is arguable that the potential result of such impartiality was to distance audiences from the realities of the war – in itself a political outcome).

Turning to the present period, the proliferation of news outlets on the internet raises questions about the extent to which mass-market television news will retain its socially cohesive role. It can be argued that the development of the internet as a news source, and the generation of news content by users directly, marks the beginning of the end of such dominance of 'traditional' news norms, and the possible development of a much less mediated news culture. However, such developments are unlikely to catalyse any change in the need for domestically refracted news. So far, the dominant source of news on the Web for UK users is the BBC – its News site received some 6 million unique users in September 2006, nearly three times more than its nearest competitor, *Guardian Unlimited*. *Yahoo! News* was third, with 1.9 million visitors (Ofcom 2007). The UK regulator Ofcom's audience research shows that television news-channel websites are the most commonly visited sources of news on-line; the desire for a known brand, providing news from a societally specific perspective, appears to be strong. Audiences tend to want narrative and explanation. Research in the UK suggests that people want more 'people like me' on screen. Among a variety of news topics, those that are defined as news by most, and those that are of most personal interest, are local and regional news. Audiences express a desire to be informed about things that affect them. It therefore seems likely that at a national level, at least, there will continue to be key providers of news narratives, tailored to common language, assumptions and understandings. This clearly raises issues and challenges for thinking about any transnational European sense of news values.

The Death and Funeral of Diana, Princess of Wales

A more recent case study that brings together elements from the discussion so far was the death and funeral of Diana, Princess of Wales in August and

September 1997. The television coverage of the events following Diana's death combines elements of rolling news, disaster coverage, standard news practices and media event coverage. The coverage also goes to the heart of some of the issues raised in this chapter – relating to the 'live' moment, eventfulness, the historical and the notion of the 'imagined community'. At the same time it also helps us to understand the kinds of conflict that such events can generate. As such, the case study of Diana in the British context ties in directly to the three key tensions which have been explored in this chapter: the relationship between the ordinary and the extraordinary; the tension between unity and division; and between live and recorded programming.

The death of Diana in a car crash in the early hours of Sunday 31 August 1997 in Paris began a week of intense media activity and apparently high public emotion in the UK – and was an event that seemingly sent shock waves around the world's media. The princess had been at the centre of press and media attention since just before her wedding to Prince Charles in 1981, and after years of controversy and bitter infighting with the British royal family she was still a glamorous figure and attracted much popular and international attention. In the week before her death the UK tabloid press was full of images of her relaxing on holiday in the south of France with her new boyfriend, Dodi Al Fayed. Her death in a high-speed car crash at the age of 36, while apparently being pursued by press photographers, was as shocking as it was unexpected.

This extraordinary news event disrupted and dominated the schedules of the main British television services. BBC1 ran rolling news throughout the day, with BBC2 simulcasting until mid-afternoon, and ITV ran coverage until the early evening before screening popular television drama. The live, rolling news coverage was delivered by sombre and at times visibly distressed newsreaders. Updates and bulletins replayed images of the crumpled Mercedes car in which the princess was a passenger, and early blame for the accident was attributed to the aggressive practices of the paparazzi. Earl Spencer, the Princess's brother, issued a scathing live statement from outside his home in South Africa denouncing the press for their intrusions into her life and their 'direct hand in her death'. Television reporters and presenters sought to distance themselves from tabloid press practices, and studio speculation focused on whether stronger press regulations and privacy laws should be imposed. The coverage of the aftermath of the accident had much in common with what Tamar Liebes (1998) has described as 'disaster marathons'. Liebes argues that such coverage is dangerous to proper democratic process because it emphasises blame and recrimination and can prompt ill-considered and hasty governmental responses.

The rolling news coverage also featured tributes to the princess, in news packages and clips about the princess's life and work, with eulogies and tributes from political leaders such as UK Prime Minister Tony Blair. That morning Tony Blair, in a live scene from outside his church in his parliamentary constituency, referred to a 'nation united in mourning' and described Diana as the 'People's Princess'. World figures, such as Nelson Mandela and Mother Teresa (who died later that week), also paid tribute. There was also speculation about the impact of Diana's death on the royal family. Reporters and camera crews were stationed outside the Queen's holiday residence in Balmoral in Scotland, and the coverage followed Prince Charles and Diana's two sisters as they boarded a flight to Paris to collect the princess's body. Later in the afternoon, images of the plane leaving Paris for the return journey, taking off into the setting sun, and pictures of the coffin being carried off the aircraft back in Britain were particularly poignant. A key element in the coverage was the images of people starting to gather outside London palaces to leave flowers. Some of the news footage included angry and emotional members of the public, and commentators spoke of the princess's popularity among a wide range of people. The focus on members of the public during the day may have arisen out of standard operational news practice; journalists and camera crews often visit the scene of a disaster to give the news a visual centre (Doane 1990). As the Paris authorities were quick to clear the car wreckage and open up the underpass where the accident took place, there was little visual centre. The veteran BBC correspondent Kate Adie noted (in Gibson 1998) that when she arrived at the scene in the afternoon, the images only looked like a local traffic report. In Adie's view, news images focused on crowds and flowers because they were 'something else to look at . . . not that concrete, smelly, traffic-ridden underpass'.

Throughout the day, the images of the crowds, the flowers, the tributes and the eulogies were played and replayed. An air of unreality hung over proceedings as well as footage of Diana in life, attending gala ceremonies, visiting people with AIDS or accompanying the two young Princes William and Harry on a theme park ride, were intercut with images of the wrecked car and the flowers. Although Diana was dead, she was still on television. The television coverage that Sunday can therefore be characterised by four main features (Turnock 2000). It was extraordinary (an extraordinary disruption of the schedules by an extraordinary event), it was extensive (day-long rolling coverage), it was emotive (including emotional displays, eulogies and a narrative of tragedy) and it was emphatic (emotional footage and responses were repeatedly used throughout the day).

The coverage also set up the narratives and conflicts for the week that followed, as the television schedules returned to more normal and familiar output. However, the death of the princess and its consequences continued to dominate news, and also a wide range of other programme forms such as daytime talk and magazine programmes. There were four main narratives. The first was the continuing pursuit of the cause of the accident. This was particularly the case when it was discovered on the Monday that the princess's chauffeur had been driving while over the legal alcohol limit. This calmed the accusations against the tabloid press, and coincided with an enormous rise in the consumption of newspapers that week. The UK tabloid the *Sun* 'reputedly' sold an extra million copies the day after Diana died (Higham 1997). Nonetheless, seven paparazzi were charged with manslaughter for impeding the rescue operation after the crash. The second major news narrative was the preparation for the funeral. As Diana was divorced from the heir to the throne, there was some ambiguity as to the level and status of her funeral – constitutionally it should not be a 'royal' funeral. There were also debates as to how public the funeral should be, and permission was only given to the BBC and to ITV on the Tuesday evening to broadcast the service from Westminster Abbey. As the week progressed, news coverage focused on the nature of the service, the length and make-up of the procession and other preparations. The third news narrative focused on increasing criticism of the royal family. In many of the obituaries and tributes to Diana much was made of the princess's unhappiness and the difficulties she had had with them. This was exacerbated by the Queen's refusal to leave Balmoral to return to London, which was read as evidence of royal indifference to the Princess's death and of the royal family being out of step with the apparent wave of public feeling. So stinging was the press criticism later in the week that the Queen was effectively forced to make a live television address to the nation on the evening before the funeral.

The fourth narrative that week focused on the public response. The wave of apparent public displays of emotion was hailed as 'unprecedented', with members of the public queuing for hours to sign books of condolence or leave flowers outside London palaces and other public places. Yet there was also a silent section of the British public who were uninterested in the life and death of Diana. This silent audience became increasingly frustrated by the continuing television coverage of the event and alarmed at the widespread public rhetoric of 'grief' and 'national unity'. In a survey conducted by the British Film Institute (BFI), 50 per cent of respondents claimed that they were not personally affected by the princess's death, and 70 per cent did not participate in any kind of public display of sentiment (Turnock 2000). Many of those who did not participate could not understand the apparent public response, taking a more traditional 'stiff upper-lip' view that mourning should not be a public thing. Others were dismayed by what they saw as 'mass hysteria' or media-induced participation. What is clear, however, is that the media exaggerated both the depth and extent of public feeling (Thomas 2002). This was done by news cameras focusing on images of people crying in the queues to leave flowers, for example, whereas most people were silent or solemn. It has been suggested (see Merck 1998) that many people in the streets were more interested in witnessing the apparent public event or participating in history, or were tourists and others enjoying the last days of summer rather than expressing strong feelings towards Diana. Yet cameras focused on a crying member of the public and zoomed out to see a homogenous mass of people, implying that all the people were crying (Kitzinger 1998). Many of the BFI's respondents claimed to feel isolated and alienated by such coverage. Some recorded family arguments about the princess's death, while others felt that they could not speak out in public for fear of censure from friends, family and colleagues. In many respects, divisions around Diana and mourning responses occurred along generational and gender lines, with women being more interested in Diana and older people more uncomprehending about the public displays of grief and sentiment. There may also have been national differences within the UK, with the Princess being referred to in the press as 'England's Rose' and not 'Britain's Rose' (Thomas 2002).

After a week marked by drama and conflict, the funeral of Diana on Saturday 6 September seemed an inclusive, conciliatory and cathartic event. Divorced from the heir to the throne, yet mother of the next in succession, the Princess's status was ambiguous. A Buckingham Palace spokesman described the planned funeral as 'a unique event for a unique person', but the senior correspondent John Simpson stated on the BBC evening news on 1 September, 'It may not technically be a royal funeral, but it will certainly look like one.' The route of the funeral cortège was expanded in the preceding days to allow more people to line the route and watch, and details were publicised in the national press and on television in advance. Television screens were erected in Hyde Park for members of the public, and cameras set up along the route, including BBC and ITV (with worldwide syndication arrangements) installed in Westminster Abbey.

The coverage followed the funeral cortège on its two-hour journey, through silent streets lined with people, passing the symbolic landmarks of royalty and the state, Buckingham Palace and Whitehall. A sense of formality and historical continuity was provided in the BBC coverage by the commentary of David Dimbleby, the son of the famous broadcaster Richard Dimbleby who had commentated for television at the Queen's Coronation in 1953 and Winston Churchill's funeral in 1965. The cortège arrived at the Abbey before 11.00 a.m. and the coverage continued through the service. The service inclusively mixed the religious and secular, reflecting the light and popular touch of Diana herself. It included traditional hymns and prayers alongside readings and an address by the princess's brother Earl Spencer, and a live rendition of the pop song 'Candle in the Wind' by Elton John (Davies 1999). The inclusive and popular nature of the event was particularly felt when crowds in Hyde Park watching the television coverage on the large screens started applauding Earl Spencer's speech, and the sound was heard inside the Abbey, causing members of the congregation also to start applauding (Davies 1999). After a national one minute's silence, the main broadcasters followed the hearse through London streets lined with people clapping and throwing flowers, and then from the air as it drove to Diana's burial place.

The television coverage was watched by 32 million people throughout the UK, and had an estimated worldwide audience of 2.5 billion. In the UK the event was perceived as inclusive because it allowed access for the public at a number of levels, to watch the live coverage, to attend the streets in London, and because of the traditional and popular appeal of the funeral service. The event was conciliatory because there was a shared ritualistic moment of togetherness, an apparent moment of national unity, and the monopolistic coverage of the funeral focused on the positive attributes of tradition and unity. The event was also conciliatory and cathartic because funeral rites function as a celebration of group survival (Walter 1999) and as a removal of the body, which symbolises the disruptive potency of death (Richardson 1999). As a result, the Princess's funeral marked the emotional and symbolic closure to a week of conflict, distress and disruption.

The Princess's funeral conforms to both the idea of the 'imagined community' (Anderson 1991) and the model of media events proposed by Dayan and Katz (1992). In the first sense the broadcasts marked a shared moment for people in Britain, articulated through the rhetoric of 'the People's Princess' (the idea of the 'nation united in grief'). The news and the moment in history was shared and articulated by the media, and by television especially, with its instantaneity and liveness. The broadcasting of the funeral and the minute of national silence were key moments in the articulation of the imagined community. In terms of media events, the funeral marked a disruption to the normal schedules, it was monopolistic in that it dominated the media and it was pre-planned and primarily organised by institutions outside the media (although television was clearly central to the way the event was staged). It also marked the symbolic closure of a period of trauma and conflict (Turner 1982). Dayan and Katz (1992: 139) also argue that the large audiences that these events generate articulate a loyalty to the core values expressed by the event. As such, events can act as a 'confirmation of loyalty, as a reiteration of the social contract between citizens and their leaders'.

Yet in the case of the funeral of the Princess of Wales there are some factors which complicate this view. There were nearly 25 million people in the UK who did not watch the funeral (Thomas 2002). In the survey conducted by the BFI, 50 per cent claimed they were affected by the princess's death, but this means that 50 per cent were not (Turnock 2000). Nonetheless, 70 per cent of the BFI sample watched the funeral, so many of those who watched it were not particularly interested in Diana or moved by her death. What the BFI sample reveals is that many watched the funeral because the shops were closed and many other sporting and public events had been cancelled, and there was nothing else on television. Some viewers watched the funeral not because of Diana herself, but because they wanted to watch a televised 'historic' event. Interestingly, many of those not interested in Diana, or who had been dismissive of the coverage throughout the week, found the broadcast of the funeral moving and poignant. What this suggests is that such events generate uneven and complex responses, and that such responses might be prompted by the formal structure and aesthetics of the broadcast event as well as or instead of the nature of the event being represented (Turnock 2000).

Indeed, Stephanie Marriott (2007) has shown that despite the differences among television audiences, BBC and ITV particularly strove to make the coverage inclusive, solemn and recuperative, avoiding as much as possible the discord and disharmony of the week. This was in contrast, however, to the more irreverent and lively discussions held by American commentators during the live feeds to the USA.

Television Events in Europe

The case studies in this chapter have explored a number of tensions and issues that impact on the thinking about a range of different kinds of event that are broadcast on television. Three related key tensions were identified at the outset. These were the tension between live and recorded programming, between the extraordinary event and ordinary or routine television programming, and between the social cohesion and potential division that events can engender. It is difficult to draw broad conclusions here, but some of the complex and multifaceted strands discussed in this chapter overlap.

This chapter has mainly looked at live events, but we have also seen that recorded programming can constitute or make up parts of major events. Past European events can be fictionalised and presented as recorded television drama, as in the example of the US mini-series *Holocaust*. The entry of this recorded television drama in the West German and Austrian public sphere made its transmission a remarkable event in its own right. News events can also be circulated in both live feeds and recorded film and videotapes – something that has been facilitated by the developments in communications technologies. During the Bosnian war, the same news footage was used in packages and inserted into different news bulletins in different ways. This also raises questions about how footage translates across borders and cultures. Furthermore, the rolling live news in the aftermath of the death of Princess Diana heavily relied upon recorded footage. The live coverage depended on stock footage of the Princess while she was alive to explore her life in pictures and to support eulogising and speculation. Interviews with famous people and members of the public, and images of people attending and leaving flowers were also used and reused in packaged reports. The packages were shown partly because they articulated the news story powerfully, but also because live rolling news needs to fill airtime in the absence of 'new' news. The transmission of images of Diana over and over again served to undermine the idea that television could capture the sudden and violent discontinuity of her death.

Televised events have promoted unity yet also secured a sense of difference and conflict. The case of the European Song Contest has shown how it emphasised Finland's geopolitical and cultural isolation, and how at the same time it also created conflict over how best to represent Finnish culture. The coverage of the Romanian national day also aimed to represent national unity. Yet there was clearly a separation between the public action of people in the streets and the viewership of people in private. This raises questions about how to understand media events within the contexts of totalitarian regimes. The television coverage in the aftermath of the death of Princess Diana emphasised a rhetoric of national mourning while promoting conflict within its news agendas. The coverage dwelt first on apportioning blame, and later it juxtaposed the apparent popular displays of emotion against the reluctance of the Queen to return from Scotland to make a personal public statement. By comparing the Romanian national-day coverage with the death of Diana it is possible to see the television techniques that are deployed to imply mass and collective actions. In Romania this was through the use of the long shot and bird's-eye views of crowds and banners; in Britain it was through close-ups on individual mourners crying that were placed amid medium or long-shots which implied that everyone in the queue or crowd was also crying (Kitzinger 1998). As with the Romanian coverage, there was also some discrepancy between the public displays on the streets of London and the feelings of many viewers at home. Many of those watching television had not been interested in Diana, and they found the intense coverage of apparent public sentiment bewildering and isolating. Nonetheless, the coverage of the Princess's funeral was deliberately conciliatory and inclusive.

The meanings of such media texts can be especially unstable, however, when they cross international borders. The Eurovision Song Contest is open to a wide range of complex and multifaceted readings when it is transmitted simultaneously around Europe. The conciliatory tone of the UK broadcasters in the coverage of Diana's funeral was also undermined, for example, by the more conflictual, sensational and irreverent commentaries in the USA over the British live feeds. This refraction and domestication of news event content was seen during the Bosnian war, with different countries accentuating different aspects of the footage to accord with national news tastes and agendas. There were even instances where the use of the same footage imputed blame for a shelling to different combatants, and this was dependent on the national allegiances of the broadcaster. There were also conflicts and disagreements about *Holocaust*. US critics and viewers were concerned with issues of quality and taste, while some East Germans expressed surprise at some of the reactions to the series by their West German neighbours (while also dismissing the commercial nature of US programming).

The case studies here have also circled around the tension between ordinary and extraordinary. Most of what is on television is of a routine, habitual and familiar nature. Despite Dayan and Katz (1992) claiming that events like the Olympic Games and football World Cup constitute media events because they are based on interruption and disruption, this chapter has suggested that such events can also be considered part of the routine and ordinary cycle of sporting programmes. The Romanian national-day events were also expected annual occasions. Those events and representations of events that do cause an unusual, unexpected and extraordinary stir are often the result of routine, rationalised and professional practices. *Holocaust* was a television drama produced by professionals using standardised industry practices within the context of a commercial entertainment-based network. Despite the subject matter, the US television industry had already shown itself interested in controversial histories with the production of *Roots*, a historical drama about black-American slavery which aired on ABC the previous year (Morey 2004). Even the British news coverage of the death of Princess Diana, itself a remarkable and unexpected event, used standardised news practices and can be contextualised within an emerging genre of 'disaster marathons'.

However, to draw attention to the routine and standardised aspects of the textual properties and production practices of these occasions is not to deny the interest, controversy, depth of emotion, commitment or sense of anxiety and extraordinariness that these events can generate. What it should point to, however, is the very constructed quality of those texts. The transmission and portrayal of any event is necessarily dependent on the 'attitude' or 'demeanour' of the broadcasting institution (Scannell 1996). No event is value-free and neither is its mediation or interpretation. Historically, and across cultures and borders, values change. The problems of understanding this become even more acute when programming and events intersect with the range of factors such as gender, class, religion, ethnicity and cultural and social variations that impact on viewing practices and experiences. The claims made by broadcasters and the values of the event texts they produce may be assimilated, appropriated or rejected by audiences in complex, divergent and paradoxical ways in a multitude of different contexts.

References

Anderson, B. (1991) *Imagined Communities: Reflections on the Origin and Spread of Nationalism*. London, Verso.

Babbili, A. (1996) 'United States of America'. In: Gow, J. et al. (eds.) *Bosnia by Television*. London, BFI, pp. 176–8.

Baudrillard, J. (1995) *The Gulf War Did Not Take Place*. Sydney, Power Publications.

Berry, D. (2004) *The Romanian Mass-Media and Cultural Development*. Burlington, Ashgate.

Bourdon, J. (2000) 'Live television is still alive: on television as an unfulfilled promise'. *Media, Culture & Society* 22, 531–56.

Boyd-Barrett, O. (1996) 'Global news wholesalers as agents of globalization'. In: Srebreny-Mohammadi, A. et al. (eds.) *Media in a Global Context*. London, Arnold, pp. 131–44.

Davies, Douglas (1999) 'The week of mourning'. In: Walter, T. (ed.) *The Mourning for Diana*. Oxford, Berg, pp. 3–18.

Dayan, D. and Katz, E. (1992) *Media Events: The Live Broadcasting of History*. Cambridge, MA, Harvard University Press.

Dayan, D. and Katz, E. (1995) 'Political ceremony and instant history'. In: Smith, A. (ed.) *Television: An International History.* Oxford, Oxford University Press, pp. 169–88.

Diem, P. (1980) 'Die Wirkung der Fernsehserie "Holocaust" auf die Zuseher in Österreich'. *Rundfunk und Fernsehen* 28, 574–82.

Doane, M. A. (1990) 'Information, crisis, catastrophe'. In: Mellencamp, P. (ed.) *Logics of Television: Essays in Cultural Criticism.* London, BFI, pp. 222–39.

Ellis, J. (1982) *Visible Fictions: Cinema, Television, Video.* London, Routledge.

Ellis, J. (2000) *Seeing Things. Television in the Age of Uncertainty.* London and New York, I. B. Tauris.

Gibson, J. (1998) 'TV news "has heart" since Diana's death'. *Guardian*, 31 August, p. 6.

Gow, J., Paterson, R. and Preston, A. (eds.) (1996) *Bosnia by Television.* London, BFI.

Hallin, D. and Mancini, P. (1991) 'Summits and the constitution of an international public sphere: the Reagan–Gorbachev meetings as televised media events'. *Communications* 12, 249–65.

Harle, V. and Moisio, S. (2000) *Missä on Suomi? Kansallisen identiteettipolitiikan historia ja geopolitiikka.* Tampere: Vastapaino.

Higham, N. (1997) 'Change in the air'. *Ariel*, 9 September, p. 7.

Hobsbawm, E. and Ranger, T. (1983) *The Invention of Tradition.* Cambridge, Cambridge University Press.

Khandriche, Z. (1996) 'Algeria'. In: Gow, J. et al. (eds.) *Bosnia by Television.* London, BFI, pp. 126–7.

Kitzinger, J. (1998) 'Image'. *Screen* 39:1, 73–9.

Langer, J. (1998) *Tabloid Television.* London, Routledge.

Liebes, T. (1998) 'Television's disaster marathons: a danger for democratic process?' In: Libes, T. and Curran, J. (eds.) *Media, Ritual and Identity.* London, Routledge, pp. 71–84.

MacGregor, B. (1997) *Live, Direct and Biased? Making Television News in the Satellite Age.* London, Arnold.

McNair, B. (2003) *News and Journalism in the UK.* London, Routledge.

Marriott, S. (2007) 'The BBC, ITN and the funeral of Princess Diana'. *Media History* 13:1, 93–110.

Marvin, C. (1988) *When Old Technologies Were New: Thinking about Communications in the Late Nineteenth Century.* New York and Oxford, Oxford University Press.

Merck, M. (ed.) (1998) *After Diana: Irreverent Elegies.* London, Verso.

Morey, A. (2004) 'Holocaust'. In: Newcomb, H. (ed.) *The Encyclopedia of Television* (2nd edn). New York, Fitzroy Dearborn, pp. 1111–12.

Noam, E. (1991) *Television in Europe.* Oxford, Oxford University Press.

Ofcom (2007) *New News Future News.* London, Office of Communications.

Pajala, M. (2006) *Erot järjestykseen! Eurovision laulukilpailu, kansallisuus ja televisio-historia.* Jyväskylä, Nykykulttuurin tutkimuskeskus.

Pajala, M. (2007) 'Finland, zero points: nationality, failure, and shame in the Finnish media'. In: Raykoff, I. and Deam Tobin, R. (eds.) *A Song for Europe: Popular Music and Politics in the Eurovision Song Contest.* Burlington, Ashgate, pp. 71–82.

Parks, L. (2001) 'As the earth spins: NBC's wide wide world and live global television in the 1950s'. *Screen* 42:4, 332–49.

Paterson, C. (1996) 'Global television news services'. In: Srebreny-Mohammadi, A. et al. (eds.) *Media in a Global Context.* London, Arnold, pp. 145–60.

Preston, A. (1991) *The Impact of Technology on Current British Television News Bulletins*. MA thesis, Institute of Communications, University of Leeds.

Preston, A. (1996) 'Introduction to Part Four'. In: Gow, J. et al. (eds.) *Bosnia by Television*. London, BFI, pp. 119–25.

Preston, A. (2000) *The Development of the UK TV News Industry 1982–1998*. PhD thesis, University of Stirling.

Ratesh, N. (1991) *Romania: The Entangled Revolution*. New York, Praeger.

Richardson, R. (1999) 'Disposing with Diana: Diana's death and British funerary culture'. *New Formations* 36, 21–33.

Salokangas, R. (1996) *Aikansa oloinen: Yleisradion historia 1946–1996*. Helsinki, YLE.

Saur, K.-O. (1979) 'Holocaust – nur ein Cornflakes-Melodram?' *Süddeutsche Zeitung*, 22 January, p. 21.

Scannell, P. (1996) *Radio, Television and Modern Life: A Phenomenological Approach*. Oxford and Cambridge, MA, Blackwell.

Schudson, M. (2005) 'Four approaches to the sociology of news'. In: Curran, J. and Gurevitch, M. (eds.) *Mass Media and Society* (4th edn). London, Hodder Arnold, pp. 172–97.

Silverstone, R. (1994) *Television and Everyday Life*. London, Routledge.

Spigel, L. (1992) *Make Room for TV: Television and the Family Ideal in Postwar America*. Chicago and London, University of Chicago Press.

Szajkowski, B. (1991) *New Political Parties of Eastern Europe and the Soviet Union*. Harlow, Longman.

Taranger, M. (1996) 'France'. In: Gow, J. et al. (eds.) *Bosnia by Television*. London, BFI, pp. 133–5.

Tatulici, M. (ed.) (1990) *Revolutia Romana in Direct*. Bucharest, Combinatul Poligraphic.

Taylor, P. M. (1992) *War and the Media: Propaganda and Persuasion in the Gulf War*. Manchester, Manchester University Press.

Thomas, J. (2002) *Diana's Mourning: A People's History*. Cardiff, University of Wales Press.

Tsagarousianou, R. (1996) 'Greece'. In: Gow, J. et al. (eds.) *Bosnia by Television*. London, BFI, pp. 136–40.

Turkovic, H. (1996) 'Controlling national attitudes: war and peace in Croatian TV news'. In: Gow, J. et al. (eds.) *Bosnia by Television*. London: BFI, pp. 72–80.

Turner, V. (1969) *The Ritual Process: Structure and Anti-Structure*. Ithaca, NY, Cornell University Press.

Turner, V. (1982) *From Ritual to Theatre: The Human Seriousness of Play*. New York, PAJ.

Turnock, R. (2000) *Interpreting Diana: Television Audiences and the Death of a Princess*. London, BFI.

Walter, T. (1999) 'The questions people asked'. In: Walter, T. (ed.) *The Mourning For Diana*. Oxford, Berg, pp. 19–47.

Williams, R. (1990) *Television, Technology and Cultural Form*. London, Routledge.

Yleisradion vuosikertomus 1964 (YLE annual report).

8

European Television Audiences:
Localising the Viewers

Mats Björkin, with Juan Francisco Gutiérrez Lozano

. . . the economic difference between viewers and non-viewers is diminishing and almost certainly the same is true of occupational and educational levels. The time is coming, if indeed it has not already come, when there will be little to distinguish the television public from a cross-section of the population . . .
(Emmet 1956: 284)

In the audience research conducted by BBC's Audience Research Department during the first part of the 1950s it rapidly become more and more obvious that the economic and educational difference between the television audience and the British public in general was becoming reduced. In relation to class, this, according to the BBC researchers, meant that the television audience was no longer dominated by the upper and lower middle class. The working class was going to take over. It seems that classification of audiences has been a major preoccupation of television audience research from the very beginning. This is not surprising, since most audience research has been conducted or commissioned by the broadcasters themselves. Public service broadcasters have had, and still have, a need to legitimate their (often privileged) position, and justify why taxes or licence fees should go to them. Commercial television broadcasters must have knowledge about their audience in order to argue why advertisers should use their medium rather than go to a competitor.

This means that we know a great deal about particular audience preferences, for example which programmes have been preferred at a certain time. Again, since most audience research has been carried out in the interest of broadcasters, it has been focused on knowledge that could be of interest for programme development and scheduling. Based on quantitative and (gradually) qualitative methods broadcasters wanted to get to know their audiences, and while creating knowledge of audiences they created their audiences in the image of that knowledge. Definitions and classifications created typical audience behaviours and typical viewers, for which broadcasters could create programmes. Simultaneously, from the 1950s onwards, sociologists and other researchers interested in contemporary society began seeing television as an object worth studying for its impacts, its effects on viewers. This could include effects related to political issues, effects of advertising, often the effects on children and viewers thought to be more easily affected or seduced by television, that is, children, women and working-class people. Most commonly this was linked to the statistically dominating working-class audience. This academic image of the audience was as static and passive as the broadcasters' conception of their audience.

Independent of perspective, whether the audience was active or passive, or could be described as 'audience-as-market' or 'audience-as-public', whether the view of television could be labelled 'optimistic' or 'pessimistic' (Morley 1992), the struggle over the television audience seems to have been constructive for media research as long as television has existed. Academic research has successfully connected programmes, formats and genres to particular audience categories, but mainly on a national level. On the other hand, most of the published introductions to audience research are very generalising and unspecific, though most often, directly or indirectly, building on American and/or British examples (Hay, Grossberg & Wartella 1996, Dickinson, Harindranath and Linné 1998). It is as if those television systems that have contributed the most programmes and programme formats have also 'exported' not only theories and methods of audience research, but also the questions asked in this field of study.

The prefatory quotation above from the 1956 article on the British television audience not only indicates the characteristics of this television audience, but it equates the television audience with 'a cross-section of the population'. If that is a reasonable conclusion, studying the television audience is studying the population, with television as a contributing factor. Studying the relations between text and viewer is one thing, while studying all aspects of the television viewer is something completely different. The latter is of course not possible, or rather, that is what different national statistical agencies are doing all the time, but they rarely include attitudes and experiences of television in their studies. If it is not possible to distinguish the television audience from other constellations of individuals, television audiences are not individuals as a whole, but something most people are to some degree from time to time. Following John Hartley, this could be described in the following way:

> The TV audience doesn't exist as such. Instead, 'the audience' is a discursive construct of (among others) media organizations, government regulators and academic criticism, all of which make a metaphorical extension from the tradi-

tional idea of the audience as a self-present assembly and apply this metaphor to unknown populations of, for instance, individuals-in-families at home. Those who construct audiences in this way go on to use what they 'know' about them to authorize acts undertaken in institutions from which audiences-as-people are routinely excluded, including government, media and academic/critical institutions. (Hartley 1999: 491)

The next step is to make a distinction between individuals viewing television and television audiences.

For a European comparative perspective this is particularly important. The 'discursively' constructed audience differs with programming (and other textual) traditions and the 'real' people differ with national, regional and local traditions. Understanding television audiences thereby becomes an issue of finding methods of making meaningful connections between television viewing and other human activities.

Qualifying Quantitative Information

One example of the problems of interpreting survey material is Mark A. Wolfgram's research based on audience surveys in GDR in the 1970s. It is always necessary to discuss the reliability of any statistical material, but perhaps even more so in a totalitarian state like Communist East Germany. When asked about viewing of obviously propagandistic programmes, party members are not likely to reveal that they were not watching. Another problematic aspect was the question of anonymity, in a survey conducted through door-to-door interviews (Wolfgram 2006: 60). Here, even the survey methods can tell us something about the audience. Not all television owners had a telephone, so personal interviews were the only possible way of conducting the research. Another reason might of course have been eventual connections to other reasons for controlling citizens (on the part of the secret police, the Stasi). Notwithstanding these problems, material like this from the GDR cannot only say something about what it originally aimed at achieving, namely to document attitudes towards individual programmes, but can also contribute to an understanding of what it was like to be a television viewer in the GDR. If a person was a party member, or was striving for a bureaucratic career, to watch news or political commentaries was perhaps not only a way of knowing what was going on, it was just as much a part of a person's professional life. For those who could see West German television, which most East Germans could, a window to another, unreachable lifestyle was opened up. But it was also an act of subversion. More interesting is how the widespread possibility of watching West German television created an alternative public sphere, outside the official political system, but open to almost everyone. Studying historical audience surveys are thus not only ways of understanding television viewing, for the conditions of conducting them could tell us equally as much.

Even if, most of the time, television audiences are very much like the rest of the population, television has made a difference. Societies have changed when television has become a dominating medium. Families have changed with the presence of the television set amongst them. The question is how. It seems that descriptions of how television made a difference have suffered from the transference of results from those countries where television first made its entrance (the United States, the UK, France) to other countries as well. Television was said to have created cultural uniformity, overemphasised the nuclear family, and devalued public life and the ordinary community experience in bars, pubs, restaurants and so on.

Although television reception in many countries started with a mix of private and public viewing, because of the relative expense of television sets it soon primarily became something done in private, within the home. Television sets in public spaces, shop windows or bars were obviously important for spreading the knowledge of television, and were also a way of integrating television into already existing social contexts. It is interesting, for example, to see how soon television became a subject of discussion within education, emphasising pedagogical uses of public viewing practices, and quite often as attempts to support public television viewing outside urban areas. UNESCO's support of the community 'téléclubs' in rural France is a good example of how public viewing of television was seen as having a potential use for educational purposes, as well as the importance of finding ways of creating possibilities for an active audience (Cassirer 1960, Dumazedier 1956). But both public viewing, and the optimism of educational uses, soon became marginal in comparison to private viewing.

It is remarkable how long it took for the home and family life to become the focus of television audience studies. In, for example, David Morley's and Charlotte Brunsdon's *Nationwide* studies from the late 1970s families are present, but more at a discourse level, rather than as constituting the physical and social context of television viewing (Morley 1980, Brunsdon & Morley 1978). Home and family became the object of American studies in the early 1990s; most well known is perhaps the work of Lynn Spigel. Her emphasis was on 'how ideals of family life and domestic recreation supplied a framework of ideas and expectations about how television could best be incorporated into the home' (Spigel 1992: 11). Spigel's work seems to have been influential even in Europe, which perhaps has resulted in too much emphasis on the importance of the nuclear family, again, a transference of result rather than of questions and research methods. Using Spigel's method for European audiences requires a very keen concern for national, regional and local differences in family life.

One such example of the importance of taking the social context into consideration is the Swedish discussion during the 1950s on the nature of the television audience. As in many countries the debate focused on public service and/or commercial television. But, with its strong social democratic system, there was little room for commercial alternatives.

'Housewife's Films' as an Alternative to Commercial Television

When Swedish television officially started in September 1956 commercial television was banned. The public service system that followed would remain without competition for more than 30 years. But in 1956 commercial television was still a hot topic within Swedish business and industry as well as in the film industry. The framework for television advertising was well established, and there was certainly a demand for and public interest in commercial television. Through the debate over commercial television in Sweden it is possible to describe how integrated the idea of commercial television was, even in a semi-socialist system like Social Democratic post-Second World War Sweden.

In an advertisement from 1959, a company called Husmors Filmer AB – Housewife's Films Inc. (and we will use this literal English translation in what follows) – described the success of American television advertising and said that it would take a long time before it would be possible to broadcast television advertising in Sweden. Therefore, potential advertisers should come to Housewife's Films. Their services were, they said, even better than television advertising. They listed five reasons why this was so:

1. Their films were in colour.
2. They were screened in large-screen format with a better and sharper image.
3. They were screened in a dark space, without 'disturbing elements', that is, children.
4. The audience had come to see the films intending to pick up information (to 'see and learn') and was thereby focused on getting information about different products.
5. Housewife's Films, and their other product, Youth Films, were selective means of advertising, which reduced what they called 'contact cost', that is, the cost of reaching and making an impact on each potential customer.

After that they added one more argument. At that time, in 1959, Housewife's Films had been screened in all the major cities of Sweden, twice a year, where one in every four housewives had seen them. That, according to the advertisement, was better than most American television programmes.

So, what *were* Housewife's Films? They were not ordinary commercial films for cinema theatres. They were especially composed and carefully constructed programmes of about 60–90 minutes long, and were made up of 7–10 information and advertising films, each 5–15 minutes long. The programme was held together by a host, most often some sort of celebrity, well known from women's magazines, entertainment, cinema, and later even from television. These programmes toured around Sweden between 1954 and 1972 and were shown at cinemas, for free, during the afternoon.

It was not a coincidence that they started in 1952, at the height of the first debate about commercial television, two years before the first Swedish experiments with commercial television (Olsson 2004). But, at first, they emphasised another source of inspiration. Together with the films the company published a magazine called *Husmors-Journalen* (*Housewife's Journal*). In the very first issue the editors described the need for 'sober advertising'. By that they meant something which should be as much informative as designed for selling. Good advertising was seen as a way of making a housewife's day more efficient. It is important, here, to add that their definition of a 'housewife' was a married woman, with children, with a part-time job outside the home. Because of her life outside it, the home itself needed to be as efficient and well organised as possible. Most of all, there was little time to collect information about different products, and therefore Housewife's Films saw the need for an improved form of advertising.

What was never stated but often implied was that a housewife's part-time job gave the family more money, gave the housewife a limited form of economic independence, and thereby made her into an even more interesting and attractive consumer. When focusing on advertising, those few Swedish scholars who have studied these films have seen this development as the outcome of the post-war diffusion of American capitalist ideology. When looking at the informational aspect, they have seen the films as the result of three decades of social engineering. Both interpretations tend to disregard how Housewife's Films were embedded in contemporary discourses on media use. Housewife's Films were, from the beginning, not implemented as an alternative to television, but they came to fulfil a similar demand. Moreover, they looked like television. The products shown and the ideal of the nuclear family presented in these films are strikingly close to the ideal of the American family (as discussed by Spigel 1992).

Domestic products such as washing machines, detergents and kitchen equipment dominated the programmes of Housewife's Films. During the 1950s domestic products also seem to have been more actively advertised, and marketed in a more modern way, involving consumer and women's organisations. Their engagement in Housewife's Films was as immediate as it was serious. There are many advertisements and articles in home and women's magazines about efficient housework and new technologies for improving housework, like washing machines controlled by punchcards. New technologies, new methods, and a scientific knowledge of the functions of a household had strong roots in the 1930s debates on the functionalist home, covering everything from city planning and architecture to methods of hygiene and cooking. In consequence, companies and public organisations involved in home technology, hygiene and consumption were very active in commissioning and producing films for Housewife's Films.

An argument found everywhere in advertising and information discourses during the early 1950s was that a site for learning was also a good site for selling. It could even be better than traditional advertising. What is interesting is the widespread idea that audiovisual media in combination with human contact was the most effective means possible for both learning and selling. Another outcome of this was that issues of learning and selling were regarded as an organisational problem, or even as a spatial problem. Again, the best place to sell something must be found where people are prepared to learn things. As a consequence of the idea of contact, companies spent a great deal of resources on film, travelling exhibitions, industry fairs and public displays. Films, and slideshows with sound, became a well-known form of communication, especially among the growing middle classes and the more skilled manual workers. The 1950s was also a time of increased vocational education and new methods for education and training within companies to overcome the difficulties of finding and attracting young people. In all these areas films were used frequently. It was therefore scarcely a surprise for anyone to encounter moving images outside cinema theatres.

But even if more and more women started to work outside their homes, they were perhaps the only group that was not reached by the industrial and informational film industry. This was a good opportunity for Housewife's Films, but a problem for the advocates of television advertising. There were two categories of people and organisations who argued against television advertising. The first of these were those who argued that all forms of advertising simply tried to convince customers with false arguments and made products more expensive. In this camp we find the ruling Social Democratic Party, the Communist Party, many intellectuals and the national radio broadcaster. The second group comprised those who were afraid of losing income due to increased competition in advertising. In this group we find almost all newspapers, even the more liberal and market-friendly ones. The ever-present ghost haunting this situation was American television. It was regarded as vulgar (a common European anti-American argument), 'too commercial' and lacking in all forms of quality. The question is not whether this was a correct description (it sometimes may have been), but whether it was at all relevant for the question of whether Sweden should have commercial television or not. The advocates of commercial television either said that American television was not too bad, and rather argued that advertising even made television better; or they agreed with the view that American television was not particularly good, but that that was not a relevant issue. The United States was so different from Sweden, they argued, that any comparison between the two was irrelevant. Instead they advocated that Sweden should look to West Germany, the UK, Italy or any other European country, except Albania, that already had or planned commercial television networks.

When studying this debate today, it seems at first incomprehensible why the comparisons with West Germany and the UK were not persuasive. There are many reasons why, and the Housewife's Films can be of help to understand some of these reasons. First we have the conditions, the taken-for-granted assumptions, and views expressed on television, of those who opposed commercial television.

1. Television was seen as a medium for public information that should not compete with other channels of information.
2. Television was directed to the home. Homes in the Social Democratic, functionalist ideology were places for sobriety, contemplative reading, human interaction within the nuclear family and the education of children. In other words, the home was a site of social learning, a place where, according to contemporary psychological and pedagogical knowledge, people would have difficulties defending themselves against advertising.
3. Television would distract men from relaxing after work, women from doing the housework and children from doing their homework and playing. Commercial television would result in transforming consumption from being a rational household activity into an amusement.
4. Television was a threat to a view that separated consumption from information and learning.
5. More important here is that, while industrial and informational films had required *contact* and the films thereby became a tool for someone to inform or convince others, television was impersonal. It relied on indirect human interaction, in a situation or place where people not only were prepared for learning but also prepared for unconditional human interaction. This was sometimes described in terms of trust.

At this point we could easily compare this situation with studies of, for example, American television. But there is one important difference. Housewives were seen as a more important target for advertising outside the home, rather than inside. Even advocates of television advertising assumed women were working at least part-time. In practice this was a dangerous assumption since the majority of women actually did not work outside the home at all. Probably that is the reason why advertisers wanted to reach people in their own homes, while arguing the accepted version of this discourse. It may be one reason why Housewife's Films were so popular, since they reached both categories of women.

Urbanisation and Modernisation: Television Audiences in Milan

The early history of television in Italy is a telling example of yet another form of national and cultural appropriation of the new medium and of the social construction of an audience. Research in rural southern Italy shows that there, television's cultural impact was heavily connected to a movement from the public to the private, from bars and restaurants to the home. Research based in urban northern Italy, where the post-war economic boom, *il miracolo economico*, was more present suggests that the cultural impact of television was more complicated. A movement from public to private spaces also meant going from a primarily male context (very few women went to bars and restaurants alone) to the space of the family. John Foot (1999: 380–1) describes this complexity in an article on the introduction of television in Milan:

. Television had contradictory effects on all sectors of cultural and economic life; it encouraged atomisation of the family unit, but also promoted collective consumption in places designed for other activities. It educated and opened horizons, but also tended towards a levelling (up and down) of cultural and everyday outlooks. It both liberated and imprisoned the mind. It encouraged consumerism, as well as criticisms of that consumerism. Some effects were short-term, some are still being felt. In short, the impact of television was extremely complicated and contradictory and difficult to characterise in simplistic terms.

Foot discusses, among many things, the transformation of the *salotto* or *soggiorno*, that is, the living room. In many homes the living room was only used for special family occasions, but when it became the site of the television set it opened up and became more of an everyday space. When placed in the kitchen or the dining room the television set affected eating habits and the role of family dinners (Foot 1999: 384–6).

Television entered into a complex relationship with daily family routines. Children's bedtime became determined by popular television shows, but its influence also went in the other direction. Initially programmes aimed at children were put at a time when children should have finished their homework. Also in the first years of Italian television, 'there were no programmes at all between 7.30 and 8.45 p.m., to "allow" the family to eat' (Foot 1999: 386). Later this adaptation to family routines ended, forcing television and family life to go on simultaneously.

Early Italian television is interesting also in the way it put the focus on urban life. In comparison to American television during the 1950s, where so much attention has been focused on suburbanisation, the strong position of Milanese television connected the medium with urbanisation and industrialisation. It perhaps even affected the large migration from the south to the north during the 1950s and 1960s; perhaps not the migration itself, but views of what the migrants thought they were striving after, what they dreamt of. Despite the importance of micro-studies, of local examples, a key to understanding television audiences could just as well be to look at audiences in motion; in relation to both voluntary and involuntary migrants.

Emigration and Television Audiences in Spain

Spain is among the leading countries in Europe in terms of number of immigrants received. In 2006, residents of foreign origin accounted for 8.4 per cent of the total population (some 3,730,000 people). The situation in Spain today is entirely different to the one that prevailed there four decades ago in the 1960s, when the country exported its workforce. Thousands of young people from the more economically backward regions (notably Galicia and Andalusia) moved either to other cities in Spain or abroad in search of a brighter future. At the same time, the development of television was in its formative stages.

The phenomenon of mass emigration saw people relocate both within Spain itself, moving from the countryside to the cities, and beyond its borders, primarily to other European countries or to Latin America. According to official statistics gathered by the Instituto Nacional de Estadística (2006), a little over 1.1 million Spaniards now reside abroad. More than 600,000 of these live in Latin America and some 475,000 in Europe. However, these figures are way below those recorded during the emigration phenomenon of the 1960s and early 1970s. The foreign currency brought in by Spain's emigrants was partly responsible for the economic growth that the country experienced during this same period, the other factors being the expansion of tourism and the liberalisation of the economy, both of which were promoted by General Franco's dictatorship (1939–75).

To a certain extent, the migratory process alleviated potential domestic conflict, both economic and political, in spite of the hard times initially endured by many of those who went to work in foreign countries. Following the world economic crisis of 1973, and at the same time as the political transition towards democracy, Spain's emigrant workers began to return home to a much more highly developed society in which television was now the communication medium with the biggest following. Televisión Española (TVE), the state television channel, began broadcasting in Madrid in October 1956. Three months earlier in July, the National Emigration Institute had been set up. This body struck agreements with the governments of various different European countries (the German Federal Republic, Switzerland, France and Belgium) that would enable Spanish workers to be sent abroad to play their part in the key years of Europe's economic rebuilding process.

From the moment of its inception in Spain, television served to improve the difficult living conditions endured by most of the population due to the scarcity of economic resources and the lack of freedom that prevailed in the country. Both geographically and socially speaking, the growth of television was a gradual process. The nationwide coverage of television took a long time and reinforced the gap between the relatively few urbanised centres and the large peasant regions. For some social classes, particularly those with little formal education (manual workers, day labourers or maids, for example), television was for many years a luxury beyond their reach. In 1965, in an attempt to make it available to a wider audience, the Dictatorship, aware of the social importance that television broadcasts were beginning to acquire, abolished the luxury tax previously levied on the purchase of television sets.

As the reconstructed recollections of Spain's earliest viewers and press reports published at the time both confirm, emigration was, for thousands of

Spaniards, a phenomenon that would become crucially intertwined with television (Gutiérrez Lozano 2006). Moving abroad enabled thousands of Spanish emigrants to enjoy their first glimpse of television pictures at a time when television sets were not even available to their relatives back home in Spain. The formative experience of television for those who settled in other European countries consisted of watching programmes broadcast in a foreign tongue (German, French or Italian). The initial impact of the medium was coupled in such cases with the alienation caused by a lack of knowledge of the foreign language in question. Certain channels, such as the Italian channel RAI, became more popular with the emigrants due to the similarities between Italian and Spanish.

In any event, the language barrier encountered in other countries failed to dampen the emigrants' enthusiasm for the new-found technology and televisual entertainment. In view of the significant number of Spaniards now living in the aforementioned countries, some public channels in Europe even began to broadcast programmes in Spanish on a weekly or fortnightly basis. These broadcasts played a crucial role in easing the sense of having been uprooted that was felt by the emigrants. The newspaper for southern Spain, *Diario Sur* (3 November 1962: 3), estimated that by 1962, some 90,000 Spaniards were resident in the Federal Republic of Germany, with almost 8,000 living in Frankfurt, to quote one example. Germany's third channel, which was based in the city of Cologne, began showing a weekly programme for Spanish emigrants in 1965. This programme featured folk dancing as well as Spanish news and current affairs, as *Diario Sur* noted on 25 November 1965 (p. 1).

TVE itself, which was controlled by the Dictatorship, organised an 'artistic delegation' in the mid-1960s. This took the form of a televised tour involving famous Spanish singers and presenters, who would perform in various different cities to 'brighten up' the emigrants' lives. In the Netherlands, for example, the directors of the Philips Company lent their support to the staging of one such musical festival for its Spanish employees in December 1966. Eindhoven played host to a 'celebration of patriotic harmony' held in the city's municipal theatre which, according to press reports of the time (*Diario Sur*, 13 December 1966: 22), attracted some 500 workers and a further 1,500 Spaniards living in nearby areas, accompanied by the Spanish ambassador to the Netherlands and the chairman and director of the company, Frits Philips.

Even leaving specific examples such as these to one side, it is still clear that the nostalgia evoked by going to live so far from home was in many cases made easier to bear by television. Broadcasts of football matches, usually involving the Spanish national team or Real Madrid, were joyfully received by men and women alike. The feeling of belonging and 'national pride' ensured that these sports transmissions carried immense emotional significance for all Spanish emigrants. Whole families of emigrants, women included, would get together to see the matches. At the same time, female interest in televised football was not common back in Spain, where it was frowned upon for women to watch television in bars, whether alone or in groups. The weight of Roman Catholic religious morality, which had become the social norm under the Dictatorship, ensured that women in Spain occupied a subordinate role in the shadow of men, and this extended to watching television. For this reason, many wives whose husbands were working in other countries had to wait until their return to Spain during holidays or at Christmas before they could buy television sets for their children with the money earned abroad. Meanwhile, the habits acquired by female emigrants were not so heavily influenced by the rigid morality that constrained women living in rural areas of Spain and even in its cities.

The economic problems faced by most of the Spanish population meant that buying a television set was difficult. Emigration, however, made it possible. The cost of purchasing a set was equivalent to almost 75 per cent of the annual salary of the average middle-class employee. Foreign currency provided the families of emigrant workers with a greater capacity for saving the money required to purchase domestic appliances. Though emigration from Spain was initially undertaken primarily by young men, they were subsequently joined by their wives and children. For these emigrant families, television provided a highly effective social tool that would help their children to settle in their host countries. While the language barrier proved to be a huge obstacle for parents, many of whom lacked even basic education, television gave their children the chance to learn about and become integrated into their adopted countries. In any event, the progressive acquisition of a foreign language enabled many of these early emigrant viewers to become familiar with the programmes broadcast in their host countries. When they eventually returned to Spain, they brought with them not only the television sets purchased during their time abroad but also the habit of watching foreign channels, which in many cases also led to them being among the first to install satellite dishes in their homes in order to see foreign programmes.

In short, the recollections of television expressed by early emigrant viewers reveal their experience to have been magnified by two factors: the difficulties encountered in adapting and the benefits reaped from the experience. Emigrants recall with gratitude the years of hard work that enabled them to purchase a greater number of material goods or to provide a better education for their children. The effects of emigration were not only economic but sociological as well: it enabled many Spaniards to discover the democratic values prevalent in other European countries and witness electoral processes carried out in free conditions. This would prove crucial during the process of political transition towards democracy which began in 1975 (Sánchez López 1969: 284).

As far as television is concerned, the survival in the collective memory of experiences related to emigration goes a long way to explaining the tastes and consumption habits of more recent times. Since the 1980s, certain programmes shown in Spain on both private commercial television channels and their state-owned counterparts, particularly those with a talk-show format, have sought to attract audience attention by featuring personal accounts of emigration and contriving family reunions and other tear-jerking situations. From the 1990s onwards, due to the sociological changes that have occurred in Spain, these programmes have focused instead on immigrants working in Spain. However, the two audiences, Spanish-born and Spanish resident alike, share a vivid sense of identification with the protagonists of these programmes, which appeal directly both to their own feelings and to the experience of being uprooted and travelling far from home, a considerable ordeal for any human being.

Conclusion

Whether we are studying television audiences as discursive formations or 'real' people, the challenge is to match the extensive statistical and ethnographic material that does exist through 60 years of audience research, with new questions. If the television viewer is understood as 'ordinary' (whatever that means), as many studies show, studying television audiences becomes the cultural and social study of the difference television makes, as institution, commodity, furniture, discourse-producing machine and so on, in people's everyday lives. Moreover, 'people' are different, live differently and behave differently from each other. Due to the relative geographical immobility of programmes themselves, it should not be controversial to argue that relations between viewer and text should be studied locally. That is also what a large part of the existing body of audience research looks like, having a very specific, local character. On the other hand we have a highly mobile set of questions, theories and methods for audience research. Television's earliest years show on one hand how fruitful this could be, for example the impact in countries beyond the United States of Lynn Spigel's work on television's arrival. On the other hand, John Foot's research on the earliest years of television in Milan is a useful reminder of the importance of actually looking at the local conditions in their distinctive specificity. The link between television and sub-urbanisation, so evident in the United States, is not relevant for the Italian economic miracle. The social and demographic processes involved (sub-urbanisation and urbanisation) are essential to all aspects of people's lives, thereby affecting the role played in them by a medium as dominant as television.

Despite the call for local studies, it would also be possible to formulate a set of questions that are particularly relevant for Europe. Certainly on a macro-level the Second World War, the era of the Cold War, the European Union, the economic boom of the 1950s and 1960s, the Balkan Wars and the fall of the Iron Curtain are important. But they are so big, so large-scale that they seem to be more relevant for questions about discursive effects or institutional effects in television. They help explain what has affected television, but to what extent do they really explain what television does and has done? The lessons from local, micro-level research indicate the importance of looking not only at the relative stability of the social and cultural contexts in which most people in Western Europe have lived since the 1950s. The large waves of migration, particularly from southern to northern Europe during the 1950s, 1960s and 1970s, not only changed those who moved, but almost as much those who stayed. The struggle of creating a daily life in a new country is a major factor in people's identities. So is the development of communities to include people from other parts of Europe or other parts of the same country. This process defines a new kind of community identity, a new meaning of 'we' which affects what we buy in shops, what we eat, what detergent we buy, when we eat, how we interact with our neighbours, where and how we live, and what television does for 'us'.

References

Brunsdon, C. and Morley, D. (1978) *Everyday Television: 'Nationwide'*. London, BFI.

Cassirer, H. R. (1960) 'Audience participation, new style'. *Public Opinion Quarterly* 23:4, 529–36.

Dickinson, R., Harindranath, R. and Linné, O. (eds.) (1998) *Approaches to Audiences: A Reader*. London, Arnold.

Dumazedier, J. (1956) *Television and Rural Adult Education*. Paris, UNESCO.

Emmet, B. P. (1956) 'The television audience in the United Kingdom'. *Journal of the Royal Statistical Society. Series A (General)* 119:3, 284–311.

Foot, J. (1999) 'Television and the city: the impact of television in Milan, 1954–1960'. *Contemporary European History* 9:3, 379–94.

Gutiérrez Lozano, J. F. (2006) *La televisión en el recuerdo: La recepción de un mundo en blanco y negro en Andalucía*. Málaga, RTVA/University of Málaga.

Hartley, J. (1999) ' "Text" and "audience": One and the same? Methodological tensions in media research'. *Textual Practice* 13:3, 487–508.

Hay, J., Grossberg, L. and Wartella, E. (eds.) (1996) *The Audience and Its Landscape*. Boulder, CO, Westview Press.

Instituto Nacional de Estadística (2006) *Anuario Estadístico de España*, Madrid.

Morley, D. (1980) *The 'Nationwide' Audience: Structure and Decoding*. London, BFI.

Morley, D. (1992) *Television, Audiences and Cultural Studies*. London: Routledge.

Olsson, J. (2004) 'One commercial week: television in Sweden prior to public service'. In: Spigel, L. and Olsson, J. (eds.) *Television after TV: Essays on a Medium in Transition*. Durham, NC and London, Duke University Press, pp. 249–69.

Sánchez López, F. (1969) *Emigración española a Europa*. Madrid, Confederación Española de Cajas de Ahorros.

Spigel, L. (1992) *Make Room for TV: Television and the Family Ideal in Postwar America*. Chicago and London, University of Chicago Press.

Wolfgram, M. A. (2006) 'The Holocaust through the prism of East German television: collective memory and audience participation'. *Holocaust and Genocide Studies* 20:1, 57–79.

9

Conclusion:
Reflections on Doing European Television History

Andreas Fickers and Jonathan Bignell

In the introduction we problematised European television as our object of study by developing a set of key concepts that would offer an analytical framework for the historical investigations presented in this volume. While those introductory remarks aimed at demonstrating the richness of our theoretical and methodological approaches and at the same time highlighted our understanding of television as a complex historical phenomenon, this concluding section is intended to critically discuss the value and the benefits of the book's comparative perspective on the history of television in Europe. Closely related to this, we have to face the inconvenient question of the extent to which we can justify our claim to call this book a *European* history of television. It is one thing to proudly proclaim that this book is the result of co-operation between 28 television scholars of 15 different nationalities (27 of them being affiliated to a European university), developing historical case studies of 15 European countries and 3 European regions. But it is another thing to convincingly argue that this panorama of national or regional case studies offers more than an eclectic glimpse of cultural specificities and national traditions, thereby reaffirming the concept of Europe as 'unity in diversity'. In embedding the – undeniably heterogeneous – development of television in Europe in both a spatial and temporal context of cultural modernisation, we will try to find historical evidence for a European television culture which is characterised both by its traditional diversity (we must always think of culture as plural) and its hybrid uniformity. Reappropriating Raymond Williams's famous characterisation of television as 'flow' and by perhaps overstressing the abstract analogy between television and Europe, one could say that what keeps both television and Europe together is 'flow'; the constant change or rearrangement of different elements or entities in a given structure, following certain technological, economic, political and cultural agendas. Both television and Europe each remain projects that need to be continuously renegotiated and reinvented. Both 'Europe' and 'television' as concepts are constructed entities whose identities vary depending on the topic of enquiry and the roster

of questions of those investigating the phenomena. Europe as a discursive construction has been instrumentalised from a multitude of angles – historical,
religious, geographical, political and cultural (Landwehr & Stockhorst 2004:
264–86), and television has been – amongst other ways – approached as being
essentially a technology, an institution, an art or simply a form of popular mass
entertainment.

Stressing the analogousness of 'Europe' and 'television' as discursive constructions from an epistemological point of view by no means implies the deconstruction of historical evidence about them. On the contrary, it emphasises
their fundamental historicity. Nothing can better demonstrate this than comparative historical research. Comparative studies remind us of the 'simultaneity of the nonsimultaneity' (Bloch 1935) – or, in other words, of the breaks,
contradictions and resistances in the complex process of modernisation both
within and between different societies (Degele & Dries 2005). As a methodological tradition, comparative study forces us to look at the deeply ambivalent and sometimes paradoxical nature of historical processes. Comparison does
not simply direct our view to the differences and similarities of historical developments in different times in the same places (diachronic comparison) or at
different places at the same time (synchronic comparison), but also emphasises
the complex interconnections between television and Europe as objects of study.
Such an approach stresses the hybridity of cultural phenomena and the complex modes of cultural transfer and translation in the processes of circulation
and appropriation of cultural goods.

Without denying the power of the nation-state or language as strong
frameworks for the shaping of specific television cultures during the second
half of the twentieth century, the comparative perspective shows the simultaneous emergence of regional, national and transnational or global television
production, transmission and viewing cultures. From the early days of television, these processes of adaptation, translation or co-production have shaped
a European television culture, characterised both by a certain national domestication of programmes or formats and by the commonly shared experience
of a struggle to domesticate foreign television productions. In distinction
to the more self-sufficient American television culture, all European countries
have tried to embed 'alien' television productions into their own viewing
traditions or cultural narratives. This has been a deep ambivalence or paradox
for European television – at least during the so-called 'public service era'
(1945–75). The drive has been to present television as a 'window on the world'
(to invite unknown and unaccustomed sights to become part of the viewer's
private life) and also to propagate television as a powerful sociocultural tool
in the stabilisation of the nation as a trustworthy and reliable imagined
community (a difficult problem for many European nation-states involved in
whatever way in the Second World War). There were very different structural
conditions under which television emerged as a national institution in post-
war European countries, including different political regimes, different insti-

tutional settings, different economic systems and technological infrastructures. But television had a similar function: to mediate and sometimes catalyse the process of mental recovery of the tattered, reconstructed or newly constituted nation-state. As a symbolic cornerstone for the society, promoting conservative and thus stabilising norms and values such as the family, the home and the nation, television became the privileged vehicle of national socialisation in the golden age of capitalism. Again, what characterises the European dimension of television is rather the similarity of this symbolic function in different European countries than any analogousness of the structural conditions in which television emerged as the new leading mass medium.

While this instrumentalisation of television in the name of the national community is not an exclusively European phenomenon but rather a global one, there are a number of other distinctive factors making the European experience of television if not unique, then at least specific. In recapitulating the main arguments and cases presented throughout the different chapters of the book, we will try to systematically highlight the European dimension – sometimes by recapitulating the findings and theses of our co-authors, and sometimes by presenting auxiliary arguments and examples.

Europe Envisioning Television

In the first chapter, Knut Hickethier placed the imagination of television in the tradition of the European Enlightenment and its gradual technical realisation through the process of industrialisation. Based on a periodisation differentiating six phases of scientific reasoning and technical experimentation, each embedded in the broader sociocultural and political contexts of European history, Hickethier explicitly addressed television as a European achievement, incorporating and representing the visionary potential and the technological competence of a group of scientists and skilled technical amateurs from all over Europe. Every phase of development was marked by a sample of important ideas and practical experiments, each demonstrating the fundamental 'openness' of the innovation process and the various, often parallel emergence of technical solutions and discursive constructions of television as a communication medium. Television as a technology – as has been demonstrated by Abramson (1987), Burns (1998), Winston (1998) and others – was the result of the often uncoordinated and sometimes concerted action of hundreds of inventors, technicians, scientists and reckless entrepreneurs (who were often in personal contact with each other). Their work was driven by curiosity, ambition, fantasy or the search for profit, and often by all of these impulses at once. Despite the many attempts to instrumentalise the invention and to co-opt the inventors of television for national or nationalistic purposes, these activities must be interpreted as part of an international saga of invention and innovation. The development of television should be read as a serial technological drama, as we noted in our introduction, in which figures from many European countries participated (Fickers & Kessler 2008). As Erik Barnouw (1995: 1) has declared: 'No one country enjoyed the monopoly on the process, in fact, several countries had two, perhaps three outstanding "favorite sons".'

It is of course not our aim to dismiss any nationalistic misappropriation by substituting it with a European one. To deny the important role of Americans in the technological and economic advancement of television – especially from the 1930s onwards – would be ridiculous. But concerning the prehistory of television (1870–1930), it would be historically incorrect to 'provincialize Europe', as has recently been postulated by Dipesh Chakrabarty (2000). To exemplify the differences between European ways of imagining television and what might be termed the American way, a comparative study of the presentation of television at the World's Fairs in Paris (1937) and New York (1939) is helpful. In Paris, television was shown in two prominent locations: in the German pavilion by Telefunken and in the French 'Palais de la Radio'. In New York, three major companies exhibited the new medium: the Radio Corporation of America (RCA), Westinghouse and General Electric.

Whatever an appropriate definition of a 'World's Fair' might be – 'laboratories of modernization' (Rydell & Gwinn 1994: 1), 'international potlatch ceremonies' (Benedict 1983: 10) or 'sites of pilgrimages to the commodity fetish' (Benjamin 1978: 151) – they all must be read as specific expressions of an historical moment in a certain geographical environment. They all breathe the anxieties and hopes of their contemporaries, and the visions and traditions of their planners and exhibitors. In this respect, the Paris and the New York Fair are representations of the same moment in the ongoing global development of television. But despite their relative temporal closeness they offer two completely different discourses of modernity. The Paris World's Fair can be read as a discourse imagining the world from a European and more specifically French perspective that was eager to create a symbolic harmony between cultural traditions and the industrialised present (described as 'arts et techniques dans la vie moderne'). On the other hand, the New York Fair shaped a modernity in the making, transcending past and present, offering the fair-goers a simulation rather than a representation of the 'world of tomorrow'. In both cases, planners and designers had been motivated by the economic and political currents and problems of their time, but their creative translations of these problems into visionary concepts of a 'better' or more harmonious world were very different. In an exaggerated statement one could say that the Paris Fair was driven by the 'invention of tradition' (Hobsbawm & Ranger 1983), while the New York Fair was inspired by the will to invent the future.

The chosen mottos for the Fairs – 'Arts et techniques dans la vie moderne' and 'The world of tomorrow', respectively – and their material manifestations in architecture and industrial design are evidence of their different geographical, political, economic and cultural environments. While the Paris Fair marked probably the end of the great European World's Fairs in terms of their legacy of imperialism and national self-portrayal, the 'world of tomorrow' was not so much the result of national self-presentation, but was in the hands of the new 'global players', the big international corporations. The general design of the Paris fairground was characterised by a symbolic architecture that culminated in the confrontation between fascist and communist ideologies, whereas corporate exhibits dominated the New York Fair in scale as well as in position.

Comparative historiography is illuminating here because it is exactly within these differing historical moments and the different geographical place of their museum-like staging that 'the consequences of the technological innovation' of television become manifest (Boddy 2004: 3). Even though the programming shown on television in the German and in the RCA pavilion had few significant differences, the two versions of television were embedded in varying discourses. 'Nation' and 'education' could be isolated as the keywords of the German discourse constructed around television in Paris, while 'commercialisation' and 'entertainment' were the most significant terms in the American discourse about television in the context of the World's Fair. These findings might not be very surprising, given the history of radio broadcasting. The institutional framework of radio broadcasting shaped people's imagination when they considered the future medial identity of television (Hilmes 2002). The 'older brother' of television was the 'structuring framework' in which the professional and popular imagination of television as the new 'window on the world' took place (Olivesi 1998). But – as Raymond Williams (1962: 11) has argued – 'the moment of any new technology is a moment of choice'. At the end of the 1930s there was no such thing as a definite vision of the 'true nature' of television. In the United States, large-screen theatre television had been the chief alternative to television as advertiser-supported, network-distributed programming to the homes of American families (Spigel 1992), and the 'radio set in every household' philosophy of the Nazis was also clearly a guideline for television in the propagandistic strategy of the National Socialist Party.

But from a media-historical perspective, the comparison between the competing narratives of television at the World's Fairs offers an interesting insight. While the presentation of television as a new medium in Paris and New York was embedded in divergent economic, political and cultural environments that shaped a different narrative of television, the televised content was nearly exactly the same. The same 'programme philosophy' inspired both performances, namely the aim to demonstrate television as a multi-functional medium, and an integrative medium that could combine live transmissions with pre-produced filmed material. Even the chosen formats were the same, and consisted of live interviews with fairgoers, shots of the fairground combined with an explanatory commentary, and films. The programming and the programmes were almost identical – the 'televisual reality' was the same – but the discourse surrounding television was very different. In Paris and New York, the different narratives of television had different imagined stories about it, while the message of the medium was the same. The situation at the end of the 1930s to a great extent defined the future identity of television as a mass medium. The dominance of the public-service concept of broadcasting in the European context and the commercial patterns in the United States shaped hegemonic narrations of television on each side of the Atlantic. The World's Fairs in Paris and New York both created and represented alternative symbolic frameworks in which television as a revolutionary technology and a new mass medium was presented. They were two windows giving a slightly different view of the new electronic 'window on the world'.

Institutionalization of Television in Europe

Political and ideological contexts without doubt had an important impact on the public imagination of the new technology called television. But the concrete transformation of television from a technological possibility into a medium of mass communication was shaped by other factors. As both chapter 2 and 3 demonstrate, the emergence of television as a new medium was the result of a structural and aesthetic remediation. Television grew up in the sheltered environment of radio broadcasting and the institutionalisation of television broadcasting took place by adopting exactly the same arrangements, for the ideas about television scheduling and content followed the proven patterns of radio. Of course, radio was not the only source of inspiration for early television makers. Theatre – especially in the days of all-live television of the 1950s – and the aesthetics of film deeply influenced television production in the first post-war decade. Television as a new medium had to struggle hard to find its own identity as an audiovisual medium, and it was – in the drastic formulation of Lyn Gorman and David McLean (2003: 127) – a 'parasitical medium'. Radio must be interpreted as the 'structuring framework' of early television development. In all countries, the most prominent radio programmes were retransmitted as television adaptations, the studios and production locations were mostly run by radio people, ideas of scheduling and programming (summed up in the whole idea of television as 'flow') were copied from radio, and the familiar voices of radio commentators and speakers were to be heard on television. From the perspective of theories of innovation, the advent of television has nothing of a revolutionary character about it. On the contrary, one could describe it as a 'conservative innovation', despite the fact that the rhetoric of television advertisements was peppered with 'revolutionary' adjectives.

The predominant role of radio in the shaping of television's medial identity is true for both the American and the European continents. What differ are of course the legal, administrative and organisational traditions of broadcasting as a primarily commercial activity in the United States and as a public service in most of the European countries. The characteristic institutional structures of public service television in Europe – as has been argued by Christina Amadou, Isabelle Gaillard and Dana Mustata – radically changed with the liberalisation of national television regulations and the advent of private and commercial television stations from the mid-1970s onwards. What for more than twenty years had been an exclusive British experience in Europe, namely a dual system with both public service television (BBC) and a commercial network (ITV), became a model for most European countries in the 1980s. Nevertheless, it is interesting to notice the quite different appreciation of the advent of commercial television in Central and Eastern European countries, where public service television under communism or socialism was identical with a state-owned and controlled institution. Here, after the end of the Cold War in 1989, private or commercial television was embraced as the herald of freedom of opinion and a window on to the western world. While the apologists of the public service monopolies in most Western European countries caricatured commercial television as a corruption of civic norms and values and therefore as a threat to civil society, the advocates of private television in Eastern European states presented themselves as the true defenders of freedom of opinion and as a mouthpiece for the entertainment-seeking masses.

Although the effects of the competition between public and private providers vary from country to country, it can be concluded that most European countries have managed to settle down with a plural television culture, combining the more serious or intellectual offer of the public service channels with the more popular and easily digestible formats of the private channels. The public debate surrounding the advent of commercial television in most European countries was centred on quality issues, in a certain way recapitulating the high- versus low-culture discussion during the implementation era of television in the 1950s. The resistance to 'light' entertainment and popular formats of mass entertainment is deeply rooted in European intellectual history, and the debates about commercial television represent just one facet of this recurring discourse about 'consumption versus culture' (Slater 1997: 63–99, Lusted 1997, Sassoon 2006). The fierce, sometimes embittered literary campaign of cultural pessimists – both from the conservative and the leftist intellectual tradition – against television as a form of popular mass entertainment was without doubt a particularly European phenomenon (Thompson 1995). As the examples of France or the Netherlands show, this hostile rhetoric towards television as a mass medium could have a retarding impact on the dynamic of television implementation. A remark in the weekly newspaper *Gereformeerd Gezinsblad* (*Protestant Family Newspaper*), made by one of the protestant churches in the Netherlands on 9 October 1956, demonstrates the sometimes belligerent attitude of moral authorities towards the potential threat of television: 'Television is a powerful tool in the hands of the devil, used to tempt faithful people from God's commandments. By means of television, he makes his entry into the home. The enemy is at the door and we need to carefully watch for his artful slurs.'

But it would be historically wrong and historiographically distorted if we failed to give credit to those who enthusiastically welcomed and energetically devoted their time and energy to making television a daily reality. Both from an ideological and institutional point of view, the professional guild of television engineers and technicians (often forgotten in scholarly media historical publications, at least) has had an unquestionably prominent role in the creation and building of a transnational and European television infrastructure. Since the creation of the International Broadcasting Union in 1925, a professional group of radio experts had been working in a non-governmental organisation in order to secure practical communication by radio signals on a global scale. Although the European Broadcasting Union, founded in 1950 as the Western European successor to the IBU, was 'the result of the splitting of Europe into an eastern and western bloc' (Zeller 1999: 38), it has become one of the main architects of the European television landscape ever since. Like its Eastern European sister organization, the Organisation Internationale de Radiodiffusion et de Télévision (OIRT), the EBU was the main platform for the technical realisation of transnational television activities, and slowly but steadily expanded its activities beyond mere technical concerns such as the standardisation of transmission systems. Initiated and headed by the Swiss Marcel Bezençon, in 1953 the EBU created a television programme committee for promoting and organising programme exchange between the member bodies. Bezençon's plan was not immediately welcomed by all members, especially Britain and France, who as the most advanced television nations of the time feared losing their predominant role. However, the successful transmissions of the coronation of Queen Elizabeth II (1953) and the first Eurovision week in 1954 convinced all critics that exactly these kinds of European television events would be the best advertisement of television as such. The EBU became a central actor in the international television business, on the basis of three kinds of development. The first was the expansion of technical activities. In 1956, the Eurovision Control Centre in Brussels was inaugurated; in 1962 a permanent sound network was established; and this was joined by a permanent vision network in 1968. The second development was the supply of new exchange facilities. From 1958 onwards, the Eurovision News Exchange collected and distributed news items on a daily basis in the early evening. Finally, the EBU stimulated the invention of new European programmes, most notably the Eurovision Song Contest, which began in 1956.

Similar action – although somewhat delayed – was taken by the Eastern European broadcasting union, the OIRT. In 1956 the first discussions about programme exchanges started, but it took another four years before the first Intervision transmission took place in February 1960. Starting with four original members (Czechoslovakia, the German Democratic Republic, Hungary and Poland), the USSR joined one year later, followed by Romania and Bulgaria in 1962. Finland (the only country with a dual membership in both the EBU and the OIRT) joined in 1965, Mongolia in 1972, Cuba in 1979 and Afghanistan and Vietnam in 1982. Geographically speaking, Intervision was the largest land network in the world. Despite the fact that the Cold War greatly affected the relationship between the EBU and OIRT, especially in the early 1950s, relations began to thaw from the late 1950s onwards. As Ernest Eugster (1983) has documented in his authoritative study of television programming across national boundaries, the communication and practical co-operation between the two bodies is an astonishing example of cross-boundary collaboration in what has been called the 'Age of Extremes' by Eric Hobsbawm (1995). The linking of the Eurovision with the Intervision network, first realised in the West–East direction during the Rome Olympics in 1960 and memorably repaid with the coverage of the cosmonaut Yuri Gagarin's Moscow welcome in April 1961, marked a crucial step in television becoming a truly global medium.

European Programmes and Programming

From an institutional point of view, both the EBU and the OIRT exerted a tremendous influence on the shaping of the European and international broadcast space. But we must also ask about the programmes circulating on the Eurovision or Intervision exchange lines and the programmes co-produced by them, in order to assess whether the EBU or the OIRT have been important actors or mediators in the construction of a European television culture or identity. As the authors of chapter 4 have demonstrated, it is hard to identify typical European programmes, genres or formats. While some trends in the programming or scheduling of television – especially in the 'public service era' – could be characterised as Europe-wide phenomena, we still know very little about the circulation of nationally produced formats or programmes on a European scale. As the example of the German crime appeal show *Aktenzeichen XY* presented in chapter 4 has revealed, the comparative analysis of the circulation and appropriation of a single programme in the European context tends to sharpen our attention to the differences rather than the communalities of television cultures. While certain television formats easily travel between national television cultures, others do not. Historical drama or documentary, often produced to reflect or stimulate debates about national or regional identities, do not seem to communicate effectively in foreign reception contexts. Their inherent semantic codes, encrypting political, cultural and social meanings, make them hard to customise for a non-domestic public. Other commercial formats, as the popular entertainment programmes *Who Wants to Be a Millionaire*, *The Weakest Link* or *Big Brother* have demonstrated, have been sold to a great number of different television stations and successfully embedded in differing television cultures. Eggo

Müller characterises such television formats explicitly produced for an international market as hybrid formats, as products incorporating the economic reality of a globalised television market and transcultural phenomena (Müller 2002: 456–73). Transculturalism, according to James Lull (2000: 242), 'refers to a process whereby cultural forms literally move through time and space where they interact with other cultural forms and settings, influence each other, produce new forms, and change cultural settings . . . Transculturalism produces cultural hybrids – the fusing of cultural forms.'

But, as Müller rightly warns us, the concepts of 'hybridisation' or 'convergence' tend to play down the different contexts of accommodation and appropriation of such travelling formats or products. In order to underline the necessity of an active process of embedding 'alien' formats into a national or culturally homogenous television culture, he proposes to characterise them as a 'flexible matrix'. The flexible matrix of these successfully travelling programmes enables processes of adaptation, assimilation and appropriation (Müller 2002: 469). As well as this flexible matrix, which bears a certain resemblance to the concept of 'interpretative flexibility' introduced by the Dutch sociologist and historian of technology Wiebe Bijker (1995) to describe alternative modes of development and intellectual appropriation of new technologies, the format's characteristics are of crucial importance for its transferability. Michael Skovmand has argued that what makes quiz or game shows so easy to circulate and appropriate is the fact that they address the television audience in a specific and direct manner. Unlike television sitcom or drama, 'game shows foreground the fact that they are a cultural practice rather than a "text"' (Skovmand 1992: 85). The participatory impetus of game, talk and quiz shows, in other words the fact that their attraction relies on their invitation to viewers to be part of the playing, discussing and guessing, makes them a social situation rather than an ordinary one-way communication process. This ability to embrace a large, socially and culturally unspecified public undoubtedly explains the successful spread of such transcultural programme formats.

The central motivation behind the production of such transcultural formats – often by multinational firms or in international co-operation between both public service and commercial broadcasters – is of course to make economic profit. At international programme trade fairs like MIPTV in Cannes, founded in 1963, the big business of television is staged. In the same year as the launch of this industrial Mecca, however, the EBU inaugurated the 'EBU Screening Sessions', based on the idea of a bilateral exchange of television programmes, free of charge. Based in Milan, where the 'Mercato Internationale del Film, del TV e del Documentario' (MIFED) had established a tradition of film and television trade mainly to promote the export of Italian productions, the EBU Screening Sessions were initiated as a non-profit business in order to facilitate the exchange of television programmes between EBU members. While some of the big broadcasting companies like the BBC or the German ARD initially reacted with a certain aloofness to the plans, the smaller member organisations strongly supported the initiative. From their perspective, the EBU Screening Sessions not only offered the possibility to show and thereby promote their television productions to an international audience of television professionals, but to make attractive bilateral programme exchange deals with the international programme providers currently dominating the market. The formula proved to be a success as the following figures show: within the first ten years of its existence, the screening of presented programmes doubled (from 118 to 247 hours), and the number of affiliates quadrupled to a total of 263 in 1976 (Henrich-Franke 2005). Right from the beginning, the documentary format largely dominated the character of the EBU Screening Sessions, averaging around 60 per cent of all screened material. Since cost-saving for member organisations was one of the central motivations behind the Screening Sessions, documentaries were by far the most popular programmes included because of the relatively low post-production costs involved in adapting them for broadcast in another country. As a counterweight to the exploding costs of commercial television trade in the 1960s and based on the EBU solidarity principle, the Screening Sessions – at least until their end in 1985 – provide a good example of television as a platform for transcultural communication beyond the ideology of capitalism.

Questions of European Identities

The expansion of television in Europe in a geographical sense is characterised by two parallel tendencies. On the one hand, each country slowly but steadily expanded the technical infrastructures of television on a national scale and thereby increased the density of viewers and households equipped with a television set. On the other hand, these efforts to make television the legitimate successor of radio as the 'national theatre of the air' were foiled by the medium's promise to function as a 'window on the world'. In other words, television became increasingly available as a dominant means of identity formation that might regularise what people's identities could be. But at the same time it was a conduit for the circulation of images of what might be alien, unfamiliar and foreign to that regularised sense of identity. This ambivalent identity of television as an agent of 'private mobilization' (Williams 1974) challenges our understanding of television programmes as texts, because it suggests a double process of encoding and decoding of cultural meanings, both in the processes of production and circulation and in the processes of reception and appropriation.

To deal with this complex phenomenon in a historical perspective, the authors of chapter 5 decided to focus their work on the concept of identity. The concept of identity is – as the authors themselves point out – not an uncontested or easy one to handle. Developed as a theoretical concept in the context of psychoanalytical and sociological studies in the 1940s, identity was primarily understood as a psychological process of self-definition and self-development (Erikson 1959). As the result of a constant mediation between the individual and the social roles available to the self, identity functions as a kind of balance between the distinctive singularity of each individual and the social environment in which he or she is embedded. As Anthony Giddens (1991: 5) has shown in his work on modernity and self-identity, the process of identity building must be understood as a reflexive project of the self, 'which consists in the sustaining of coherent, yet continuously revised, biographical narratives'. Both psychological and sociological conceptualisations of identity as a key element of human self-consciousness point to a crucial ambiguity in its meaning and to the paradoxical function of identity as something that is both fixed and also mobile. Identity is a flexible, dynamic – thus historically changing – entity since it offers a stable and structuring framework for the continuous reinvention or redesign of the self in a changing world (Schütz 1932). The easy switching between or simultaneous overlap of regional, national, transnational or political, religious and ethnic identities is both influenced by the concrete historical situation in which an individual acts and by larger macro-historical processes of change (Schmidt-Gernig 1999: 163–216).

Since the 1970s, the subject-oriented theory of identity, explicitly dealing with the challenging experiences of contingency, differentiation and strangeness felt by the modern individual, has been transferred to the level of collective or group identities, inaugurating a real boom in identity research. Aleida Assman and Heidrun Friese (1998: 11) go so far as to diagnose an epidemic spread of the term: cities, regions and nations defend their specific identities, firms and public administrations promote their corporate identities, ethnic minorities and gender groupings are in search of their identities, and – last but not least – media constantly shape 'imagined communities' and thereby new 'spaces of identity'. It is in any case more accurate to speak of multiple identities, following the concept of 'multiple realities' introduced by Alfred Schütz (1945) or Goffman's (1967) concept of 'patchwork identities'. While most people would find it hard to 'define' their own personal identity, the analytical potential of the identity concept as a collective phenomenon often seems to be in inverse proportion to its popularity (Straub 1998: 73–104). Some scholars therefore simply deny the possibility of the creation of a kind of collective personality or identity, stressing the fact that such a collectivising construct always implies an unjustified harmonisation or normalisation of social, cultural or political differences. As the German historian Lutz Niethammer (1994: 378–99) has argued, this collectivisation is mainly the result of an action 'from outside', often initiated and rhetorically staged by a small but powerful elite. He shows that the term has often been pressed into service for ideological and manipulative purposes and therefore argues for a critical use of the term in historical writing as well (Niethammer 1995: 25–50). Nevertheless, a whole range of scholarly works within the field of media studies have used the concept of identity to describe and analyse the importance of media in the creation or stabilisation of 'imagined communities', mainly as a national phenomenon of self-imagination. As Alexander Schmidt-Gernig has suggested in his brilliant research essay on the possibilities for a European identity, the concept of identity can be fruitfully applied as a theoretical tool when used as a constructivist rather than essentialist category. Studying the public discourses about European identity, especially in mass media, allows us to avoid the trap of essentialism when undertaken with the necessary critical reflexivity (Schmidt-Gernig 1999: 163–216).

But we have been concerned to ask questions about what constitutes the 'Europeanness' of this constructed identity. Precisely because it lacks, and has arguably always lacked, the rigid territorial boundaries and more or less centralised governing institutions of nation-states, 'Europe' can be considered a notoriously inaccurate referent of academic inquiry, particularly when studied over any relatively lengthy time period. Assuming that 'Europe' is – and always has been – a discursive construction, the problem begins with the very definition of Europe. As Achim Landwehr and Stefanie Stockhorst (2004) have shown, the concept of Europe has been an object of continuously negotiated meaning in respect of whole range of different perspectives. In all these dimensions, for example religious, spatial, political or historical ones, there are multiple definitions of where or what Europe is (Strath & Malmborg 2002: 1–26). We propose that Europe might best be characterised as a never-ending story, or – in the words of the German sociologist Richard Münch (1993) – as an ongoing project. Lutz Niethammer (2000: 111) has even argued that the meanings of 'Europe' and the bases of European identity represent no more than 'a plurality of synchronous monologues' and that to seek any form of unity in them distracts from, rather than contributes to, understanding the processes and power relations involved. The problem becomes evident when looking at programmes that often are presented as showcases of European identity in the making: the Eurovision programmes. But we have been concerned to debate in this book whether watching programmes like the *Eurovision Song Contest* or *Jeux Sans Frontières* actually makes audiences European – or at least makes them feel European.

European Events

As Rob Turnock, Mari Pajala, Alexander Hecht, Dana Mustata and Alison Preston have argued in their chapter on European events, the participatory promise is one of the strongest attractions of television, especially under the conditions of live broadcasts of media events. Early Eurovision transmissions undoubtedly were surrounded by the aura of the extraordinary. As concrete performances of the promise of television as a 'window on the world', Eurovision programmes functioned both as a stage for the promotion of the new medium and as a new media platform constructing a European public sphere. This double attraction of Eurovision programmes in the 1950s and 1960s assures them a pivotal and privileged place in the television memories of the first generation of television viewers in Europe. According to Jérôme Bourdon (2003: 14), they would fit into the category of 'event memories', or evocations 'not so much of the event itself as of the process of reception and the emotions that were triggered in the viewers at that time'. While the public discourse concerning early Eurovision programmes is in general dominated by a rhetoric of pride and confidence about the shining future of European collaboration in television matters, the internal debates both in the EBU programme committee and in the leading broadcasting institutions involved in Eurovision reveal a less enthusiastic or harmonious picture.

Two months before the official inauguration of Eurovision in June 1954, BBC controller of television Cecil McGivern gave a speech on Eurovision at the Radio Industries Club Luncheon in London.

> When we first, and extremely airily, began to talk about an exchange of European programmes, one of the television critics coined the word 'Eurovision'. The other day a colleague of mine – one of my bosses – was in my office when I was talking for quite a long time to one of the European countries who are going to give us some programmes, and when I put down the phone with a worried brow, he said: 'You shouldn't call it Eurovision; you should call it Neurovision'. I think he is quite correct, for at present the emphasis is much more on the nerves than on the vision. (BBC Written Archives Centre, henceforth BBC WAC, T23/26)

McGivern's scepticism derived from the technical problems that both the BBC and the French RTF had encountered during their first transnational television transmissions in 1950 (the Calais experiment) and 1952 (Paris week) presented by the different line standards used in the broadcasts. It was a difficult enterprise that strained the nerves of the participants.

The first European television exchange was the biggest experiment in international television collaboration of its time. Over 4,000 kilometres (almost 2,500 miles) of radio circuits linked 44 relay transmitters in eight countries (Britain, France, Germany, Italy, Denmark, the Netherlands, Belgium and Switzerland). The challenge of line standard conversion and sound transmission was enormous. In Breda (in the Netherlands), a converter point was established for the conversion from either French or Belgian 819-line or British 405-line pictures to 625 lines. The RTF team in Paris managed the conversion from either 625 or 405 lines to 819 lines, while BBC staff in Dover made the conversion from either 625 or 819 lines to the British 405-line standard. Because no electronic converter systems existed at that time, the technical solution to the problem of changing from one line standard to another was simply to place a 405-, 625- or 819-line camera in front of a 405-, 625- or 819-line receiver in order to re-televise the picture in the line standard used by that camera's pick-up tube.

The following description of the journey of a British 405-line picture taken in London to different countries of destination, which is a transcription from the BBC documentary *The Expansion of Television* (1961), might help demonstrate the complexity of the technical endeavour underlying the first Eurovision transmission:

> The programme left London and travelled in a series of hops via Wrotham and Dover across the Channel to Cassell, France, where it was taken over by the RTF and carried to Lille. Here the programme was divided: in one direction it went to Paris for conversion to 819 lines and distribution on the French network; in the other direction it went over a series of links installed in Belgium to Holland. In the Netherlands [at Breda], the British 405 line picture was converted to the continental standard of 625 lines and then distributed in one direction to Belgium and in the other to the Dutch network and then onwards to Cologne over new relay stations especially installed for this purpose. Here the signals joined the Western German TV network and were fed to all the German transmitting stations. From Hamburg, a series of special links continued the circuit as far north as Copenhagen, while from the southern end of the German network near Baden Baden a link was established to Chasseral, Switzerland. From this point the signals travelled to Zurich for transmission on the Swiss network and also separately across Switzerland to Italy, the intermediate relay points being on the Jungfrauenjoch and Monte-Generoso before finally descending to Milan. At Milan the signals joined the Italian network and found their way as far south as Rome.

It was not only the pictures that had to travel, but sound too. For BBC controller Cecil McGivern, sound transmission was even more complicated due to the different languages involved, as a briefing handout for the press explained (BBC WAC T23/26). Because of the limited bandwidth, it was not possible to transmit in parallel the voices of the commentators from all seven participating countries. On each filming location, only two or three commentators were actually on the spot describing the action and directing the camera operators. For the large majority of programmes, local commentaries were added in each of the receiving countries based on the picture seen by the commentator on a monitor receiver. To assist the commentator in these cases, a 'guide' at the programme end passed on information and advice either in English or French to the commentator. This, of course, could not be heard by the viewers.

While the technicians were worried about the enormous technical complexity and the administrative and organisational effort required (Fickers & Lommers 2009), the programme committee saw itself confronted with the question of future programme content that might be of international interest. At an EBU television forum held in Sandpoort in 1954, the year following the broadcast of Queen Elizabeth's coronation, journalists from the eight European countries involved in the Eurovision project had serious problems in finding even a handful of subjects of common interest, which caused one British journalist to make the ironic suggestion: 'Another Coronation'. While the technical realisation of Eurovision as a material performance of 'Europe' was generally celebrated as an historic milestone in television history and European integration by both its makers and the public, the programmes themselves mainly reflected national partialities and often mirrored stereotyped images of national customs and traditions. As Cecil McGivern concluded with a hint of desperation in his speech at the Radio Industries Luncheon: 'Every country is typical – France, Versailles and the revue; Germany, the youth camp on the Rhine, etc., and it was impossible to get away from that' (BBC WAC T23/26).

Most of the original Eurovision programmes of the 1950s and 1960s like the *European Song Contest* or *Jeux Sans Frontières* perfectly illustrate McGivern's disenchantment, though not the transmission of major events like the Olympics or Football World Cup via the Eurovision or Intervision network. The European narrative presented by the former kind of programmes is one of Europe as a bundle of nations or national representatives competing against each other, with either artistic (in the *Song Contest*) or physical weapons (in *Jeux Sans Frontières*). What is celebrated is not the idea of European integration or a shared European identity, but the staging of national stereotypes. In this sense, the popularity of such Eurovision programmes is to be explained by its catalytic function in the creation of a national imagined community ('we' against 'the others'), and not by assuming a positive identification with Europe as a commonly shared set of cultural norms and values. It is a bitter but true historical judgement that all Eurovision attempts to develop 'serious', 'high-culture' programmes explicitly aimed at bridging national differences and creating a transnational and European experience failed. As Wolfgang Degenhardt and Elisabeth Strautz (1999) have shown in their study of Eurovision programmes from 1954 to 1970, programmes like *The Largest Theatre in the World* (beginning in 1963), a series of simultaneously broadcast theatre plays based on a script by one European writer but staged and directed in different ways by the participating television stations, perfectly met the cultural ambitions of the programme committee but dismally failed to attract a broad European audience.

While programmes like the *Eurovision Song Contest* or *Jeux Sans Frontières* offered good entertainment for a broad audience, *The Largest Theatre in the World* flagrantly manifested the crucial obstacle or even impracticability for a genuinely European programme: the language problem. Although EBU programme committee director Marcel Bezençon recognised the language factor as the central limitation of Eurovision's ambitions, he strongly believed in the cultural mission of Eurovision as an important tool in the construction of a European identity. 'Eurovision must not be just a toy,' he declared in an article in the *EBU Review* (Bezençon 1964: 8), 'but an instrument as well. An instrument to be used for what purpose? To build Europe, for example.

The suggestion has already been made, and Eurovision has at times applied itself to this task.' Without questioning Bezençon's belief in Europe and his personal commitment to promoting the European idea, it is a historical fact that the Eurovision network most successfully operated as unilateral platform for the distribution of television pictures (especially of sports events), but that its role as an agent of transculturalism by organising a large-scale exchange of programmes remains limited. With the exception of the Eurovision News Exchange, which, incidentally, organises the exchange of pictures and original background sound but not linguistic commentary, a truly European programme exchange has not been achieved.

Europeanisation and/or Americanisation

This rather pessimistic or critical appreciation of television's role in the construction of a European identity – whatever this might be – is not intended to dismiss the role of television as a mediator of transcultural communication in general. Since the quantum leap in transborder television transmission provoked by satellite technology, television has like no other medium (until the advent of the internet) both mirrored and fostered the process of globalisation. But long before the private satellite channels sent their signals around the Earth, Europe discussed the phantom of cultural imperialism with fighting talk about 'Americanisation'. As the authors of chapter 6 have concisely demonstrated, the United States has acted as both the hated and the celebrated 'other' in European media and culture in general. In a 1965 survey of the current state of television in Western Europe, the German television critic Gerhard Eckert (1965: 27) stated that Europe, in spite of its longer television tradition, was on the point of becoming a beachhead for American popular culture. He lamented that European viewers had no chance to see the best television productions from Britain, Italy or the Federal Republic of Germany, but instead were flooded with imports of American series like *The Flintstones*, *Father Knows Best* or *Lassie*. Poorer countries especially, like Spain or Finland, he feared, would become addicted to the American way of life instead of integrated into the European family.

Without entering the delusive dichotomist debate about the virtues or dangers of American culture, it is a fact that American television programmes have had – both on a quantitative and qualitative level – a tremendous impact on all television cultures in Europe. But it would be distorting the historical reality to give privileged credit only to television from the United States, which was part of a process that reaches back to the end of the nineteenth century, starting with vaudeville amusement culture and continuing with popular magazines, radio and of course Hollywood films. In the long history of transatlantic cultural transfer – which of course was not a one-way traffic from the

United States to Europe but a process of mutual interference – television simply created a new locus for the exchange of (mainly visual) cultural narratives. As a new agent in the mass-media ensemble, American television programming without doubt challenged the imagination of a large group of European viewers, but its impact on the formation of a new lifestyle, characterised by consumption and individualisation, has perhaps been overestimated when compared to the influence of films and music. This is certainly true for a group of people generally referred to as most attracted by the American lifestyle in the post-war years, namely the baby-boom generation that formed the youth audiences of the 1950s and 1960s (Sirinelli 2002). As works by Lynn Spigel (1997) or Detlef Siegfried (2006) have shown, the rather conservative attitude of most television institutions concerning youth, alternative or counter-culture movements has turned the juvenile public towards film or radio as mediators of American cultural industries. Television, with its strong domesticating function and family commitments, assuredly accommodated the wants of the middle and older generations – including young families with small children, but only partly did so for teenagers. For them, both the site of the cinema and the portable technology of the transistor radio offered the possibility of de-domesticated media use, combining the wish for social mobility with the appropriation of films or music with an American imprint.

The process of 'Americanisation' or 'Westernisation' of European culture and lifestyle was paralleled by a process of 'Europeanisation'. As comparative social histories of Europe have shown, the barriers dividing European societies both on economic and social levels have step by step been levelled in the process of European political integration, starting in the West with the European Coal and Steel Community in 1952. This process of convergence of the different economies had deep impacts on the quality of daily life. The unprecedented rise in production levels and economic welfare during the so called 'golden age of capitalism' led to the post-war years being described as a *Wirtschaftswunder* (economic miracle) in West Germany and the *trentes glorieuses* (three glorious decades) between the mid-1940s and 1970s in France, for example. This gave birth to a European consumer society, marked by mobility (tourism played a crucial role in the discovery of Europe by Europeans), migration and secularisation (Kaelble 2007). Television both acted as a mirror of these political and social changes (documentaries and travelogues were a very popular genre on television) and as a catalyst for the Europeanisation of national cultures (cookery programmes are a perfect example of this, documenting the spread of foreign eating and drinking habits). Also, the political process of European integration was often portrayed and commented on in television news or in specific programmes initiated either by Eurovision such as *The European Journal* (beginning in 1964) or by national broadcasters like the BBC series *With Europe in View* (1959). Introducing the BBC's new programme in the *Radio Times* (18 September 1959: 1), Aidan Crawley, the editor responsible for the series, declared:

Live television is still largely national . . . Night after night we entertain and talk among ourselves . . . And yet on the Continent of Europe there are probably more intelligent and interesting people than in any other part of the world . . . It is to make use of this talent, to broaden our own perspective and enjoy the company of our neighbours, that we have planned this new series 'With Europe in View' . . . For a little while each Wednesday you will now be able to watch and listen, if not as Europeans, at least 'With Europe in View'.

Again, this quote is a perfect example of the ambivalence of the process of Europeanisation and of the role of television in it. Television can and was to be used to open up people's minds, to make them sensitive or interested in Europe, but does it from (in this case) a familiar and slightly arms-length British perspective.

Europe Watching

The big challenge for all television historians, and more generally for historians of all media, is of course to reconstruct who actually watched those programmes, not to mention the problem of reconstructing the meaning viewers gave to the content they viewed. It is relatively easy to collect and present statistical material on the expansion of television in terms of television sets produced, officially registered viewers (at least in countries where set owners had to pay a licence fee), the average number of households equipped with a set and therefore the average density of television coverage in relation to the population, or the average number of hours that people have turned on their sets. But as with all statistics, the numbers presented need to be carefully read in order to avoid misinterpretation. Of course the number of officially registered television sets was – certainly in the early years of television – far from being the real number of television viewers. While the usual viewership of a single set in the 1950s and 1960s was the family group, viewing culture has turned into a much more individualised and singularised reception situation. During the implementation phase of television in the post-war years, southern European countries especially were known for their public and collective television-viewing habits. This had both economic and social causes. Receivers were too expensive for private ownership, and television was embedded in traditions of public gathering. In Italy, the popular quiz programme *Lascia o raddoppia* (*Double or Quits*), broadcast on the public service channel RAI between 1954 and 1959, attracted an estimated public of 10 million viewers with only 250,000 sets officially registered (Eckert 1965: 45). Each television set thus had an average viewership of 40. In France, the 'Télé-Clubs' tried to promote the new medium as a means of public education and entertainment. Started in 1950 by the treasurer of the Ciné-Club of Château-Thierry, a village with 10,000 inhabitants in the north of France (l'Aisne, Picardie), more than 170 Télé-Clubs existed only five years later. Depending on the dynamism of the local organising committees, television screenings were set up in primary schools or other public buildings, introduced by short lectures or speeches by the local teacher, mayor or priest and followed by a public debate. The phenomenon of the Télé-Clubs attracted the attention of UNESCO, who published a detailed study on this form of collective television viewing for educational purposes (Dumazedier 1956). But we still know very little – certainly from a comparative European perspective – about the concrete contexts of domestic television reception and its role in the routines of daily life in which it is so deeply embedded.

As the latest EU monitoring report on television has shown, television is still the leading medium in terms of media consumption. While some declared the death of television with the internet boom that began in the early 1990s, television has maintained its massive appeal to viewers, with average viewing time for adults increasing from 195 minutes per day in 1995 to 217 minutes per day in 2003 (Open Society Institute 2005: 39). In Western Europe, the south has always scored highly in television watching, while the Nordic countries have always had the lowest viewing rates. But besides a general increase of viewing time despite the competition with other new media, each country presents specific viewing habits, making any European generalisations problematic. An interesting fact revealed by this latest European survey by the Open Society Institute is nevertheless its confirmation of the fact that television remains the main source of information for people. News on public service channels especially – with the exception of the Czech Republic, Slovakia and Hungary – attracts more viewers than news on private channels. The reliance on public television channels' news is reinforced by the fact that their on-line services are among the most frequented when people look for additional information on actual news events. From the very beginning of television news, both its makers and the public were concerned about the reliability of information and its presentation on different media platforms. At the end of the 1930s, it was television that seemed to endanger the authority of radio news broadcasts. In 1938, the BBC published an announcement to explain to their television viewers the inconveniences of overlapping radio and television broadcasts, in particular in reaction to the radio news broadcast. The BBC therefore proposed to include a radio news broadcast at the end of the daily television broadcast. Viewers who would appreciate this solution were asked to express this by sending a postcard to the Director of Television. In the response to the announcement on 14 March 1938, 91 viewers were in favour of such a radio news bulletin after the regular television broadcast, and 12 were against it. Due to changed television broadcast schedules, this extra service stopped only a few months after it had started (BBC WAC, T16/116/1).

This example also reflects a typically British or BBC approach to audience response. Audience research at the BBC had started in 1936 as 'listener research' in the Home Intelligence Department of its Public Relations Division. In June

1950, 'in a highly symbolic change prefiguring the ascendance of television over radio' (Nicholas 2006: 14), the BBC Listener Research Department became the Audience Research Department. The importance of audience research for the BBC was dramatically formulated in the Beveridge Report: 'Broadcasting without study of the audience', the report stated, 'is dull dictation; it is not responsible public service' (Committee on Broadcasting 1950: 49). While the BBC inaugurated a tradition of qualitative audience research, based on daily interviews with a sample of viewers and processed into a 'Daily Audience Barometer', the commercial network ITV engaged both a British (Television Audience Measurement, TAM) and an American (A. C. Nielsen Co.) company to conduct audience research based on an automatic measurement system for quantitative analysis. The TAM-Meter (now known as the 'Peoplemeter') automatically registered the viewing time and the channel to which the set was tuned. While the BBC saw the qualitative audience research as a feedback mechanism and instrument for programme planning, the quantitative method was an indispensable tool for the commercial channels in order to inform their sponsors about ratings. In the public service era of European television (1945–75), BBC-style qualitative audience research clearly dominated in those countries which had introduced audience research of any kind. In Germany (ARD), France (RTF), Italy (RAI), Sweden (SRT), Belgium (RTBF/BRT) and Spain, qualitative audience research was introduced mainly based on regular telephone interviews. The second German channel (ZDF) which started in 1963 was the first public service institution to start with quantitative research methods (Eckert 1965: 52). With the emergence of commercial television in Europe and the establishment of a dual broadcasting system, quantitative methods have begun to dominate the business of audience research. Ratings have become the hard currency for television programming and scheduling all over Europe.

But, as Tim O'Sullivan (1988) has convincingly argued in an essay on television memories and cultures of viewing, 'viewing culture' is not only characterised by a certain temporality (the effects of scheduling on daily life routines and time management), but by two other factors, namely technology and space. While the socio-spatial aspects of the domestication of television have been described and analysed by authors like Lynn Spigel (1992), Roger Silverstone (1992) or – focusing on the Austrian case – Thomas Steinmaurer (1999), phenomena of collective and ambient television reception have rarely been studied (an exception is McCarthy 2001). In addition to that, the geographical spread of television coverage and the topography of television reception remain unknown territory in television history. The expansion of television in all countries witnesses a remarkable lack of homogeneity between urban centres and the countryside, and between industrialised and agrarian regions. Depending on the geological structure or geographical extent of countries, the development of a television infrastructure assuring the reception of television signals had a very unequal spread, creating favoured and disadvantaged television regions. Speaking of a national television audience in the 1950s and 1960s is – at least for most European countries – highly problematic.

From a European perspective, border regions would be a very interesting object of study, challenging the idea of television as a tool in the construction of a national identity or national imagined community. We have noted the techno-political instrumentalisation of television, resulting in the different line standards for black-and-white television or the different transmission systems for colour television which have hindered the emergence of a European television space (Fickers 2007). Moreover, those European countries especially which were situated between or alongside the bigger and more advanced television nations in the 1950s and 1960s – such as Denmark, Belgium, the Netherlands, Finland, Luxemburg or Switzerland – often profited from the reception of television programmes broadcast from their neighbours. In Belgium, for example, provided that they had a multi-standard receiver and depending on their geographical situation, people could watch not only the two Belgian channels (the French-speaking RTBF and the Flemish-speaking BRT), but also programmes originating from West Germany (for those in the east of the country), the Netherlands (for viewers in the north), or France and Luxembourg (in the south). Whether or not such interfering reception areas shaped or at least facilitated the emergence of a transnational or European identity remains to be researched.

Watching Out for Europe

This last example is just another case of the fragility or even the impossibility of Europe as an essentialist concept. From a political perspective, the history of European integration – which more or less coincides with the life span of television in Europe – can most accurately be described as an ongoing project (Münch 1993). Just like the gradual expansion of Europe as a political union of now 27 sovereign nation-states, television has expanded from local, regional and finally national coverage to a transnational and global media space. But Europe as a political actor has played a surprisingly minor role in the shaping of television as a cultural phenomenon. All of the political initiatives to use the medium of television for the promotion of Europe as an 'imagined community' by setting up an institutional framework for a common television station (in 1972 by the European Council and in 1980, 1981 and 1985 by the European Parliament) came to nothing (Zeller 1999). This 'failure' to establish a European television station or to embed television as a permanent institution within the political agenda of the European Union has been interpreted as lack of political commitment by some critics, and explained as the result of the inherent national or linguistic logic of television by others. The panorama of case studies and the paths of reasoning presented in this book suggest that television, because of its hybrid nature as a technological, social, political, economic and cultural phenomenon, cannot function as a kind of common European 'cultural currency' (Rüsen 2000: 76).

Television, just like the concepts of Europe and of identity, may be best characterised by means of Williams's definition of 'flow'. Each of these entities can be understood as simultaneously an enunciation of stable and fluid elements, as a continuously changing entity and as the result of periodical reinvention. From a constructivist and radical historicist position, all 'taxonomic exercises' (McDonald 2000: 90) attempting to catalogue or map all possible variations of 'television' or 'Europe' are necessarily doomed. Instead of trying to identify 'core shared European experiences', the anthropologist Sharon McDonald advocates the study of European culture as a multivocal phenomenon, paying tribute to the multifarious nature of individual experiences and interpretations of television in daily life.

Against this constructivist agenda, sociologists and historians, economists and political scientists have stressed the fact that despite all differences in cognitive perception and meaningful interpretation of 'Europe' and 'television' by individuals, people do share the spatial or temporal dimensions of certain events, making them – willingly or not, consciously or unconsciously – historical coevals. Television undoubtedly created a 'European experience space' (Heinen 2000: 103–11) and thereby at least potentially created occasions for an imagined European identity. Acting as a platform for the transnational circulation of symbolic visual and sonic icons (for example the Eurovision hymn and graphical logo), television has left its traces on the individual and collective memory of Europeans. It has achieved this both at particular moments in time by its synchronising power during media events, and also over extended periods of time by its ritualising impact on the rhythms of daily life. Of course these traces vary according to the different generations of television viewers who have experienced them. But in a 'longue durée' perspective, television deserves its place in the 'invention of Europe', just as Europe can claim its role in the development of television. As a result of a process of mutual co-construction, a European television culture has emerged that is more than the sum of its (national) attributes. This becomes evident when comparing the European case with other television cultures, for example with television cultures in Africa, Asia or the Americas. Such a drastic change of perspective often reveals the many communalities of European cultures when confronted with the 'other'.

This positioning of the specifically European within the global, or the effort to 'provincialize Europe' – in the provocative words of Dipesh Chakrabarty (2000) – is without doubt one of the most interesting perspectives for a future European historiography. This book has been designed as a first attempt to demonstrate the intellectual fruitfulness of a comparative approach to television as an object of media history. While the theoretical and methodological challenges are far from being exhaustively discussed and have only been partly put into practice, the future of comparative television history will to a large extent depend on a rather mundane question: the extent of the availability and accessibility of sources. Everyone who has ever tried to work with audio-visual sources in a serious way will acknowledge the practical limitations that confront television history. Fortunately, this problematic situation, in which availability and accessibility become the criteria defining a research agenda instead of that agenda being the result of an academic debate, slowly seems to be changing.

This book is in some ways the direct result of a European co-operation, launched by the European Television History Network (ETHN). Started in 2005 at the initiative of Sonja de Leeuw and Andreas Fickers from the de-partment of Media and Culture Studies at the University of Utrecht in the Netherlands, the network has grown into a vibrant community of European television scholars from over twenty European countries. One of the central aims of this network is to stimulate and – if possible – institutionalise the communication and co-operation between television scholars and audiovisual archives. A first remarkable success of this initiative is the EU-funded project 'VideoActive. Creating Access to Europe's Television Heritage' (www.videoactive.eu). In developing an internet portal on the history of tele-vision in Europe with at least 10,000 items on-line, based on archive mater-ial from 13 audiovisual collections from 11 European countries, VideoActive will be the first internet platform explicitly dealing with the history of tele-vision in Europe from a comparative and cultural history perspective. In close collaboration with the academics of the ETHN, the streamed television programmes will be enriched by contextualising information and historical background information in order to offer a pedagogic environment for the original source material. Along with other open archive initiatives of national archives or public service broadcasting institutions like the French Institut National de l'Audiovisuel (www.ina.fr), projects like VideoActive might open the door to real comparative research, based on a rich collection of available on-line sources.

It is our hope that this book might further stimulate the fruitful discussion between audiovisual archives and the academic community as well as contributing to the challenging dialogue about European and media history. The next section of this book, therefore, is a brief expert discussion of the nature and context of audiovisual archives across Europe. It is followed by a schematic listing of the main organisations and institutions holding archival material as they existed in 2007. The listing demonstrates what a rich set of resources there is already for continuing some of the lines of inquiry presented here. It also suggests that, as digital technology and public as well as academic inter-est in television history burgeon, these resources will most likely become better documented and more accessible. A final comment on European tele-vision historiography, therefore, must be that the ambitious comparative questions that we have begun to pose and discuss will undoubtedly advance in directions which we cannot as yet predict. It follows that our conclusions will undoubtedly be disputed, and this situation is of course a reason for optimism. We look forward to the continuation of the dialogues that have made this book possible.

References

Abramson, A. (1987) *The History of Television, 1880 to 1941.* Jefferson, NC, Mc Farland.

Assman, A. and Friese, H. (1998) *Identitäten.* Frankfurt a. M., Suhrkamp.

Barnouw, E. (1995) *Tube of Plenty: The Evolution of American Television.* New York, Oxford University Press.

BBC Written Archives Centre, Caversham, file T16/116/1, 'News'.

BBC Written Archives Centre, Caversham, file T23/26, 'TV Publicity, Eurovision, 1953–1955'.

Benedict, B. (1983) *The Anthropology of World's Fairs: San Francisco's Panama–Pacific International Exposition.* London, Scolar Press.

Benjamin, W. (1978) 'Paris: capital of the nineteenth century'. In: Demetz, P. (ed.) *Walter Benjamin. Reflections, Essays, Aphorisms, Autobiographical Writings.* New York, Harvest, pp. 146–62.

Bezençon, M. (1964) 'Eurovision, or the price of fame'. *EBU Review* 92:8.

Bijker, W. (1995) *Of Bicycles, Bakelites, and Bulbs: Toward a Theory of Sociotechnical Change.* Cambridge, MA, MIT Press.

Bloch, E. (1935) *Erbschaft dieser Zeit.* Zürich, Oprecht & Helbling.

Boddy, W. (2004) *New Media and Popular Imagination: Launching Radio, Television and Digital Media in the United States.* Oxford, Oxford University Press.

Bourdon, J. (2003) 'Some sense of time: remembering television'. *History and Memory* 15:2, 5–35.

Burns, R. W. (1998) *Television: An International History of the Formative Years.* London, Peregrinus.

Chakrabarty, D. (2000) *Provincializing Europe: Postcolonial Thought and Historical Difference.* Princeton, NJ, Princeton University Press.

Committee on Broadcasting (1950) *Report of the Committee on Broadcasting, 1949.* London, HMSO.

Degele, N. and Dries, C. (2005) *Modernisierungstheorie.* Munich, Wilhelm Fink.

Degenhardt, W. and Strautz, E. (1999) *Auf der Suche nach dem europäischen Programm: Die Eurovision 1945–1970.* Baden-Baden, Nomos.

Dumazedier, J. (1956) *Television and Rural Adult Education: The Tele-clubs in France.* Paris, Unesco.

Eckert, E. (1965) *Das Fernsehen in den Ländern Westeuropas: Entwicklung und gegenwärtiger Stand.* Gütersloh, Bertelsmann.

Erikson, E. (1959) *Identity and the Life-cycle: Selected Papers.* New York, International University Press.

Eugster, E. (1983) *Television Programming across National Boundaries: The EBU and OIRT Experience.* Dedham, MA, Artech House.

Fickers, A. (2007) *'Politique de la grandeur' versus 'Made in Germany': Politische Kulturgeschichte der Technik am Beispiel der PAL-SECAM-Kontroverse.* Munich, Oldenbourg.

Fickers, A. and Kessler, F. (2008) 'Narrative topoi in Erfindermythen und technona-tionalistischer Legendenbildung: Zur Historiographie der Erfindung von Film und Fernsehen'. In: Bodenmann, S. and Splinter, S. (eds.) *Mythos – Helden – Symbole: Legitimation, Selbst- und Fremdwahrnehmung in der Geschichte der Naturwissenschaft, Medizin und Technik*. Munich, Martin Meidenbauer, pp. 71–82.

Fickers, A. and Lommers, S. (2009) 'Eventing Europe: broadcasting and the mediated performance of Europe'. In: Badenoch, A. and Fickers, A. (eds.) *Europe Materializing? Transnational Infrastructures and the Project of Europe*. Basingstoke, Palgrave Macmillan.

Giddens, A. (1991) *Modernity and Self-identity: Self and Society in the Late Modern Age*. Stanford, CA, Stanford University Press.

Goffman, E. (1967) *Interaction Rituals: Essays in Face to Face Behavior*. Chicago, Aldine.

Gorman, L. and McLean, D. (2003) *Media and Society in the Twentieth Century: A Historical Introduction*. Malden, MA, Blackwell.

Heinen, A. (2000) 'Towards a European "experience space"?' In: McDonald, S. (ed.) *Approaches to European Historical Consciousness: Reflections and Provocations*. Hamburg, Edition Körber Stiftung, pp. 103–12.

Henrich-Franke, C. (2005) 'Wandlungen des europäischen Markts für Fernseh-programme 1963–1985'. *Rundfunk und Geschichte* 31, 17–25.

Hilmes, M. (2002) *Only Connect: A Cultural History of Broadcasting in the United States*. Belmont, CA, Wadsworth.

Hobsbawm, E. (1995) *The Age of Extremes: A History of the World 1914–1991*. New York, Pantheon Books.

Hobsbawm, E. and Ranger, T. (eds.) (1983) *The Invention of Tradition*. Cambridge, Cambridge University Press.

Kaelble, H. (2007) *Sozialgeschichte Europas: von 1945 bis zur Gegenwart*. Munich, Beck.

Landwehr, A. and Stockhorst, S. (2004) *Einführung in die europäische Kultur-geschichte*. Paderborn, Schöningh.

Lull, J. (2000) *Media, Communication, Culture: A Global Approach*. Cambridge, Polity Press.

Lusted, D. (1997) 'The popular culture debate and light entertainment on television'. In: Geraghty, C. and Lusted, D. (eds.) *The Television Studies Book*. London, Arnold, pp. 175–90.

McCarthy, A. (2001) *Ambient Television: Visual Culture and Public Space*. Durham, NC, Duke University Press.

McDonald, S. (2000) 'Historical consciousness "from below": anthropological reflections'. In: McDonald, S. (ed.) *Approaches to European Historical Consciousness: Reflections and Provocations*. Hamburg, Edition Körber Stiftung, pp. 86–102.

Müller, E. (2002) 'Unterhaltungsshows transkulturell'. In: Hepp, A. and Löffelholz, M. (eds.) *Grundlagentexte zur transkulturellen Kommunikation*. Konstanz, UVK, pp. 456–73.

Münch, R. (1993) *Das Projekt Europa: Zwischen Nationalstaat, regionaler Autonomie und Weltgesellschaft*. Frankfurt a. M., Suhrkamp.

Nicholas, S. (2006) *BBC Audience Research Reports. Part 1: BBC Listener Research Department, 1937–1950. A Guide to the Microfilm Edition with an Introduction by Sian Nicholas*. Wakefield, Mircofilm Academic.

Niethammer, L. (1994) 'Konjunkturen und Konkurrenzen kollektiver Identität: Ideologie, Infrastruktur und Gedächtnis'. *Prokla. Zeitschrift für kritische Sozialwissenschaft* 24, 378–99.

Niethammer, L. (1995) 'Diesseits des "Floating Gap". Das kollektive Gedächtnis und die Konstruktion von Identität im wissenschaftlichen Diskurs'. In: Platt, K. and Dabag, M. (eds.) *Generationen und Gedächtnis: Erinnerungen und kollektive Identitäten*. Opladen, Leske & Budrich.

Niethammer, L. (2000) *Kollektive Identität: heimliche Quellen einer unheimlichen Konjunktur*. Reinbek bei Hamburg, Rohwolt.

Olivesi, S. (1998) *Histoire politique de la télévision*. Paris, L'Harmattan.

Open Society Institute (ed.) (2005) *Television across Europe*. Budapest, Open Society Institute.

O'Sullivan, T. (1988) 'Television memories and cultures of viewing, 1950–1965'. In: Corner, J. (ed.) *Popular Television in Britain: Studies in Cultural History*. London, BFI, pp. 159–81.

Rüsen, J. (2000) '"Cultural currency": the nature of historical consciousness in Europe'. In: McDonald, S. (ed.) *Approaches to European Historical Consciousness: Reflections and Provocations*. Hamburg, Edition Körber Stiftung, pp. 75–85.

Rydell, B. and Gwinn, N. (eds.) (1994) *Fair Representations: World's Fairs and the Modern World*. Amsterdam, VU University Press.

Sassoon, D. (2006) *The Culture of the Europeans: From 1800 to the Present*. London, Harper.

Schmidt-Gernig, A. (1999) 'Gibt es eine "europäische Identität"? Konzeptionelle Überlegungen zum Zusammenhang transnationaler Erfahrungsräume, kollektiver Identitäten und öffentlicher Diskurse in Westeuropa nach dem Zweiten Weltkrieg'. In: Kaelble, H. and Schriewer, J. (eds.) *Diskurse und Entwicklungspfade: Der Gesellschaftsvergleich in den Geschichts- und Sozialwissenschaften*. Frankfurt a. M., Campus, pp. 163–216.

Schütz, A. (1932) *Der sinnhafte Aufbau der sozialen Welt: eine Einleitung in die verstehende Soziologie*. Vienna, Julius Spinger.

Schütz, A. (1945) 'On multiple realities'. In: Natanson, N. (ed.) *Collected Papers of Alfred Schütz*, Vol. 1. The Hague, Martinus Nijhoff.

Siegfried, D. (2006) *Time Is On My Side: Konsum und Politik in der westdeutschen Jugendkultur der 60er Jahre*. Göttingen, Wallstein.

Silverstone, R. (1992) *Consuming Technologies: Media and Information in Domestic Spaces*. London, Routledge.

Sirinelli, J.-F. (2002) *Les baby-boomers: une generation 1945–1969*. Paris, Fayard.

Skovmand, M. (1992) 'Barbarous TV international'. In: Skovmand, M. and Schroder, K. (eds.) *Media Cultures. Reappraising Transnational Media*. London, Routledge.

Slater, D. (1997) *Consumer Culture & Modernity*. Cambridge, Polity Press.

Spigel, L. (1992) *Make Room for TV: Television and the Family Ideal in Postwar America*. Chicago, University of Chicago Press.

Spigel, L. (ed.) (1997) *The Revolution Wasn't Televised: Sixties Television and Social Conflict*. New York, Routledge.

Steinmaurer, T. (1999) *Tele-Visionen: Zur Theorie und Geschichte des Fernsehempfangs*. Innsbruck, Studienverlag.

Strath, B. and Malmborg, M. (eds.) (2002) *The Meaning of Europe: Variety and Contention Within and Among Nations*. Oxford, Berg.

Straub, J. (1998) 'Personale und kollektive Identität: Zur Analyse eines theoretischen Begriffs'. In: Assmann, A. and Friese, H. (eds.) *Identitäten: Erinnerung, Geschichte, Identität 3*. Frankfurt: Suhrkamp, pp. 73–104.

Thompson, J. B. (1995) *The Media and Modernity: A Social Theory of the Media*. Cambridge, Polity Press.

Williams, R. (1962) *Britain in the Sixties: Communications*. Harmondsworth, Penguin Books.

Williams, R. (1974) *Television, Technology and Cultural Form*. Oxford, Oxford University Press.

Winston, B. (1998) *Media Technology and Society. A History from the Telegraph to the Internet*. London, Routledge.

Zeller, R. (1999) *Die EBU – Union Européenne de Radio-Télévision: European Broadcasting Union*. Baden-Baden, Nomos.

10

European Television Archives and the Search for Audiovisual Sources

Andy O'Dwyer

Contexts

To understand the current status of audiovisual sources in Europe for television studies, it is helpful to have a general overview of the historical influences and processes that have brought us to where we are now in acquiring access to them. This requires a brief discussion of the prevailing barriers that exist both technically and culturally, and the current European initiatives that are under way to promote long-term preservation of television material and enable on-line delivery for academic and public access.

The introduction of television across Europe was made over a prolonged period, using different broadcasting technologies. It is worth remembering that early live television could not practically be recorded and the only method that emerged for capturing programmes was telerecording. Developed in the 1940s, this worked by pointing a camera at a television screen and capturing the black-and-white image on film. This process enabled broadcasters to capture their live output and repeat it later. It was a universal format and gave broadcasters the opportunity to sell and distribute material abroad. Videotape emerged in the 1950s and grew in popularity to become the dominant recording technology in numerous formats and recording standards across Europe.

Film had a secure place in television until the early 1980s, particularly with location crews and in news, because film cameras could be made light and portable, while early videotape machines were large, very expensive, and not at all portable. For news production, film had the key advantage of simplicity in a time-sensitive environment. The process of capture, development and editing prior to broadcast was routinely achieved within a few hours, without the need for specialist skills and the expensive electronic apparatus required for early videotape. The familiarity of film among European news agencies and the key element of being a 'universal format' for duplication and movement across borders ensured that film stayed in news production well after videotape had become established in general programming. Film for news-gathering started to be replaced by some broadcasters with U-Matic, a cassette format which marked the end of open-reel videotape. It was relatively portable and enabled news departments a quicker turnaround from capture to broadcast. So in the holdings of European television archives, the two decades from the early 1960s to the early 1980s are represented essentially by a mixture of film and videotape materials.

Television started in Germany and in the UK before the start of the Second World War, with experimental services in some other countries. The only remaining material from that very early period is from traditional film footage shot in studios during television production. Television launched or re-launched across Europe after the Second World War, with many countries establishing television broadcasting within a few years of 1955. Television started in different European countries at different times, and the introduction was not a single step but usually several steps. The first was the creation of a single national broadcaster, usually with a 'public service' remit and with some sort of public or government funding. Second, the start of commercial broadcasting occurred. The third key moment was the start of formal archiving within individual broadcasting companies (whether public service or commercial). Finally, we observe the start of national archiving of television material.

These steps did not occur in the same sequence in each country, but they are important as they all affect what television material has been archived, and in which format. As many researchers know, making a videotape recording in broadcasting was no guarantee of long-term preservation. Early videotapes were hugely expensive, and often used for 'time-shifting' and repeats of live productions, and for pre-recording productions. After transmission and repeats, the videotape was erased for reuse by some broadcasters. Many television companies did not introduce formal archive policies until they had been broadcasting for a considerable period. So the history of archived television programming has been a case of 'accidental preservation', where some programmes survived due to the process of copying them on to modern formats for repeat purposes or commercial activities. Indeed, even now archives with programmes stored on videotape need to be vigilant, and many of the replay machines for some formats are no longer being supported by their manufacturers. To avoid the obsolescence trap of having master videotapes and no machine on which to replay them, archives need to periodically review their processes and plans for migrating their 'at risk' formats. This vigilance is needed equally for older and what are considered relatively new professional video formats. Some of these professional formats are not expected to last a decade in serviceable use.

Archiving often had little to do with history, heritage or future research. The archives existed (as they mainly do today) within the broadcast company itself, strictly to serve the needs of the broadcaster. The principal needs were to hold material for repeats or for resale elsewhere, or to provide footage for reuse. The footage reuse is largely either of specific news items that may acquire a current relevance, or 'stock shots' of general items (locations, personalities, vehicles, buildings and so forth) that can fitted into many different programme contexts. The catalogues associated with these collections were aimed at these categories of reuse, and were used by professional librarians, programme makers and 'film researchers' (a title still in use, despite the obsolescence of film). Hence material of historical interest, such as drama, was given very little attention by the cataloguers (except perhaps for a note of the title and cast), whereas news material might be described down to the specific details of every shot.

European countries are starting to develop 'heritage' television collections, held outside the domains of the broadcasters themselves, either in a new 'sound and vision archive' institution (such as INA, the French Institut National de l'Audiovisuel or the Dutch Beeld and Geluid), or as a part of an existing institution (such as the television archives of the British Film Institute). For television research this can have the advantage of centralising collections in an environment that specifically supports access for non-industry users.

As a final point about context and access generally, some countries have (relatively recently in most cases) extended legal deposit legislation to cover broadcasting. This is a requirement for broadcasters to provide a copy of their programmes to the archive, and has led to comprehensive collections of television material being gathered through a mandatory process. It is hoped that this will be followed by further arrangements to make some of this content (rights of ownership permitting) available for research and general public access. The Swedish national audiovisual archive, for example, has some six million hours of broadcast recordings acquired through legal deposit. That is more than the total number of hours of programming found in ten major European broadcast archives by the Presto project.

However, the sheer volume of material produced by 'saving everything' can overwhelm the ability to provide detailed description of content. But this is beginning to change, due to modern television production techniques which focus on tagging all the components which go into television content with metadata. This information can include key information such as title, date, director, contributors, scripts and the essential rights information, and these details can be embedded within the copy of the programme. This information, when made available, will lead to a more efficient research process.

The Technical Divide

The decisions about which of the various broadcasting technologies and video formats to adopt for recording and broadcasting television by a particular European country depend on several factors. The key ones include the country's time of entry into the television arena, the prevailing technology, and economic and political dimensions. There are numerous examples of the crucial choices being dominated directly by political and domestic interests rather than clear technical reasoning. Choosing a different line standard from that of a neighbouring country, for example, prevented citizens receiving 'foreign' broadcasts. In another common example, choosing technologies to match the products made by a country's television receiver-manufacturing industry helped to maintain employment in an expanding area of the national economy.

These choices made at the implementation of television have a bearing on what still exists and ultimately the availability and ease of access for research. These technical divides affected programme exchange between European countries because incompatible formats and recording technologies meant that costly line-standard conversions were necessary. As well as this affecting European exchange, these recording differences have also impacted on programmes from the USA, which use the NTSC format. However, modern technology for line-standard conversion has made these differences all but irrelevant for programme exchange today.

European Access Initiatives

The search techniques used by researchers seeking access to audiovisual media usually begin with querying catalogues, indexes and databases. The quality of these manual or electronic records varies enormously, and since they are often written for in-house purposes they do not lend themselves to being used by researchers from outside the broadcasting institutions. Apart from the obvious language barrier, there is no uniformity in the way information is organised and presented. This is starting to be overcome with the introduction of 'user-friendly', externally facing on-line catalogue services, where the production of these new services is often driven by commercial or public value initiatives. Both INA (France) and the BBC (in the UK), for example, are making available thousands of hours of audiovisual material for access via the internet.

The European Community is very active in promoting both the need for preservation and also access to audiovisual content. Since March 2005 they have funded many initiatives under the IST eContent Plus Programme which supports EU-wide co-ordination of collections in libraries, museums and archives and the preservation of digital collections so as to ensure availability of cultural, scholarly and scientific assets for future use. Television archives in Europe have joined some of the initiatives and the benefits are starting to be realised in the public, academic and cultural heritage communities. The PrestoSpace project is a good example, as it directly addresses the need to identify the path to preservation for all audiovisual media stored in broadcast archives across Europe. Following an assessment of what exists and the formats on which content is stored, PrestoSpace has built up a 'best-practice' approach from the expertise available, to enable the migration of content on to modern digital formats to take place as funding becomes available.

For researchers, the benefits of a co-ordinated EC approach to preservation and access are clear. It offers the opportunity for a consistent approach which is likely to prevent another 'technical divide' occurring due to different preservation standards. The EC approach also has a multilingual element in on-line interfaces and in the descriptive metadata that support the content in their projects. This is something which is unlikely to have happened without a European initiative and funding. Projects such as Birth of TV and VideoActive are making archive television available on-line. Supporting numerous European languages, these portals are ensuring that catalogues can be searched (and content viewed) by more EU citizens in their native languages.

In parallel with initiatives by the EU on access to television content for research, professional organisations in television such as FIAT (the International Federation of Television Archives) promote research and education particularly though their Television Standards Commission. The Commission's aim is to explore and advance issues relating to the use of television archive material in scholarly studies and educational environments. FIAT also participates in formulating professional standards and guidelines, and assists member archives with best practice in access and programme-preservation policies.

The European Broadcast Union (EBU), founded in 1950, was instrumental in early programme exchanges and has a useful audiovisual and document archive for anyone interested in the formative years of collaboration between broadcasters in Europe. Its archive also contains papers from the founding organisation, the International Broadcasting Union (IBU), and its Eastern European equivalent, the International Organisation for Radio and Television (OIRT). The EBU archives contain documents from 1925 up to the present day. Two members of the Eindhoven University of Technology, Alexander Badenoch and Suzanne Lommers, wrote an informative account in the EBU magazine *Diffusion* on the rich material on European television held in their archives while working on the 'Transnational Infrastructures and the Rise of Contemporary Europe' (TIE) project.

Documents about television and related political influences are often held in government departments, and their archives can be a useful entry point in discovering the reasoning and thinking of key players in television. It is common, also, for the larger cultural archives to hold audiovisual content. In the UK, for example, the National Records Office keeps comprehensive records about the setting up of television transmitter networks, and documents from the Post Office which was responsible for the transmitters. These papers offer a useful insight into policy decisions taken by the government about the expansion of post-war television. A useful starting point for research in this area is the UNESCO archives online directory, which categorises archive sources by country and type of archive.

Another dimension influencing access to television content is the issue of copyright. It is complex, with no uniform agreement about access to material, even for research. Traditionally programme rights cover areas including artistic performances, music, and literary and broadcasting rights. Copyright affects to a large extent what can be made available for public and academic access and there are agreements in place in some EU countries to provide limited access, often through a formal education body. Even then, access is dependent on the availability of a copy of the master tape, and cost. It is very likely that physical access to such copy or 'preview' material will soon become a thing of the past, as on-line services expand. However, these services are a long way off for some collections. Film, for example, still needs to go through a process of scanning via a telecine camera to create a high-quality digital broadcast file. From this file, low-quality preview copies can be distributed electronically, but the process is a two-stage one and is comparatively expensive.

Providing access for research is a labour-intensive service with real technical costs for archives. These either have to be met directly via the state or by charging individual users. For smaller television archives the costs of providing preview material for all but commercial activities can be prohibitive. The EU is aware of this and has projects such as the European Digital Library Project (EDL) and DigiCult, which are investigating how best to supply preview access to audiovisual material for cultural heritage collections. With the correct application of technology and a co-ordinated European approach to access and preservation there is a real opportunity to place more content on-line, targeted at the needs of cultural and academic interests. There are some challenges, but with the political will many of these can be overcome.

Information Sources on the World Wide Web

These web pages comprise a mixture of official, academic and enthusiast-produced sites about archival and technical issues, and were current in November 2007.

BBC audiovisual archives: http://catalogue.bbc.co.uk/catalogue/infax/
Beeld en Geluid audiovisual archives: http://portal.beeldengeluid.nl/
BFI audiovisual archives: www.bfi.org.uk/
Birth of TV project: www.birth-of-tv.org
British national archives: www.nationalarchives.gov.uk/
DigiCult project: www.digicult.info
EBU: www.ebu.ch/
EBU   archives: www.ebu.ch/en/union/diffusion_on_line/EBU/tcm_6-45879.php
eContent   Plus: http://ec.europa.eu/information_society/activities/econtentplus/index_en.htm

EDL project: www.edlproject.eu/
FIAT: www.fiatifta.org/
INA audiovisual archives: www.ina.fr/
IRTO: http://en.wikipedia.org/wiki/International_Radio_and_Television_Organisation
Metadata: http://en.wikipedia.org/wiki/Metadata
Presto archive survey: www.cultivate-int.org/issue7/presto/
PrestoSpace: prestospace-sam.ssl.co.uk/index.html
Telecine: www.en.wikipedia.org/wiki/Telecine
Telerecording: http://en.wikipedia.org/wiki/Telerecording
TIE project: www.tie-project.nl/
U-Matic: http://en.wikipedia.org/wiki/Umatic
UNESCO directory of archives: www.unesco.org/webworld/portal_archives/pages/Cool/
VideoActive project: www.videoactive.eu

Index

Abramson, Albert 55, 56, 73
acceleration of vision and perception
    58–9
acculturation 176
aesthetics 33, 34, 127
    of early television 106–13
Aksoy, A. 48, 237
Aktenzeichen XY . . . Ungelöst, European
    circulation of 113–17, 123, 124
Al-Jazeera 3, 42–3, 133
Algerian War 89, 121–2
Altman, Rick 4
American agenda-setting 159–61
Americanisation 7, 22, 33, 96, 97, 117,
    155–8, 245–6
    aesthetic and cultural clash 161
    children, anxieties concerning 171–2
    as cultural invasion 22, 155, 156
    popular fascination with America 155
    positive view of 156–7
Ampère, André Marie 57
Andalusian broadcasting 145–50
Anderson, Benedict 18, 187
animation 17
archiving 5–6, 252, 257–63
Ardenne, Manfred von 66
Arte 118, 167
audiences 215–28
    active audience 26
    classification 215, 216
    commodification 23
    discursive formations 216–17, 227

emigrant viewers 224–7
event television 185, 188
flow phenomenon 4
fragmentation 24, 188
historicisation 25
imagined communities 13, 15, 18,
    23, 129, 156, 187, 209, 230, 241,
    250
interpellation 25
niche audiences 95
passive audience 40
ratings 103, 185
research 6, 227, 248–9
social construction 219–23
women 162
young 170
audiovisual consciousness 6
Austria 114, 115, 133
    event television 193, 194–5
average viewing time 248

Baird, John Logie 64, 65, 66
Barker, Chris 1–2, 7, 16, 25, 40–1
Barnaby 17
Barthélémy, René 70
Basque television 112
BBC 19–20, 25, 27, 64, 66, 69, 72,
    86, 104, 107, 110, 111, 116, 163,
    171, 199–200, 210, 215, 242,
    248–9
    British–American co-productions
    162–3

children's television 171, 173
crime-appeal television 116
funding 25
national unification project 129
news broadcasting 41–2
pre-war service 72–3
public service ideology 20, 110
radio broadcasting 111, 162
BBC World 41–2
Belgium 3, 39, 75, 129
   Flemish broadcasting 14, 106,
     110–11, 112, 129, 139–41
Bélin, Edouard 64
Berlin Olympic Games (1936) 24, 71
Berlusconi, Silvio 120
Berman, M. 47
Bidwell, Shelford 60, 64
Big Brother 14, 37, 38, 39–40, 124,
   164
black-and-white line standards 15,
   69–70, 72, 73, 91
border regions 75, 250
Bosnian war 200–4
Bourdon, Jérôme 4, 92, 101–26, 242
Bouyssonnie, Jean-Pierre 82
Braun, Ferdinand 61
Britain 14, 163
   American cultural influences 157, 170
   American imports 163, 164–5
   animation 17–18
   black-and-white line standards 15, 91
   British–American co-productions 154,
     161–3, 164
   children's television 17–18, 172, 173
   commercial television 75, 169
   drama production 107, 108, 109–13,
     134, 135, 158, 163, 181
   foreign-language programmes,
     resistance to 2
   heritage concept 35
   national identity discourse 16, 129
   programming 104
   public service broadcasting 19–20,
     105, 129
   television development 1, 15, 67, 69,
     72–3, 75, 76
   'theatre television' 23

wartime broadcasting 18
see also BBC
British Cultural Studies 6
broadcasting, concept of 19
Brooks, Peter 159, 160
Brunsdon, Charlotte 3, 218

cable networks 32, 164
Cable News Network (CNN) 41, 42,
   131–2, 200, 203
Canal Plus 122
Canal Sur 146
Canary Islands 146
capitalism 27, 37
Cartier, Rudolph 109, 110
Catalonia 3, 146
Caughie, John 135, 136
Ceauşescu, Nicolae 87, 177, 178, 195,
   196, 197, 198–9
censorship 21, 80, 86–7, 88–9, 98, 177
children's television 17–18, 171–3, 223
   Americanisation, concerns over 171–2
   anti-authoritarian and creative 180
   playful education concept 171
citizenship 128, 130
Claes, Ernest 139, 140
Coca-Colonisation 155–6
Coe, Jonathan 148
Cohen, Évelyne 41
Cold War 75, 133
collective memory 134
collective viewing experiences 13, 23–4
   see also public viewing
colour television 15, 28, 65, 73, 74
Columbia Broadcasting System (CBS)
   20, 66
commercial television 4, 14, 19, 20–1,
   75, 105, 118–19, 235
   audience fragmentation, impact of
     24–5
   challenge to national broadcasting
     21–2, 129–30, 155
   and democratisation 21
   public service–commercial television
     duopoly 162, 167, 199–200, 235
   see also individual countries and
     television channels

commercials 2, 24–5, 146, 176, 177
communication spaces 15, 28
communism, collapse of 197–8
comparative historical methodology
  9–12, 46, 48, 101–2, 112, 230,
  233, 251–2
consumerisation 40
convergence 45, 46
Cooke, Alistair 163
copyright issues 262
Coronation of Elizabeth II (1953) 8,
  13, 27, 185, 236
Coronation Street 105, 181
Crawley, Aidan 246
crime series 163, 168
crime-appeal television 105, 113–18,
  123–4
Crimewatch UK 101, 116–17
Crone, Vincent 31
CSI: Miami 8
cultivation theory 176
cultural identity 1–2, 36, 128
  American 'threat' to 167
  see also national identities
cultural imperialism 7–8, 33, 245
cultural pessimism 235
cultural stereotypes 14, 146, 147, 161,
  244
cultural transfer 10, 11, 33
cultural uniformity 218
culture
  elite 164, 165
  free trade notions 166–7
  high 24, 91, 92, 123, 156, 160
  hybridisation 44, 158, 238
  multivocal phenomenon 251
  national 156, 164
  popular 156, 169–70
current affairs programmes 121
Cyprus 134
Czech Republic 34, 248
Czechoslovakia 21

Dallas 159, 164, 165, 166, 179
Dayan, Daniel 36, 185, 187, 188, 195,
  197, 209, 211
De Bens, E. 8, 9

De Paiva, Adriano 60
De Smaecle, H. 8, 9
Degenhardt, Wolfgang 27, 244
Delaunay, Gabriel 41
Delavaud, Gilles 165
democratisation 21, 24, 37, 40, 41
Denmark 75, 133
  anti-Americanisation 157, 160, 169,
    172
  children's television 172, 173
  Disney programmes 170
  drama 158, 160, 168
  pop programmes 170
deregulation 33, 103, 104, 130
Dhoest, A. 110–11
Diana, Princess of Wales 186, 204–10,
  211, 212
diasporic communities 48, 132,
  223–7
digital revolution paradigm 46
digital streaming 32
Disney 170–1
Doane, Mary Anne 186
domestication of television 24, 249
drama
  aesthetics of 106–13, 123
  costume drama 135, 167
  direct address 109
  early 106–13
  historical 130, 134–45, 167, 237
  liveness 106, 108, 109, 123
  melodrama 159–60, 161
  mini-series format 158, 160, 163,
    164, 192, 210
  national discourse 130, 134–45, 158,
    168
  performative events 186
  social realism 135, 138, 139–40,
    141, 163, 168, 176, 181
  see also specific countries
dramatic narratives of television 30, 31,
  32
dumbing down 37, 117

Eastern Europe
  American cultural invasion 154
  censorship 21

democratisation of television 37
  Soviet influences 21
  transition to western models 21
  see also specific countries
Eckert, Gerhard 62, 76, 245
Edison, Thomas Alva 58
Elämänmeno (*The Way Life Goes*)
  136–8
electricity 57–8
electromagnetic wave theory 58
electronic newsgathering (ENG) 199
Ellis, John 24, 186, 188, 189
EMI-Marconi 69, 70, 72
English-language television programmes
  2
entertainment programmes 37, 91–2,
  129–30, 157, 237
  see also specific types of programmes
Estonia 133, 134
Eurofiction project 157, 158
Euronews 132, 133
European Audiovisual Observatory 8
European Broadcasting Union (EBU)
  8, 27, 28, 36, 79, 90, 91, 132,
  236, 237
  European identity project 91, 92
  Eurovision News Exchanges (EVN)
    133
  news exchange facilities 157, 236
  programme exchange, promotion of
    236, 238–9, 261
  public broadcasting missions 91, 92,
    95
  Screening Sessions 238–9
European Free Trade Association 22
European identity 1–2, 48, 79, 91, 92,
  102, 241, 245
European Television History Network
  (ETHN) ix, 49, 252
European Union 2, 130, 157
Europeanisation of the national space
  97, 156, 246
Eurovision 8, 28, 36, 145, 237,
  241–4
Eurovision Song Contest 36–7, 91, 157,
  164, 170, 187, 188–92, 210, 211,
  236, 244

event television 35–7, 184–212, 241
  contribution to historical change 185
  disaster marathons 185
  domestication of international events
    201–3
  extraordinary–ordinary tension 35–7,
    184–5, 190, 206, 210, 211–12
  historical events 185
  impact on government policy 185,
    205
  invented traditions 187
  liveness, ideology of 35–6, 186, 200,
    210
  national experience 187
  television's organization of 186

Faraday, Michael 57
Farnsworth, Philo 64, 66, 68
Federal Republic of Germany 40, 75
  American imports 175
  children's television 172
  crime-appeal television 113–18
  democratisation 41
  event television 193, 195
  public service broadcasting 20, 86
Fernseh AG 67, 73
film 4, 45, 60, 63, 66, 67–8, 80, 108,
  112, 166, 175
Finland 75, 133, 134
  drama production 135–9
  event television 190, 191, 210
  national broadcasting 129
  television development 189
Fiske, John 34
flow characterisation 4, 38, 229, 251
Foot, John 223, 227
foreign-language programmes 2–3
formatted television 115, 124
Foucault, Michel 35
France 5, 41, 103, 134
  American imports 93, 166
  anti-Americanisation 117, 155, 164–8
  anti-television rhetoric 235
  black-and-white line standards 15, 73,
    91
  censorship 87, 89
  crime-appeal television 116–17

France (*cont'd*)
  drama production 106–7, 108–9,
    158, 159, 165, 167–8
  event television 201
  film industry 112, 166
  foreign-language imports 2
  funding 82, 93–4
  German–French wartime collaboration
    73–4, 82
  historical documentary 118, 119,
    121–2, 123
  nationalisms 91, 129
  news channels 133
  political broadcasting 13–14
  private television 93, 94
  propaganda 86
  public service broadcasting 20, 21,
    90, 92–4, 98, 166
  radio broadcasting 82, 83, 89, 93, 94
  state control 82, 86, 89, 102
  television development 15, 24, 70,
    73–4, 75, 76, 80, 82–3, 247–8
  wartime broadcasting 18, 82
free-market economy in
    communications 22
Front Line Family 162

Galvani, Luigi 57
game shows 4, 38–9, 105, 186, 238
Gaulle, Charles de 89, 165
Gauss, Carl Friedrich 57
genres 103, 105, 123, 124
  see also individual genres, e.g. drama
German Democratic Republic 173–80
  event television 194
  official anti-Americanism 175
  Soviet influences 174–5
  West German television viewing 217
Germany
  Big Brother 39
  black-and-white line standards 15, 91
  drama production 158, 159, 160,
    161
  public service broadcasting 90, 98,
    105
  television development 65, 68,
    69–72, 75, 76

'theatre television' 23–4
under National Socialism 23–4,
    70–2, 114
wartime broadcasting 18
see also Federal Republic of Germany;
    German Democratic Republic
Gibraltar 75
Giddens, Anthony 10, 22–3, 187, 240
global broadcasting 28, 41–2 *see also*
    transnational broadcasting
global consumerism 15–16
global village thesis 58
globalisation 7, 8, 9, 15–16, 19, 22,
    33, 44, 130, 156, 157, 158, 170
glocalisation 158, 170
Goebbels, Joseph 72
Golden Rose festival 33–4
Gramme, Zénobe Théophile 58
Gray, Frank 64
Greece 134
  censorship 80, 87, 88–9
  digital channels 95
  drama production 16
  national identity discourse 16, 91
  private television 94–5, 98
  propaganda 88
  public service broadcasting 92, 95
  state–television relationship 80, 81,
    87–9, 92
  television development 75, 80–2,
    87–8
Grimme, Adolf 41
Gulf War (1991) 132, 200

Habermas, Jürgen 15
Hall, Stuart 3, 16, 25
harmful effects of television 31
Hartley, John 34, 216–17
Hebdige, Dick 157
Heimat 47, 134, 144, 158, 161, 180
Hellenic TV 3
heritage, concept of 35, 46
Hertz, Heinrich 58
Hilmes, Michele 11, 12, 19, 33, 64
'histoire croisée' concept 10, 11, 46
historical documentary 105–6, 118–23,
    124

historiographies of European television 5–9, 101–2
history of television 55–76
  cultural context 56
  European style, shaping of 76
  experimentation and breakthroughs 64–7, 108
  first television programmes 68–74
  impact of radio 62–4
  multi-authored invention 60–1
  patents 61
  periods 55–6
  political and institutional approach 6
  postwar 74–6
  prehistory 5, 55, 57–60, 232
  technical and cultural developments 57–62
  television coverage, expansion of 15, 75–6, 249
Holocaust 159, 160, 192–5, 210, 212
Hood, Stuart 190
Hoskins 134
Housewife's Films 219–20, 221, 222
Hulten, Olof 44, 45
Hungary 21, 134, 248

identity 3, 4, 239–41
  collective 36
  deconstruction 3, 25
  essentialist notions 130
  Europeanness 1–2, 48, 79, 91, 92, 102, 241, 245
  formation 25, 128, 240
  hybridity 128
  multiple 240
  negotiated 14, 128
  reflexivity 240
  regional 145–50, 151
  subject-oriented theory of 240
  see also cultural identity; national identities
Iliescu, Ion 198, 199
imagined communities 13, 15, 18, 23, 129, 156, 187, 209, 230, 241, 250
In Retrospect 143–4

infrastructure development 15, 27–8, 249–50
institutionalisation of television 55, 79–98, 234–7
instrumentalisation of television 15, 231
  techno-political 15, 20, 250
interactivity 25–6
intermediality 45, 46
International Broadcasting Union (IBU) 27, 28, 91, 236
interpretative flexibility 238
intertextuality 45
Intervision 236–7
Ireland 75
Israel 124
Italy 24, 112, 134
  children's television 223
  foreign-language imports 2
  historical documentary 119, 120–1
  television development 24, 75, 222–3, 247
ITV 18, 75, 104, 112, 163, 210

Japan 70, 80
Jenkins, Henry 45, 46
Judt, Tony 155

Kaelble, Hartmut 9, 10
Karolus, August 63, 64, 65
Katz, Elihu 36, 185, 187, 188, 195, 197, 209, 211
Kneale, Nigel 109, 110
Korn, Arthur 63, 64

La Cinq 166, 167
Lang, Mirek 17
Levitas, R. 29–30, 31, 32
licence fees 25, 82, 83, 94
Liebes, Tamar 185, 205
Liesegang, Edmund 61
literate and oral codes of television 34
Lithuania 133
liveness 4, 35–6, 40, 106, 108, 186, 200, 210
localisation 9, 44 *see also* glocalisation
Ludwig 17
Luxembourg 75

McDonald, Sharon 251
McGivern, Cecil 242, 243, 244
McLuhan, Marshall 58
makeover television 37, 38, 41
Malta 75
Marconi, Guglielmo 59, 63
Maxwell, James Clerk 57
May, Joseph 60
media ownership concentration 26
migration 130, 223–7, 246
Mihály, Dénes von 64, 65, 66
modernisation 44, 56, 127
Monaco 75
monopolies 44, 128, 154
The Moomins 17–18
Morley, D. 9, 21–2, 31, 44, 46–7, 150,
    218
Morse, Margaret 38
Morse, Samuel F. B. 59
MTV 37, 43, 132, 170
multi-channel television 24, 104
Murdoch, Rupert 28
music culture 169–70

nation-state construction, television and
    156
national broadcasting 19, 21, 22,
    128–30, 156
  regional programming of 145–50
national community, sense of 190
national identities 16–17, 18, 36, 106,
    118, 128, 129, 130
  broadcasting's shaping and promotion
    of 83–5, 90, 91, 110, 112, 124,
    128, 130, 147–8, 165
  discursive formations 16
  fracturing of 17
  post-modern perspective 130
national imaginary 138, 140, 147–8,
    150, 158, 159
nationalism 2, 22
  cultural 111, 139
  see also national identities
NBC 20, 192
Netherlands 5, 133
  anti-television rhetoric 235–6
  Big Brother 14, 39

crime-appeal television 115–16
drama 141–5, 168
foreign-language imports 2
ideological differentiated broadcasting
    129
public service broadcasting 20, 141
television development 15
news 130, 131–4, 248
  classic model 131
  culturally specific 130, 151
  disaster marathons 185, 205, 212
  domestication of international news
    211
  ethnic channels 132
  Euronews 132
  event television 199–204
  flagship programmes 131
  negotiated readings of 42
  partiality 204
  political 2, 13–14, 73
  radio broadcasts 41–2, 248
  regional 151
  soap opera elements 186
  transnational flows 29, 41–2, 130,
    131–3
news agencies 29, 59, 257
Nipkow, Paul 61, 71
Nohain, Jean 82–3
Nordvision network 191–2
Norway 45
  children's television 172, 173
  television development 75

Olympic Games 24, 71, 187, 211
ontological security, television's
    contribution to 187
Organisation Internationale de
    Radiodiffusion et Télévision
    (OIRT) 27, 28, 91, 95, 236,
    236–7
Ørsted, Hans Christian 57
'Other' 47, 154

panoramas and dioramas 59
The Partisans 142–3
patents 55, 61
paternalism 20, 21, 37, 110, 156, 160

pay channels 158, 164
Perosino, Carlo 60
Pfaffenberger, Bryan 30
Phoenix TV 3
Poland 174
  American influences 175–7
  commercial television 176–7
  film production 175
  foreign imports 2, 176
  'social realism' cultural policy 176
political broadcasting 2, 13–14, 73, 96
Polonia 3
pop programmes 169–70
'popular' television 34
Portugal 39, 75, 133
postmodernism 32, 38, 130
postmodernity 31–2
Presley, Elvis 169
prime time 37, 105, 131, 157
  access prime time 105, 131
  national 157
private television 79, 94–8, 235 *see also*
  commercial television
producer-*auteur* model of production
  164
'programme' 103
programming 103–6
  American model 157
  competitive model 103, 104, 155
  complementary 104
  courteous model 103
  cultural aspirations 156
  democratic 113–14
  European model 157
  events television 187
  horizontal 103, 104, 105
  and identity discourses 128
  multicultural 47
  pluriformity 141
  public service programming 118, 119,
    156
  regional 145–50
  social and political context 102, 103
  vertical 103, 104
propaganda 24, 71, 72, 80, 84, 86, 90,
  98, 133, 177
ProTV 96, 97, 179, 180

public service broadcasting 6, 19, 22,
  90–4, 105
  centralised model 20
  differing notions of 90, 92, 98
  local practices 90–4
  paternalist 20, 156
  'pillarised' model 20, 141
  public service–commercial television
    duopoly 162, 167, 199–200, 235
  radio–television association 82, 83
  see also individual countries and
    channels
public service ideology 23, 76, 90–1,
  156
public sphere
  alternative 217
  communication-based 15, 156
  democratic 199
  European 132, 156
  political 28
  public–private relationship 12–14, 28,
    33, 197, 222–3
public viewing 23–4, 73, 218, 247–8
Punto y Medio 147

quality issues 32–5, 106, 110–11, 235
Quatermass serials 109–10
quiz shows 157, 186, 238
quotas and subsidies 9

radio 4, 12–13, 56, 233, 234
  early history 12–13, 19, 56, 58, 63–4
  funding 83
  illegal radio 83, 94
  imaginative power 12–13
  news broadcasts 248
  radio–television medial similarity 68,
    80, 234
Radio Corporation of America (RCA)
  20, 62, 63, 65, 66, 67, 68, 69, 70,
  73
Radio Free Europe 196
Radio Television of Andalusia (RTVA)
  146
Radio Televisión Española (RTVE) 146
Radiodiffusion-Télévision Française
  (RTF) 13, 27, 41

reality television 13, 37, 38, 39, 124, 164
   crime-appeal television 113–18
reflexivity 10–11
regionalisation 130, 145–50
regulatory environments 14, 37, 45
   liberalisation 235
Reith, John 156
Reitz, Edgar 161
remediation 45, 46
Richards, Jeffrey 16, 17
Robins, K. 9, 21–2, 31, 44, 46–7, 48, 150
Romania 134
   American imports 98, 179, 180
   Americanisation of content 96, 97, 177, 178, 179, 180
   censorship 90, 177
   decrease in broadcasting hours 178–9
   Europeanisation of broadcasting 97
   event television 195–9, 210, 211
   liberalisation 87, 96, 97, 178
   national discourses 83–5, 87, 91
   private television 95–8
   propaganda 87, 177
   public broadcasting 87, 96, 97, 177–80
   radio broadcasting 84–5
   Romanian Revolution, broadcasting of 197–9
   state control 21, 84–5, 86, 87, 96, 98, 177, 179
   television development 80, 83–6, 87
Roots 159, 164, 212
Rosing, Boris L. 62

Sarnoff, David 66, 68, 69, 70
satellite broadcasting 28–9, 32, 41, 83, 134
Scannell, Paddy 12, 13, 28, 190
scheduling 4, 103, 105 *see also* programming
Schröter, Fritz 64
screen size 108
Second World War 18, 56, 74, 141, 143, 144
selfhood, culture of 37–8, 40

Senlecq, Constantin 60
September 11 terrorist attacks 185
Sesame Street 171–3
Shakespeare, televised 123
Siemens, Werner von 58, 60
Silverstone, Roger 187
Simon, Georg 57
Sims, Monica 173
Sinclair, John 18–19, 47–8
Siune, Karen 44, 45
Sky 43, 95, 200
Slovakia 248
Slovenia 134
Smith, Willoughby 60
soap operas 105, 147, 159, 181, 186
Spain 39, 134
   crime-appeal television 117
   historical documentary 119–20
   migrant audiences 223–7
   state–broadcasting relationship 21
   television development 75, 224
specificity of television 106, 108, 130
Spigel, Lynn 218, 227, 246, 249
sporting events 13, 157, 187, 211, 225–6, 244
Stahr, Jimmy 171
standardisation of time 59
Sutton, Henry 61
Sweden 40
   audiovisual archive 259
   children's television 172, 173
   commercial television 219
   drama production 158
   television development 75, 219
Switzerland 3, 40, 75, 114, 115
Szczepanik, Jan 61

talk shows 103, 147, 157, 186
technologies 19, 24, 26–9, 30, 32, 55, 231
   and early television 57–62
   performative nature of 30
   preconditions 26
   techno-nationalistic instrumentalisation 61
Télé Clubs 24, 218, 247–8
'tele-vision' 56, 127

telecinema 63
telegraphy 19, 56, 57–9, 63
telerecording 108
Telesur 146
Televisión Española (TVE) 145, 146, 224, 225
television nations 15, 127
television ownership 15, 247
television spheres 14–15
Television without Frontiers Directive (1989) 22
'theatre television' 23
Tilly, Charles 9–10
Time to Live 144–5
top-down philosophy of communication 98
totalitarianism 40, 211
transculturalism 238, 245–6
translation 2, 45, 230
transmediality 45
transnational broadcasting 3, 41–4, 47–8, 133
transnational symbolic spaces 47
trust in television 134
Turèll, Dan 180
Turkey 48, 203

unifying power of television 129
    see also national identities; nationalism
universality, ideologies of 47
USA 154–83
    Big Brother 14
    British imports and adaptations 163
    British–American co-productions 154, 161–3, 164
    commercial television 4, 20–1, 22, 23
    drama 8, 159–60, 161, 164, 192–5
    entertainment genres 157
    flow phenomenon 4

foreign-language programmes, resistance to 2
media hegemony 8–9, 18
pay channels 158, 164
Public Broadcasting Service (PBS) 158, 163
rock 'n' roll culture 169–70
television development 20, 65–6, 67, 69, 70, 74–5
'TV freeze' 74
    see also Americanisation
uses and gratifications theory 23
utopian discourses 29–30, 31, 32, 47, 190

viewership culture 247, 249 *see also* audiences

Wagenführ, Kurt 41
Wales 3, 147–50
Wasko, Janet 170
Watson, Barnard L. 59
Weber, Wilhelm Eduard 57
Weiller, Lazare 61, 64
Werner, Michael 10–11
Wij, heren van Zichem (*We, the Lords of Zichem*) 139–41
Williams, Raymond 4, 157, 229
Wolfgram, Mark A. 217
World's Fairs 23, 65, 232–4

YLE (Finnish Broadcasting Company) 189, 191
youth culture 169

Zimmermann, Bénédicte 10–11
Zimmermann, Eduard 114–15
Zworykin, Vladimir K. 62, 64, 65–6, 67, 68–9